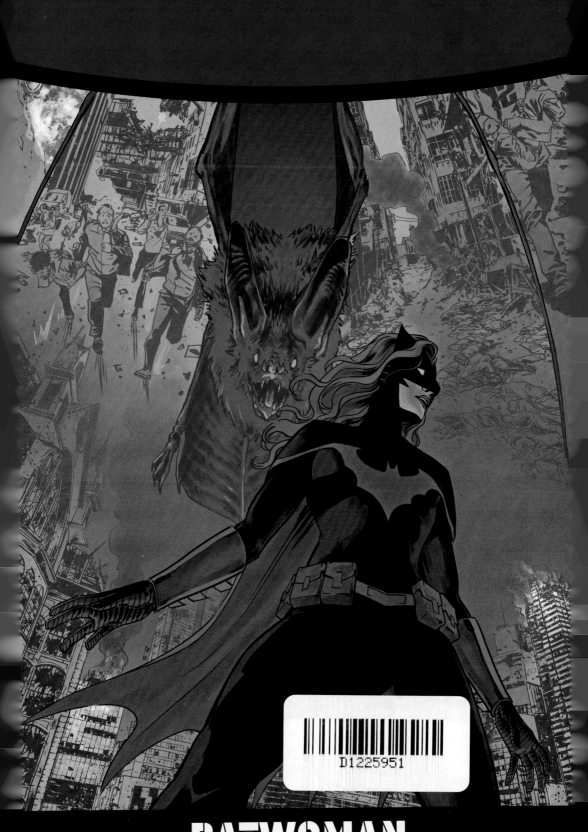

BATWOMAN

VOL.3 FALL OF THE HOUSE OF KANE

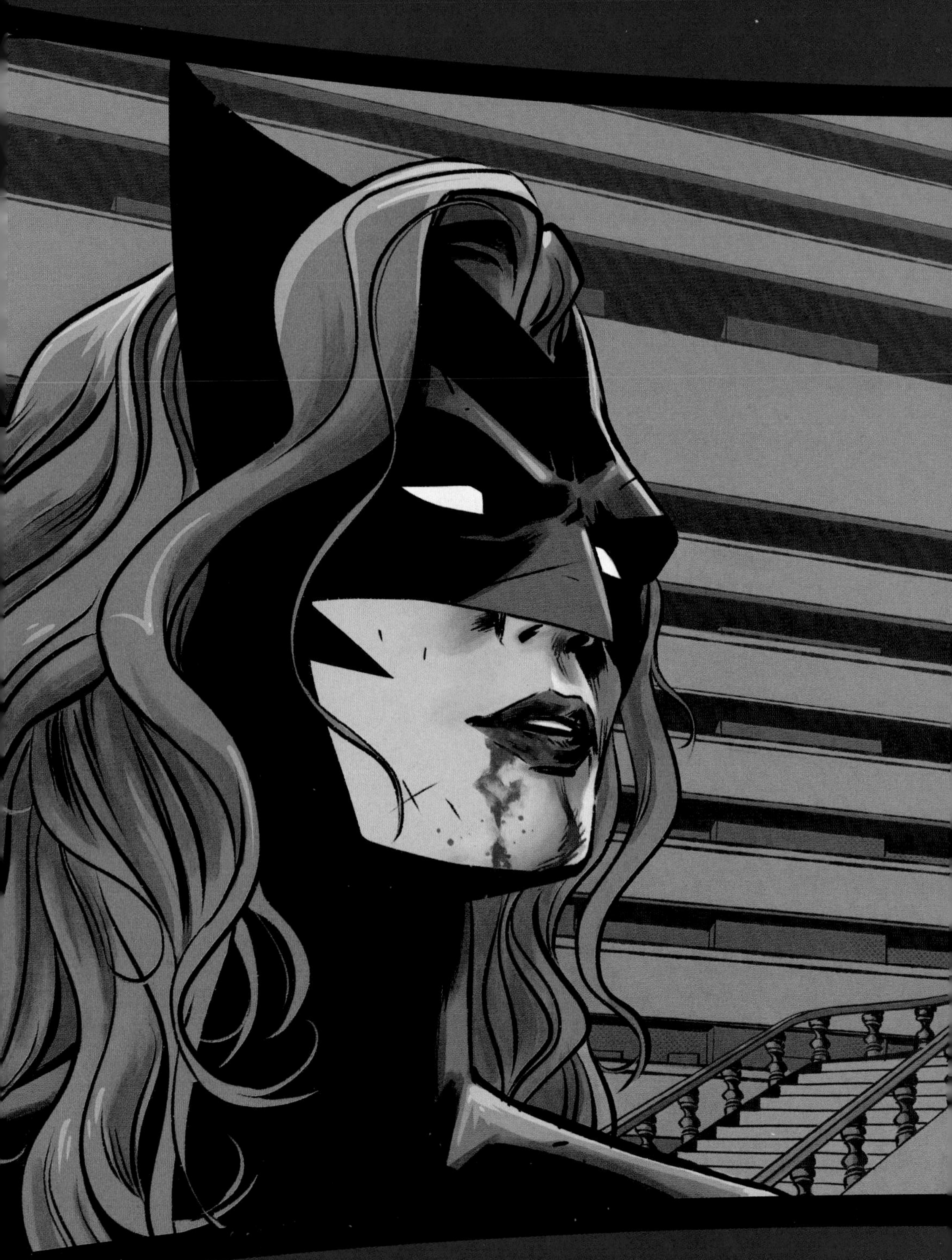

BATWOMAN

VOL.3 FALL OF THE HOUSE OF KANE

MARGUERITE BENNETT
writer

FERNANDO BLANCO
SCOTT GODLEWSKI
artists

JOHN RAUCH
colorist

DERON BENNETT
letterer

LEE BERMEJO
collection cover artist

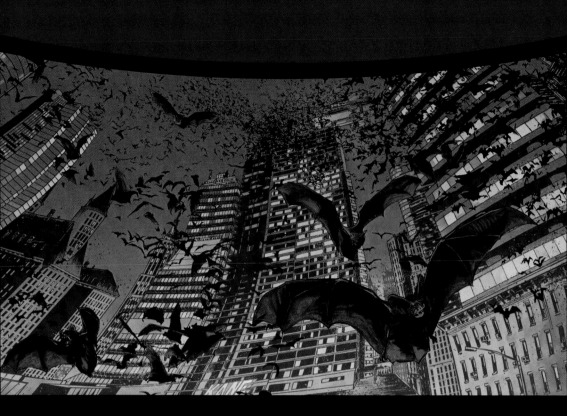

KATIE KUBERT BRITTANY HOLZHERR Editors - Original Series
JEB WOODARD Group Editor - Collected Editions * **ROBIN WILDMAN** Editor - Collected Edition
STEVE COOK Design Director - Books * **SHANNON STEWART** Publication Design

BOB HARRAS Senior VP - Editor-in-Chief, DC Comics
PAT McCALLUM Executive Editor, DC Comics

DAN DiDIO Publisher * **JIM LEE** Publisher & Chief Creative Officer
AMIT DESAI Executive VP - Business & Marketing Strategy, Direct to Consumer & Global Franchise Management
BOBBIE CHASE VP & Executive Editor, Young Reader & Talent Development * **MARK CHIARELLO** Senior VP - Art, Design & Collected Editions
JOHN CUNNINGHAM Senior VP - Sales & Trade Marketing * **BRIAR DARDEN** VP - Business Affairs
ANNE DePIES Senior VP - Business Strategy, Finance & Administration * **DON FALLETTI** VP - Manufacturing Operations
LAWRENCE GANEM VP - Editorial Administration & Talent Relations * **ALISON GILL** Senior VP - Manufacturing & Operations
JASON GREENBERG VP - Business Strategy & Finance * **HANK KANALZ** Senior VP - Editorial Strategy & Administration
JAY KOGAN Senior VP - Legal Affairs * **NICK J. NAPOLITANO** VP - Manufacturing Administration
LISETTE OSTERLOH VP - Digital Marketing & Events * **EDDIE SCANNELL** VP - Consumer Marketing
COURTNEY SIMMONS Senior VP - Publicity & Communications * **JIM (SKI) SOKOLOWSKI** VP - Comic Book Specialty Sales & Trade Marketing
NANCY SPEARS VP - Mass, Book, Digital Sales & Trade Marketing * **MICHELE R. WELLS** VP - Content Strategy

BATWOMAN VOL. 3: FALL OF THE HOUSE OF KANE

DC Comics, 2900 West Alameda Ave., Burbank, CA 91505
Printed by Times Printing, LLC, Random Lake, WI, USA. 12/14/18. First Printing.
ISBN: 978-1-4012-8577-7

Library of Congress Cataloging-in-Publication Data is available.

FSC
www.fsc.org
MIX
Paper from responsible sources
FSC® C015572

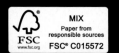

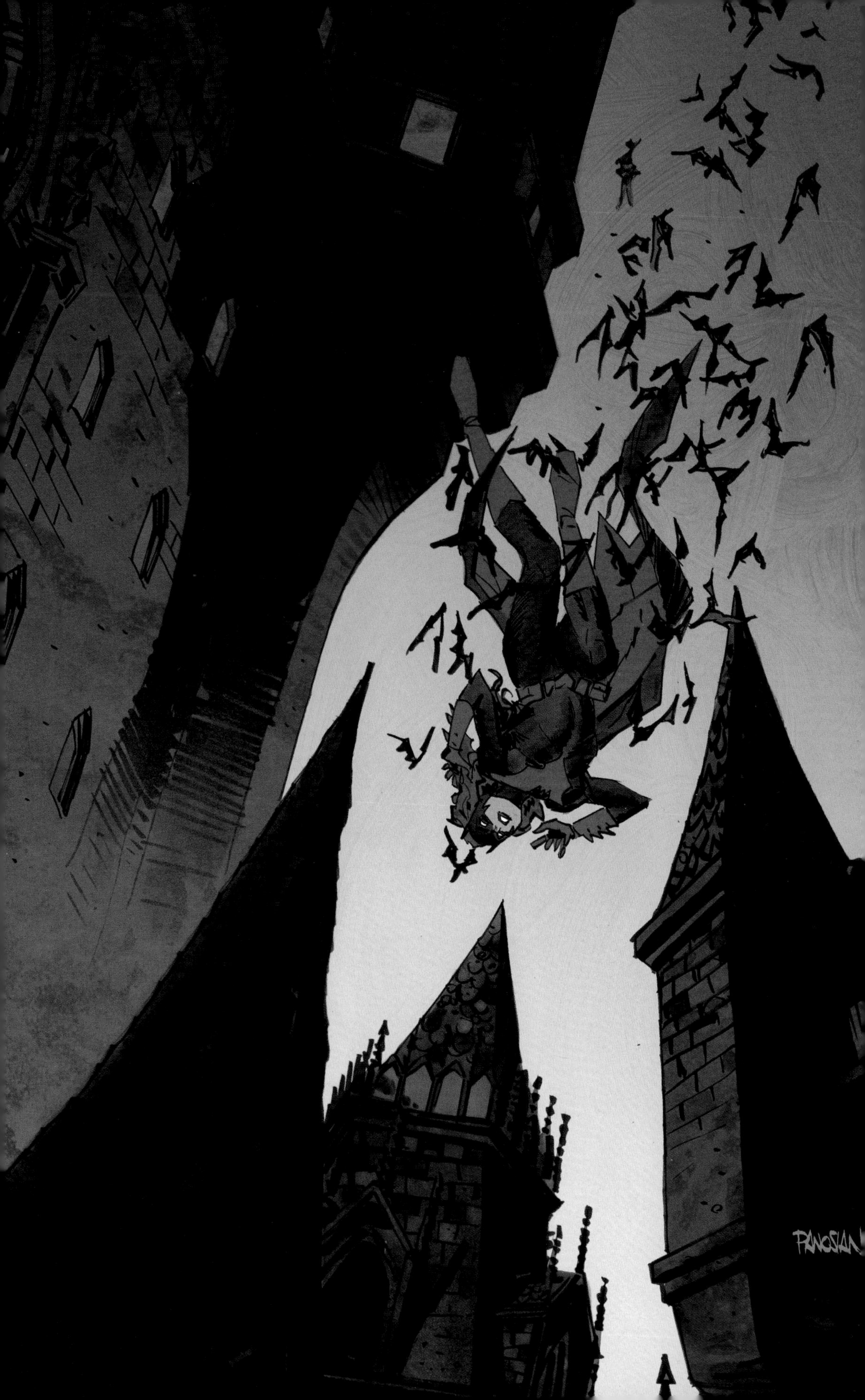
PANOSIAN

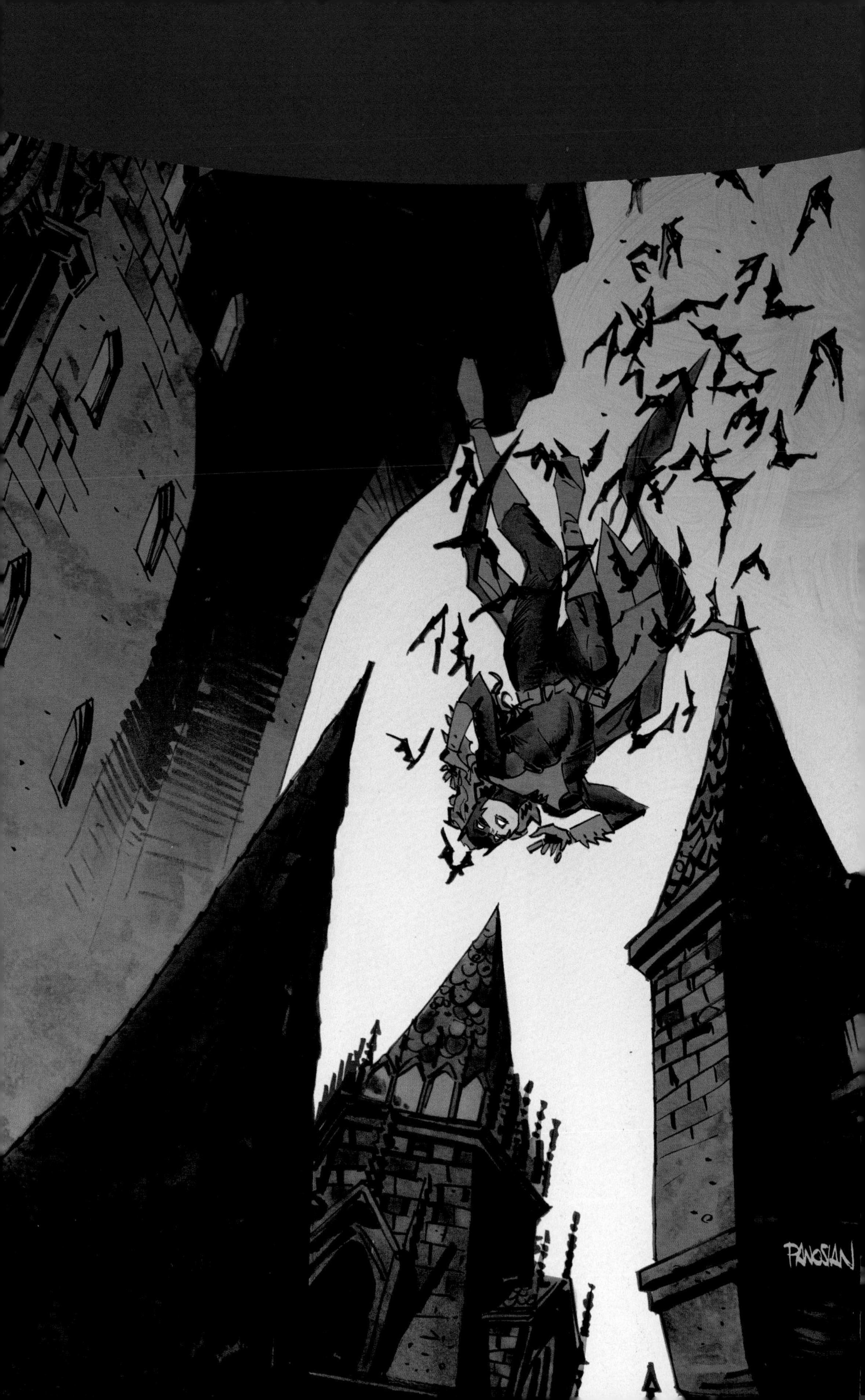
PANOSIAN

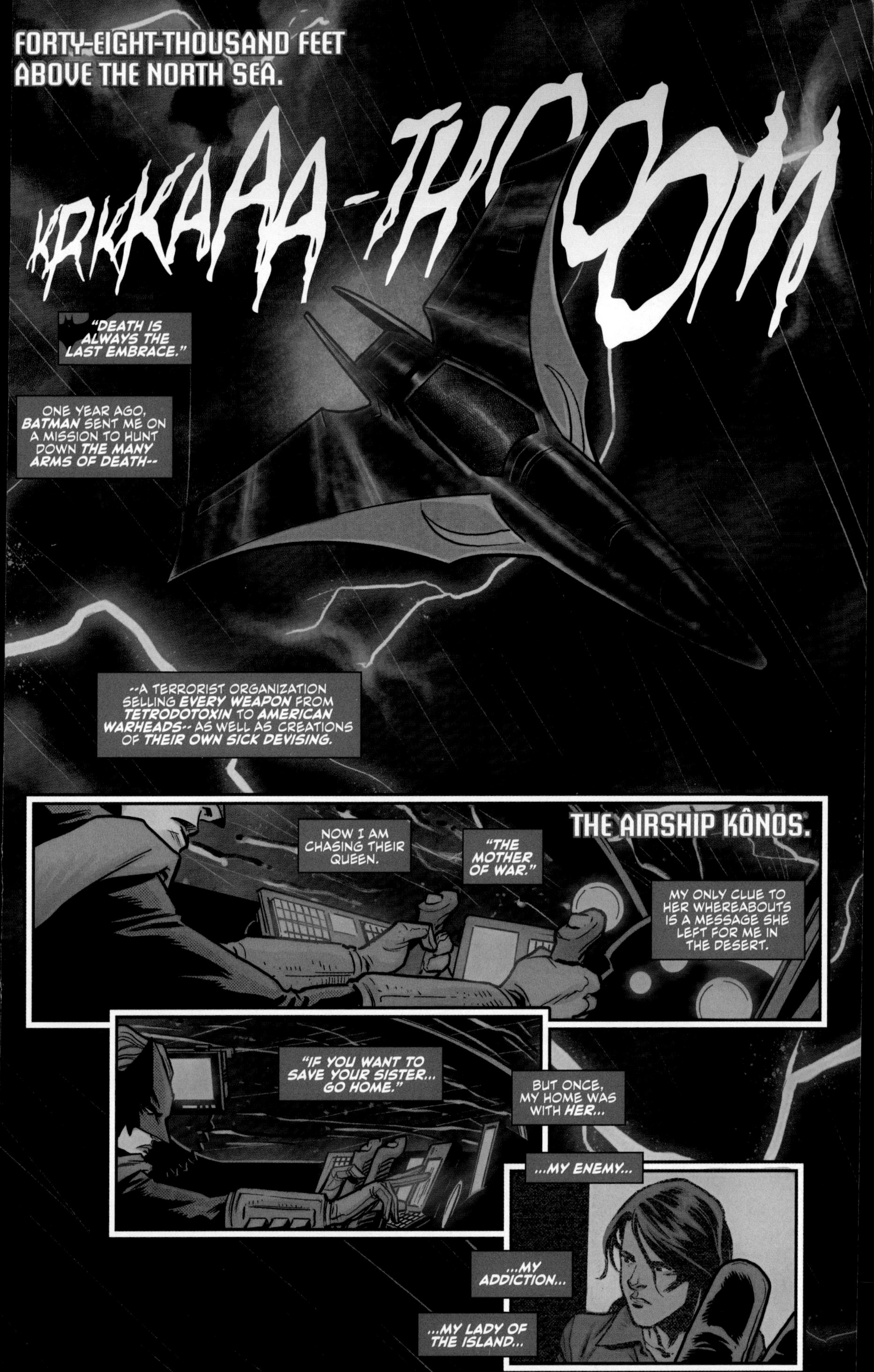

FORTY-EIGHT-THOUSAND FEET ABOVE THE NORTH SEA.
KRKKAAA-THOOM
"DEATH IS ALWAYS THE LAST EMBRACE."
ONE YEAR AGO, BATMAN SENT ME ON A MISSION TO HUNT DOWN THE MANY ARMS OF DEATH--
--A TERRORIST ORGANIZATION SELLING EVERY WEAPON FROM TETRODOTOXIN TO AMERICAN WARHEADS-- AS WELL AS CREATIONS OF THEIR OWN SICK DEVISING.
THE AIRSHIP KÔNOS.
NOW I AM CHASING THEIR QUEEN.
"THE MOTHER OF WAR."
MY ONLY CLUE TO HER WHEREABOUTS IS A MESSAGE SHE LEFT FOR ME IN THE DESERT.
"IF YOU WANT TO SAVE YOUR SISTER... GO HOME."
BUT ONCE, MY HOME WAS WITH HER...
...MY ENEMY...
...MY ADDICTION...
...MY LADY OF THE ISLAND...

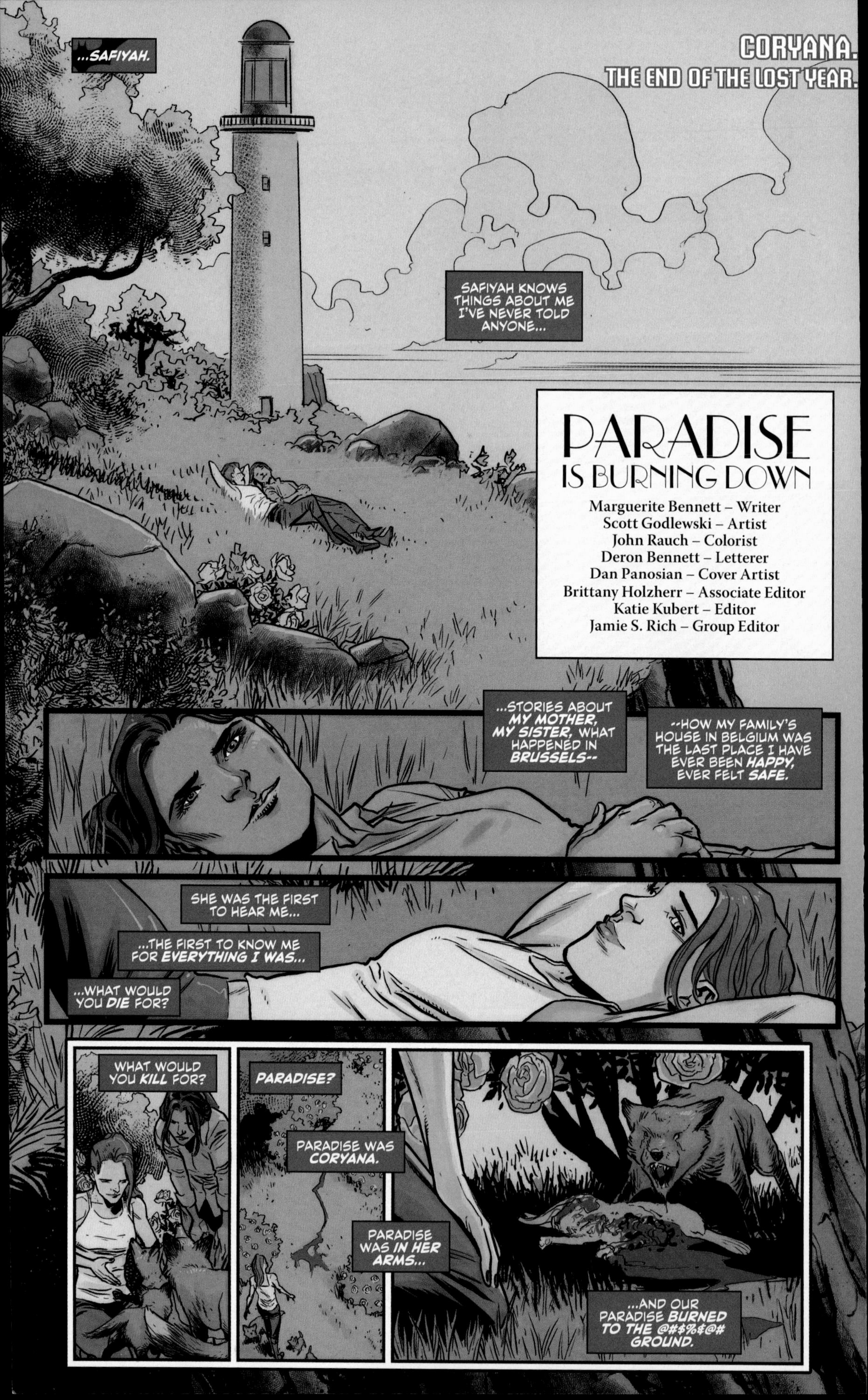
CORYANA.
THE END OF THE LOST YEAR.
...SAFIYAH.
SAFIYAH KNOWS THINGS ABOUT ME I'VE NEVER TOLD ANYONE...
PARADISE IS BURNING DOWN
Marguerite Bennett – Writer
Scott Godlewski – Artist
John Rauch – Colorist
Deron Bennett – Letterer
Dan Panosian – Cover Artist
Brittany Holzherr – Associate Editor
Katie Kubert – Editor
Jamie S. Rich – Group Editor
...STORIES ABOUT MY MOTHER, MY SISTER, WHAT HAPPENED IN BRUSSELS--
--HOW MY FAMILY'S HOUSE IN BELGIUM WAS THE LAST PLACE I HAVE EVER BEEN HAPPY, EVER FELT SAFE.
SHE WAS THE FIRST TO HEAR ME...
...THE FIRST TO KNOW ME FOR EVERYTHING I WAS...
...WHAT WOULD YOU DIE FOR?
WHAT WOULD YOU KILL FOR?
PARADISE?
PARADISE WAS CORYANA.
PARADISE WAS IN HER ARMS...
...AND OUR PARADISE BURNED TO THE @#$%$@# GROUND.

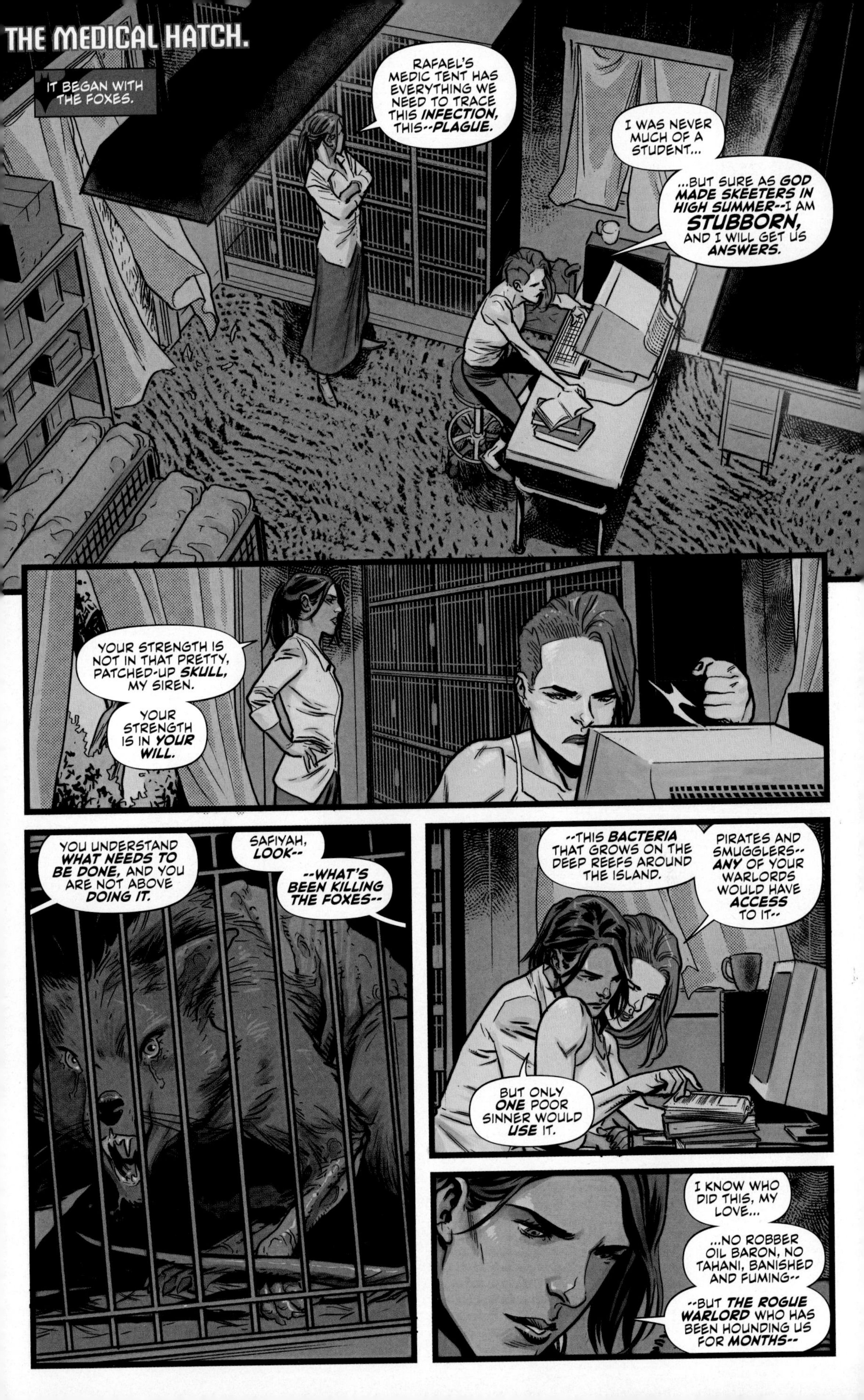

THE MEDICAL HATCH.
IT BEGAN WITH THE FOXES.
RAFAEL'S MEDIC TENT HAS EVERYTHING WE NEED TO TRACE THIS INFECTION, THIS--PLAGUE.
I WAS NEVER MUCH OF A STUDENT...
...BUT SURE AS GOD MADE SKEETERS IN HIGH SUMMER--I AM STUBBORN, AND I WILL GET US ANSWERS.
YOUR STRENGTH IS NOT IN THAT PRETTY, PATCHED-UP SKULL, MY SIREN.
YOUR STRENGTH IS IN YOUR WILL.
YOU UNDERSTAND WHAT NEEDS TO BE DONE, AND YOU ARE NOT ABOVE DOING IT.
SAFIYAH, LOOK--
--WHAT'S BEEN KILLING THE FOXES--
--THIS BACTERIA THAT GROWS ON THE DEEP REEFS AROUND THE ISLAND.
PIRATES AND SMUGGLERS--ANY OF YOUR WARLORDS WOULD HAVE ACCESS TO IT--
BUT ONLY ONE POOR SINNER WOULD USE IT.
I KNOW WHO DID THIS, MY LOVE...
...NO ROBBER OIL BARON, NO TAHANI, BANISHED AND FUMING--
--BUT THE ROGUE WARLORD WHO HAS BEEN HOUNDING US FOR MONTHS--

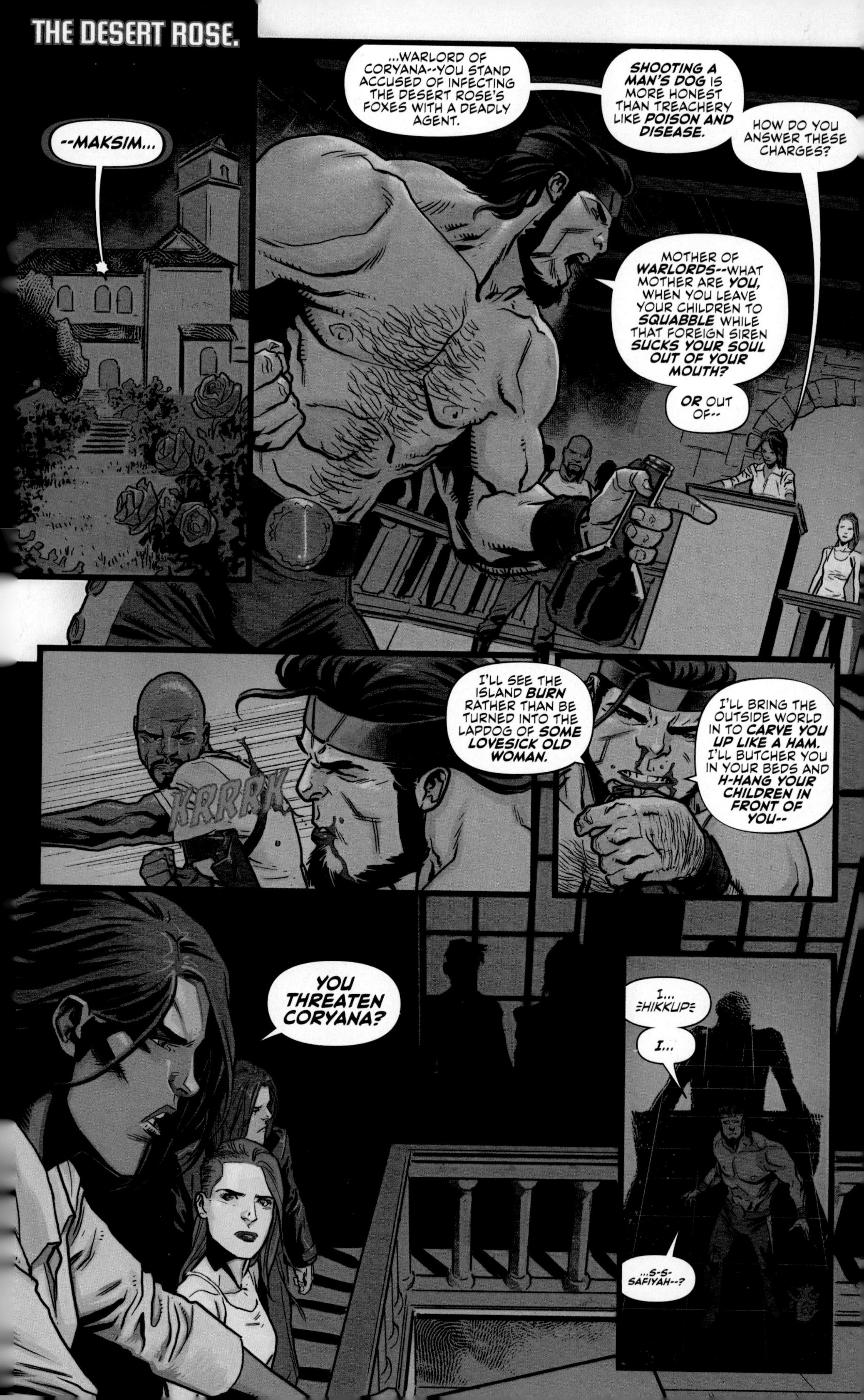
THE DESERT ROSE.
--MAKSIM...
...WARLORD OF CORYANA--YOU STAND ACCUSED OF INFECTING THE DESERT ROSE'S FOXES WITH A DEADLY AGENT.
SHOOTING A MAN'S DOG IS MORE HONEST THAN TREACHERY LIKE POISON AND DISEASE.
HOW DO YOU ANSWER THESE CHARGES?
MOTHER OF WARLORDS--WHAT MOTHER ARE YOU, WHEN YOU LEAVE YOUR CHILDREN TO SQUABBLE WHILE THAT FOREIGN SIREN SUCKS YOUR SOUL OUT OF YOUR MOUTH?
OR OUT OF--
KRRRK
I'LL SEE THE ISLAND BURN RATHER THAN BE TURNED INTO THE LAPDOG OF SOME LOVESICK OLD WOMAN.
I'LL BRING THE OUTSIDE WORLD IN TO CARVE YOU UP LIKE A HAM. I'LL BUTCHER YOU IN YOUR BEDS AND H-HANG YOUR CHILDREN IN FRONT OF YOU--
YOU THREATEN CORYANA?
I... HIKKUP
I...
...S-S-SAFIYAH--?

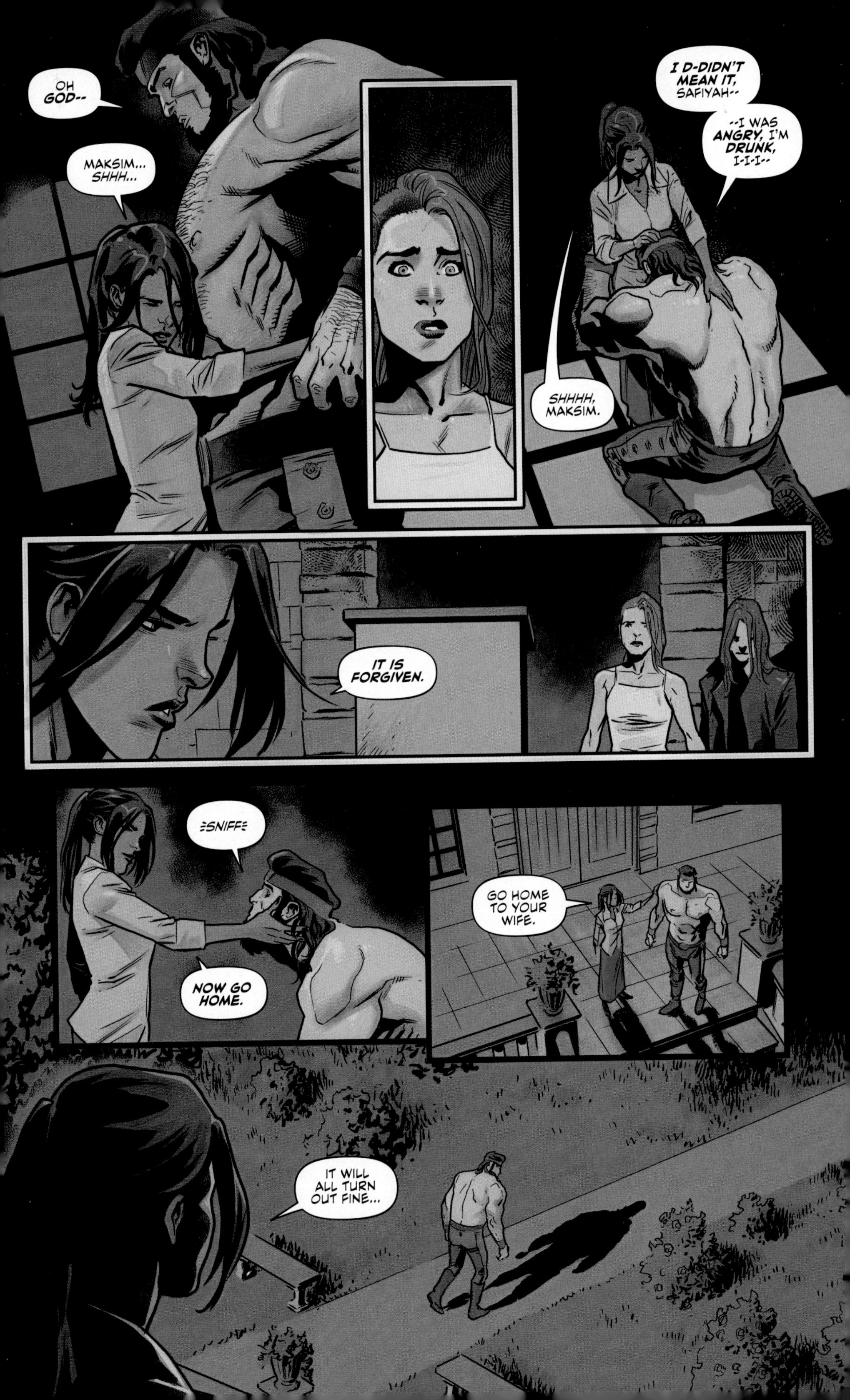
OH GOD--
MAKSIM... SHHH...
I D-DIDN'T MEAN IT, SAFIYAH--
--I WAS ANGRY, I'M DRUNK, I-I-I--
SHHHH, MAKSIM.
IT IS FORGIVEN.
SNIFF
NOW GO HOME.
GO HOME TO YOUR WIFE.
IT WILL ALL TURN OUT FINE...

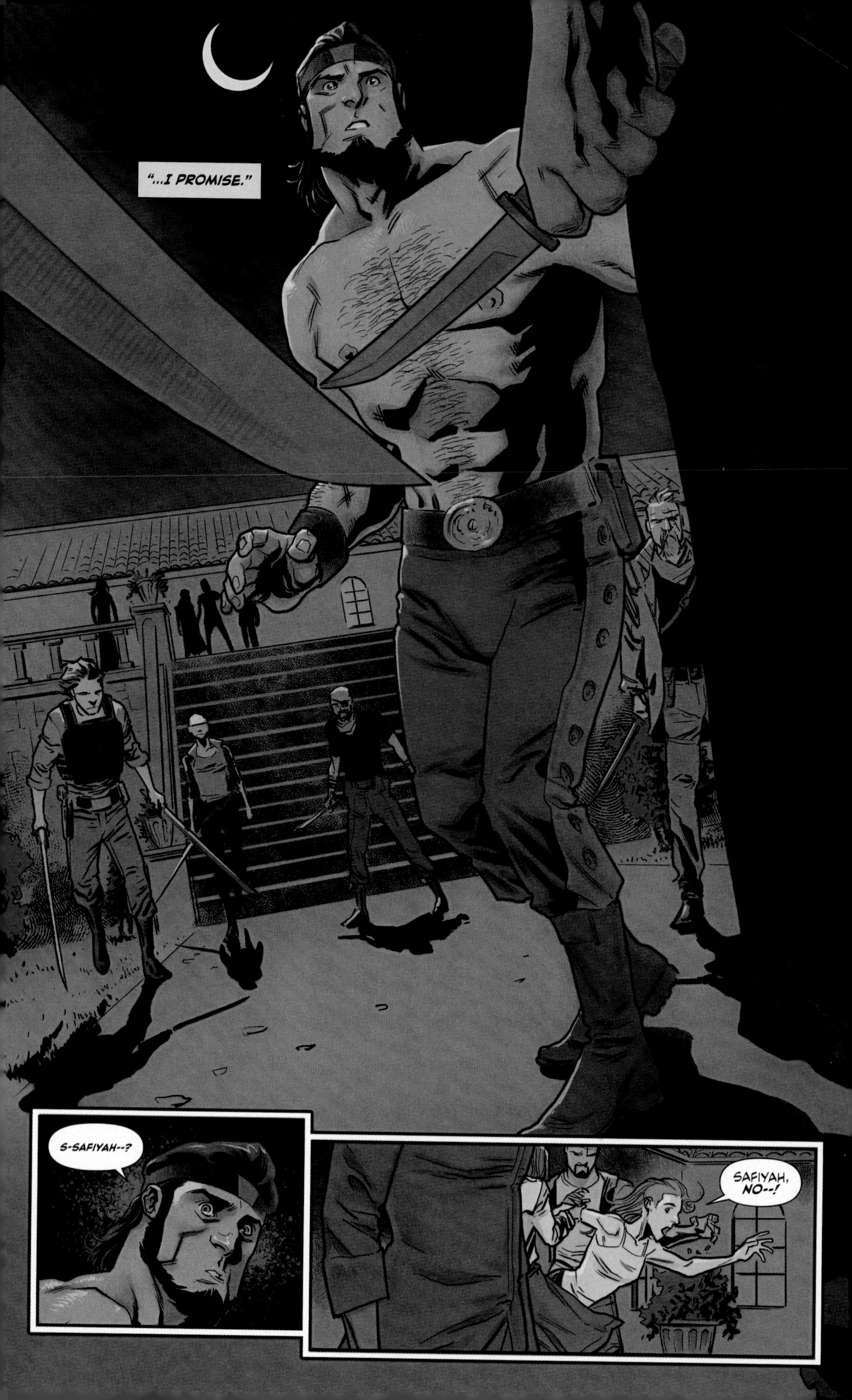
"...I PROMISE."
S-SAFIYAH--?
SAFIYAH, NO--!

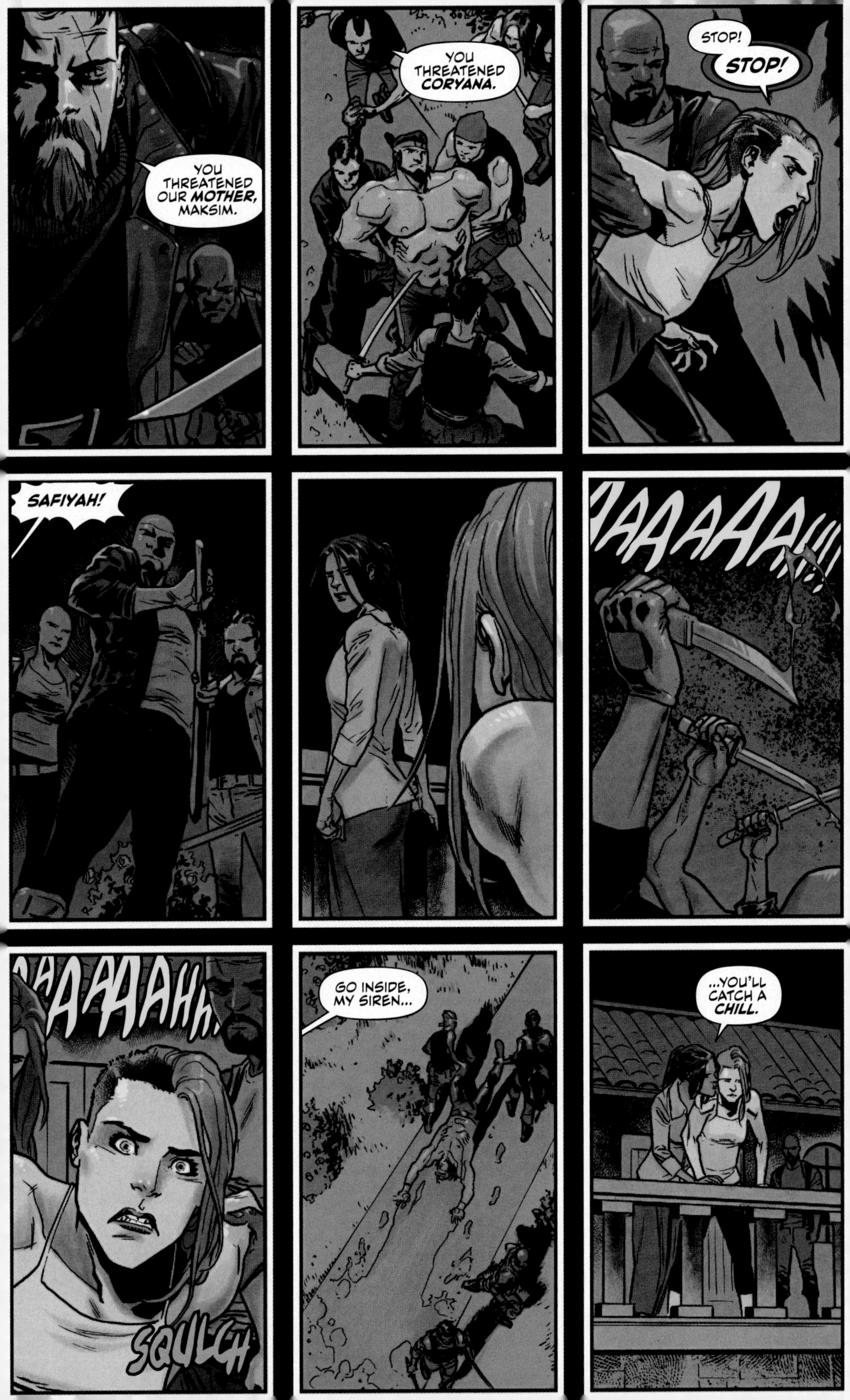
YOU THREATENED OUR MOTHER, MAKSIM.
YOU THREATENED CORYANA.
STOP!
STOP!
SAFIYAH!
AAAAAAAAH
AAAAAAHH
SQULCH
GO INSIDE, MY SIREN...
...YOU'LL CATCH A CHILL.

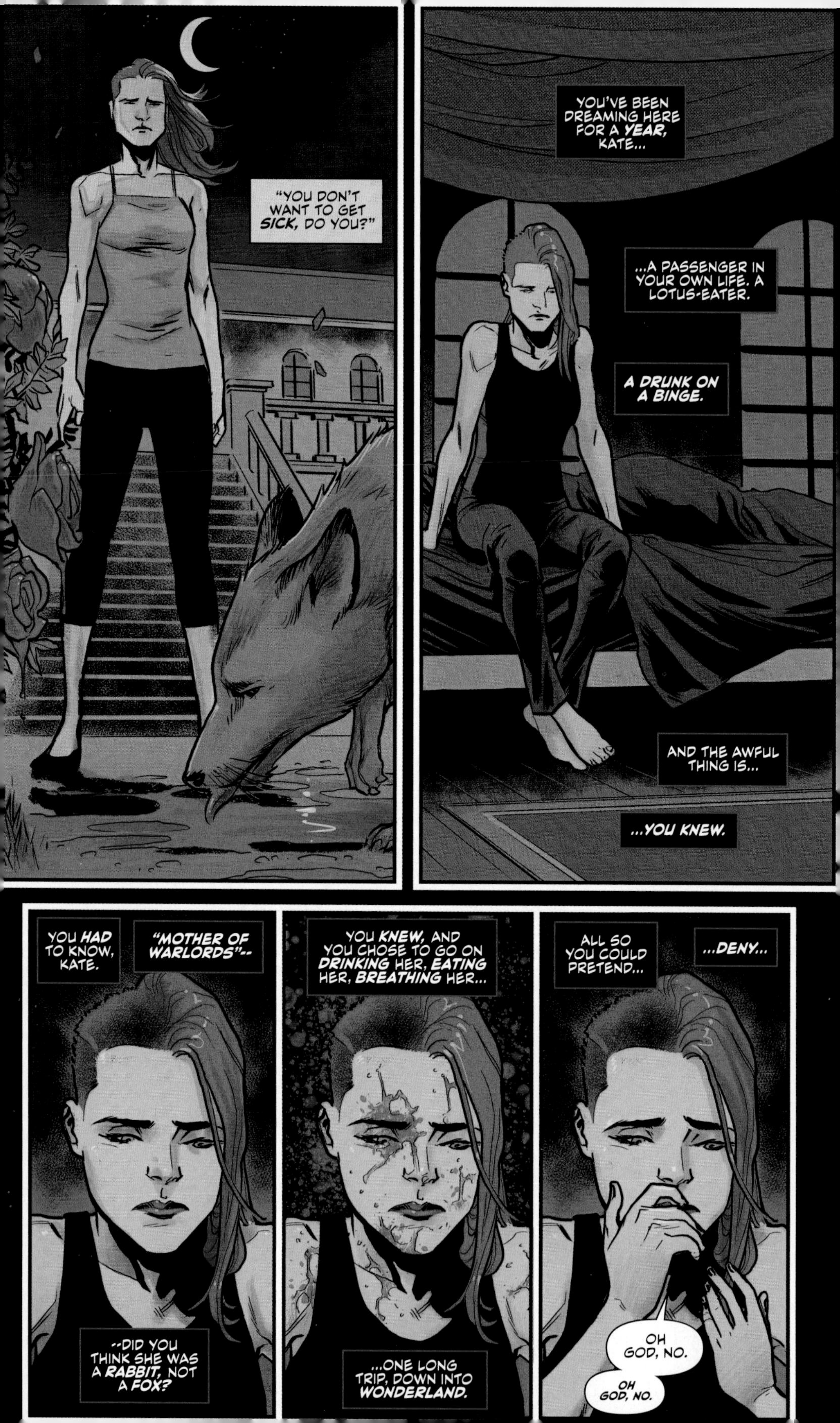
"YOU DON'T WANT TO GET SICK, DO YOU?"
YOU'VE BEEN DREAMING HERE FOR A YEAR, KATE...
...A PASSENGER IN YOUR OWN LIFE. A LOTUS-EATER.
A DRUNK ON A BINGE.
AND THE AWFUL THING IS...
...YOU KNEW.
YOU HAD TO KNOW, KATE.
"MOTHER OF WARLORDS"--
--DID YOU THINK SHE WAS A RABBIT, NOT A FOX?
YOU KNEW, AND YOU CHOSE TO GO ON DRINKING HER, EATING HER, BREATHING HER...
...ONE LONG TRIP, DOWN INTO WONDERLAND.
ALL SO YOU COULD PRETEND...
...DENY...
OH GOD, NO.
OH GOD, NO.

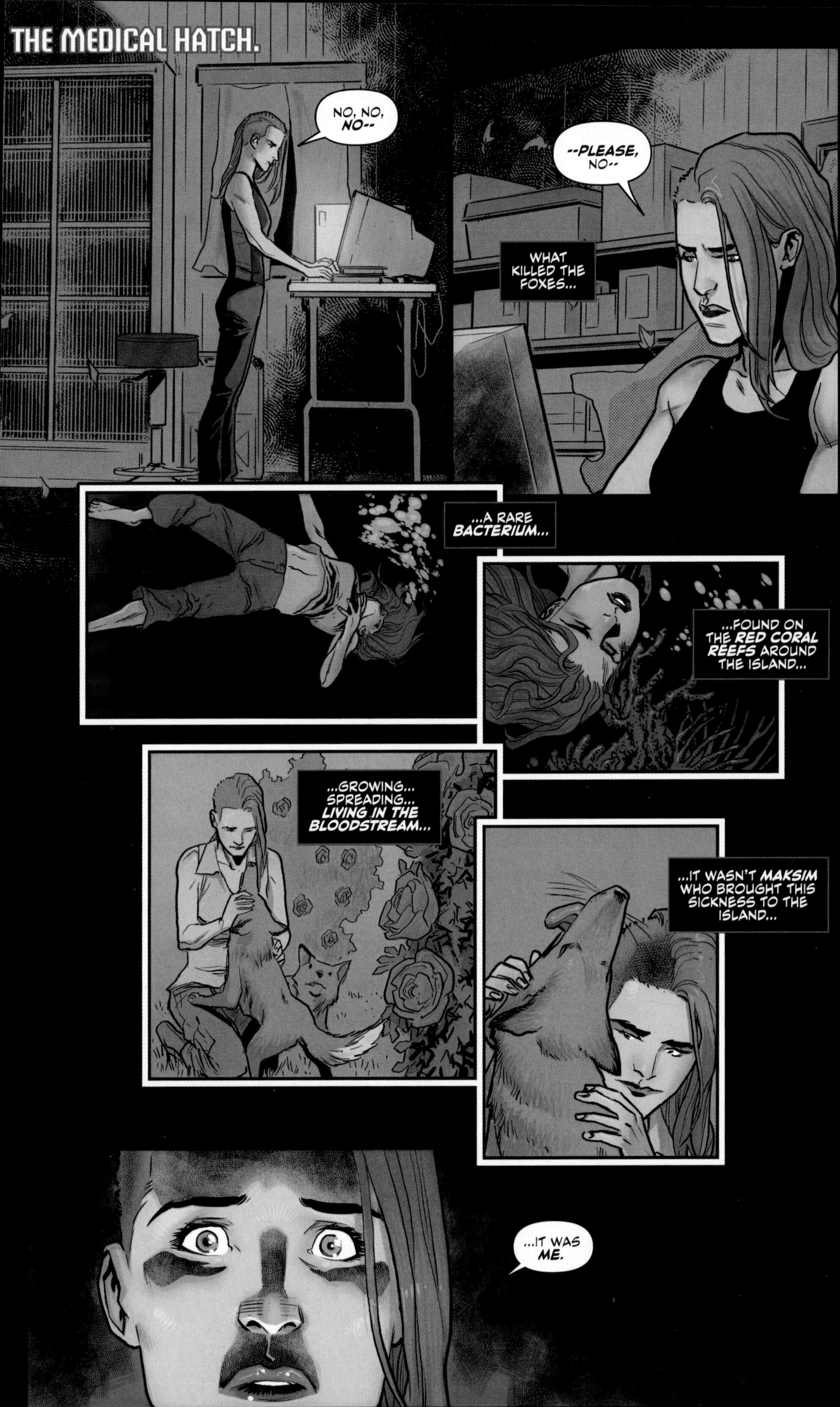
THE MEDICAL HATCH.
NO, NO, NO--
--PLEASE, NO--
WHAT KILLED THE FOXES...
...A RARE BACTERIUM...
...FOUND ON THE RED CORAL REEFS AROUND THE ISLAND...
...GROWING... SPREADING... LIVING IN THE BLOODSTREAM...
...IT WASN'T MAKSIM WHO BROUGHT THIS SICKNESS TO THE ISLAND...
...IT WAS ME.

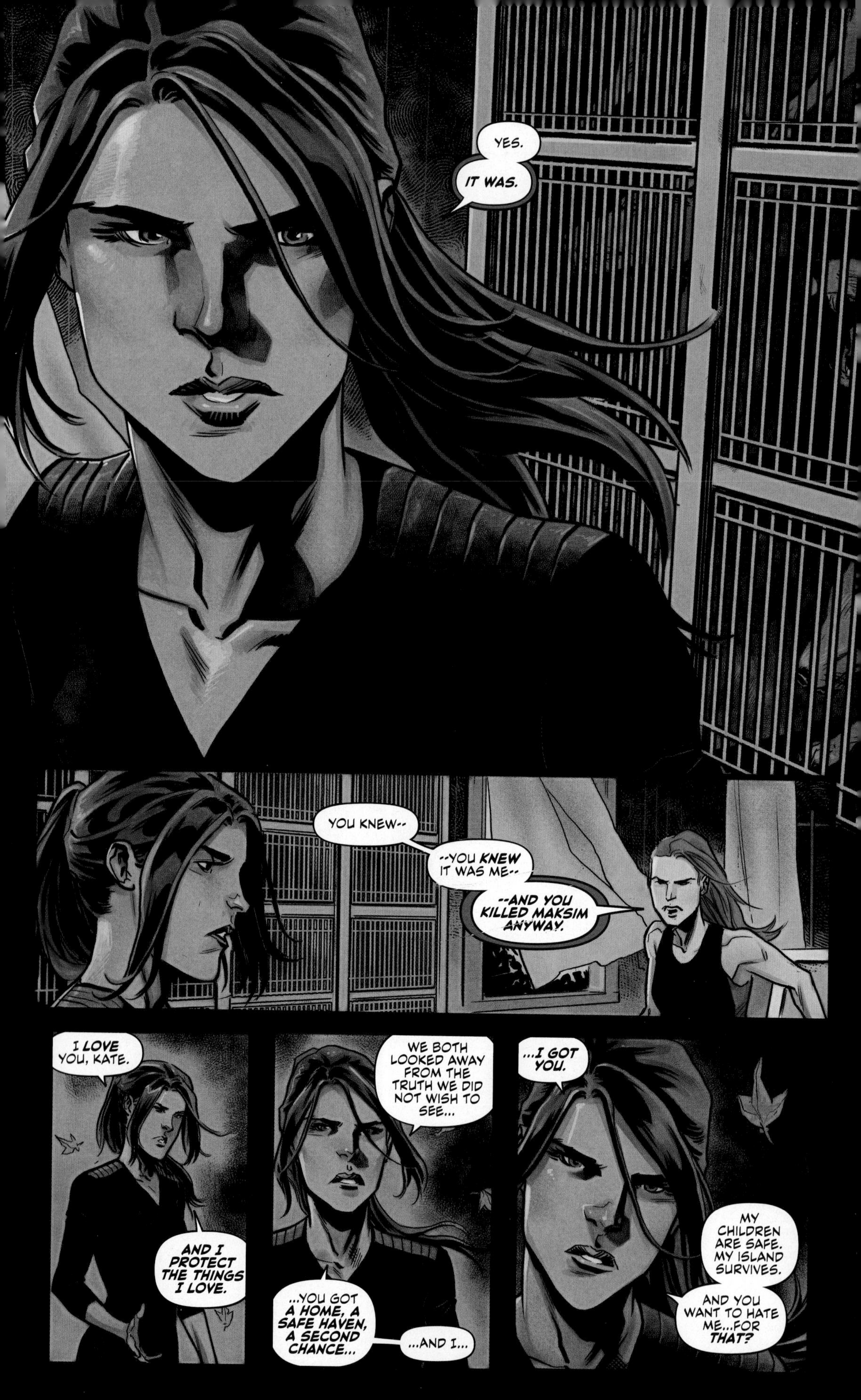
YES.
IT WAS.
YOU KNEW--
--YOU KNEW IT WAS ME--
--AND YOU KILLED MAKSIM ANYWAY.
I LOVE YOU, KATE.
AND I PROTECT THE THINGS I LOVE.
WE BOTH LOOKED AWAY FROM THE TRUTH WE DID NOT WISH TO SEE...
...YOU GOT A HOME, A SAFE HAVEN, A SECOND CHANCE...
...AND I...
...I GOT YOU.
MY CHILDREN ARE SAFE. MY ISLAND SURVIVES.
AND YOU WANT TO HATE ME...FOR THAT?

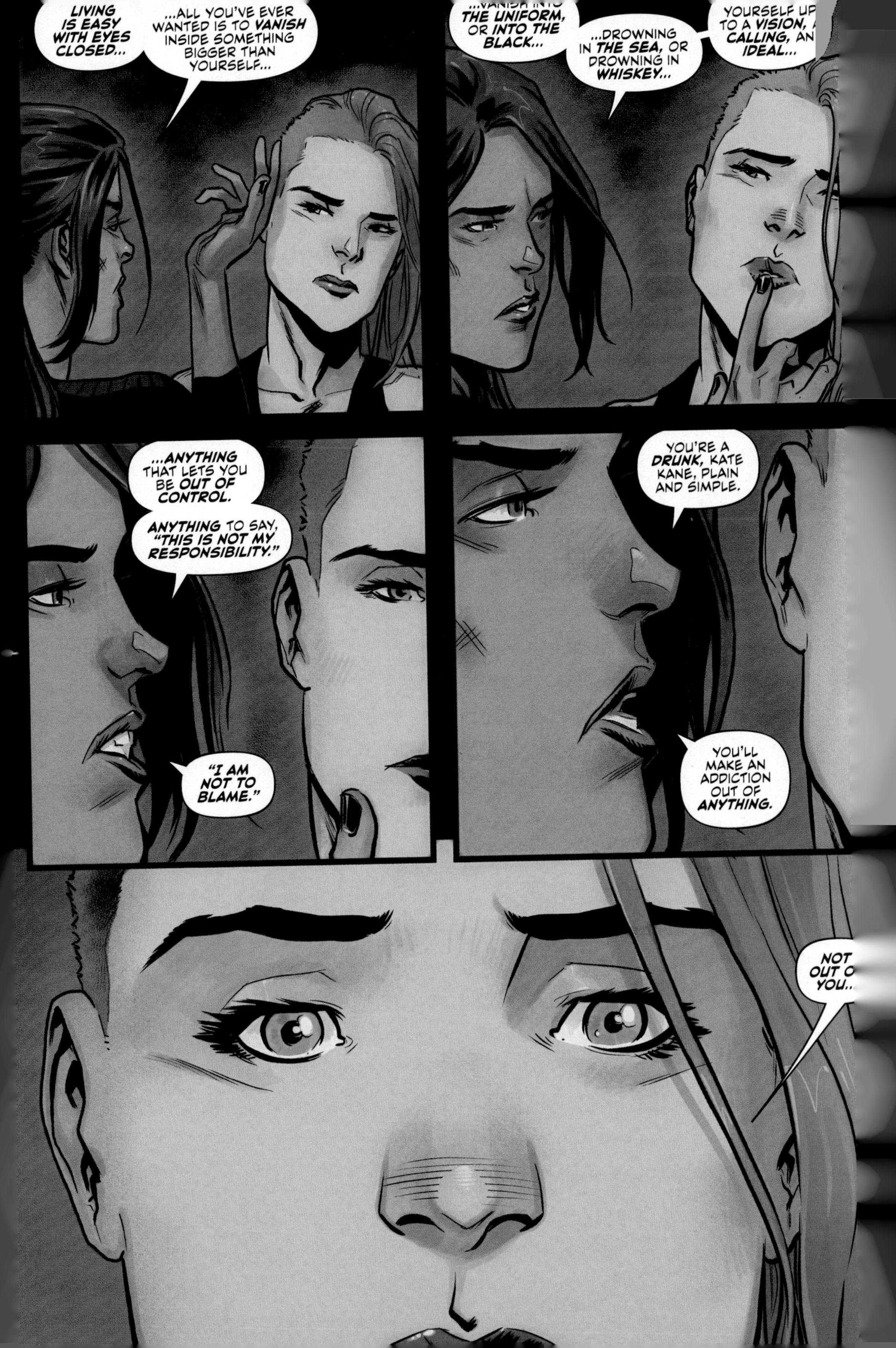
LIVING IS EASY WITH EYES CLOSED...
...ALL YOU'VE EVER WANTED IS TO VANISH INSIDE SOMETHING BIGGER THAN YOURSELF...
THE UNIFORM, OR INTO THE BLACK...
...DROWNING IN THE SEA, OR DROWNING IN WHISKEY...
YOURSELF UP TO A VISION, CALLING, AN IDEAL...
...ANYTHING THAT LETS YOU BE OUT OF CONTROL.
ANYTHING TO SAY, "THIS IS NOT MY RESPONSIBILITY."
"I AM NOT TO BLAME."
YOU'RE A DRUNK, KATE KANE, PLAIN AND SIMPLE.
YOU'LL MAKE AN ADDICTION OUT OF ANYTHING.
NOT OUT O YOU..

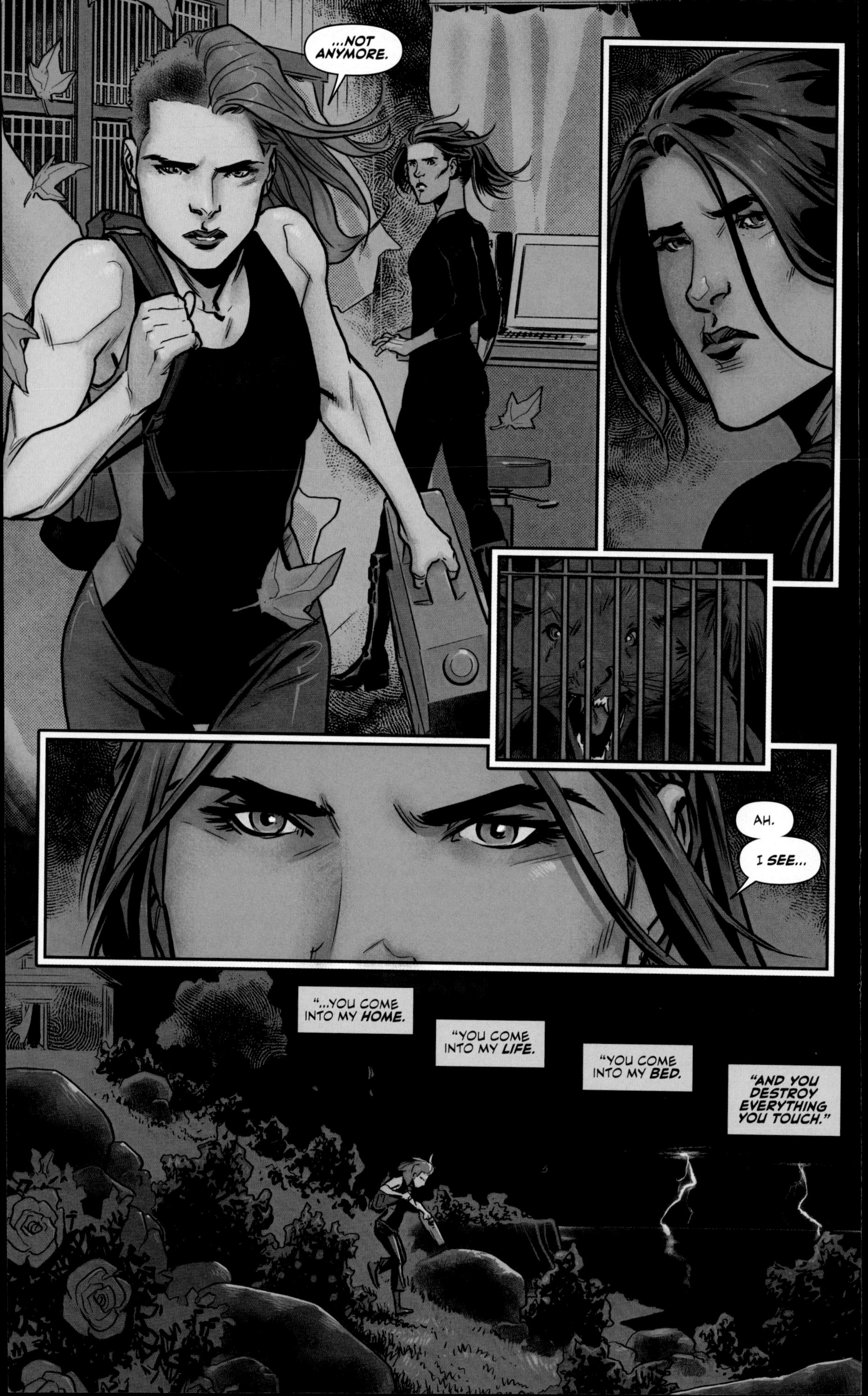
...NOT ANYMORE.
AH.
I SEE...
"...YOU COME INTO MY HOME.
"YOU COME INTO MY LIFE.
"YOU COME INTO MY BED.
"AND YOU DESTROY EVERYTHING YOU TOUCH."

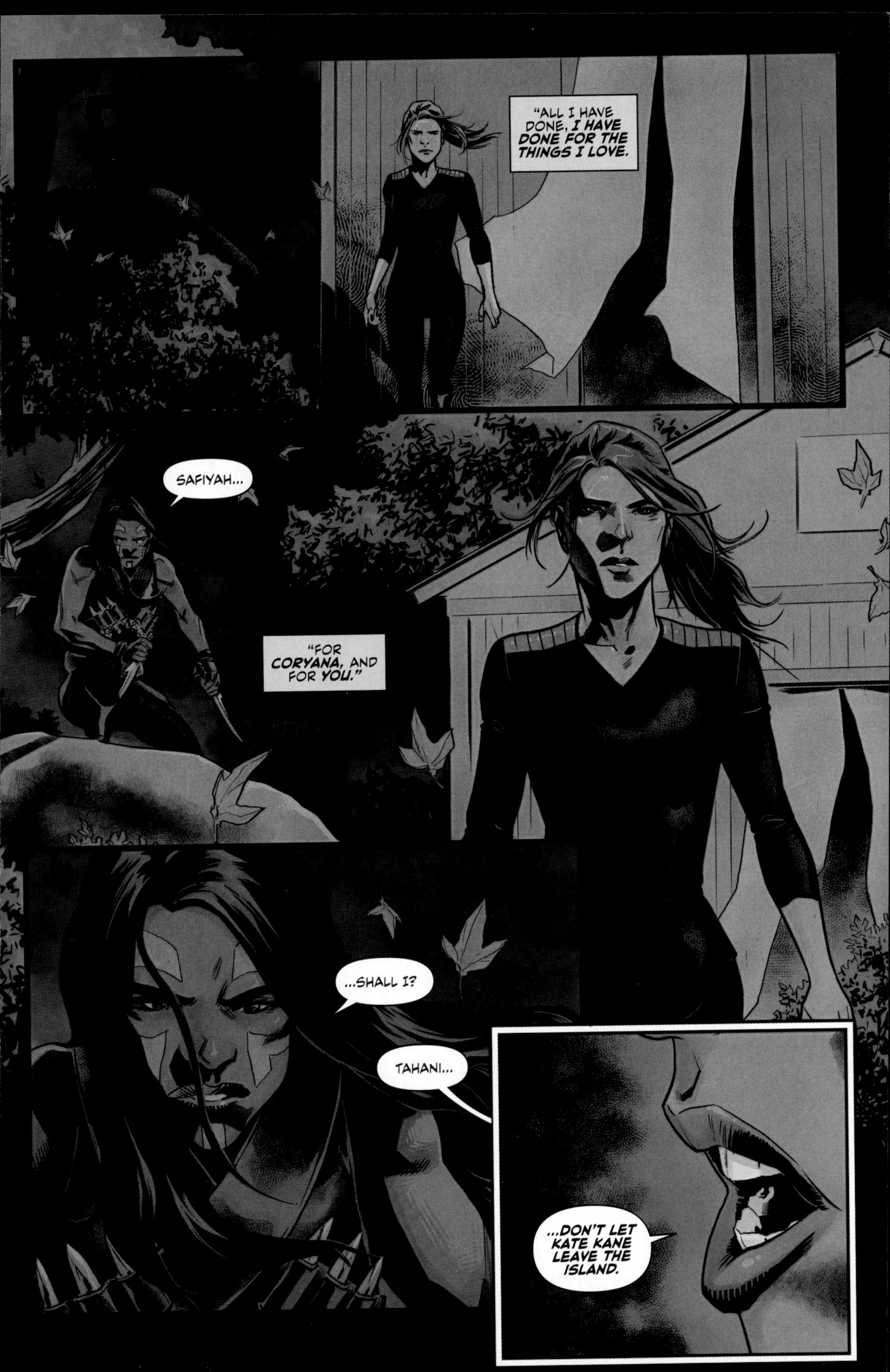
"ALL I HAVE DONE, I HAVE DONE FOR THE THINGS I LOVE.
SAFIYAH...
"FOR CORYANA, AND FOR YOU."
...SHALL I?
TAHANI...
...DON'T LET KATE KANE LEAVE THE ISLAND.

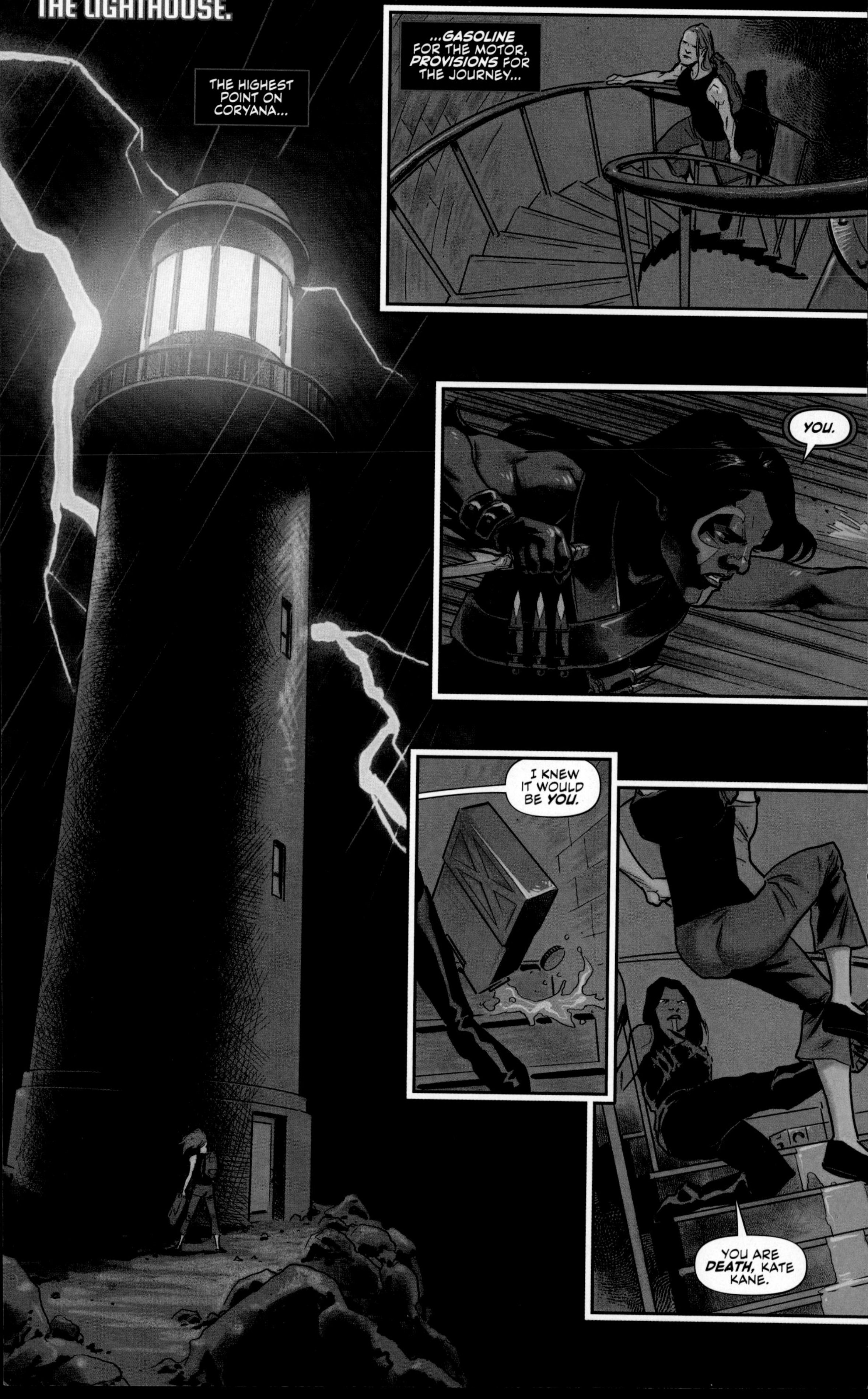
THE LIGHTHOUSE.
THE HIGHEST POINT ON CORYANA...
...GASOLINE FOR THE MOTOR, PROVISIONS FOR THE JOURNEY...
YOU.
I KNEW IT WOULD BE YOU.
YOU ARE DEATH, KATE KANE.

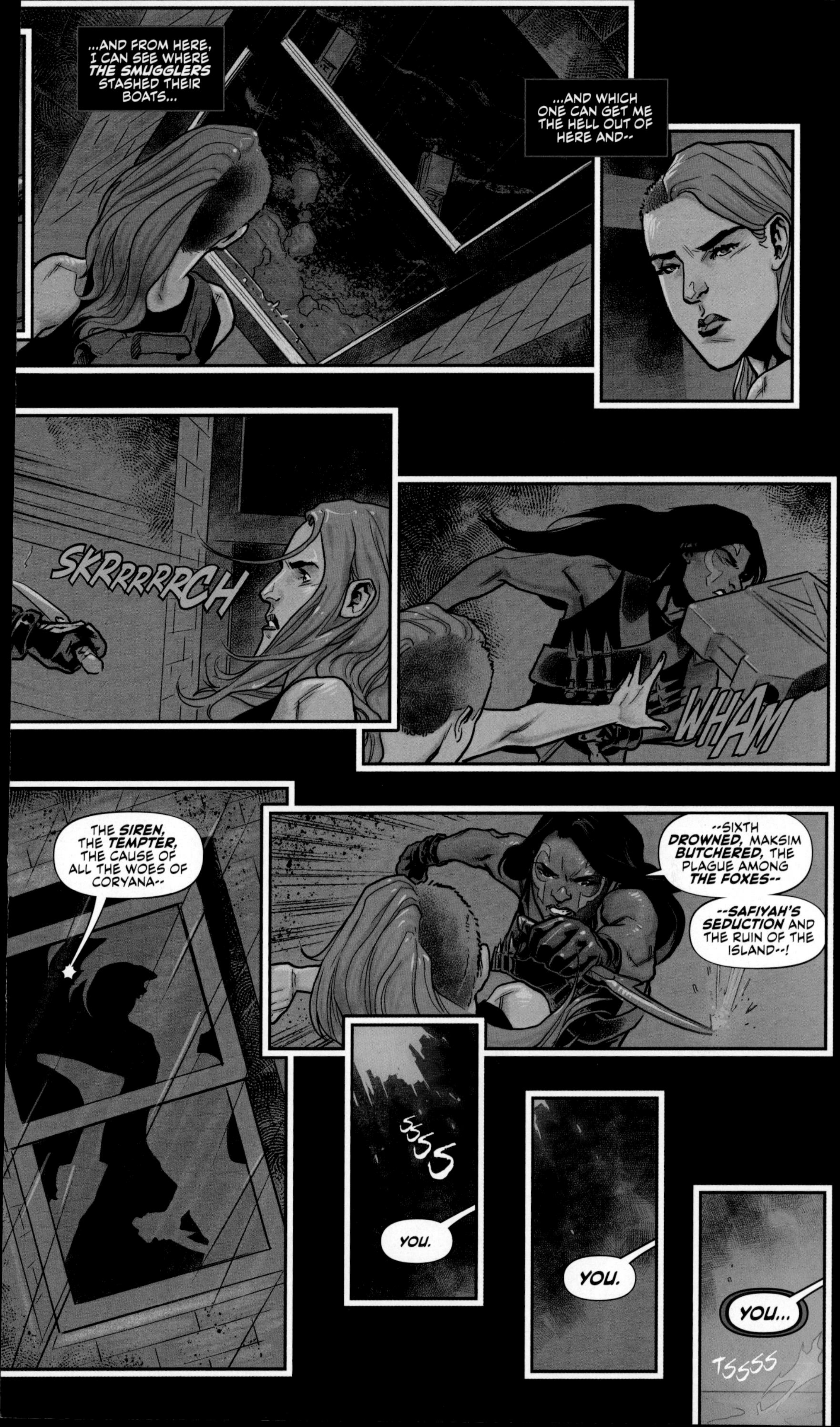

...AND FROM HERE, I CAN SEE WHERE THE SMUGGLERS STASHED THEIR BOATS...
...AND WHICH ONE CAN GET ME THE HELL OUT OF HERE AND--
SKRRRRRCH
WHAM
THE SIREN, THE TEMPTER, THE CAUSE OF ALL THE WOES OF CORYANA--
--SIXTH DROWNED, MAKSIM BUTCHERED, THE PLAGUE AMONG THE FOXES--
--SAFIYAH'S SEDUCTION AND THE RUIN OF THE ISLAND--!
SSSS
YOU.
YOU.
YOU...
TSSSS

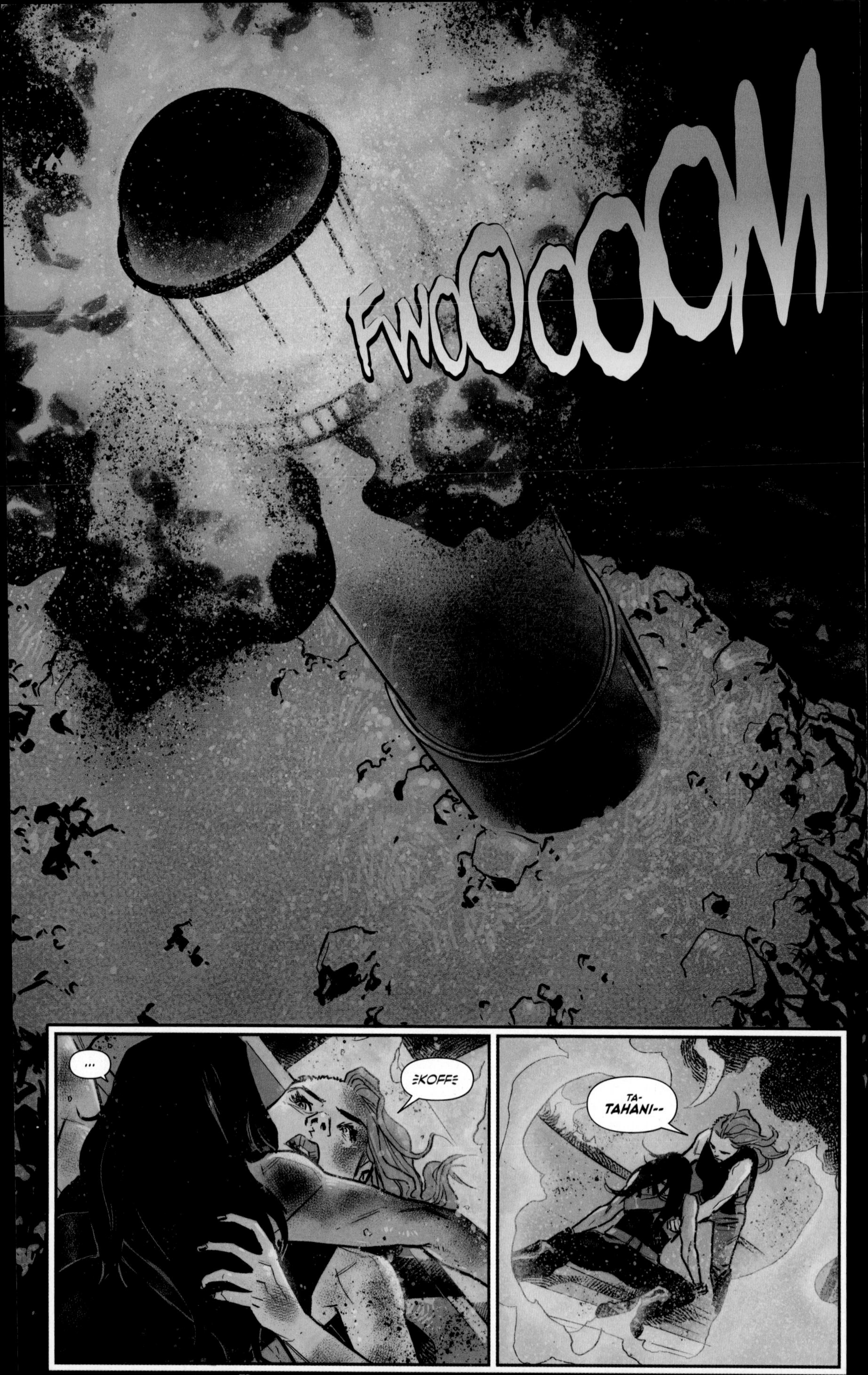
FWOOOOOOM
...
=KOFF=
TA-
TAHANI--

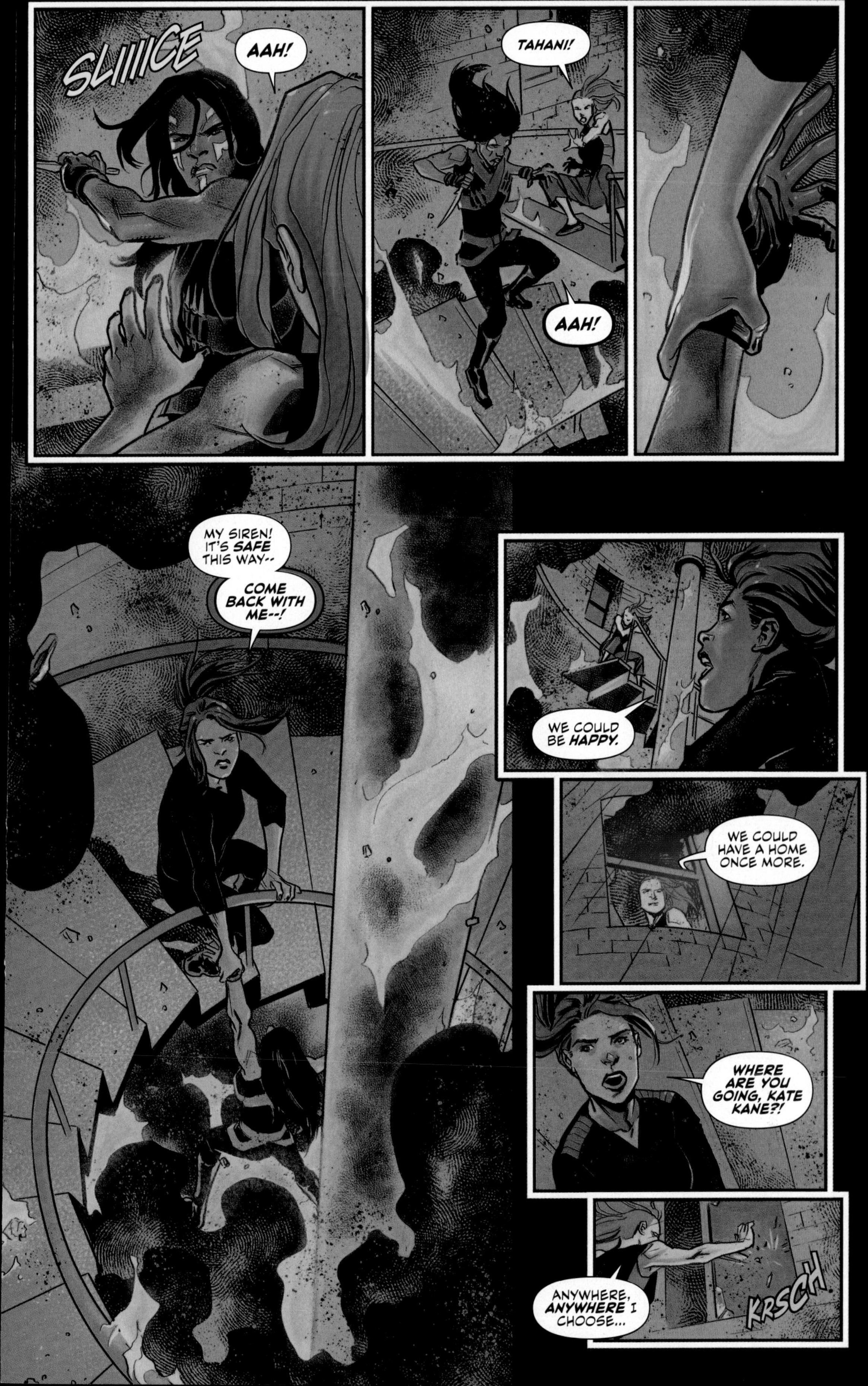
SLIIIICE
AAH!
TAHANI!
AAH!
MY SIREN! IT'S SAFE THIS WAY--
COME BACK WITH ME--!
WE COULD BE HAPPY.
WE COULD HAVE A HOME ONCE MORE.
WHERE ARE YOU GOING, KATE KANE?!
ANYWHERE, ANYWHERE I CHOOSE...
KRSCH

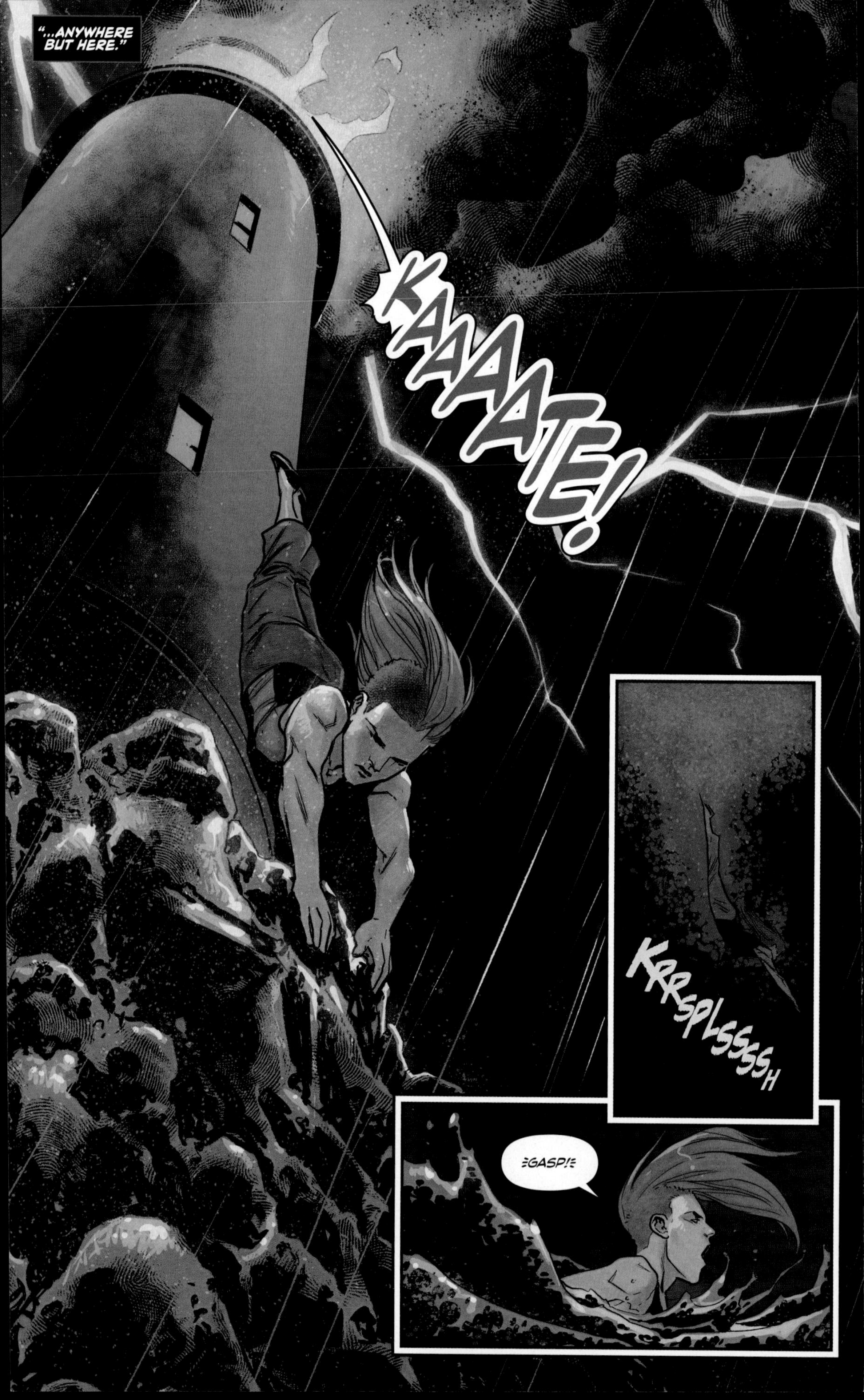
"...ANYWHERE BUT HERE."
KAAAATE!
KRRSPLSSSSH
GASP!

EACH PERSON HAS THE THING THEY WILL *KILL* FOR.

SAFIYAH...

MY SIREN...

...GO, TAHANI...

AND I HAVE THE THING *I* WILL KILL FOR.

...JUST GO.

I WILL KILL FOR *MYSELF*, THIS *ISLAND* AND *YOU.*

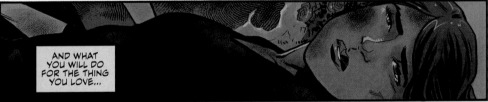

AND WHAT YOU WILL DO FOR THE THING YOU LOVE...

...ONE DAY, KATE KANE, TO YOUR SORROW...

...YOU *WILL* LEARN...

...JUST HOW FAR YOU WILL GO.

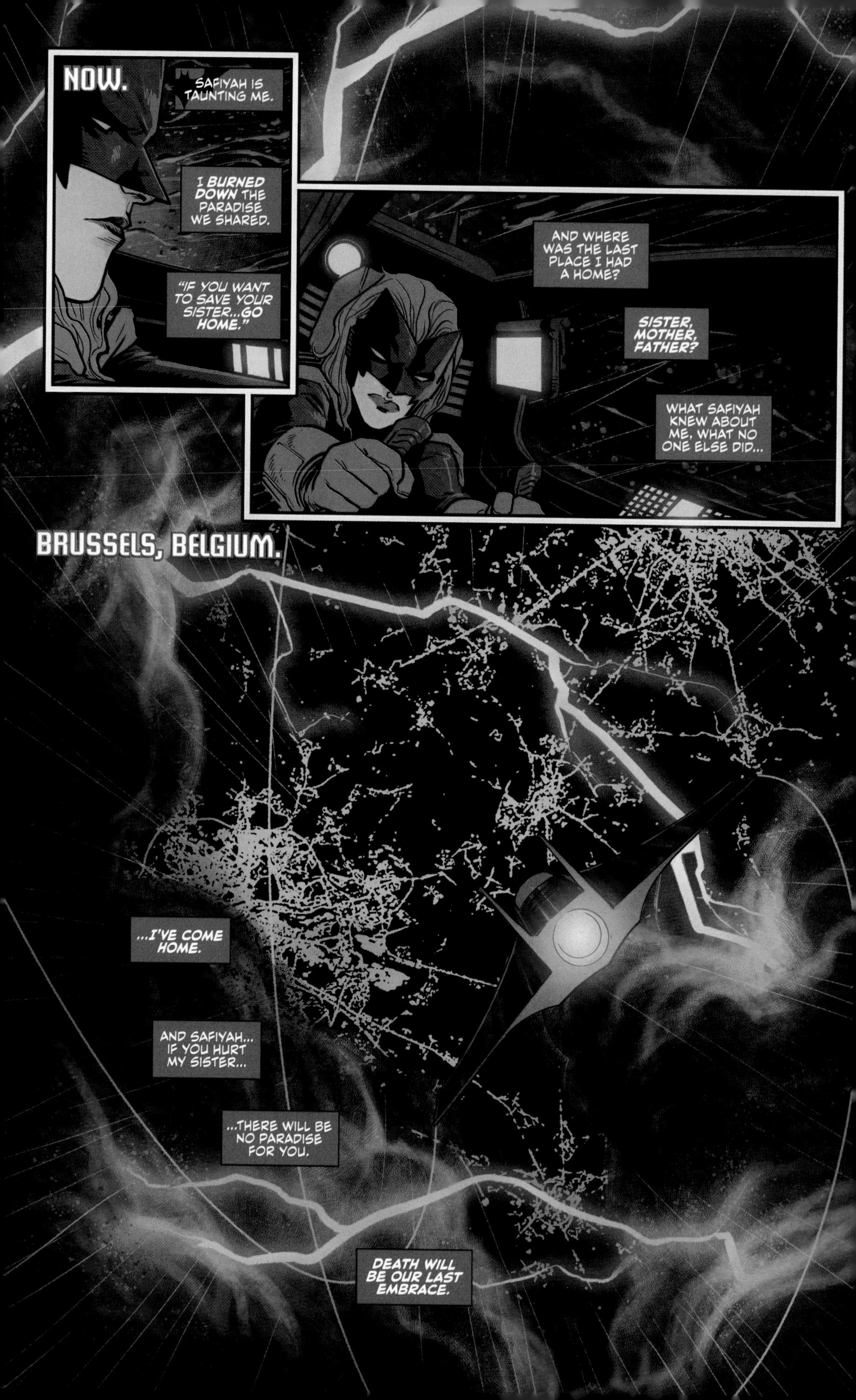
NOW.
SAFIYAH IS TAUNTING ME.
I BURNED DOWN THE PARADISE WE SHARED.
"IF YOU WANT TO SAVE YOUR SISTER...GO HOME."
AND WHERE WAS THE LAST PLACE I HAD A HOME?
SISTER, MOTHER, FATHER?
WHAT SAFIYAH KNEW ABOUT ME, WHAT NO ONE ELSE DID...
BRUSSELS, BELGIUM.
...I'VE COME HOME.
AND SAFIYAH... IF YOU HURT MY SISTER...
...THERE WILL BE NO PARADISE FOR YOU.
DEATH WILL BE OUR LAST EMBRACE.

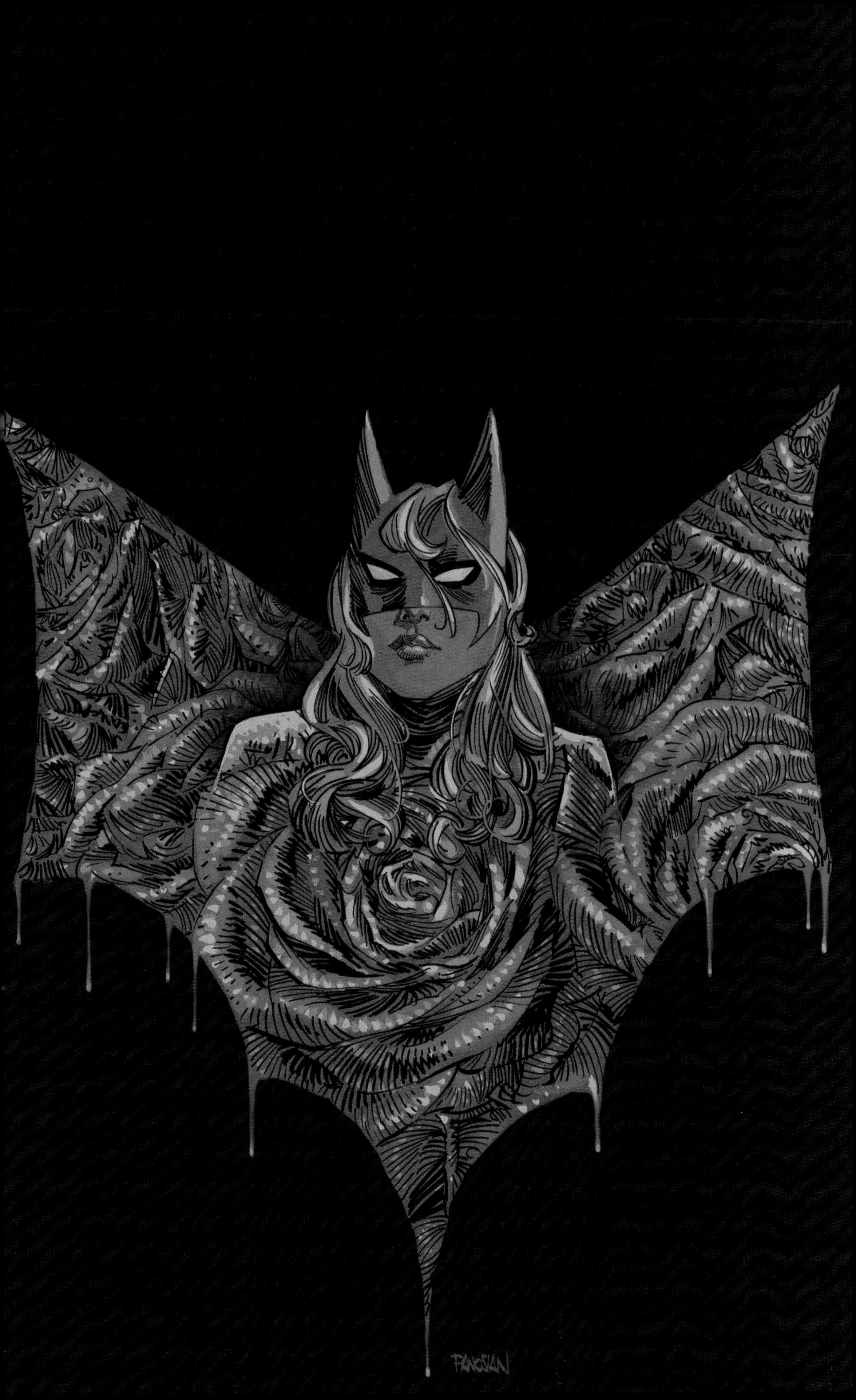
PANOSIAN

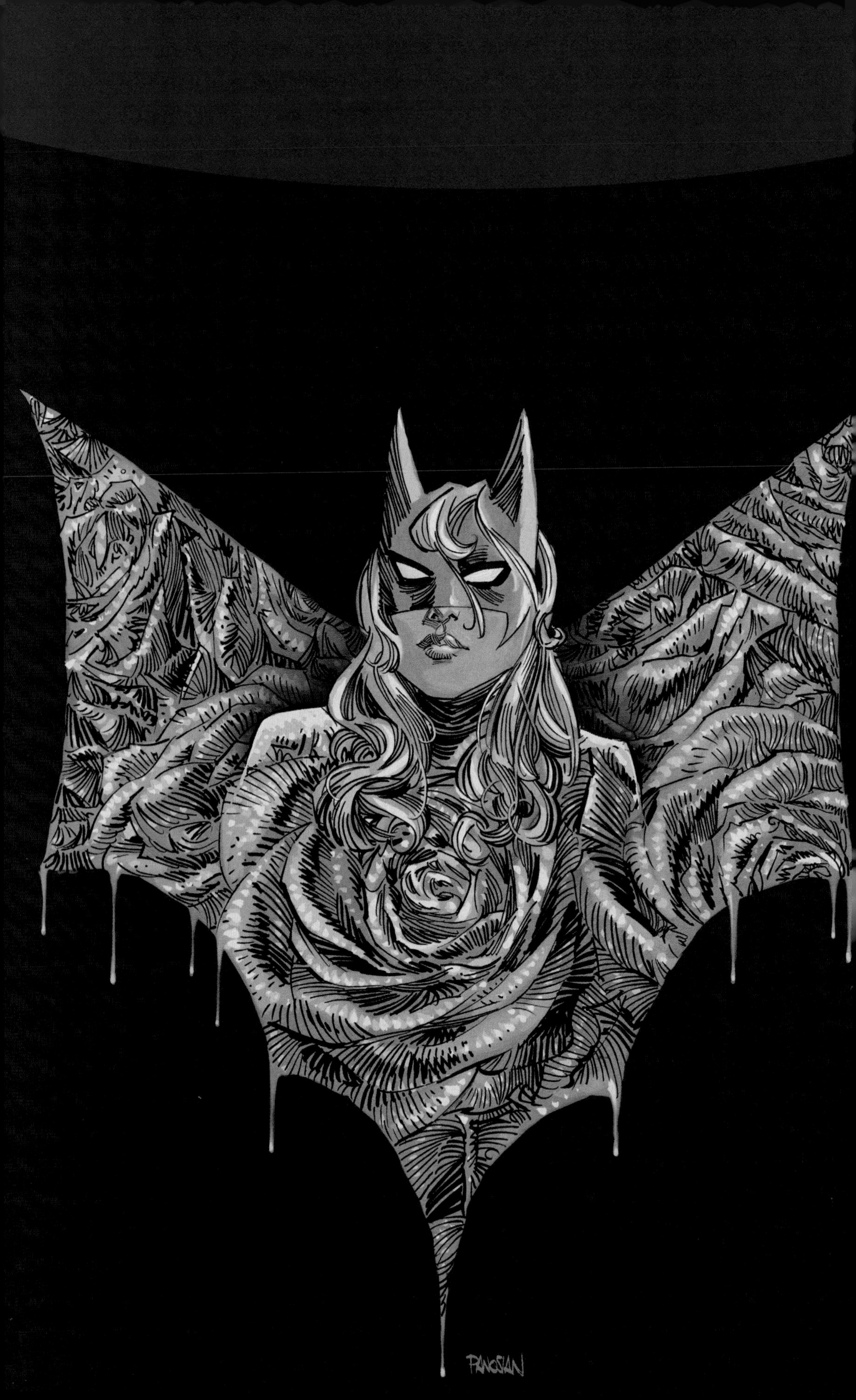
PANOSIAN

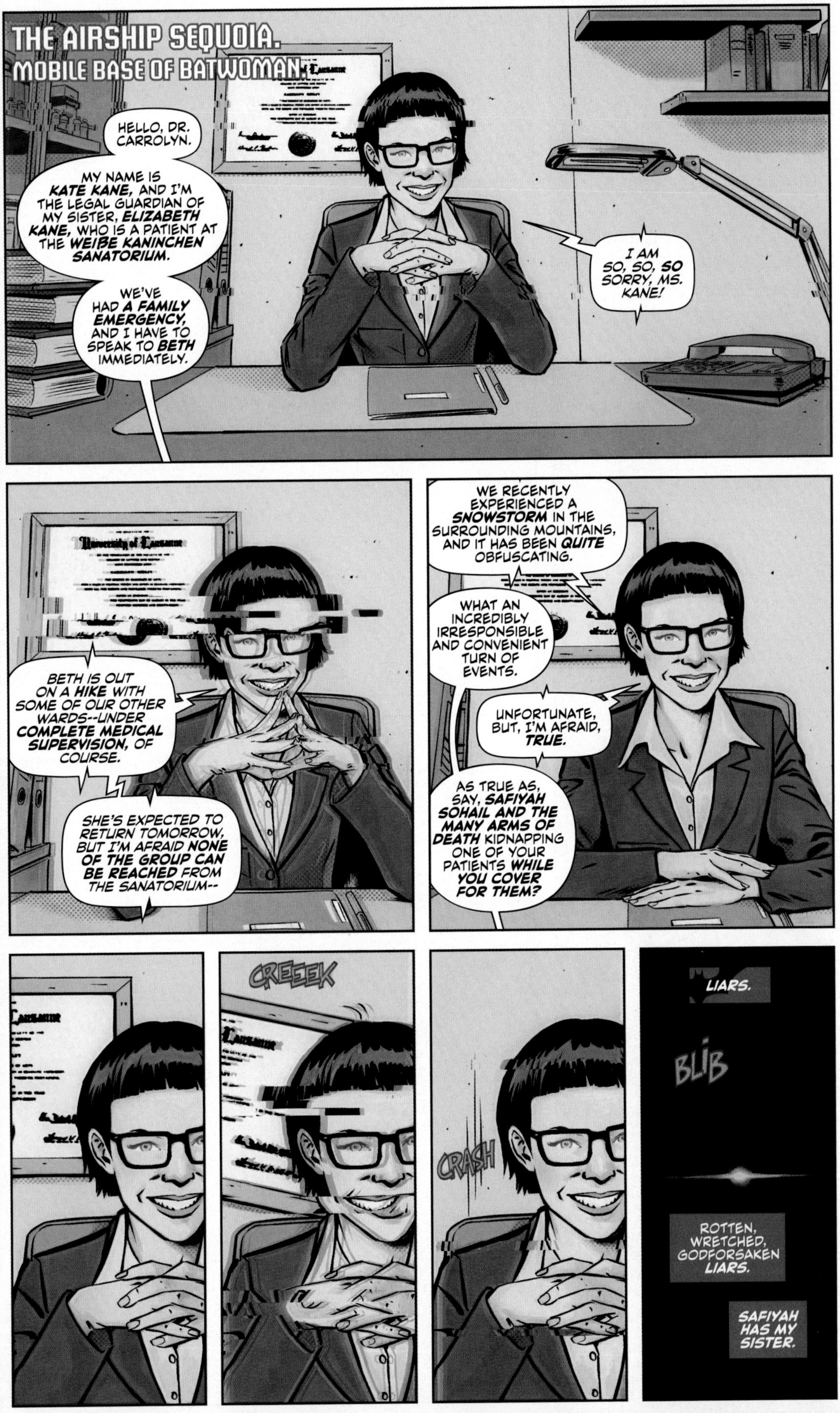
THE AIRSHIP SEQUOIA. MOBILE BASE OF BATWOMAN.
HELLO, DR. CARROLYN.
MY NAME IS KATE KANE, AND I'M THE LEGAL GUARDIAN OF MY SISTER, ELIZABETH KANE, WHO IS A PATIENT AT THE WEIBE KANINCHEN SANATORIUM.
WE'VE HAD A FAMILY EMERGENCY, AND I HAVE TO SPEAK TO BETH IMMEDIATELY.
I AM SO, SO, SO SORRY, MS. KANE!
BETH IS OUT ON A HIKE WITH SOME OF OUR OTHER WARDS--UNDER COMPLETE MEDICAL SUPERVISION, OF COURSE.
SHE'S EXPECTED TO RETURN TOMORROW, BUT I'M AFRAID NONE OF THE GROUP CAN BE REACHED FROM THE SANATORIUM--
WE RECENTLY EXPERIENCED A SNOWSTORM IN THE SURROUNDING MOUNTAINS, AND IT HAS BEEN QUITE OBFUSCATING.
WHAT AN INCREDIBLY IRRESPONSIBLE AND CONVENIENT TURN OF EVENTS.
UNFORTUNATE, BUT, I'M AFRAID, TRUE.
AS TRUE AS, SAY, SAFIYAH SOHAIL AND THE MANY ARMS OF DEATH KIDNAPPING ONE OF YOUR PATIENTS WHILE YOU COVER FOR THEM?
CREEEK
CRASH
LIARS.
BLIB
ROTTEN, WRETCHED, GODFORSAKEN LIARS.
SAFIYAH HAS MY SISTER.

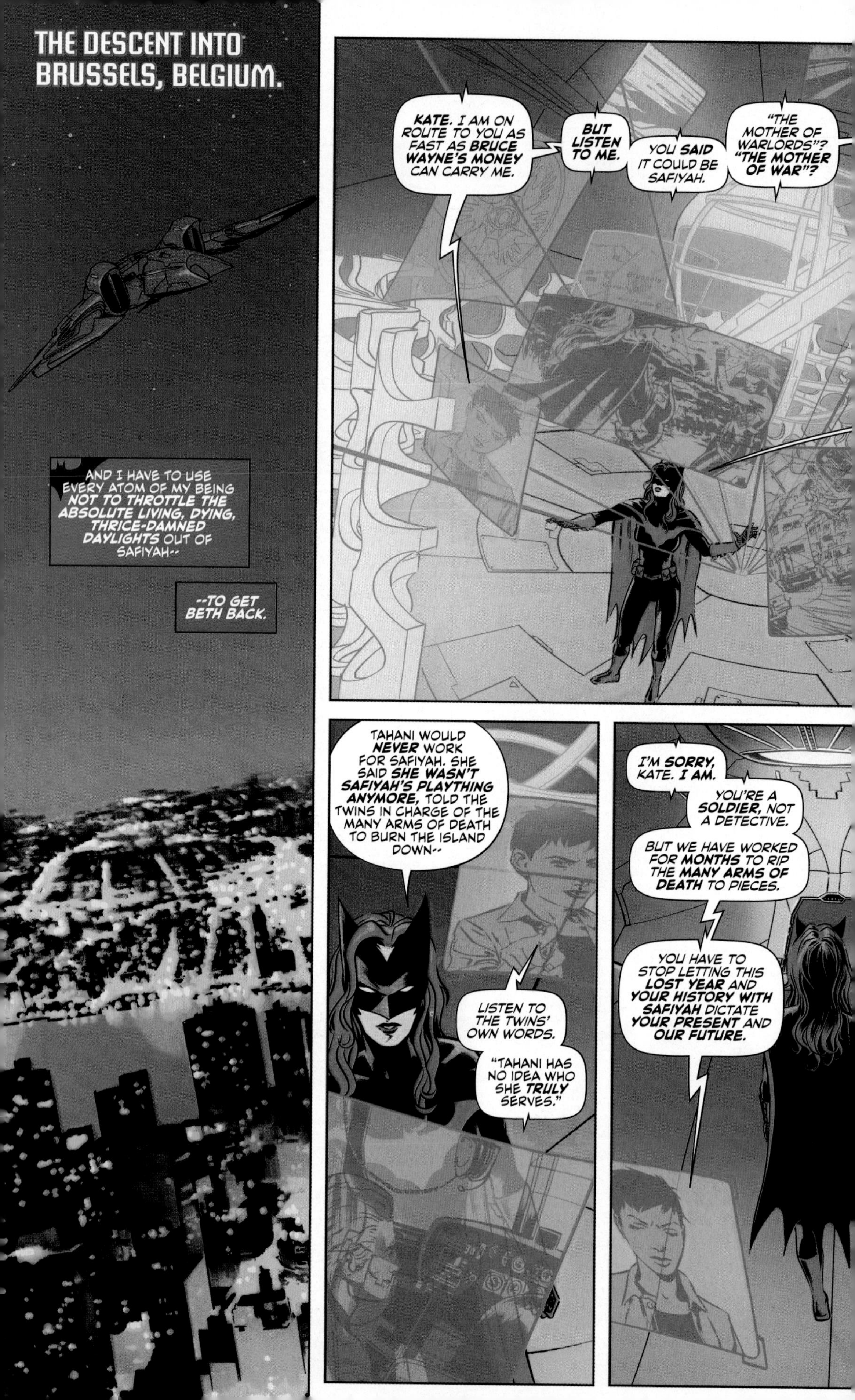
THE DESCENT INTO BRUSSELS, BELGIUM.
AND I HAVE TO USE EVERY ATOM OF MY BEING NOT TO THROTTLE THE ABSOLUTE LIVING, DYING, THRICE-DAMNED DAYLIGHTS OUT OF SAFIYAH--
--TO GET BETH BACK.
KATE. I AM ON ROUTE TO YOU AS FAST AS BRUCE WAYNE'S MONEY CAN CARRY ME.
BUT LISTEN TO ME.
YOU SAID IT COULD BE SAFIYAH.
"THE MOTHER OF WARLORDS"? "THE MOTHER OF WAR"?
TAHANI WOULD NEVER WORK FOR SAFIYAH. SHE SAID SHE WASN'T SAFIYAH'S PLAYTHING ANYMORE, TOLD THE TWINS IN CHARGE OF THE MANY ARMS OF DEATH TO BURN THE ISLAND DOWN--
LISTEN TO THE TWINS' OWN WORDS.
"TAHANI HAS NO IDEA WHO SHE TRULY SERVES."
I'M SORRY, KATE. I AM.
YOU'RE A SOLDIER, NOT A DETECTIVE.
BUT WE HAVE WORKED FOR MONTHS TO RIP THE MANY ARMS OF DEATH TO PIECES.
YOU HAVE TO STOP LETTING THIS LOST YEAR AND YOUR HISTORY WITH SAFIYAH DICTATE YOUR PRESENT AND OUR FUTURE.

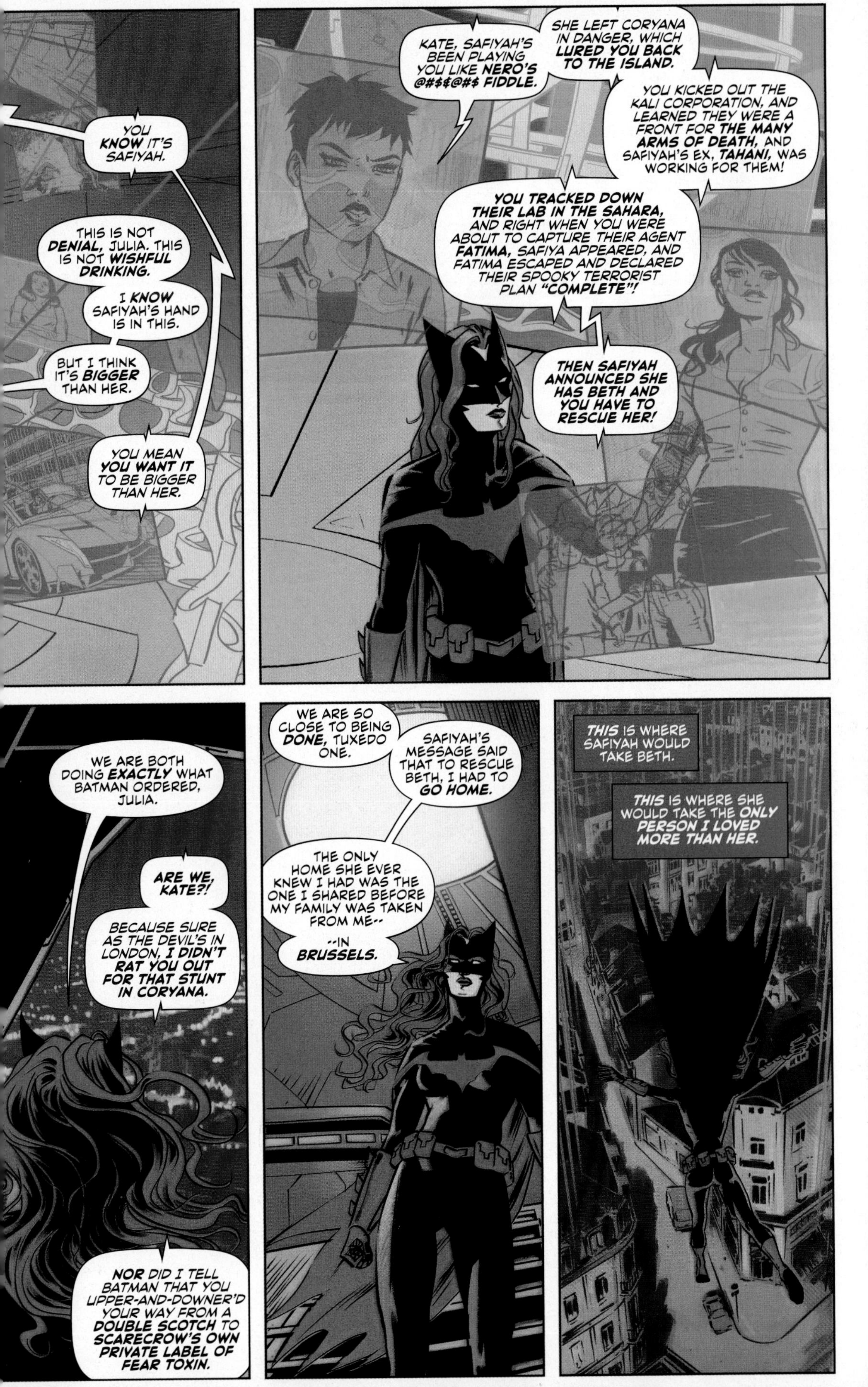
YOU KNOW IT'S SAFIYAH.
THIS IS NOT DENIAL, JULIA. THIS IS NOT WISHFUL DRINKING.
I KNOW SAFIYAH'S HAND IS IN THIS.
BUT I THINK IT'S BIGGER THAN HER.
YOU MEAN YOU WANT IT TO BE BIGGER THAN HER.
KATE, SAFIYAH'S BEEN PLAYING YOU LIKE NERO'S @#$$@#$ FIDDLE.
SHE LEFT CORYANA IN DANGER, WHICH LURED YOU BACK TO THE ISLAND.
YOU KICKED OUT THE KALI CORPORATION, AND LEARNED THEY WERE A FRONT FOR THE MANY ARMS OF DEATH, AND SAFIYAH'S EX, TAHANI, WAS WORKING FOR THEM!
YOU TRACKED DOWN THEIR LAB IN THE SAHARA, AND RIGHT WHEN YOU WERE ABOUT TO CAPTURE THEIR AGENT FATIMA, SAFIYA APPEARED, AND FATIMA ESCAPED AND DECLARED THEIR SPOOKY TERRORIST PLAN "COMPLETE"!
THEN SAFIYAH ANNOUNCED SHE HAS BETH AND YOU HAVE TO RESCUE HER!
WE ARE BOTH DOING EXACTLY WHAT BATMAN ORDERED, JULIA.
ARE WE, KATE?!
BECAUSE SURE AS THE DEVIL'S IN LONDON, I DIDN'T RAT YOU OUT FOR THAT STUNT IN CORYANA.
NOR DID I TELL BATMAN THAT YOU UPPER-AND-DOWNER'D YOUR WAY FROM A DOUBLE SCOTCH TO SCARECROW'S OWN PRIVATE LABEL OF FEAR TOXIN.
WE ARE SO CLOSE TO BEING DONE, TUXEDO ONE.
SAFIYAH'S MESSAGE SAID THAT TO RESCUE BETH, I HAD TO GO HOME.
THE ONLY HOME SHE EVER KNEW I HAD WAS THE ONE I SHARED BEFORE MY FAMILY WAS TAKEN FROM ME--
--IN BRUSSELS.
THIS IS WHERE SAFIYAH WOULD TAKE BETH.
THIS IS WHERE SHE WOULD TAKE THE ONLY PERSON I LOVED MORE THAN HER.

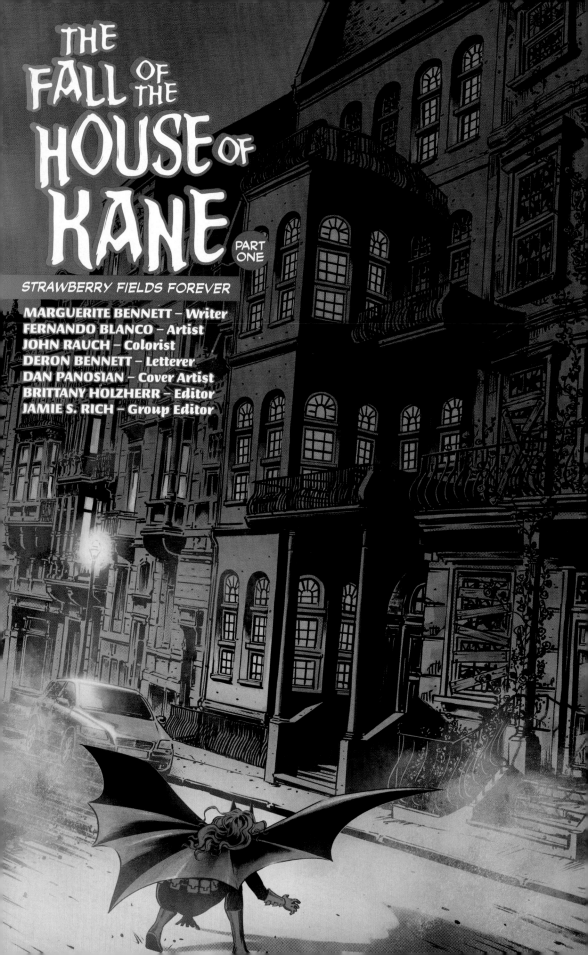

THE FALL OF THE HOUSE OF KANE

Part One

STRAWBERRY FIELDS FOREVER

MARGUERITE BENNETT – Writer
FERNANDO BLANCO – Artist
JOHN RAUCH – Colorist
DERON BENNETT – Letterer
DAN PANOSIAN – Cover Artist
BRITTANY HOLZHERR – Editor
JAMIE S. RICH – Group Editor

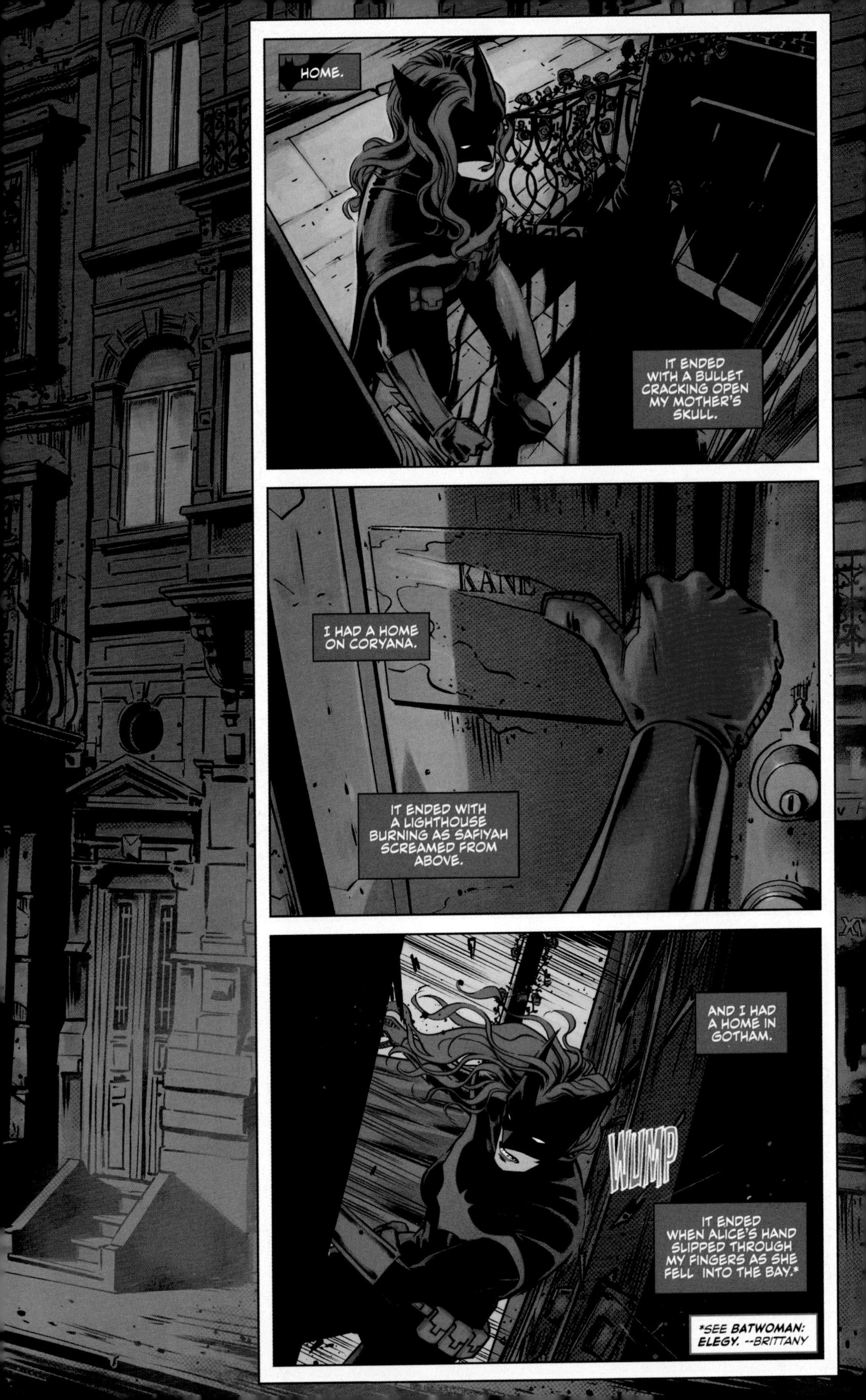
HOME.
IT ENDED WITH A BULLET CRACKING OPEN MY MOTHER'S SKULL.
KANE
I HAD A HOME ON CORYANA.
IT ENDED WITH A LIGHTHOUSE BURNING AS SAFIYAH SCREAMED FROM ABOVE.
AND I HAD A HOME IN GOTHAM.
WUMP
IT ENDED WHEN ALICE'S HAND SLIPPED THROUGH MY FINGERS AS SHE FELL INTO THE BAY.*
*SEE BATWOMAN: ELEGY. --BRITTANY

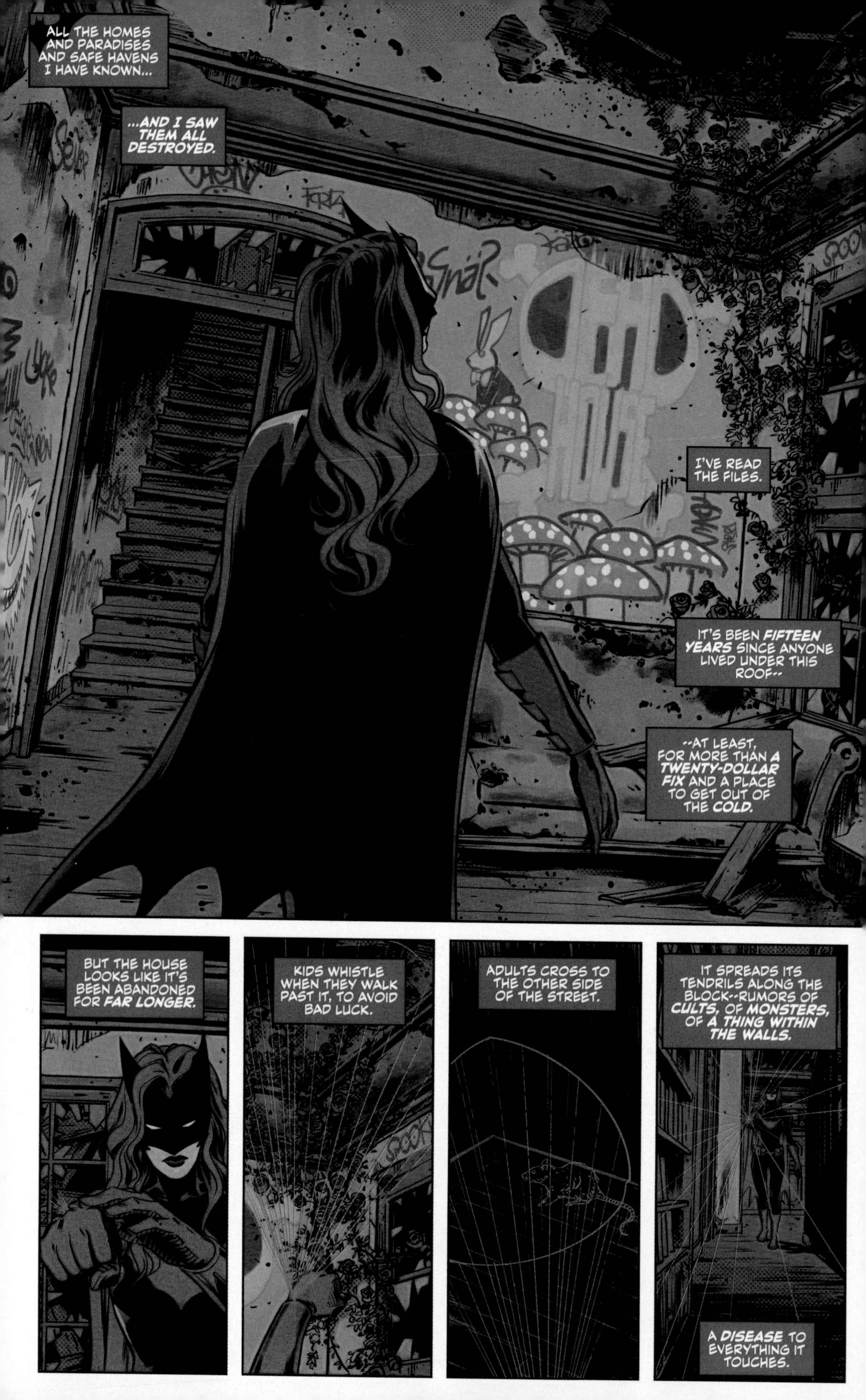
ALL THE HOMES AND PARADISES AND SAFE HAVENS I HAVE KNOWN...
...AND I SAW THEM ALL DESTROYED.
I'VE READ THE FILES.
IT'S BEEN FIFTEEN YEARS SINCE ANYONE LIVED UNDER THIS ROOF--
--AT LEAST, FOR MORE THAN A TWENTY-DOLLAR FIX AND A PLACE TO GET OUT OF THE COLD.
BUT THE HOUSE LOOKS LIKE IT'S BEEN ABANDONED FOR FAR LONGER.
KIDS WHISTLE WHEN THEY WALK PAST IT, TO AVOID BAD LUCK.
ADULTS CROSS TO THE OTHER SIDE OF THE STREET.
IT SPREADS ITS TENDRILS ALONG THE BLOCK--RUMORS OF CULTS, OF MONSTERS, OF A THING WITHIN THE WALLS.
A DISEASE TO EVERYTHING IT TOUCHES.

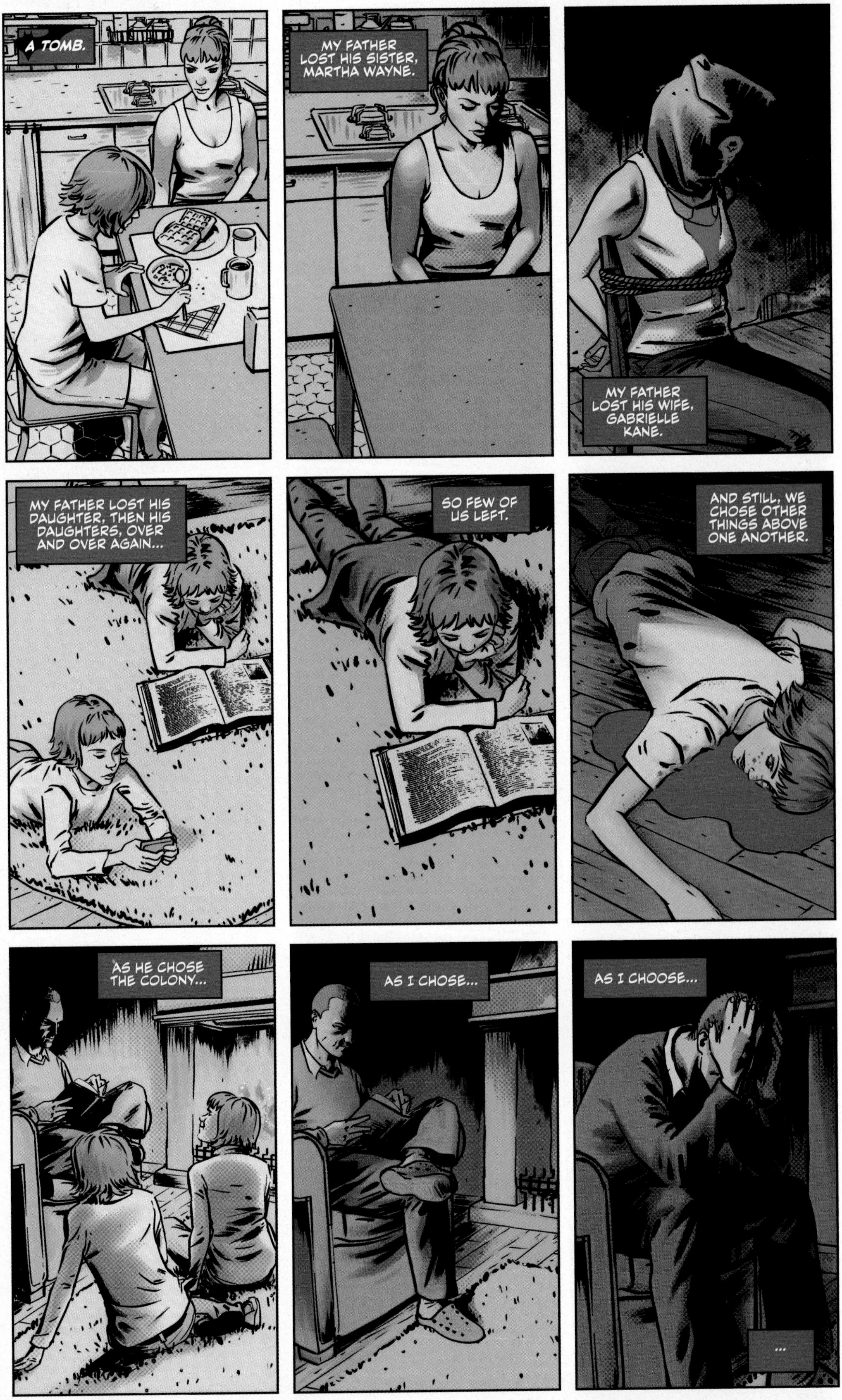
A TOMB.
MY FATHER LOST HIS SISTER, MARTHA WAYNE.
MY FATHER LOST HIS WIFE, GABRIELLE KANE.
MY FATHER LOST HIS DAUGHTER, THEN HIS DAUGHTERS, OVER AND OVER AGAIN...
SO FEW OF US LEFT.
AND STILL, WE CHOSE OTHER THINGS ABOVE ONE ANOTHER.
AS HE CHOSE THE COLONY...
AS I CHOSE...
AS I CHOOSE...
...

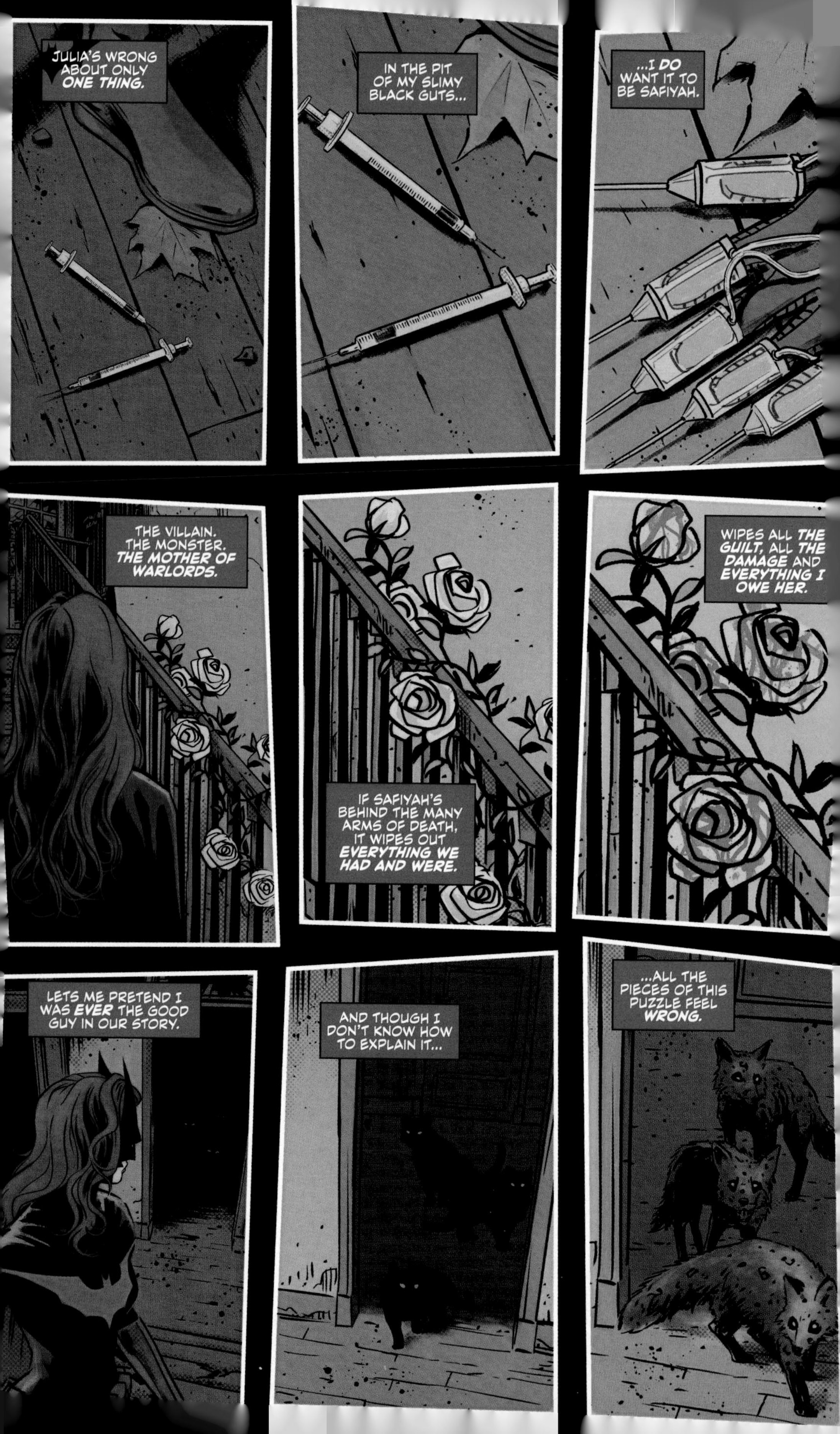
JULIA'S WRONG ABOUT ONLY ONE THING.
IN THE PIT OF MY SLIMY BLACK GUTS...
...I DO WANT IT TO BE SAFIYAH.
THE VILLAIN. THE MONSTER. THE MOTHER OF WARLORDS.
IF SAFIYAH'S BEHIND THE MANY ARMS OF DEATH, IT WIPES OUT EVERYTHING WE HAD AND WERE.
WIPES ALL THE GUILT, ALL THE DAMAGE AND EVERYTHING I OWE HER.
LETS ME PRETEND I WAS EVER THE GOOD GUY IN OUR STORY.
AND THOUGH I DON'T KNOW HOW TO EXPLAIN IT...
...ALL THE PIECES OF THIS PUZZLE FEEL WRONG.

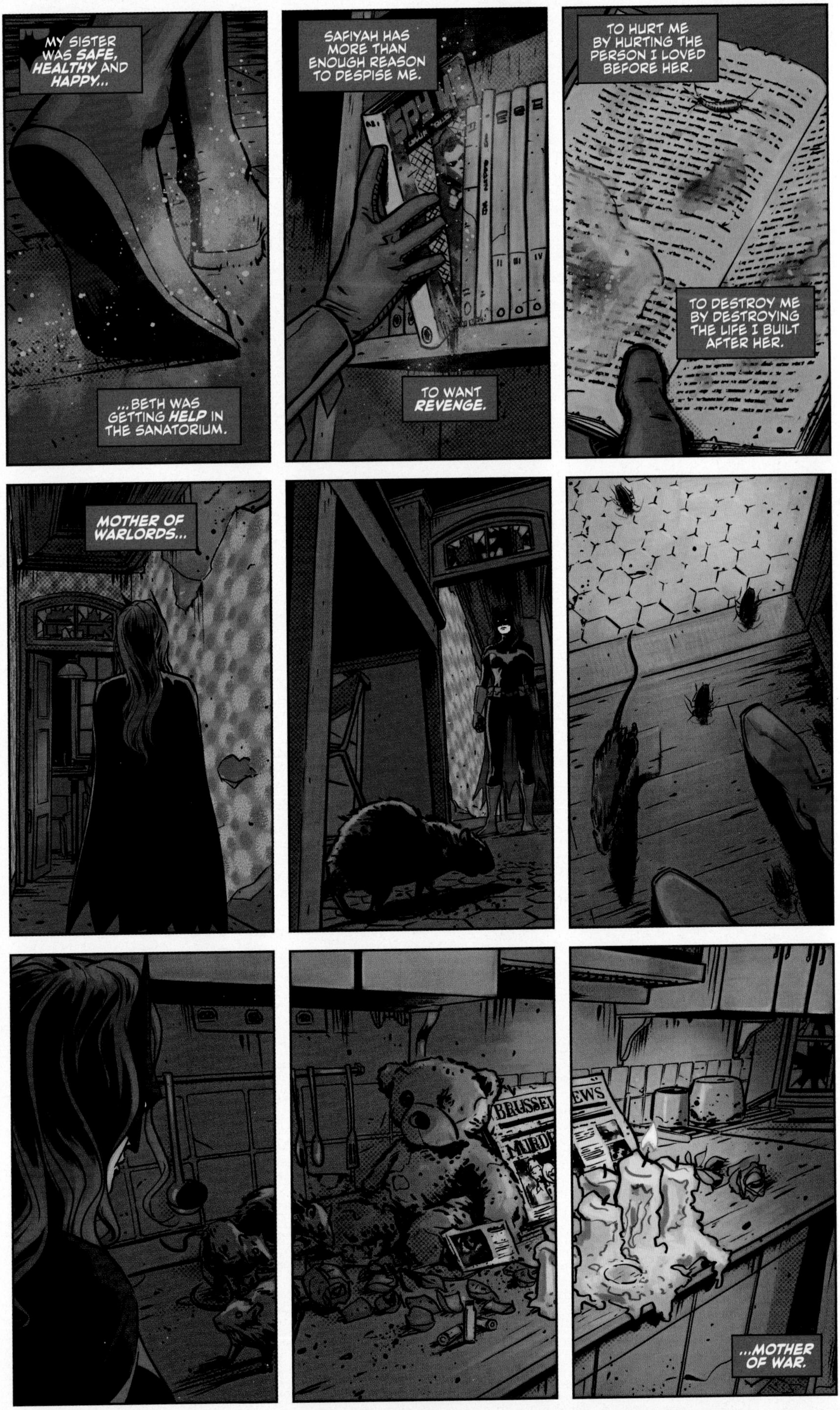
MY SISTER WAS SAFE, HEALTHY AND HAPPY...
...BETH WAS GETTING HELP IN THE SANATORIUM.
SAFIYAH HAS MORE THAN ENOUGH REASON TO DESPISE ME.
TO WANT REVENGE.
TO HURT ME BY HURTING THE PERSON I LOVED BEFORE HER.
TO DESTROY ME BY DESTROYING THE LIFE I BUILT AFTER HER.
MOTHER OF WARLORDS...
...MOTHER OF WAR.

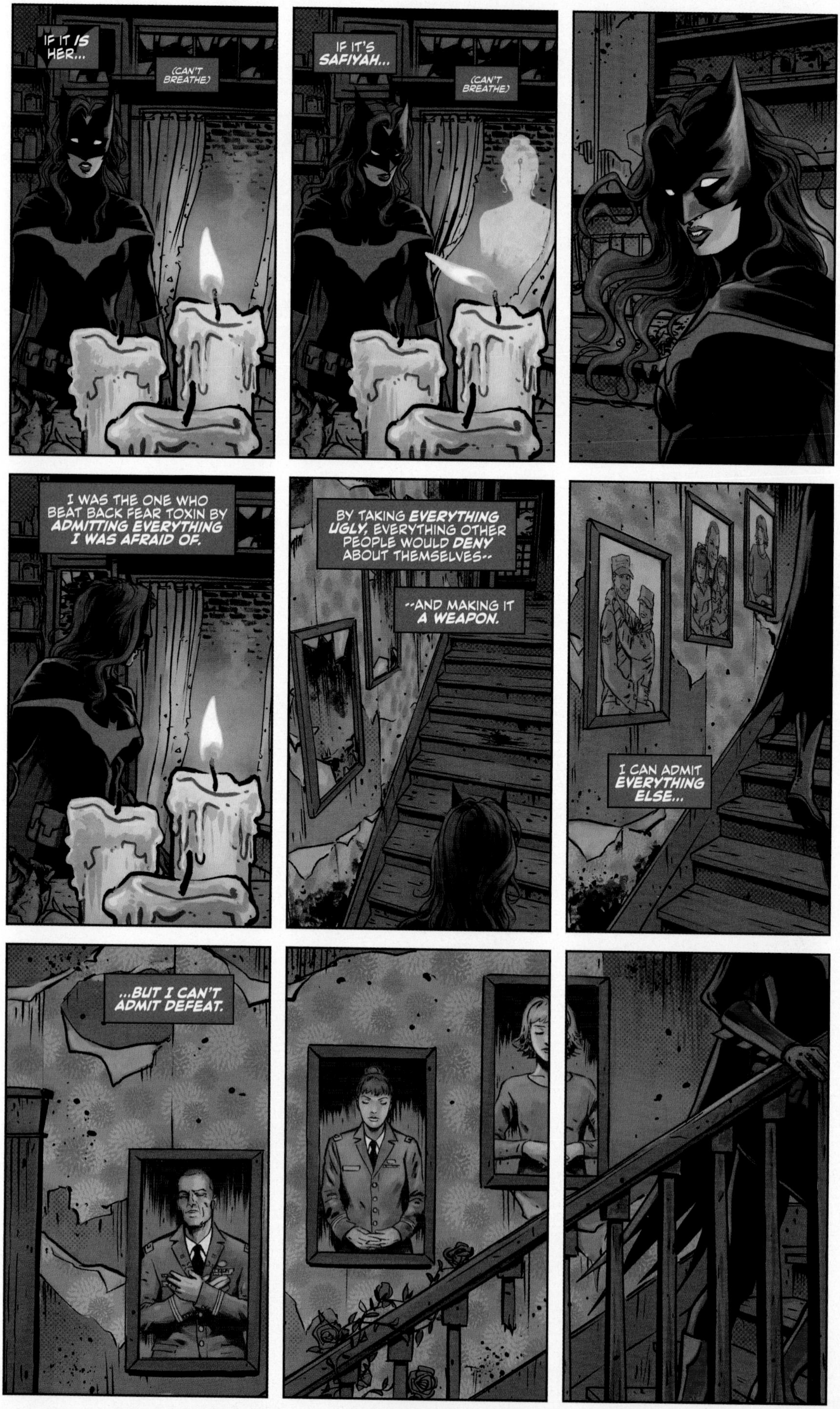
IF IT IS HER...
(CAN'T BREATHE)
IF IT'S SAFIYAH...
(CAN'T BREATHE)
I WAS THE ONE WHO BEAT BACK FEAR TOXIN BY ADMITTING EVERYTHING I WAS AFRAID OF.
BY TAKING EVERYTHING UGLY, EVERYTHING OTHER PEOPLE WOULD DENY ABOUT THEMSELVES--
--AND MAKING IT A WEAPON.
I CAN ADMIT EVERYTHING ELSE...
...BUT I CAN'T ADMIT DEFEAT.

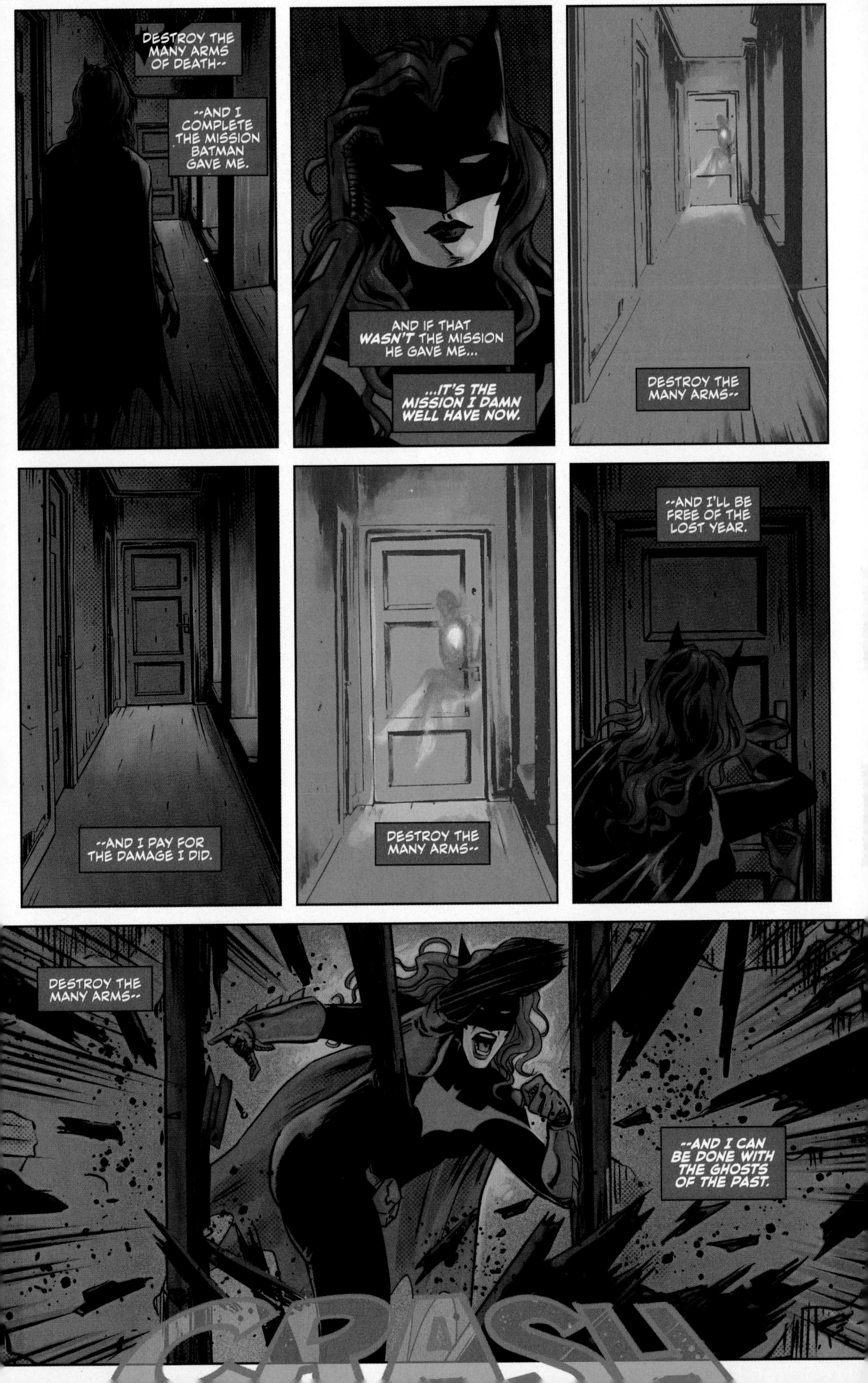
DESTROY THE MANY ARMS OF DEATH--
--AND I COMPLETE THE MISSION BATMAN GAVE ME.
AND IF THAT *WASN'T* THE MISSION HE GAVE ME...
...IT'S THE MISSION I DAMN WELL HAVE NOW.
DESTROY THE MANY ARMS--
--AND I PAY FOR THE DAMAGE I DID.
DESTROY THE MANY ARMS--
--AND I'LL BE FREE OF THE LOST YEAR.
DESTROY THE MANY ARMS--
--AND I CAN BE DONE WITH THE GHOSTS OF THE PAST.
CRASH

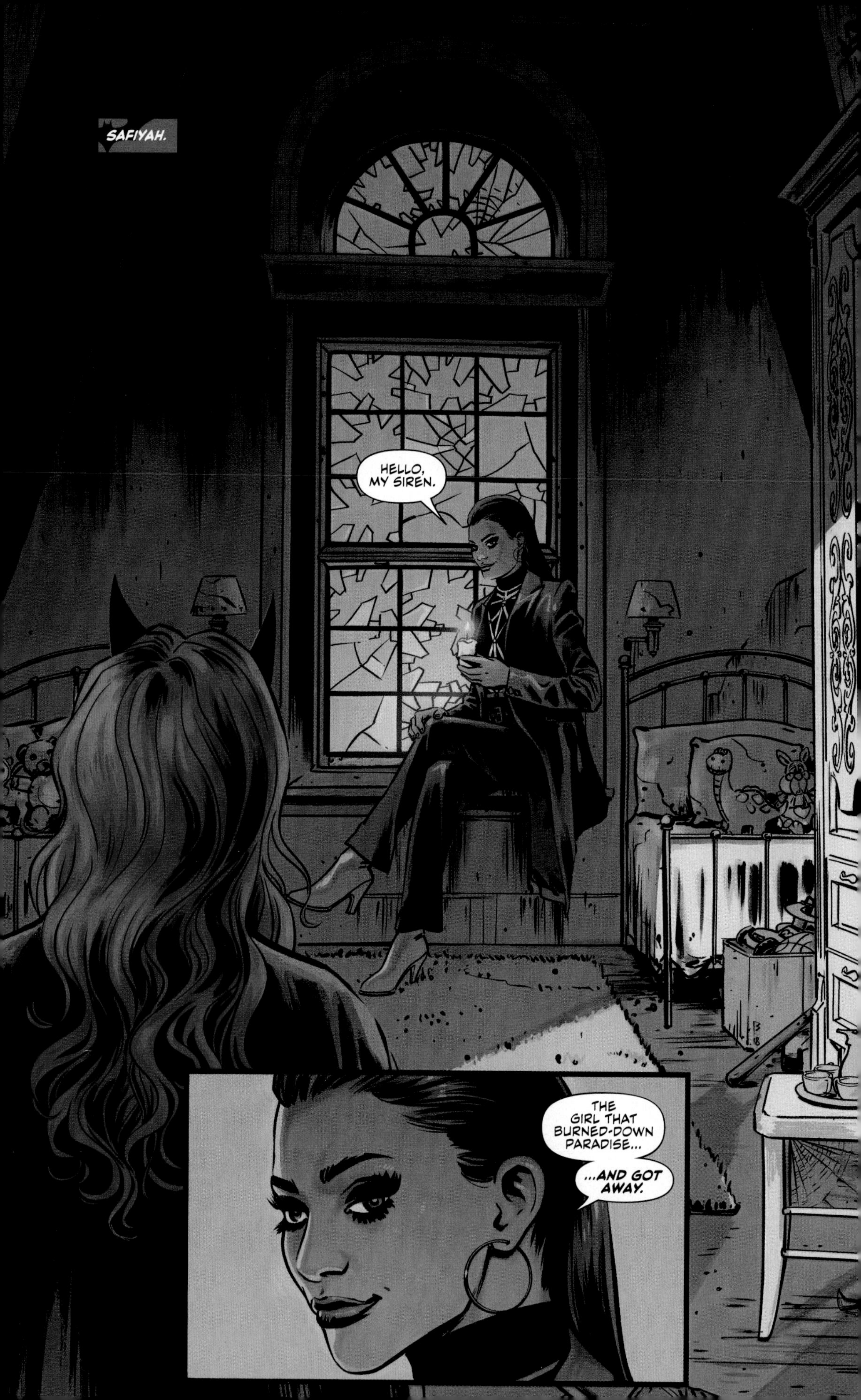
SAFIYAH.
HELLO, MY SIREN.
THE GIRL THAT BURNED-DOWN PARADISE...
...AND GOT AWAY.

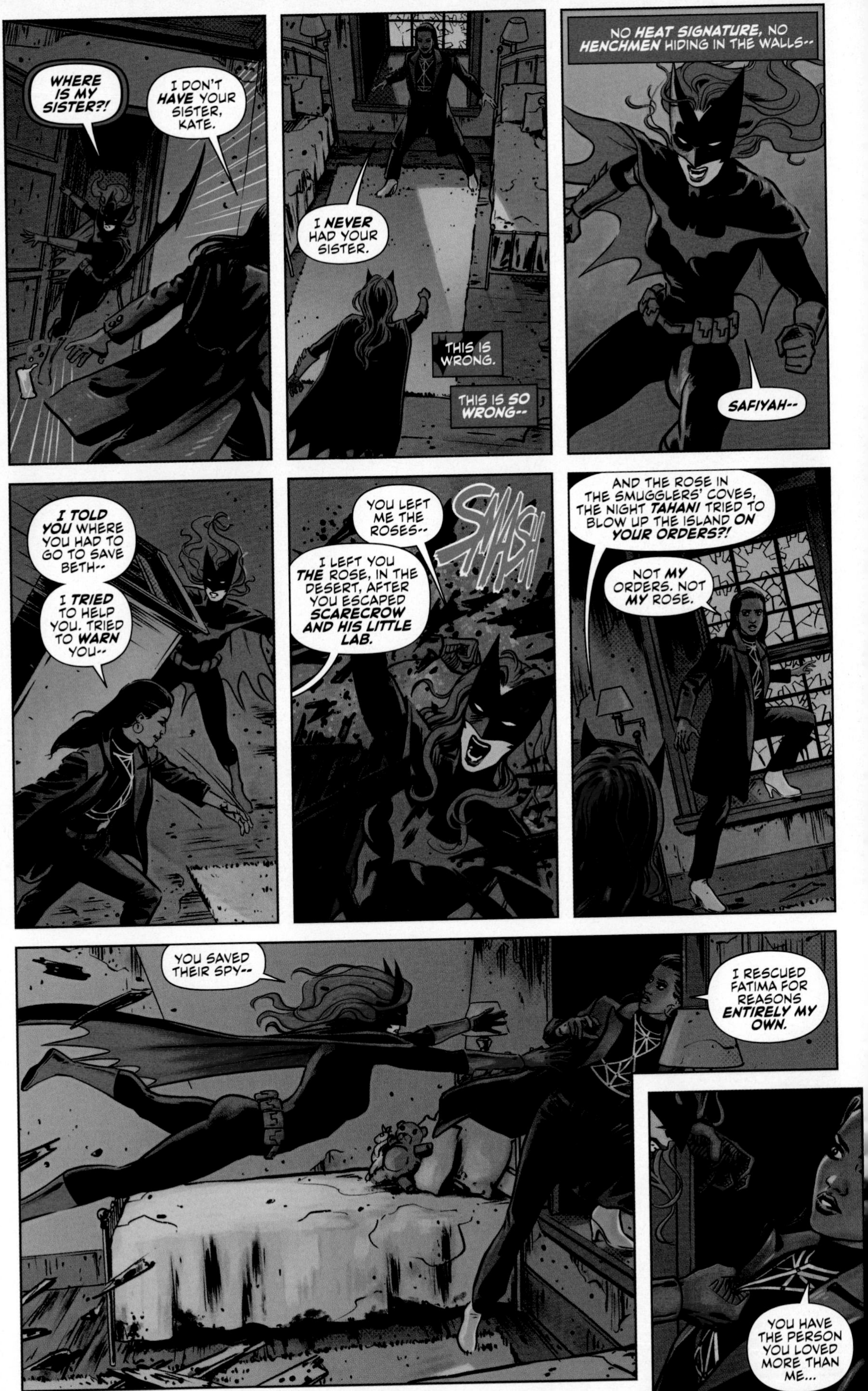

WHERE IS MY SISTER?!
I DON'T HAVE YOUR SISTER, KATE.
I NEVER HAD YOUR SISTER.
THIS IS WRONG.
THIS IS SO WRONG--
NO HEAT SIGNATURE, NO HENCHMEN HIDING IN THE WALLS--
SAFIYAH--
I TOLD YOU WHERE YOU HAD TO GO TO SAVE BETH--
I TRIED TO HELP YOU. TRIED TO WARN YOU--
YOU LEFT ME THE ROSES--
SMASH
I LEFT YOU THE ROSE, IN THE DESERT, AFTER YOU ESCAPED SCARECROW AND HIS LITTLE LAB.
AND THE ROSE IN THE SMUGGLERS' COVES, THE NIGHT TAHANI TRIED TO BLOW UP THE ISLAND ON YOUR ORDERS?!
NOT MY ORDERS. NOT MY ROSE.
YOU SAVED THEIR SPY--
I RESCUED FATIMA FOR REASONS ENTIRELY MY OWN.
YOU HAVE THE PERSON YOU LOVED MORE THAN ME...

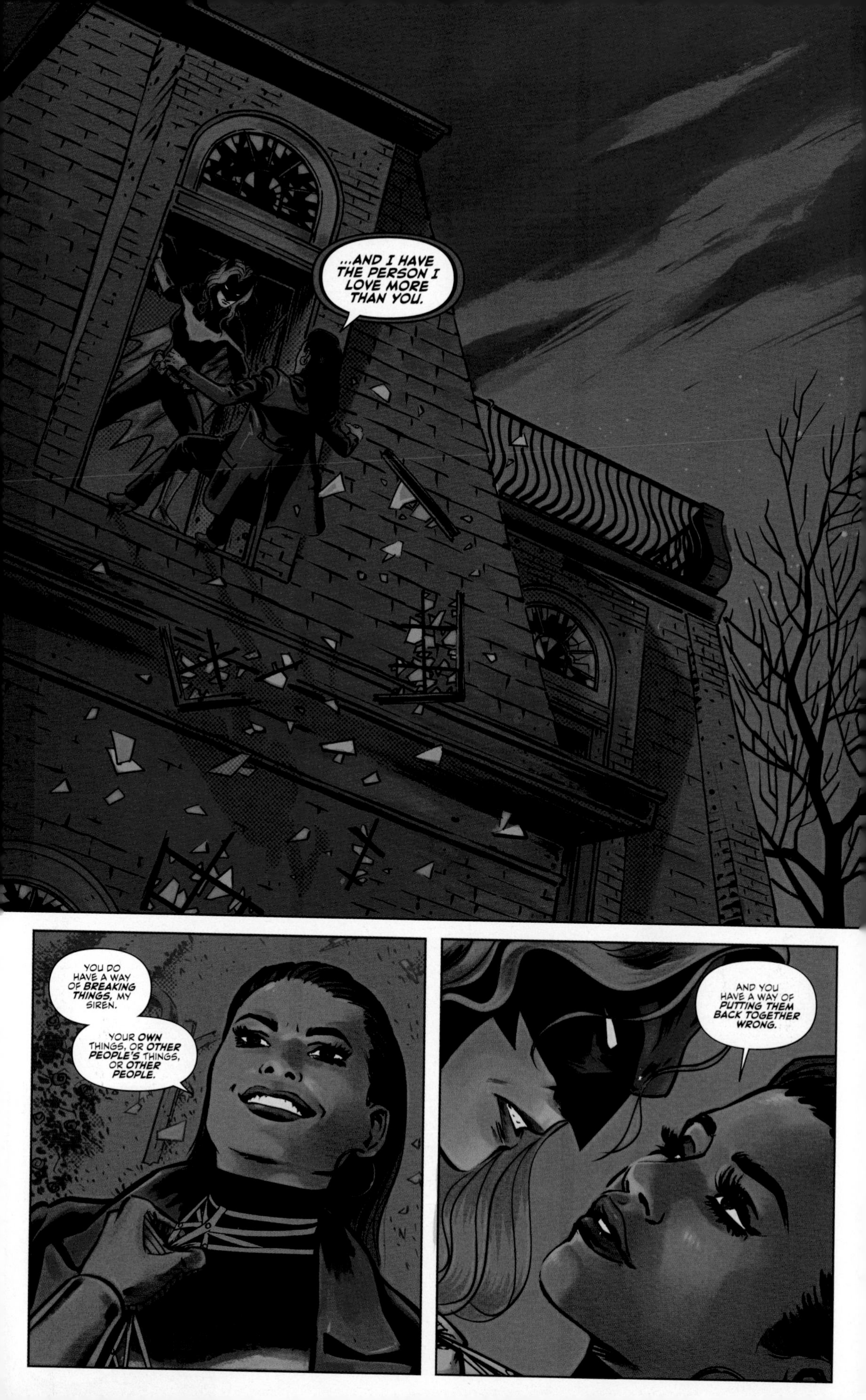
...AND I HAVE THE PERSON I LOVE MORE THAN YOU.
YOU DO HAVE A WAY OF BREAKING THINGS, MY SIREN.
YOUR OWN THINGS, OR OTHER PEOPLE'S THINGS, OR OTHER PEOPLE.
AND YOU HAVE A WAY OF PUTTING THEM BACK TOGETHER WRONG.

WHEN I REALIZED WHAT WAS HAPPENING, *I HELPED YOU*, KATE, BECAUSE I NEEDED TO SEE FOR MYSELF.

WHERE WERE YOU GOING TO *RUN*, WHEN I SAID THE WORD *"HOME"*?

TO GOTHAM? TO CORYANA?

OR WERE YOU GOING TO COME *HERE*?

I HAD HOPED, ONCE...

...BUT *NO*. I WAS WAITING *WHERE I'D* BET YOU'D BE.

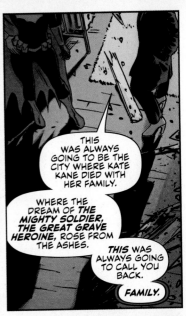

THIS WAS ALWAYS GOING TO BE THE CITY WHERE KATE KANE DIED WITH HER FAMILY.

WHERE THE DREAM OF *THE MIGHTY SOLDIER, THE GREAT GRAVE HEROINE*, ROSE FROM THE ASHES.

THIS WAS ALWAYS GOING TO CALL YOU BACK.

FAMILY.

THE GHOSTS OF THE FAMILY YOU COULD NEVER SAVE.

BLINDING YOU TO THE FAMILIES YOU COULD HAVE *CHOSEN FOR YOURSELF*.

EVEN *I* COULD SEE IT WAS *BAIT*, TO SEND YOU ON A *MISSION*.

SOMETHING TO KEEP YOU *BUSY*.

SOMETHING TO LEAVE *GOTHAM* UNDEFENDED.

WHO HATES US, KATE? WHO HATES THE TWO OF US?

ENOUGH TO TAKE *THE ONE I LOVE* FROM ME...

ENOUGH TO TAKE *THE SISTER YOU LOVE* FROM YOU...

WHO IS THE HEAD OF THE MANY ARMS OF DEATH?

WHO IS THEIR MOTHER OF WAR?

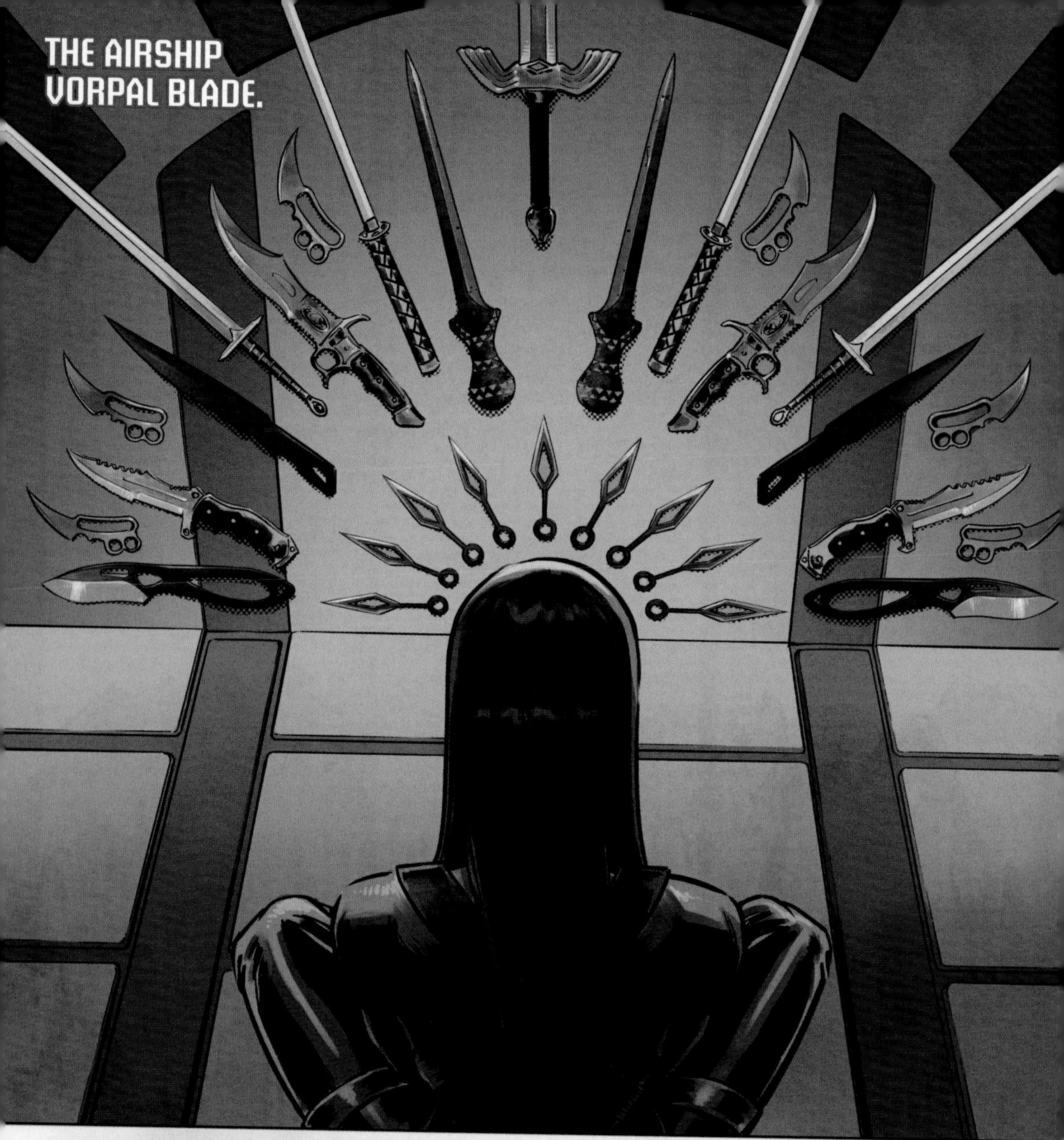
THE AIRSHIP VORPAL BLADE.

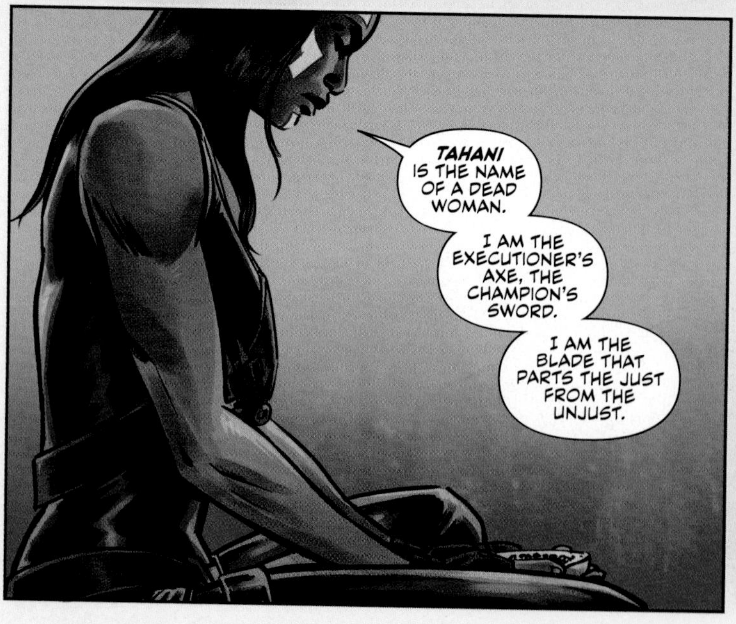
TAHANI IS THE NAME OF A DEAD WOMAN.
I AM THE EXECUTIONER'S AXE, THE CHAMPION'S SWORD.
I AM THE BLADE THAT PARTS THE JUST FROM THE UNJUST.

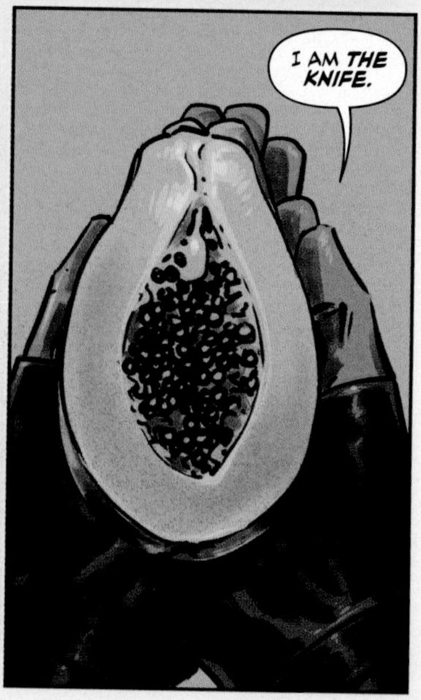
I AM THE KNIFE.

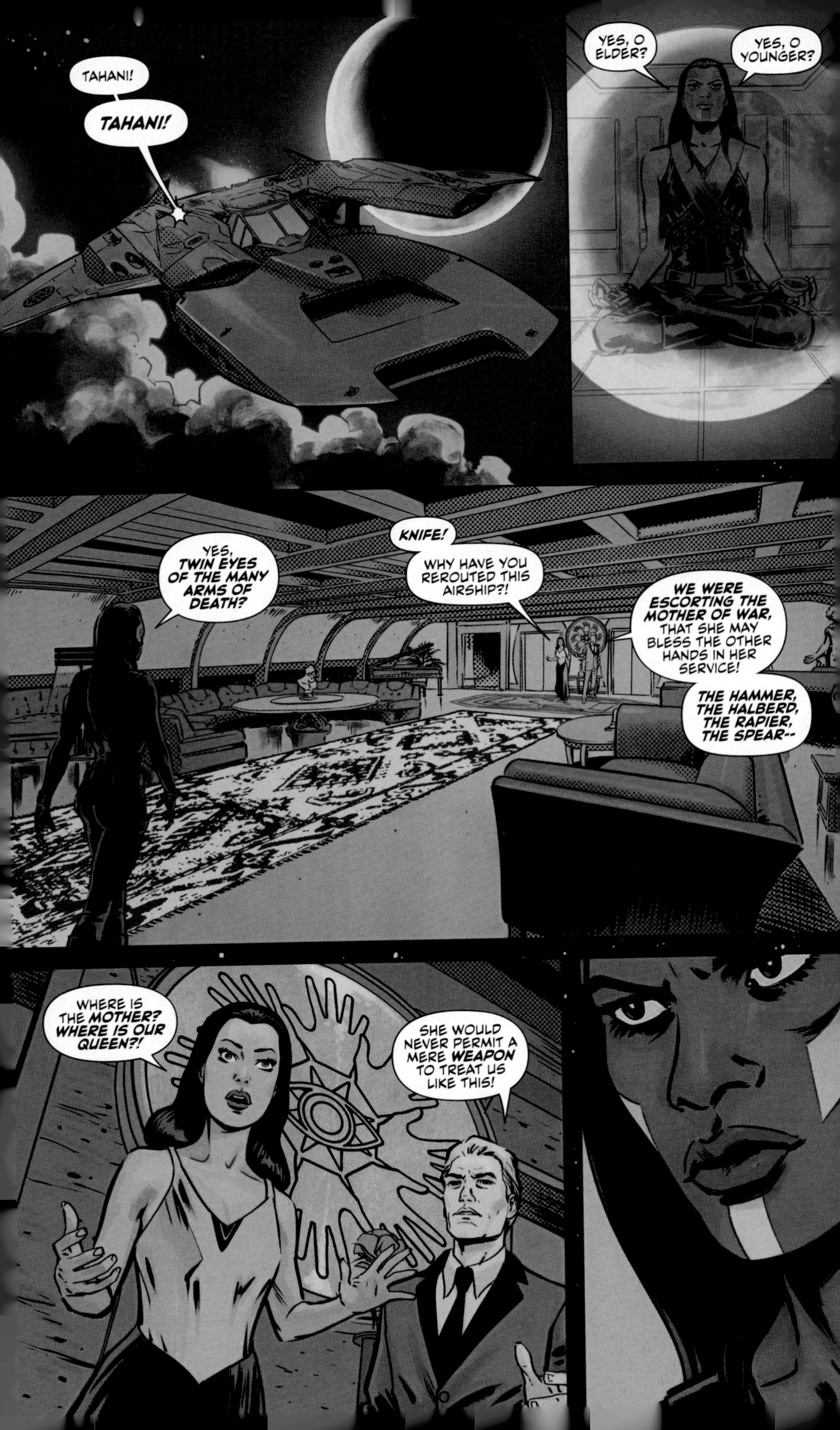
TAHANI!
TAHANI!
YES, O ELDER?
YES, O YOUNGER?
YES, TWIN EYES OF THE MANY ARMS OF DEATH?
KNIFE!
WHY HAVE YOU REROUTED THIS AIRSHIP?!
WE WERE ESCORTING THE MOTHER OF WAR, THAT SHE MAY BLESS THE OTHER HANDS IN HER SERVICE!
THE HAMMER, THE HALBERD, THE RAPIER, THE SPEAR--
WHERE IS THE MOTHER? WHERE IS OUR QUEEN?!
SHE WOULD NEVER PERMIT A MERE WEAPON TO TREAT US LIKE THIS!

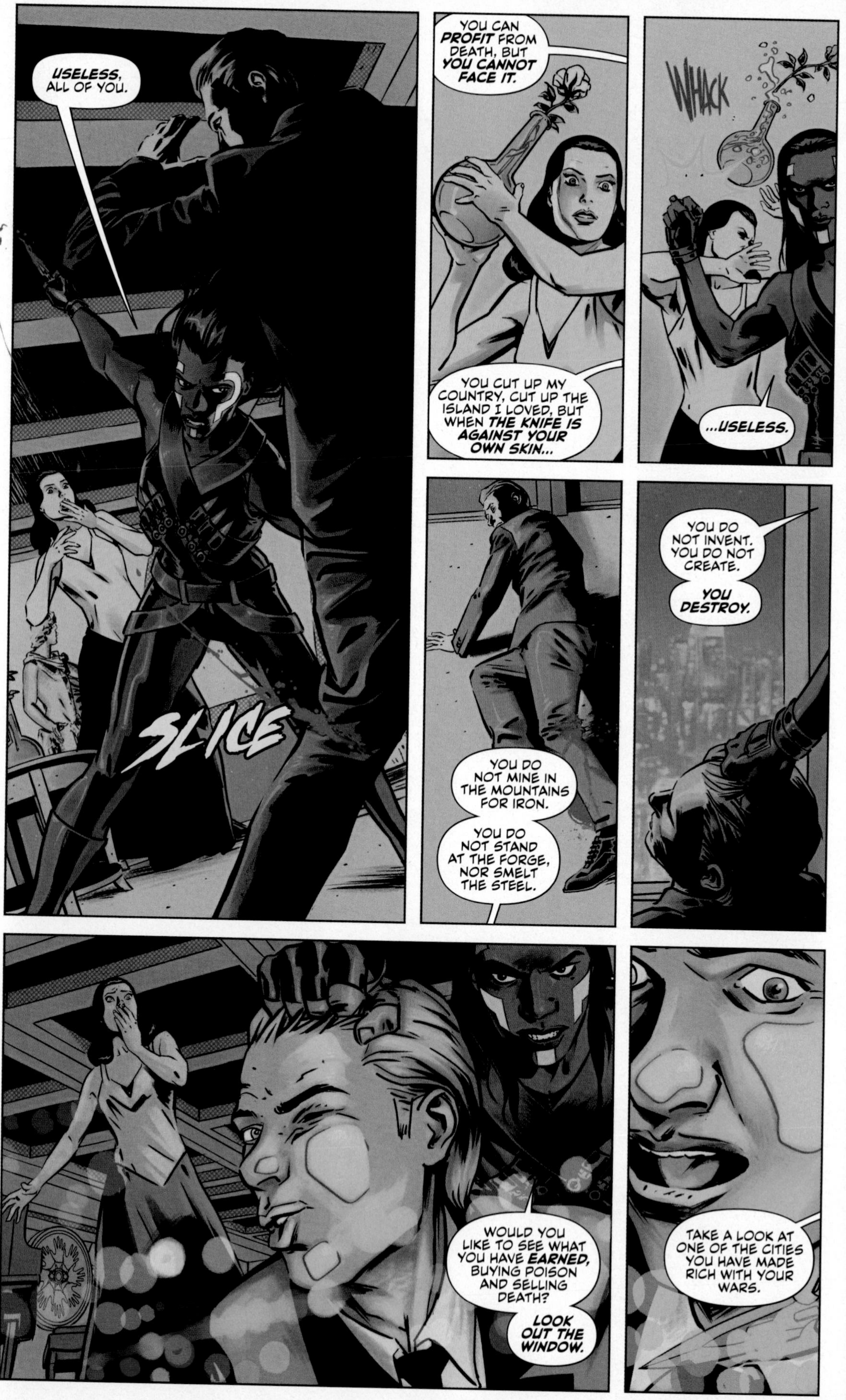
USELESS, ALL OF YOU.
SLICE
YOU CAN PROFIT FROM DEATH, BUT YOU CANNOT FACE IT.
YOU CUT UP MY COUNTRY, CUT UP THE ISLAND I LOVED, BUT WHEN THE KNIFE IS AGAINST YOUR OWN SKIN...
WHACK
...USELESS.
YOU DO NOT MINE IN THE MOUNTAINS FOR IRON.
YOU DO NOT STAND AT THE FORGE, NOR SMELT THE STEEL.
YOU DO NOT INVENT. YOU DO NOT CREATE.
YOU DESTROY.
WOULD YOU LIKE TO SEE WHAT YOU HAVE EARNED, BUYING POISON AND SELLING DEATH?
LOOK OUT THE WINDOW.
TAKE A LOOK AT ONE OF THE CITIES YOU HAVE MADE RICH WITH YOUR WARS.

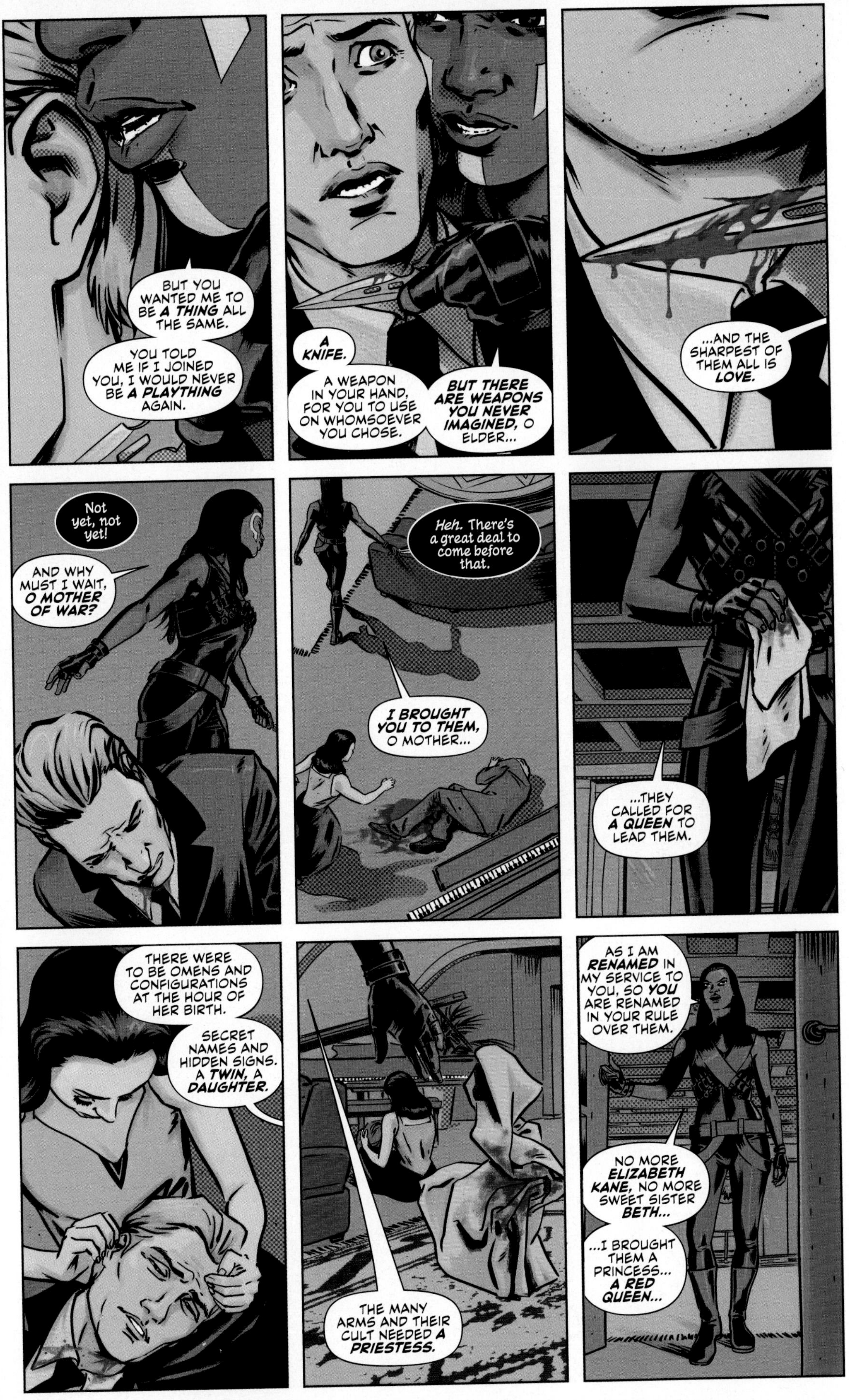

BUT YOU WANTED ME TO BE A THING ALL THE SAME.
YOU TOLD ME IF I JOINED YOU, I WOULD NEVER BE A PLAYTHING AGAIN.
A KNIFE.
A WEAPON IN YOUR HAND, FOR YOU TO USE ON WHOMSOEVER YOU CHOSE.
BUT THERE ARE WEAPONS YOU NEVER IMAGINED, O ELDER...
...AND THE SHARPEST OF THEM ALL IS LOVE.
Not yet, not yet!
AND WHY MUST I WAIT, O MOTHER OF WAR?
Heh. There's a great deal to come before that.
I BROUGHT YOU TO THEM, O MOTHER...
...THEY CALLED FOR A QUEEN TO LEAD THEM.
THERE WERE TO BE OMENS AND CONFIGURATIONS AT THE HOUR OF HER BIRTH.
SECRET NAMES AND HIDDEN SIGNS. A TWIN, A DAUGHTER.
THE MANY ARMS AND THEIR CULT NEEDED A PRIESTESS.
AS I AM RENAMED IN MY SERVICE TO YOU, SO YOU ARE RENAMED IN YOUR RULE OVER THEM.
NO MORE ELIZABETH KANE, NO MORE SWEET SISTER BETH...
...I BROUGHT THEM A PRINCESS... A RED QUEEN...

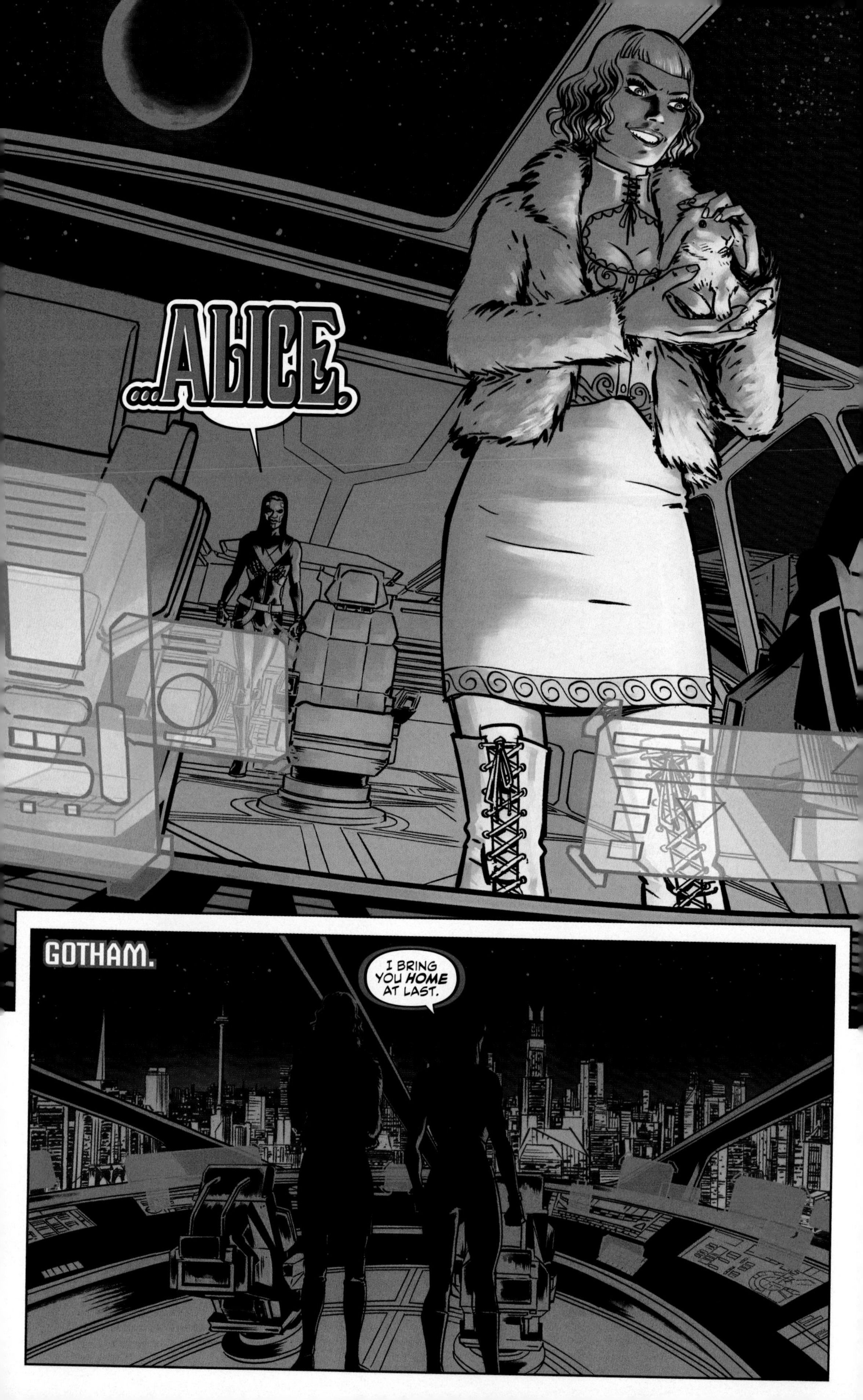
...ALICE.
GOTHAM.
I BRING YOU HOME AT LAST.

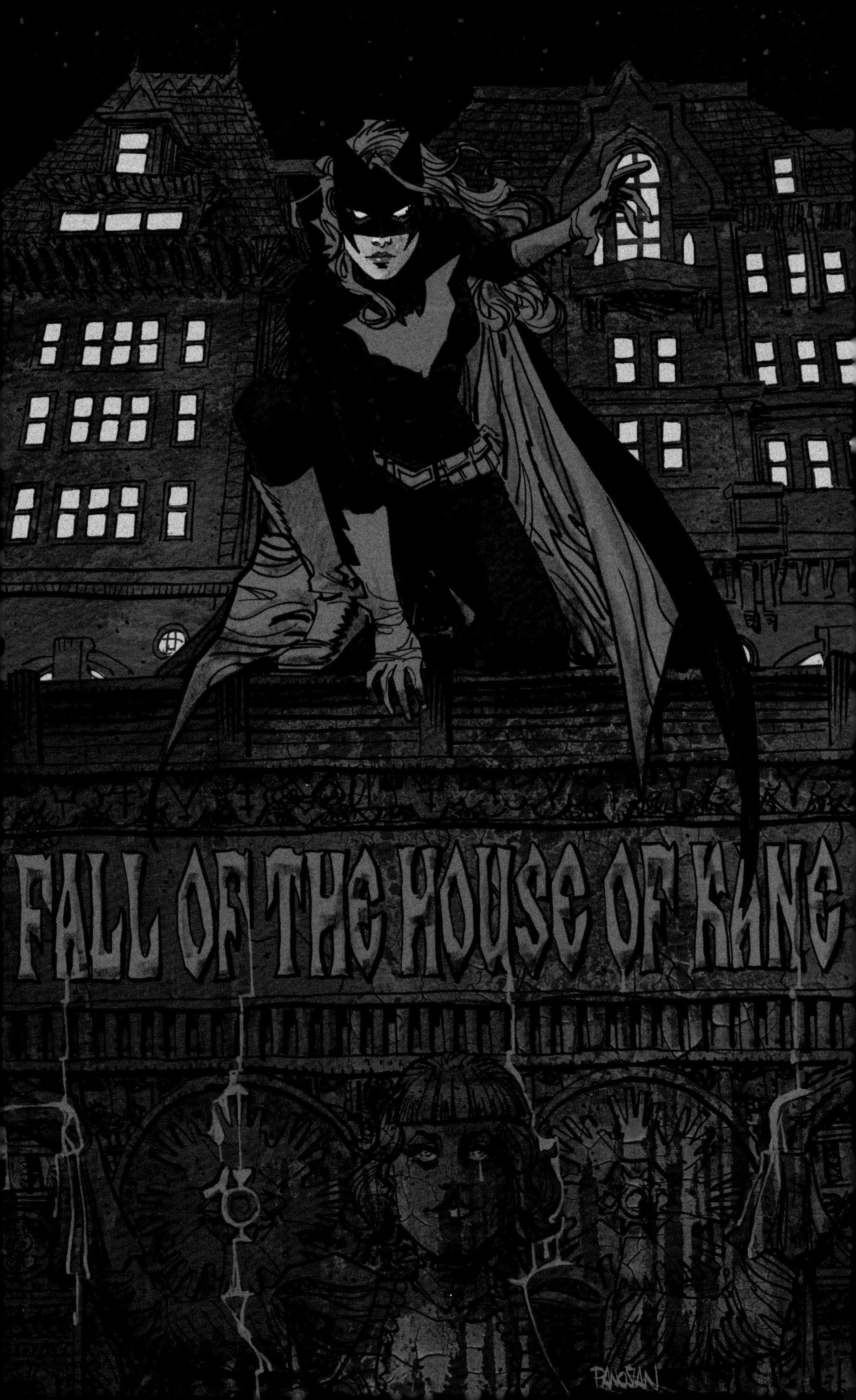
FALL OF THE HOUSE OF KANE
PANOSIAN

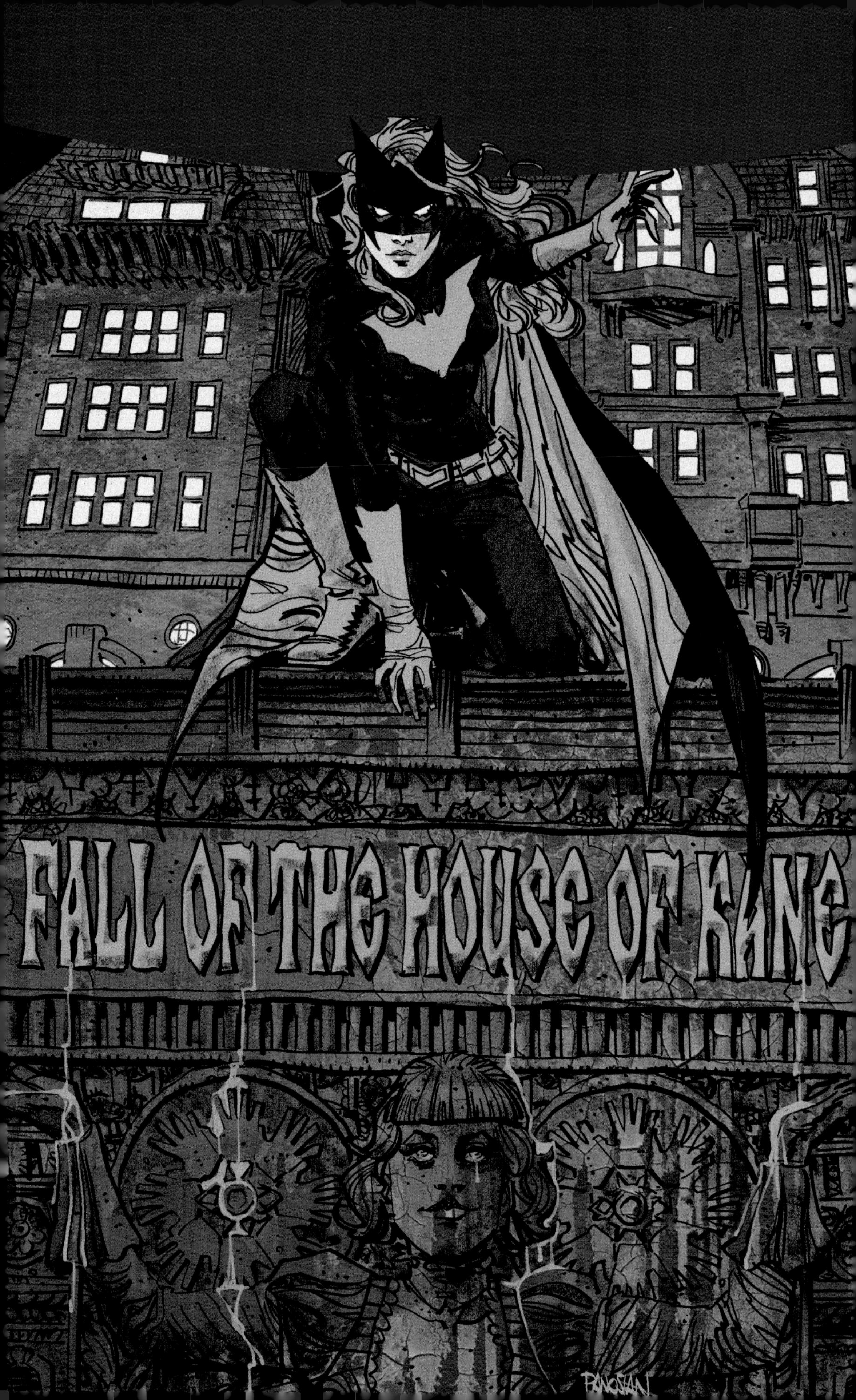
FALL OF THE HOUSE OF KANE

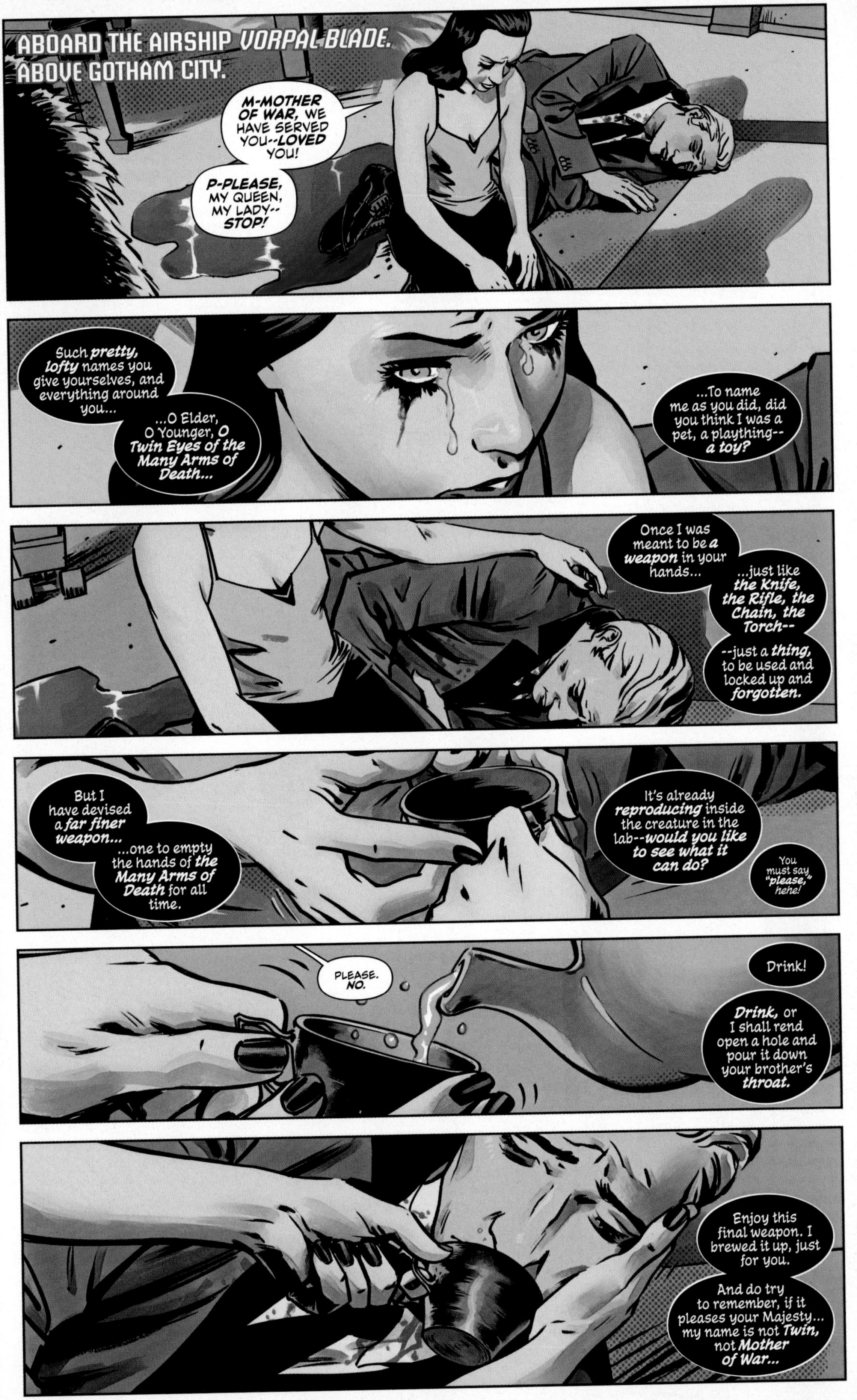
ABOARD THE AIRSHIP VORPAL BLADE. ABOVE GOTHAM CITY.
M-MOTHER OF WAR, WE HAVE SERVED YOU--LOVED YOU!
P-PLEASE, MY QUEEN, MY LADY-- STOP!
Such pretty, lofty names you give yourselves, and everything around you...
...O Elder, O Younger, O Twin Eyes of the Many Arms of Death...
...To name me as you did, did you think I was a pet, a plaything-- a toy?
Once I was meant to be a weapon in your hands...
...just like the Knife, the Rifle, the Chain, the Torch--
--just a thing, to be used and locked up and forgotten.
But I have devised a far finer weapon...
...one to empty the hands of the Many Arms of Death for all time.
It's already reproducing inside the creature in the lab--would you like to see what it can do?
You must say "please," hehe!
PLEASE. NO.
Drink!
Drink, or I shall rend open a hole and pour it down your brother's throat.
Enjoy this final weapon. I brewed it up, just for you.
And do try to remember, if it pleases your Majesty... my name is not Twin, not Mother of War...

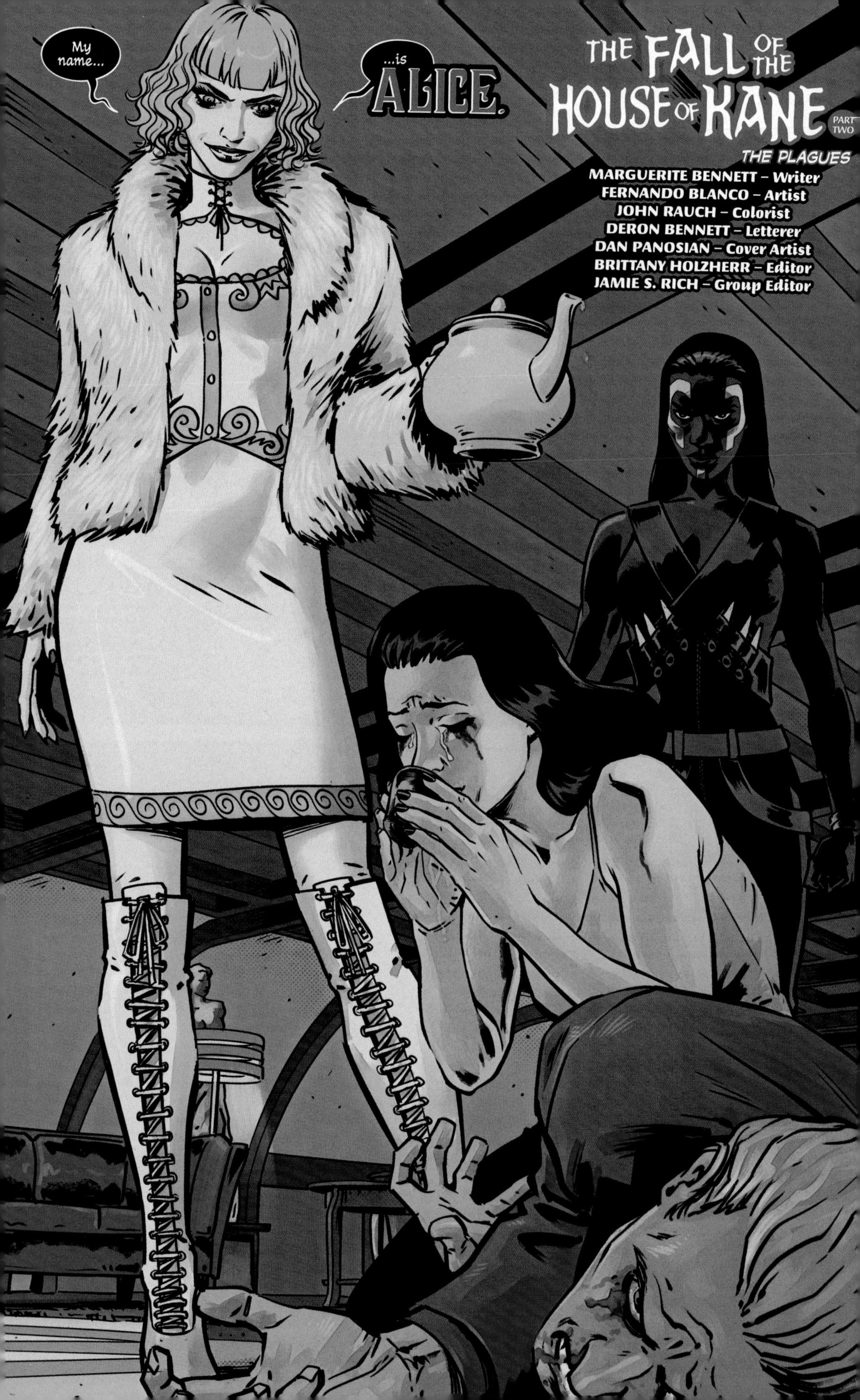
My name...
...is ALICE.
THE FALL OF THE HOUSE OF KANE PART TWO
THE PLAGUES
MARGUERITE BENNETT – Writer
FERNANDO BLANCO – Artist
JOHN RAUCH – Colorist
DERON BENNETT – Letterer
DAN PANOSIAN – Cover Artist
BRITTANY HOLZHERR – Editor
JAMIE S. RICH – Group Editor

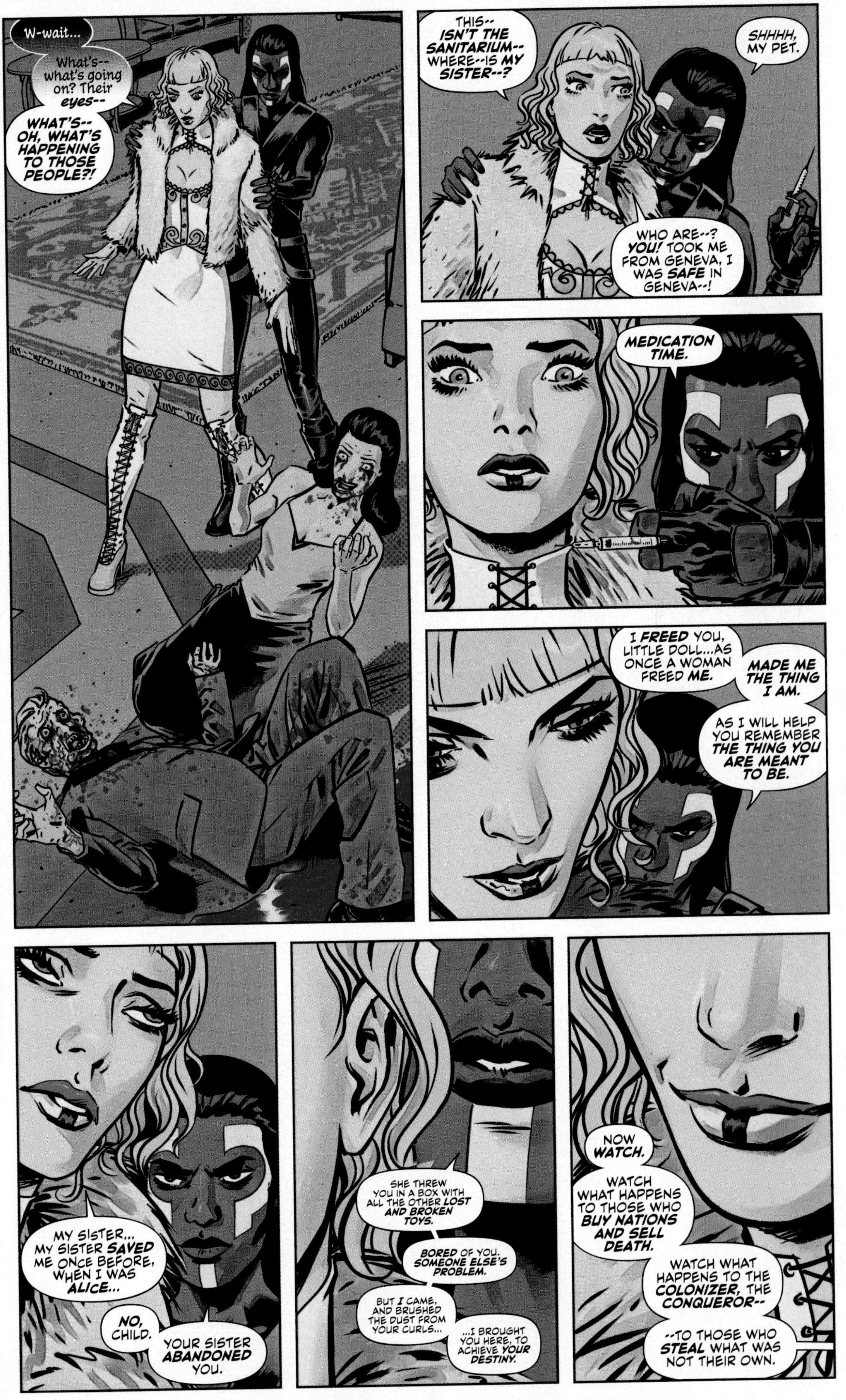
W-wait...
What's-- what's going on? Their *eyes*--
WHAT'S-- OH, WHAT'S HAPPENING TO THOSE PEOPLE?!
THIS-- ***ISN'T THE SANITARIUM***-- WHERE--IS ***MY SISTER***--?
SHHHH, MY PET.
WHO ARE--? ***YOU!*** TOOK ME FROM GENEVA, I WAS ***SAFE*** IN GENEVA--!
MEDICATION TIME.
I ***FREED*** YOU, LITTLE DOLL...AS ONCE A WOMAN FREED ***ME.***
MADE ME THE THING I AM.
AS I WILL HELP YOU REMEMBER ***THE THING YOU ARE MEANT TO BE.***
MY SISTER... MY SISTER ***SAVED*** ME ONCE BEFORE, WHEN I WAS ***ALICE...***
NO, CHILD.
YOUR SISTER ***ABANDONED*** YOU.
SHE THREW YOU IN A BOX WITH ALL THE OTHER ***LOST AND BROKEN TOYS.***
BORED OF YOU. ***SOMEONE ELSE'S PROBLEM.***
BUT ***I*** CAME, AND BRUSHED THE DUST FROM YOUR CURLS...
...I BROUGHT YOU HERE, TO ACHIEVE ***YOUR DESTINY.***
NOW ***WATCH.***
WATCH WHAT HAPPENS TO THOSE WHO ***BUY NATIONS AND SELL DEATH.***
WATCH WHAT HAPPENS TO THE ***COLONIZER,*** THE ***CONQUEROR***--
--TO THOSE WHO ***STEAL*** WHAT WAS NOT THEIR OWN.

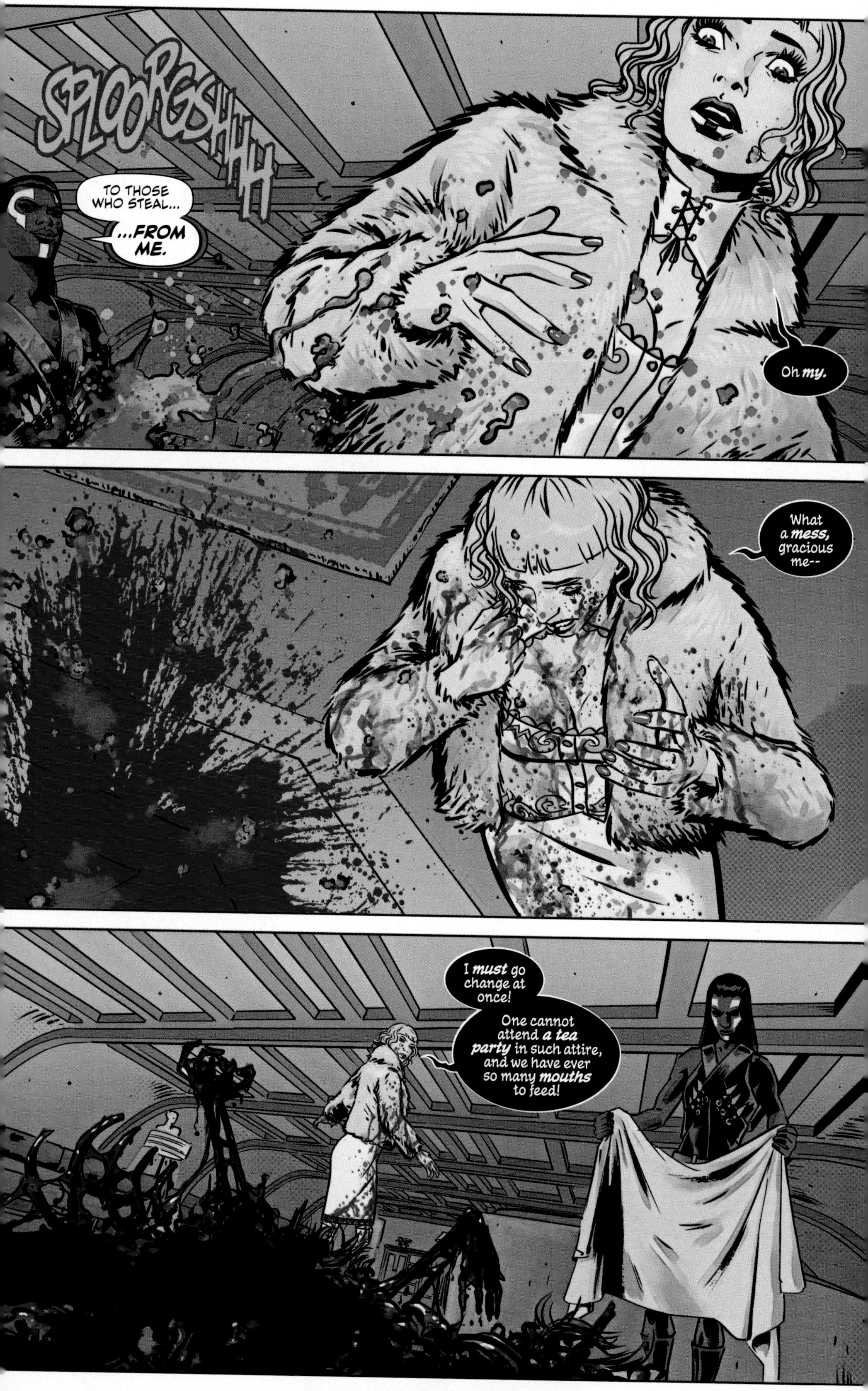
SPLOORGSHHH
TO THOSE WHO STEAL...
...FROM ME.
Oh my.
What a mess, gracious me--
I must go change at once!
One cannot attend a tea party in such attire, and we have ever so many mouths to feed!

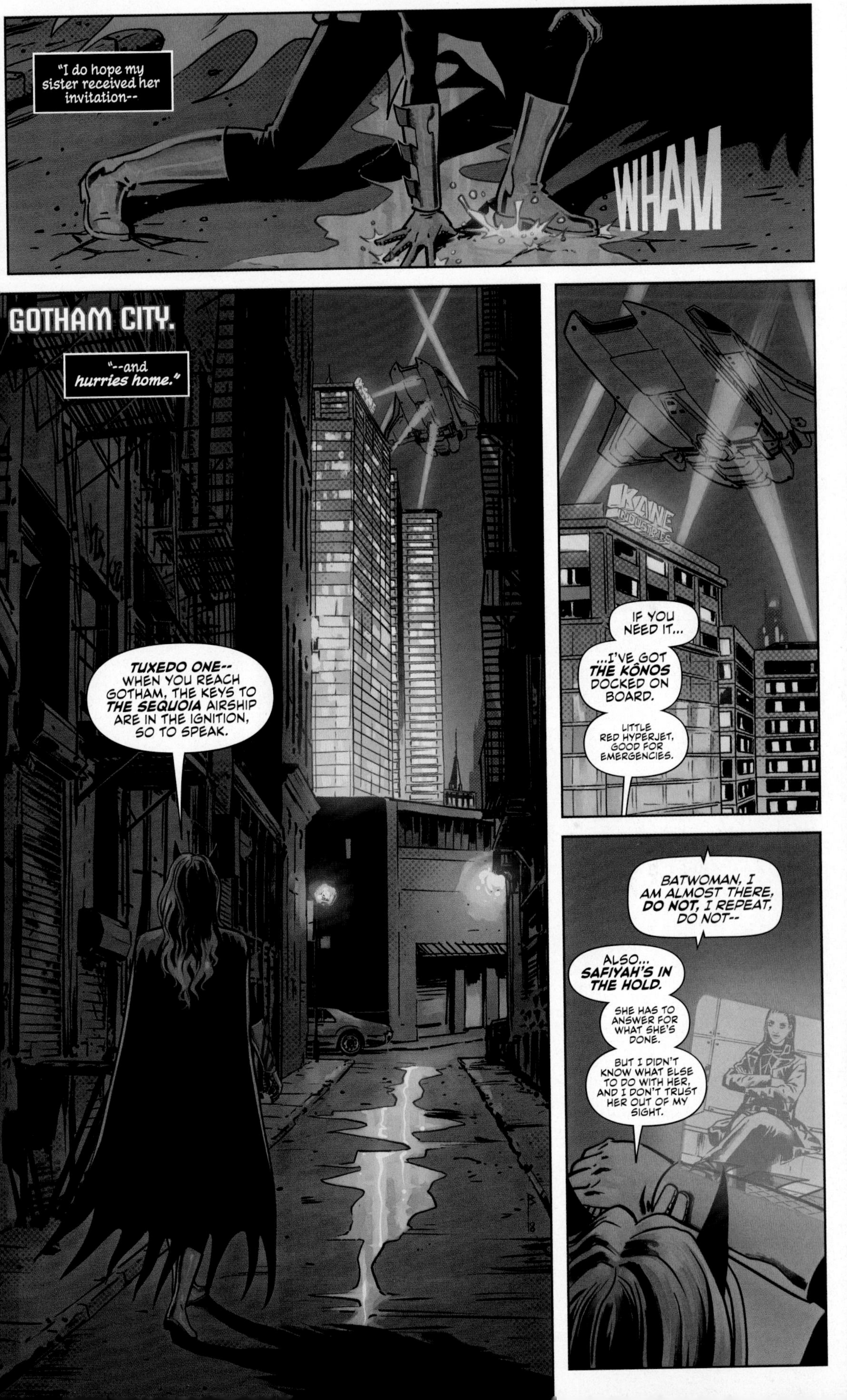
"I do hope my sister received her invitation--
WHAM
GOTHAM CITY.
"--and *hurries home.*"
TUXEDO ONE-- WHEN YOU REACH GOTHAM, THE KEYS TO ***THE SEQUOIA*** AIRSHIP ARE IN THE IGNITION, SO TO SPEAK.
KANE INDUSTRIES
IF YOU NEED IT...
...I'VE GOT ***THE KÔNOS*** DOCKED ON BOARD.
LITTLE RED HYPERJET, GOOD FOR EMERGENCIES.
BATWOMAN, I AM ALMOST THERE, ***DO NOT,*** *I REPEAT, DO NOT--*
ALSO... ***SAFIYAH'S IN THE HOLD.***
SHE HAS TO ANSWER FOR WHAT SHE'S DONE.
BUT I DIDN'T KNOW WHAT ELSE TO DO WITH HER, AND I DON'T TRUST HER OUT OF MY SIGHT.

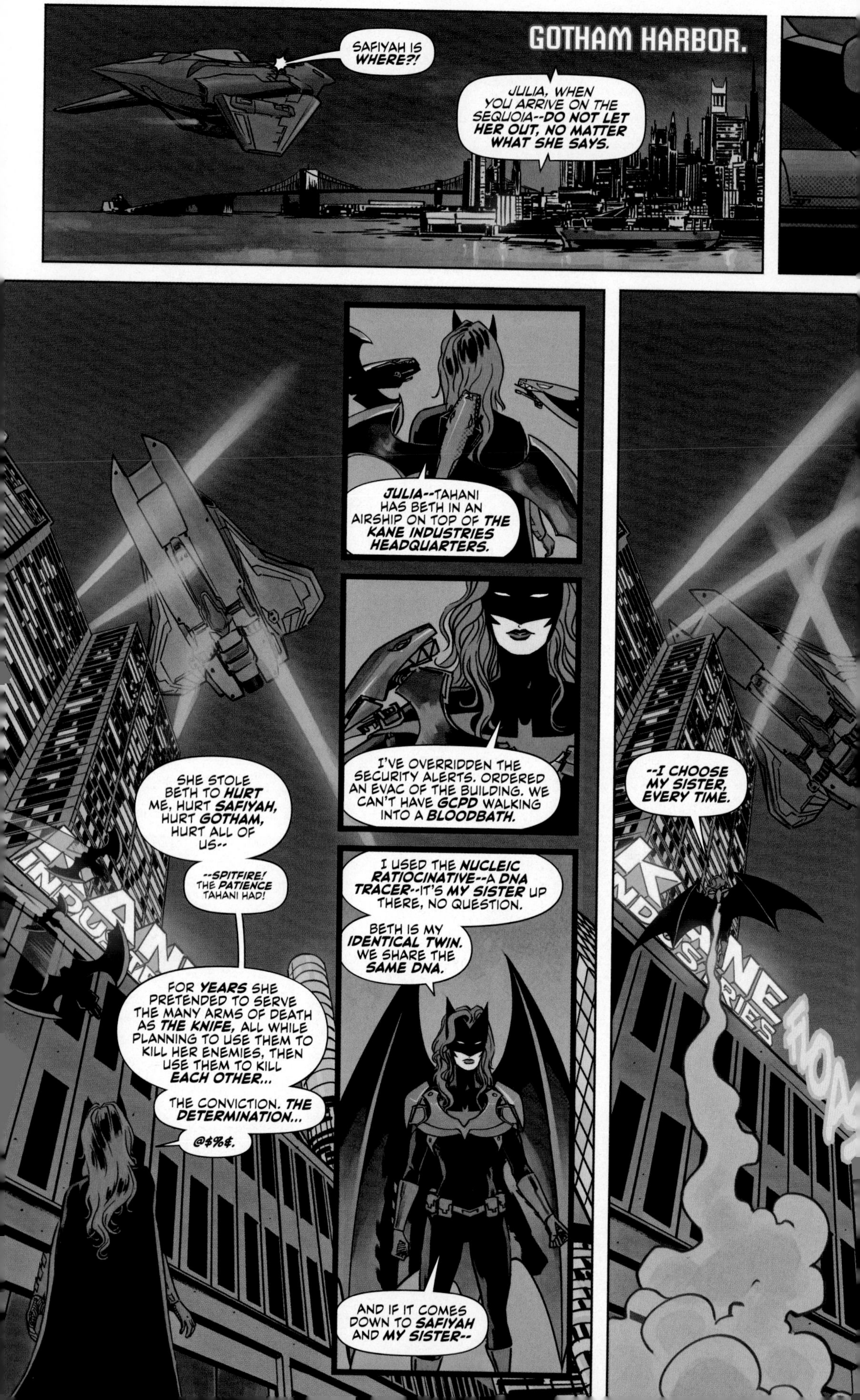
GOTHAM HARBOR.
SAFIYAH IS WHERE?!
JULIA, WHEN YOU ARRIVE ON THE SEQUOIA--DO NOT LET HER OUT, NO MATTER WHAT SHE SAYS.
JULIA--TAHANI HAS BETH IN AN AIRSHIP ON TOP OF THE KANE INDUSTRIES HEADQUARTERS.
I'VE OVERRIDDEN THE SECURITY ALERTS. ORDERED AN EVAC OF THE BUILDING. WE CAN'T HAVE GCPD WALKING INTO A BLOODBATH.
I USED THE NUCLEIC RATIOCINATIVE--A DNA TRACER--IT'S MY SISTER UP THERE, NO QUESTION.
BETH IS MY IDENTICAL TWIN. WE SHARE THE SAME DNA.
AND IF IT COMES DOWN TO SAFIYAH AND MY SISTER--
--I CHOOSE MY SISTER, EVERY TIME.
SHE STOLE BETH TO HURT ME, HURT SAFIYAH, HURT GOTHAM, HURT ALL OF US--
--SPITFIRE! THE PATIENCE TAHANI HAD!
FOR YEARS SHE PRETENDED TO SERVE THE MANY ARMS OF DEATH AS THE KNIFE, ALL WHILE PLANNING TO USE THEM TO KILL HER ENEMIES, THEN USE THEM TO KILL EACH OTHER...
THE CONVICTION. THE DETERMINATION...
@$%$.
KANE INDUSTRIES

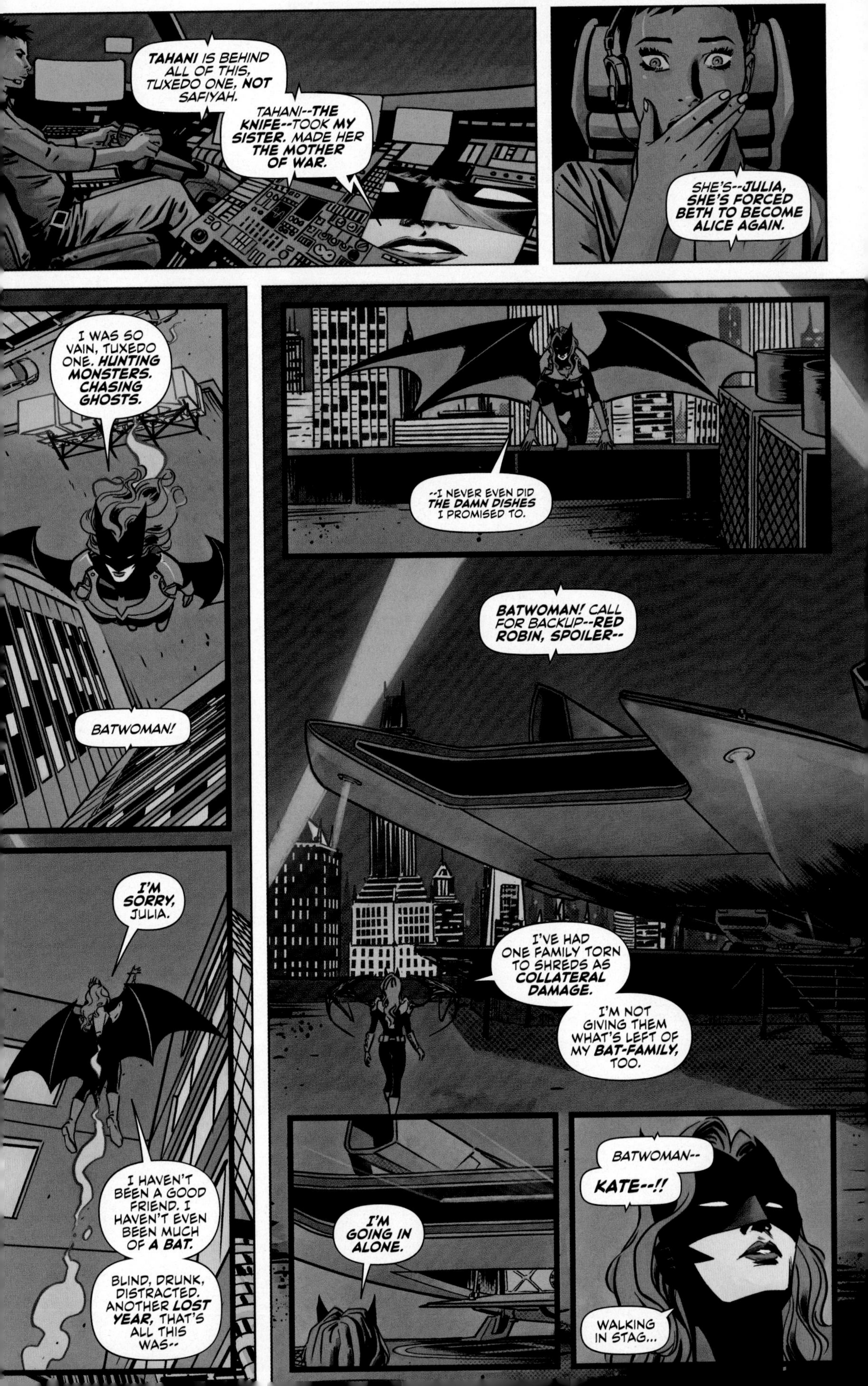
TAHANI IS BEHIND ALL OF THIS, TUXEDO ONE, NOT SAFIYAH.
TAHANI--THE KNIFE--TOOK MY SISTER. MADE HER THE MOTHER OF WAR.
SHE'S--JULIA, SHE'S FORCED BETH TO BECOME ALICE AGAIN.
I WAS SO VAIN, TUXEDO ONE. HUNTING MONSTERS. CHASING GHOSTS.
BATWOMAN!
I'M SORRY, JULIA.
I HAVEN'T BEEN A GOOD FRIEND. I HAVEN'T EVEN BEEN MUCH OF A BAT.
BLIND, DRUNK, DISTRACTED. ANOTHER LOST YEAR, THAT'S ALL THIS WAS--
--I NEVER EVEN DID THE DAMN DISHES I PROMISED TO.
BATWOMAN! CALL FOR BACKUP--RED ROBIN, SPOILER--
I'VE HAD ONE FAMILY TORN TO SHREDS AS COLLATERAL DAMAGE.
I'M NOT GIVING THEM WHAT'S LEFT OF MY BAT-FAMILY, TOO.
I'M GOING IN ALONE.
BATWOMAN--
KATE--!!
WALKING IN STAG...

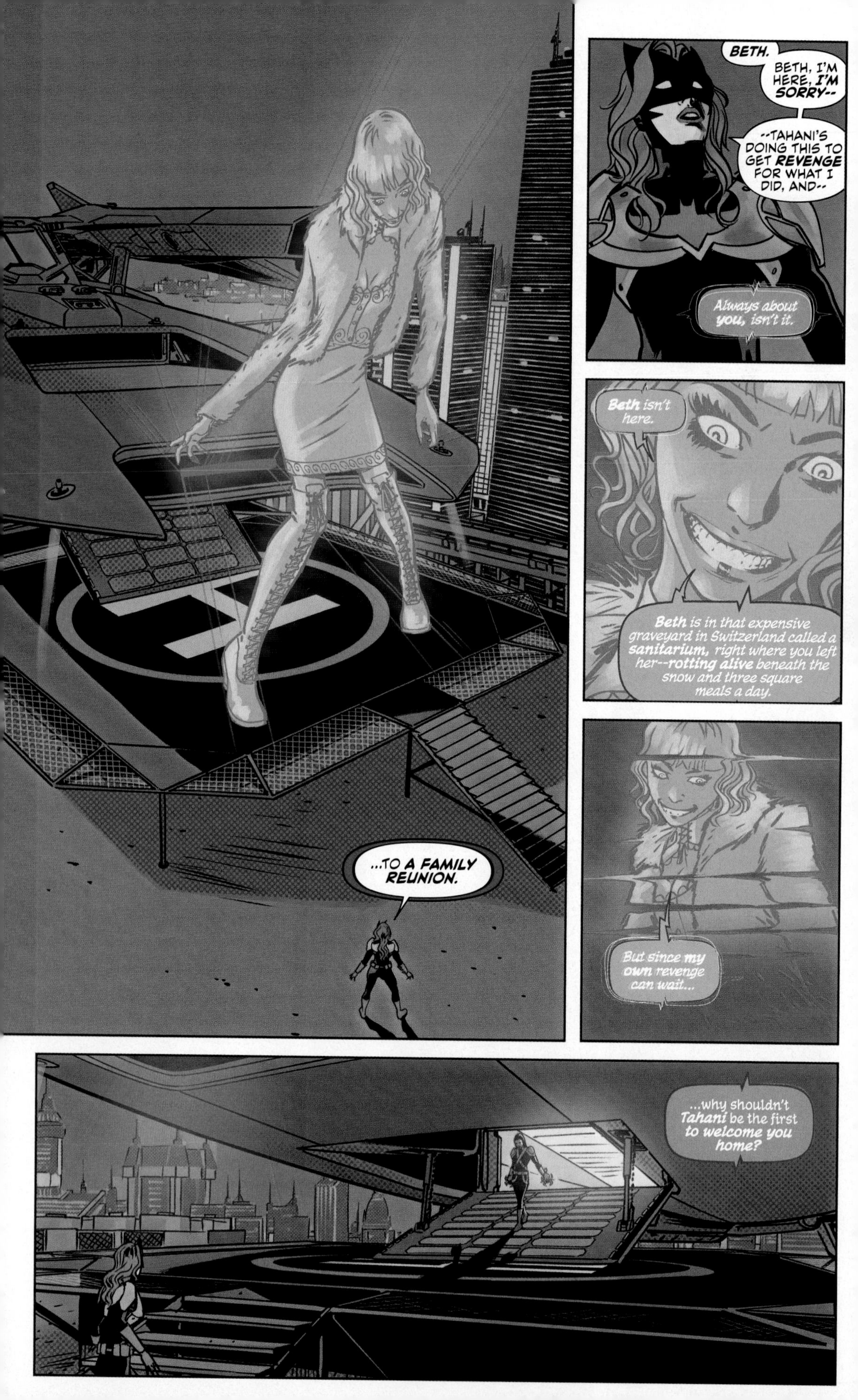
...TO A FAMILY REUNION.
BETH.
BETH, I'M HERE, I'M SORRY--
--TAHANI'S DOING THIS TO GET REVENGE FOR WHAT I DID, AND--
Always about you, isn't it.
Beth isn't here.
Beth is in that expensive graveyard in Switzerland called a sanitarium, right where you left her--rotting alive beneath the snow and three square meals a day.
But since my own revenge can wait...
...why shouldn't Tahani be the first to welcome you home?

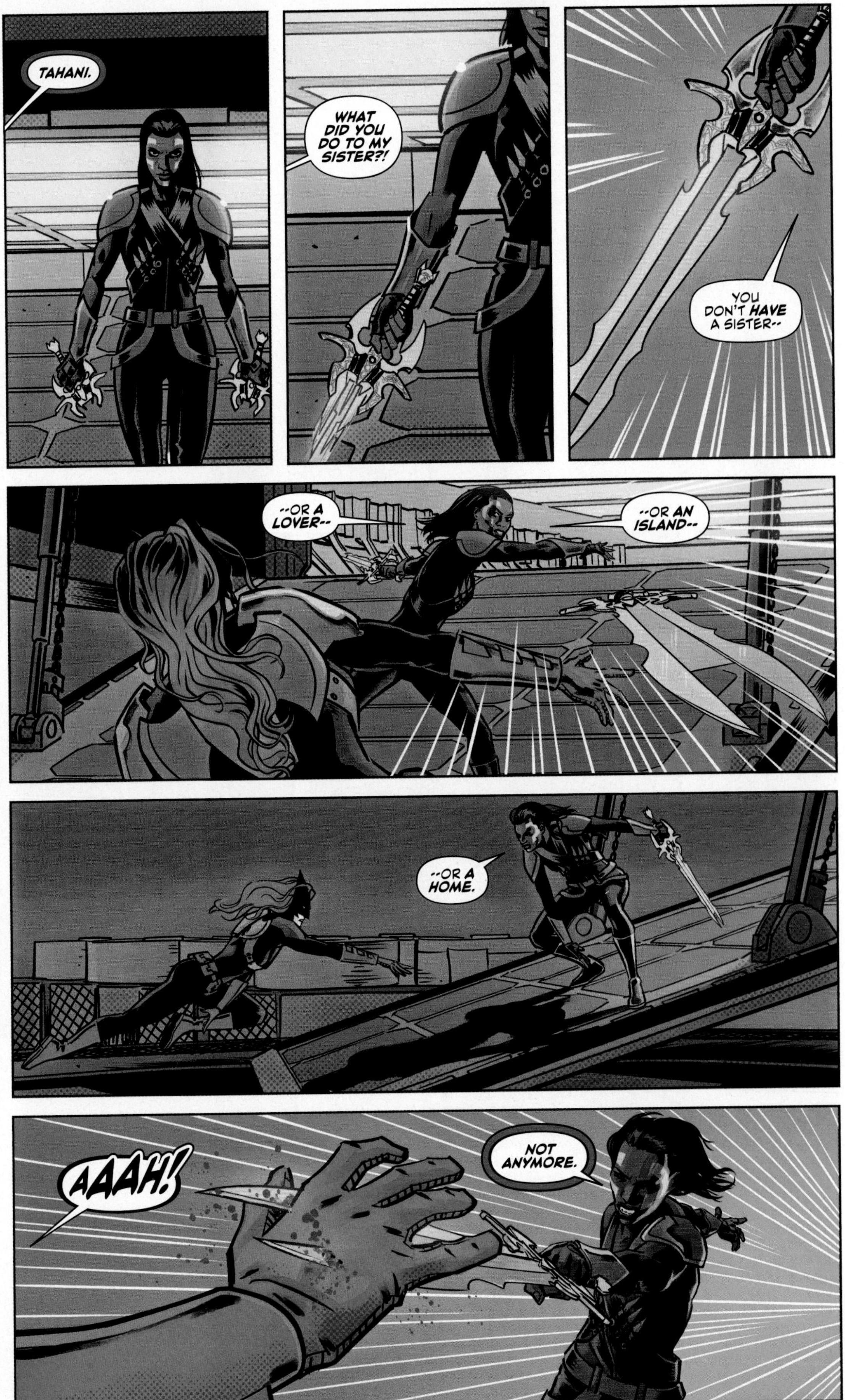
TAHANI.
WHAT DID YOU DO TO MY SISTER?!
YOU DON'T HAVE A SISTER--
--OR A LOVER--
--OR AN ISLAND--
--OR A HOME.
AAAH!
NOT ANYMORE.

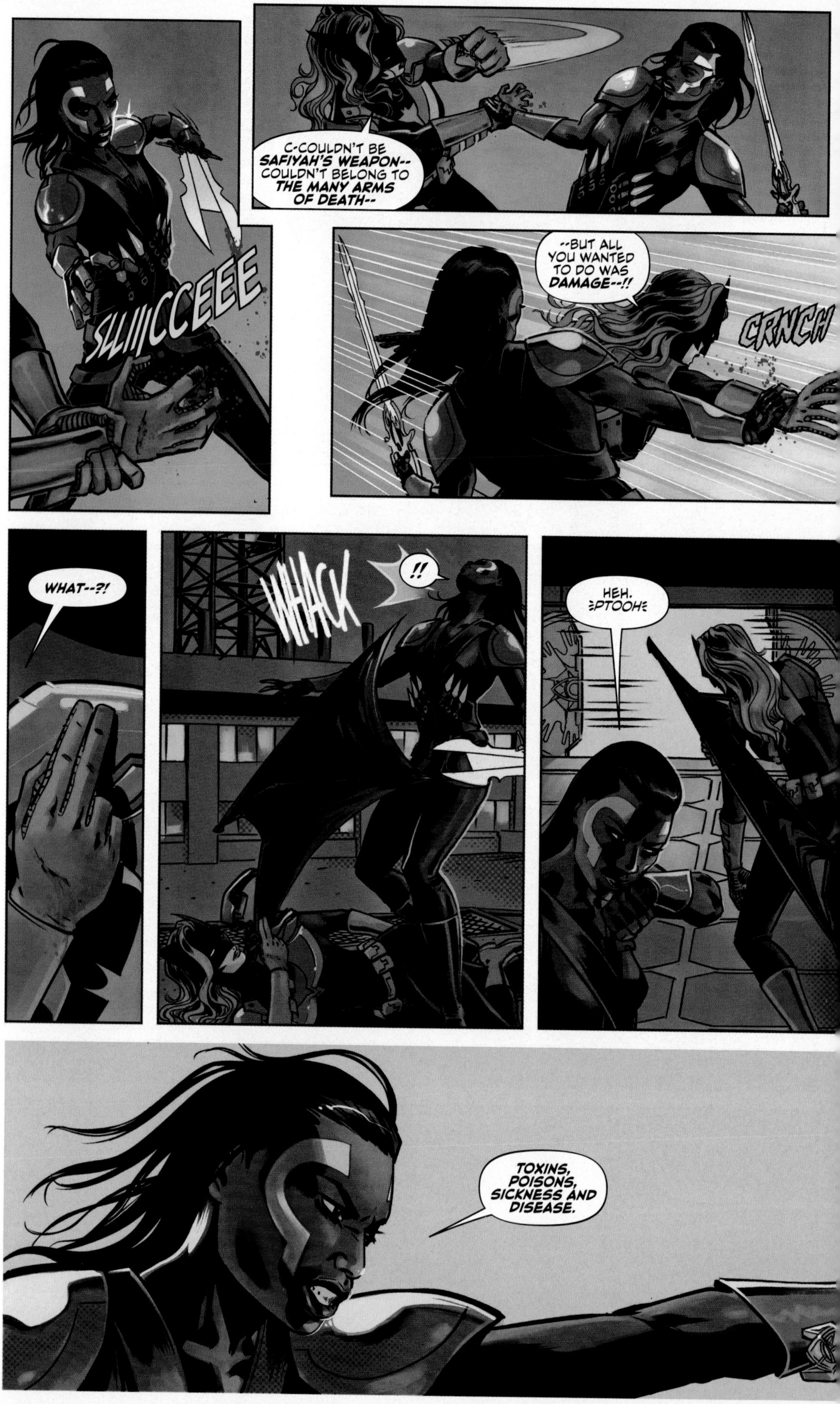
SLLIIICCEEE
C-COULDN'T BE SAFIYAH'S WEAPON-- COULDN'T BELONG TO THE MANY ARMS OF DEATH--
--BUT ALL YOU WANTED TO DO WAS DAMAGE--!!
CRNCH
WHAT--?!
WHACK
!!
HEH. PTOOH
TOXINS, POISONS, SICKNESS AND DISEASE.

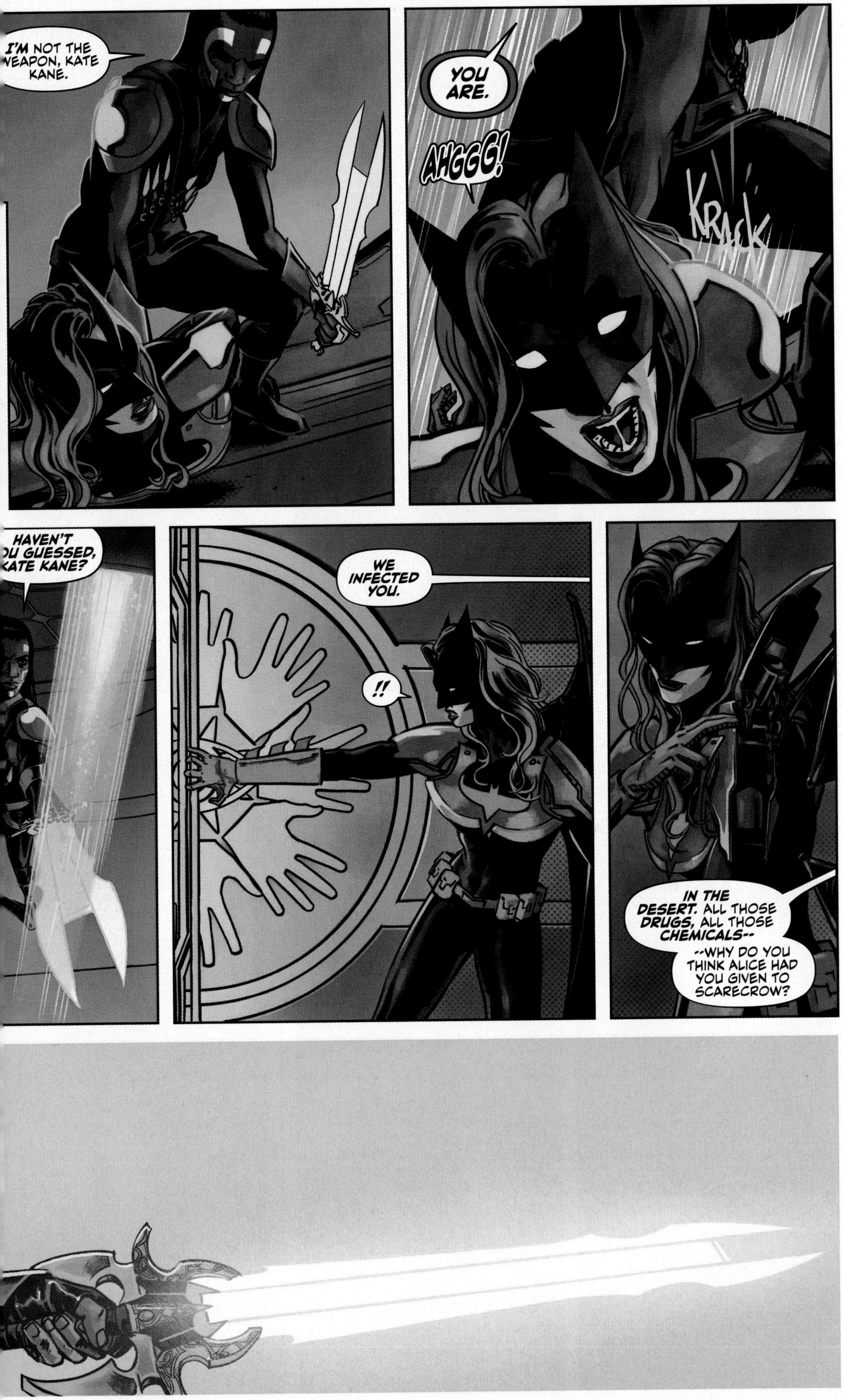
I'M NOT THE WEAPON, KATE KANE.
YOU ARE.
AHGGG!
KRACK
HAVEN'T YOU GUESSED, KATE KANE?
WE INFECTED YOU.
!!
IN THE DESERT. ALL THOSE DRUGS, ALL THOSE CHEMICALS--
--WHY DO YOU THINK ALICE HAD YOU GIVEN TO SCARECROW?

YOU WERE *AN INFECTION* ONCE BEFORE--*BREAKING* INTO CORYANA, *CORRUPTING* SAFIYAH, *KILLING* THE FOXES--

ARRRG!

--*NOW,* YOU ARE AN *INFECTION* ONCE MORE.

DO YOU *REALIZE* WHAT YOU'VE BROUGHT TO GOTHAM?

LITTLE ALICE AND I ARE *IMMUNE...*

...AS ARE *YOU,* IN A FASHION...

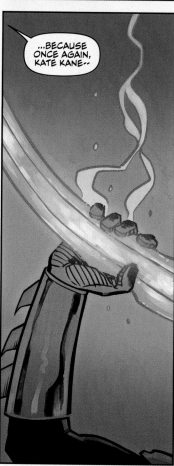

...BECAUSE ONCE AGAIN, KATE KANE--

--AAH!!

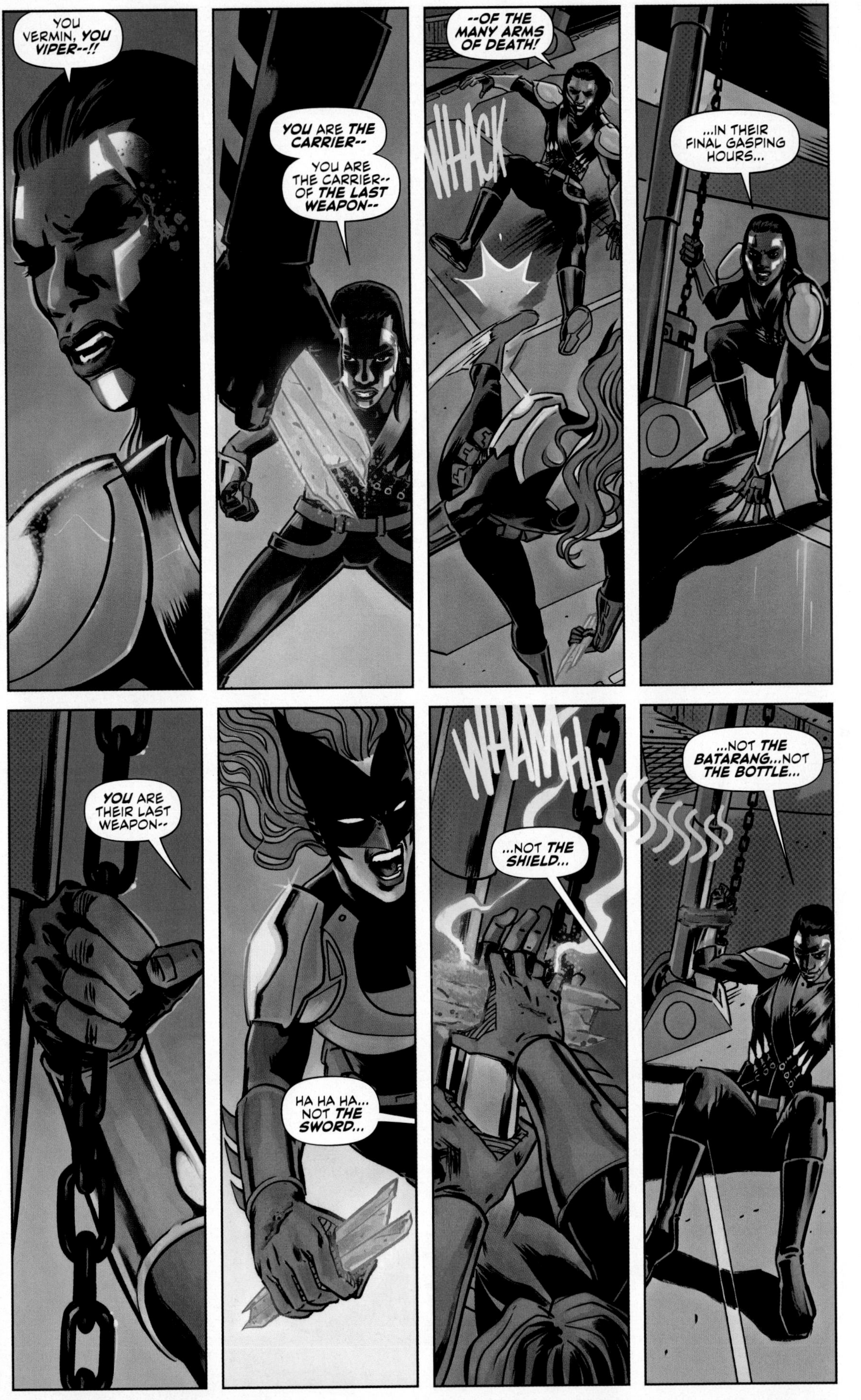
YOU VERMIN, YOU VIPER--!!
YOU ARE THE CARRIER--
YOU ARE THE CARRIER-- OF THE LAST WEAPON--
--OF THE MANY ARMS OF DEATH!
WHACK
...IN THEIR FINAL GASPING HOURS...
YOU ARE THEIR LAST WEAPON--
HA HA HA... NOT THE SWORD...
WHAMHH
HSSSSSS
...NOT THE SHIELD...
...NOT THE BATARANG...NOT THE BOTTLE...

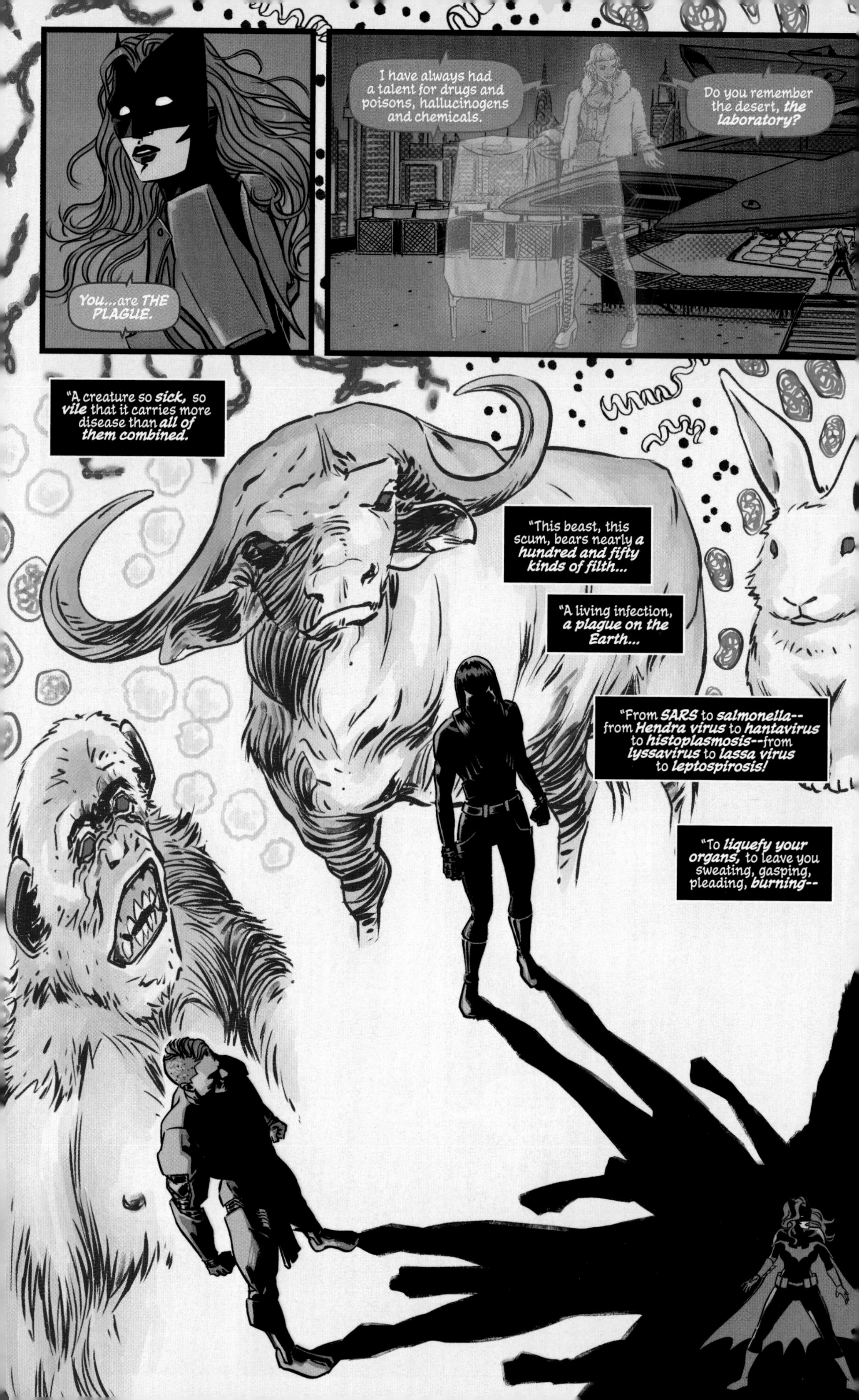

You...are THE PLAGUE.
I have always had a talent for drugs and poisons, hallucinogens and chemicals.
Do you remember the desert, the laboratory?
"A creature so sick, so vile that it carries more disease than all of them combined.
"This beast, this scum, bears nearly a hundred and fifty kinds of filth...
"A living infection, a plague on the Earth...
"From SARS to salmonella--from Hendra virus to hantavirus to histoplasmosis--from lyssavirus to lassa virus to leptospirosis!
"To liquefy your organs, to leave you sweating, gasping, pleading, burning--

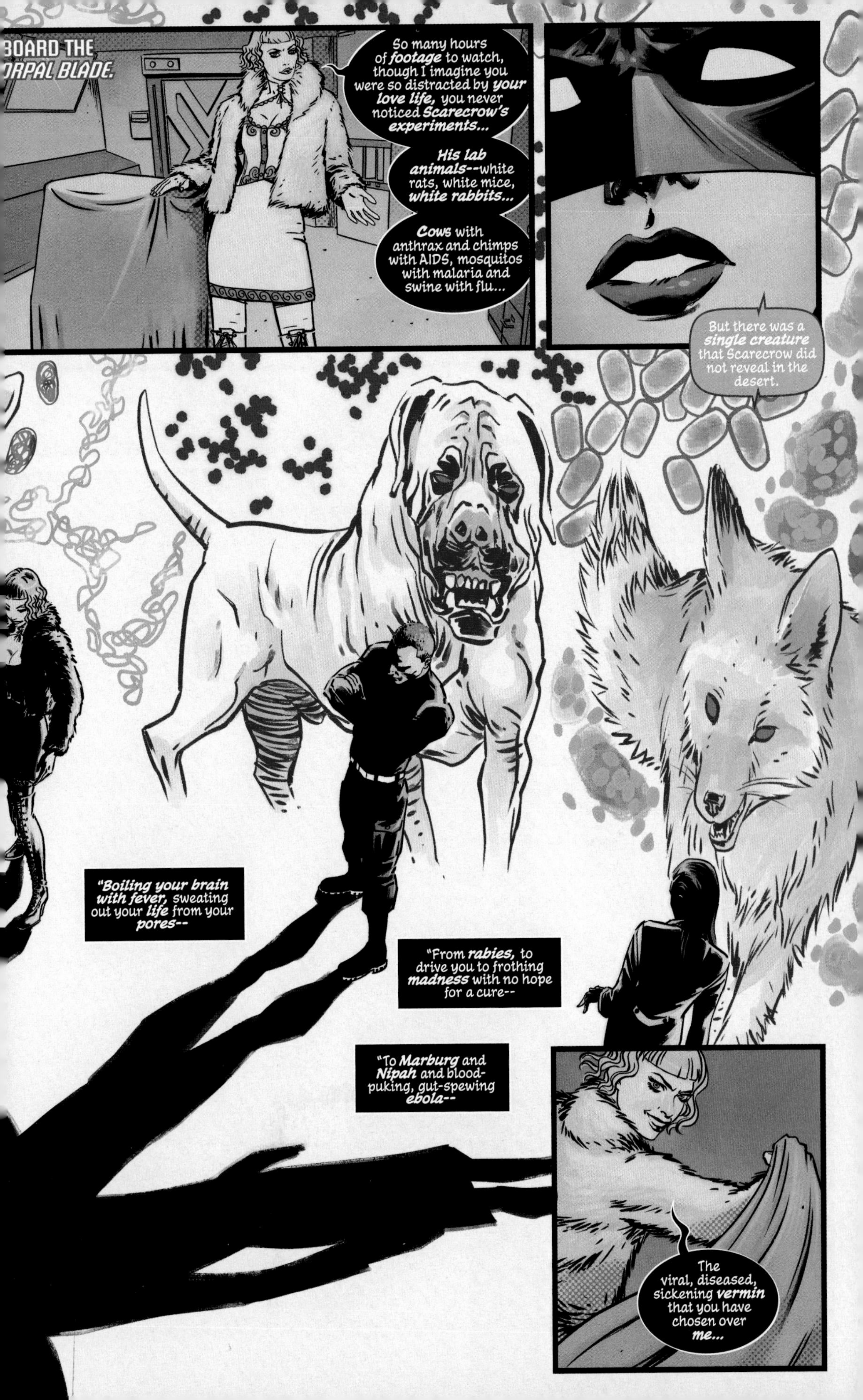

BOARD THE
ORPAL BLADE.
So many hours of footage to watch, though I imagine you were so distracted by your love life, you never noticed Scarecrow's experiments...
His lab animals--white rats, white mice, white rabbits...
Cows with anthrax and chimps with AIDS, mosquitos with malaria and swine with flu...
But there was a single creature that Scarecrow did not reveal in the desert.
"Boiling your brain with fever, sweating out your life from your pores--
"From rabies, to drive you to frothing madness with no hope for a cure--
"To Marburg and Nipah and blood-puking, gut-spewing ebola--
The viral, diseased, sickening vermin that you have chosen over me...

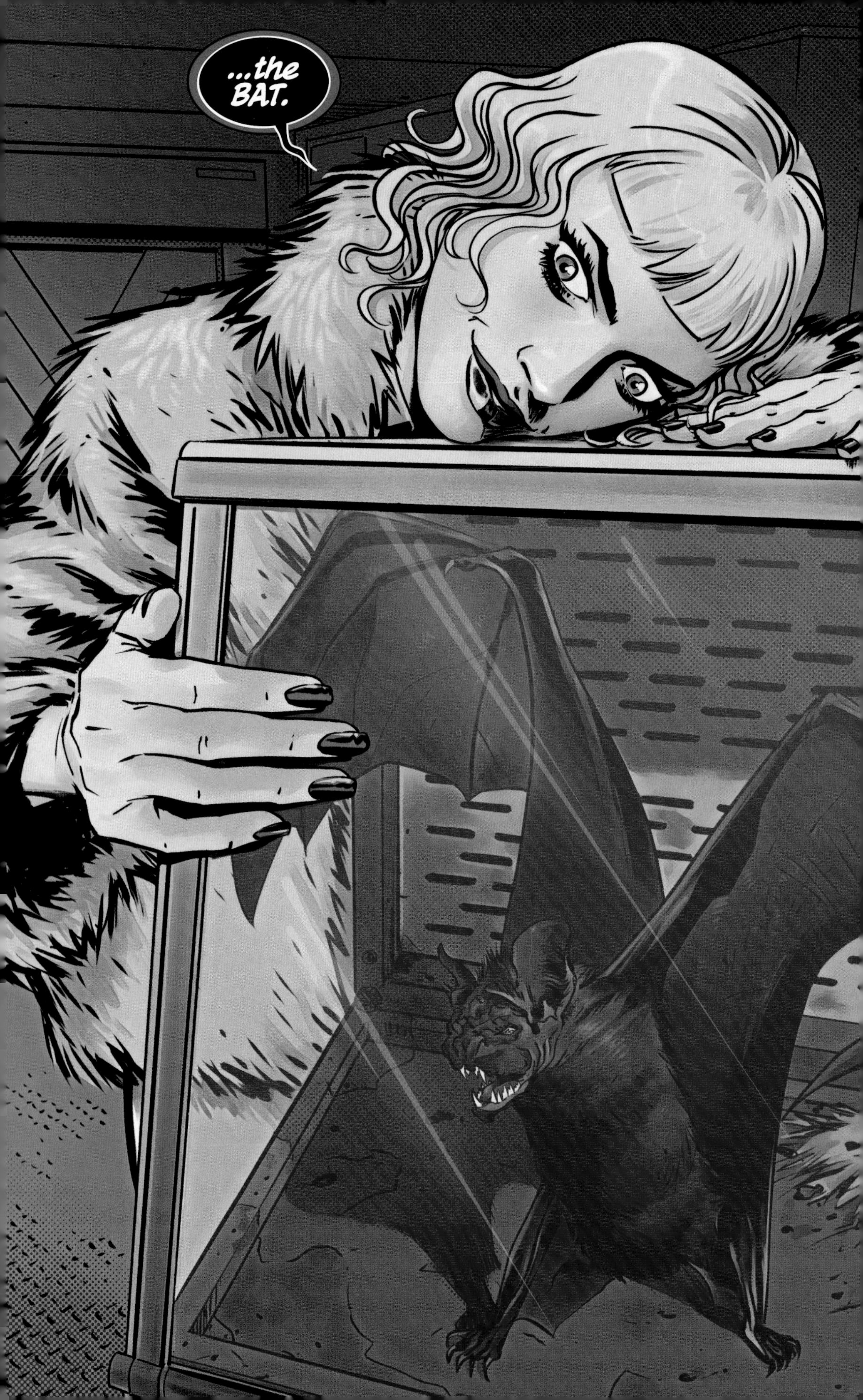
...the BAT.

But *this* bat...

...and all its *brothers and sisters* in the hold...

...they are *special.*

"I was always so good with *drugs* and *potions* and *poisons*...

"And now, with the help of what *was* the Many Arms of Death, I have crafted a draught of *something new.*

A *virus* unlike any the world has ever seen.

You loved this *thing*...this *vermin*...this *symbol*...

"...more than you loved your *own family.*

"As you took *Safiyah* from Tahani...

"...as Tahani took *Beth* from you...

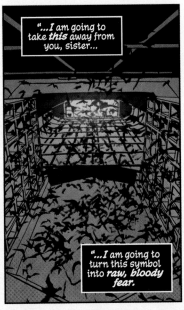

"...I am going to take *this* away from you, sister...

"...I am going to turn this symbol into *raw, bloody fear.*

"I will *destroy* what *the bat* means to *you*--and to *Gotham*--"

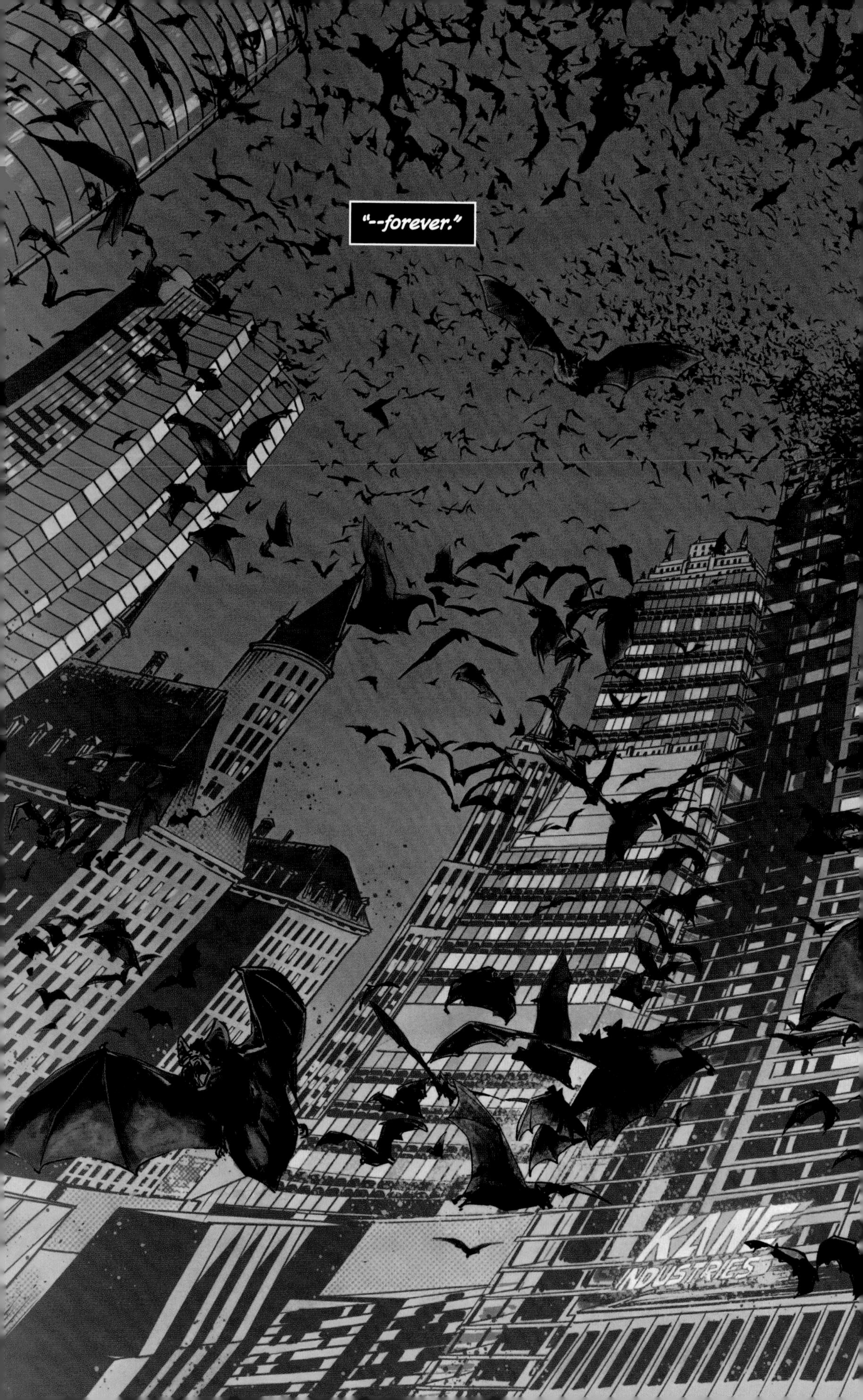
"--forever."
KANE
INDUSTRIES

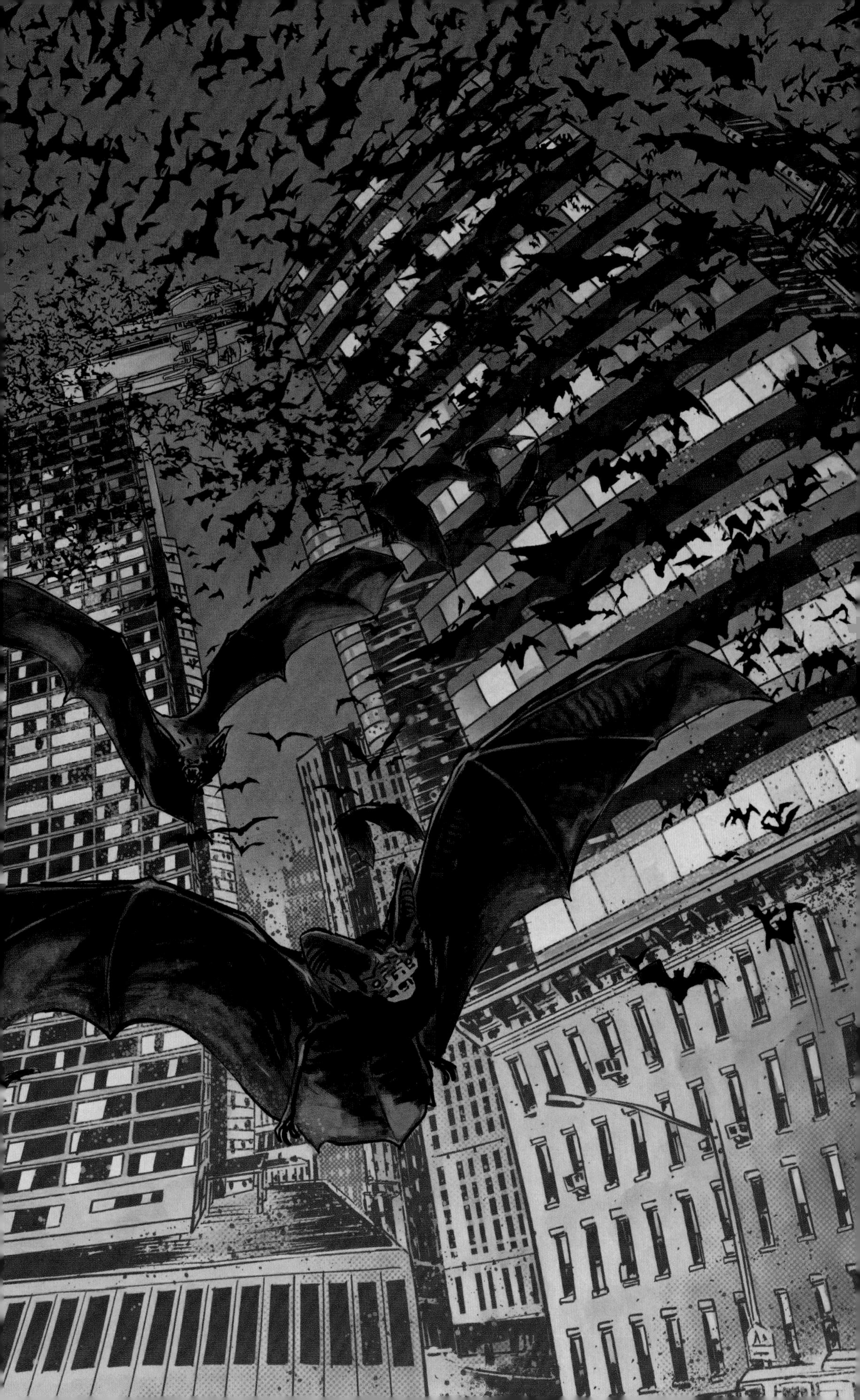

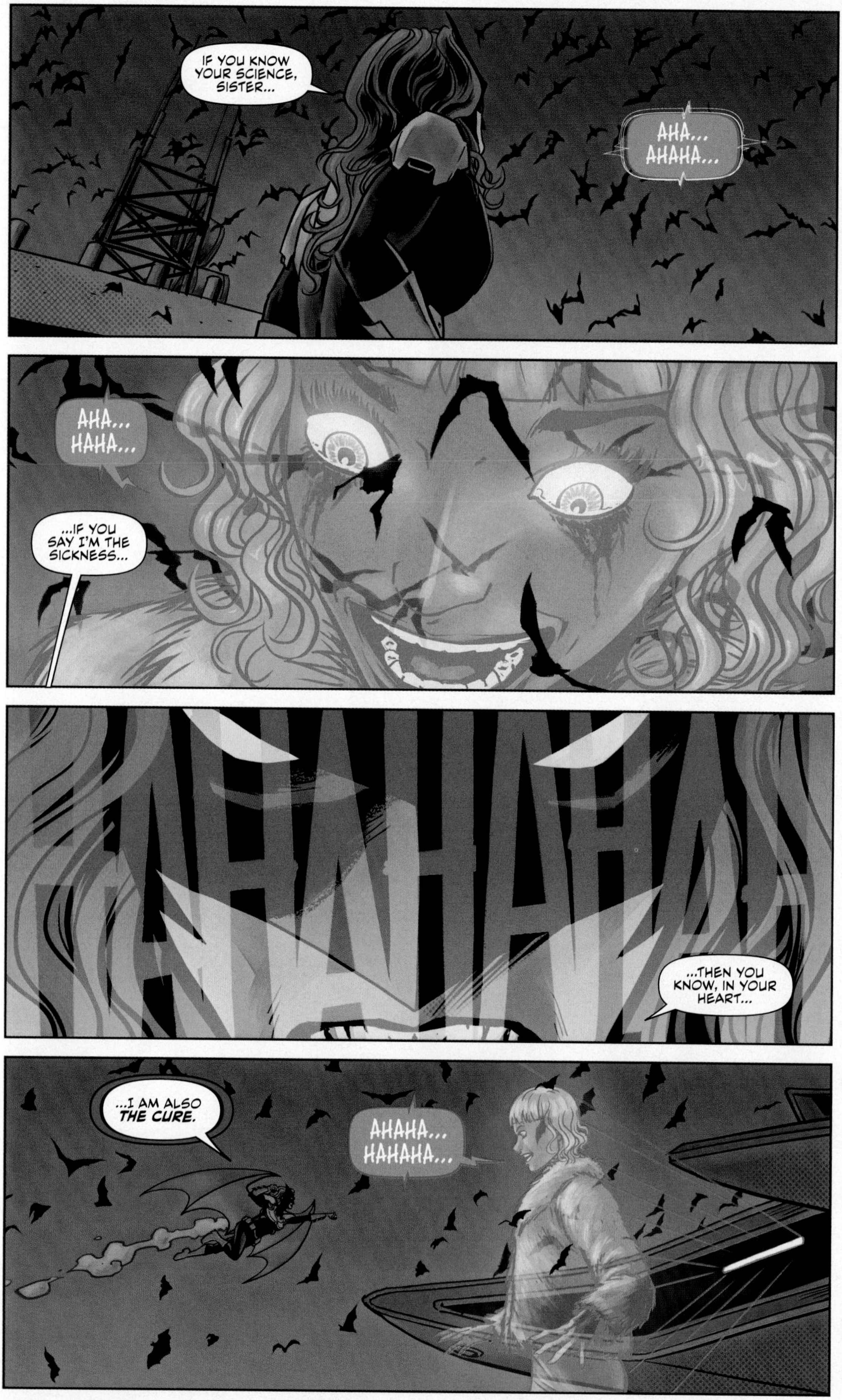
IF YOU KNOW YOUR SCIENCE, SISTER...
AHA... AHAHA...
AHA... HAHA...
...IF YOU SAY I'M THE SICKNESS...
...THEN YOU KNOW, IN YOUR HEART...
...I AM ALSO *THE CURE.*
AHAHA... HAHAHA...

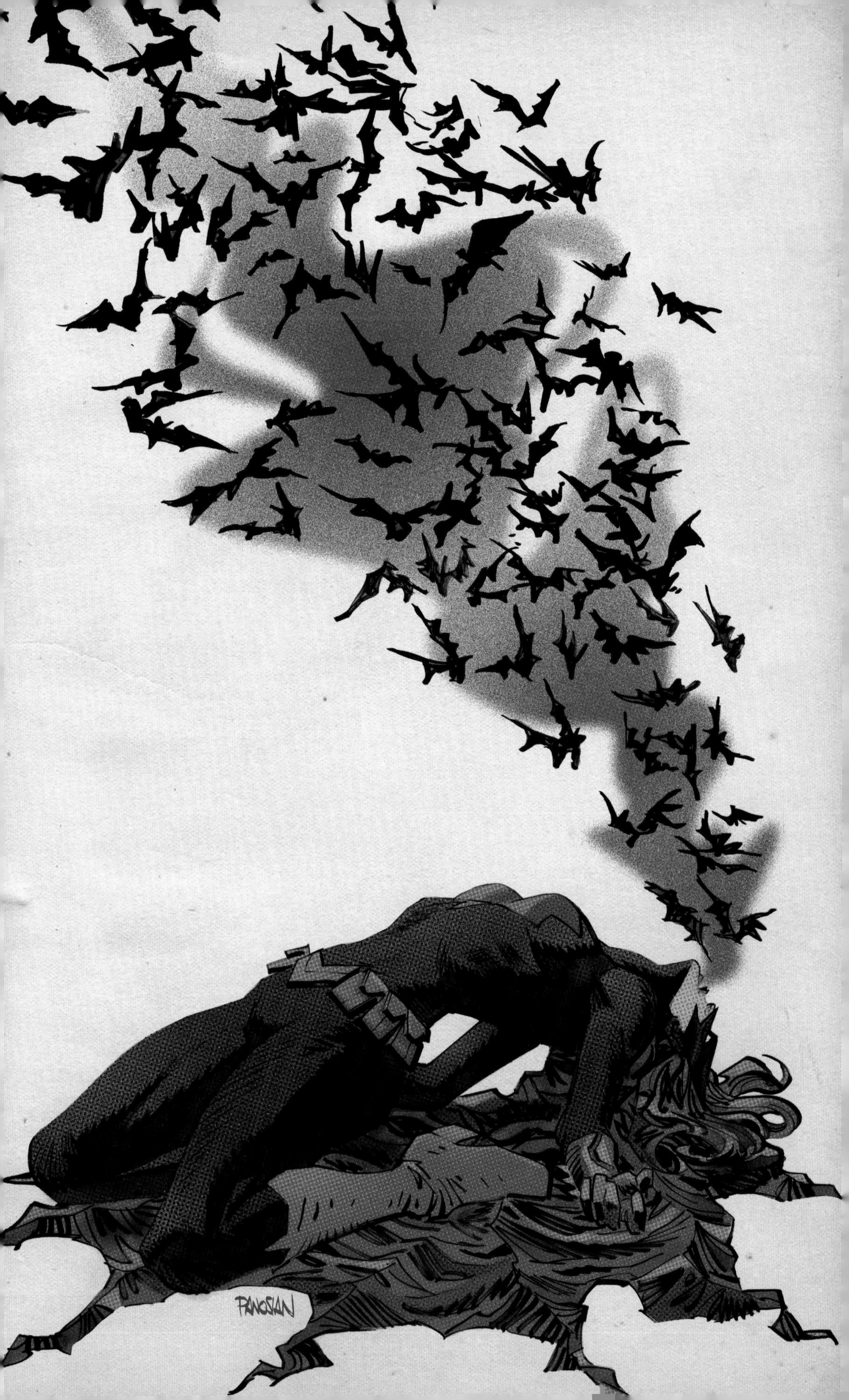
PANOSIAN

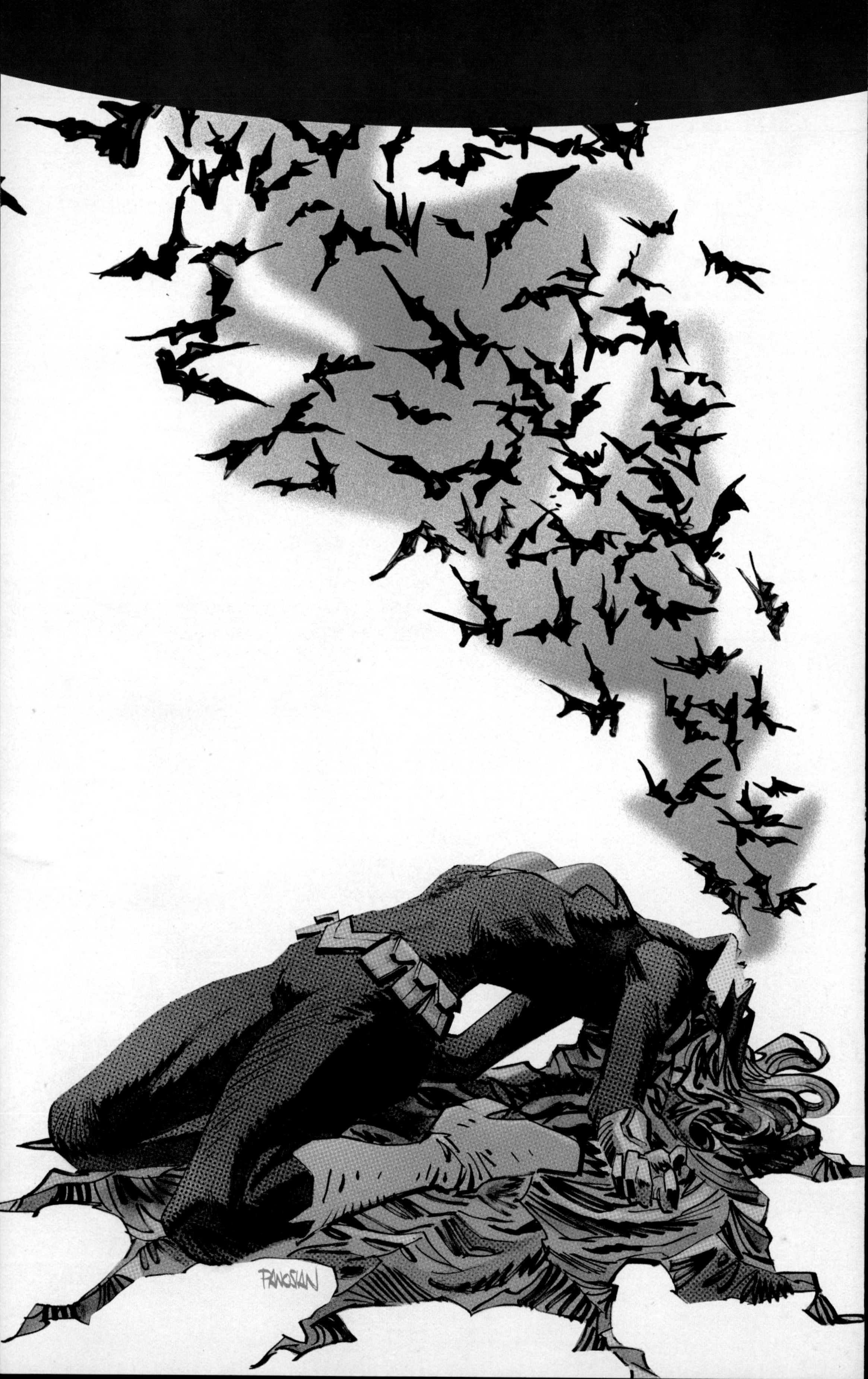
PANOSIAN

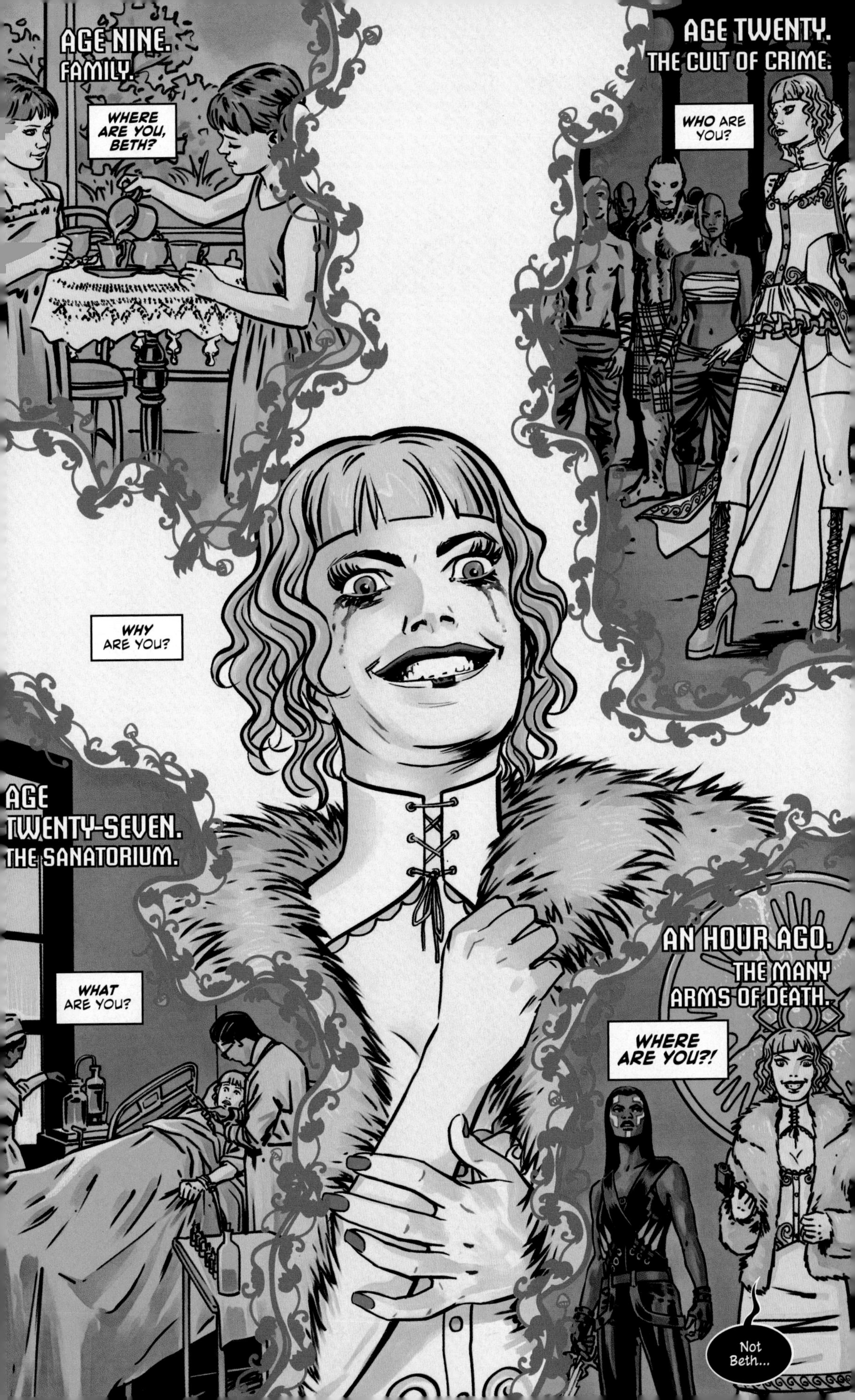
AGE NINE.
FAMILY.
WHERE ARE YOU, BETH?
AGE TWENTY.
THE CULT OF CRIME.
WHO ARE YOU?
WHY ARE YOU?
AGE TWENTY-SEVEN.
THE SANATORIUM.
WHAT ARE YOU?
AN HOUR AGO.
THE MANY ARMS OF DEATH.
WHERE ARE YOU?!
Not Beth...

This is the Story of **Little Alice.**

Once upon a time, in a great and distant country, two little princesses were born deep in a forest of silver and chrome, beneath a sacred sign.

The stars had aligned in the heavens. A thunderstorm came at midnight and the princesses were born together, holding hands. Their father the king was a mighty warrior. Their mother the queen was skilled in combat.

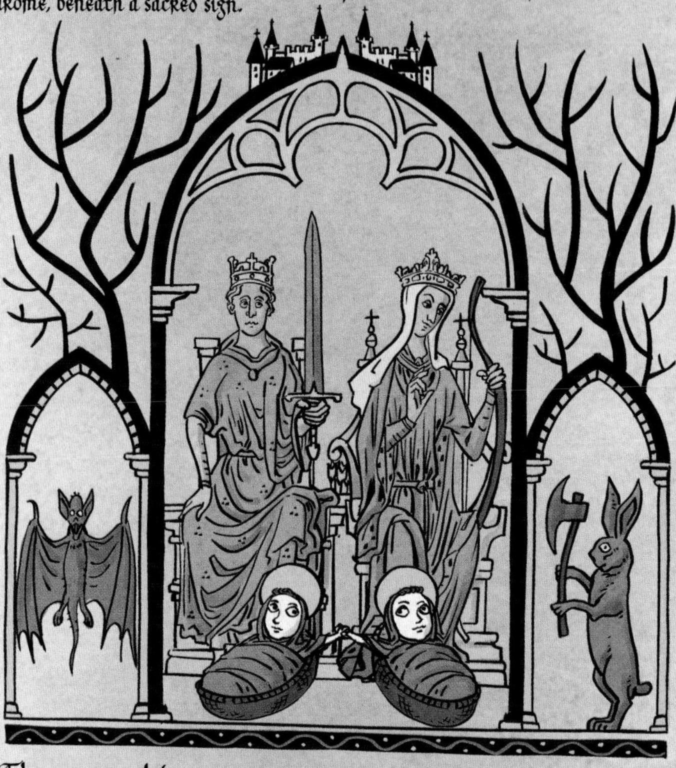

One day, a great monster with a thousand hands reached out to claim the girl-children, to have them for its servants.

But their mother the queen drove the many hands back.

And so the monster sought others who despised the king and queen. And those the monster called rose up and did as they were invited to do.

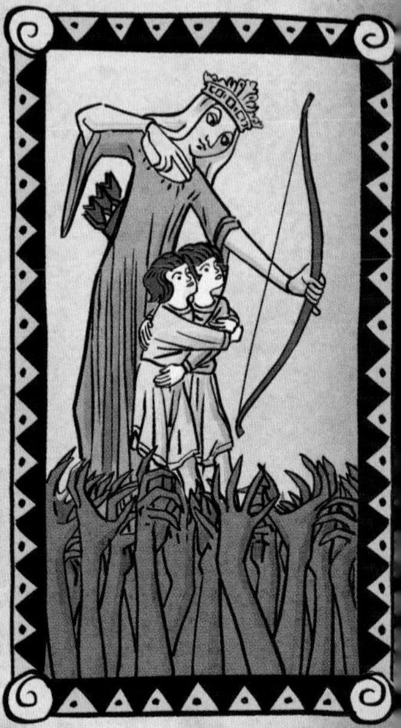

The queen was slain.

All thought the younger princess lost...

...but they were wrong.

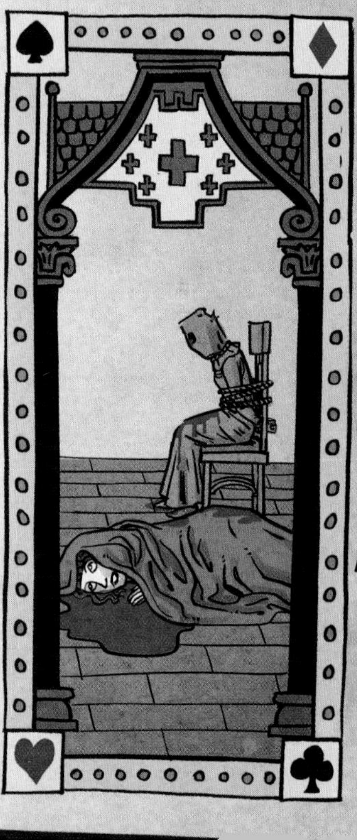

Another pair of twins was chosen to serve the monster instead.

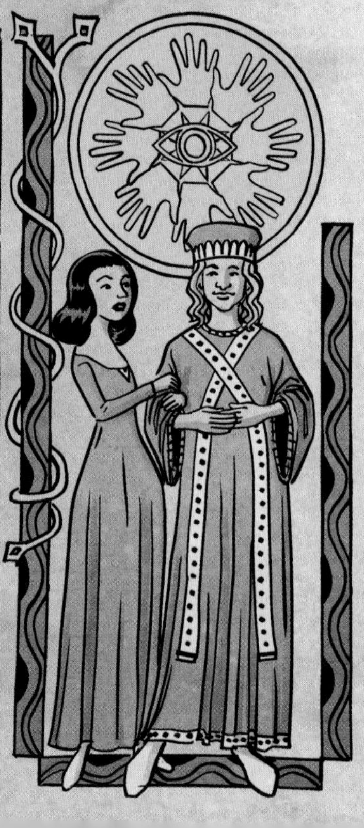

Too weak, too fragile for her birthright, the lost princess was reared in the monster's court and sent to rule a lesser land, where a cult of strange creatures did her bidding.

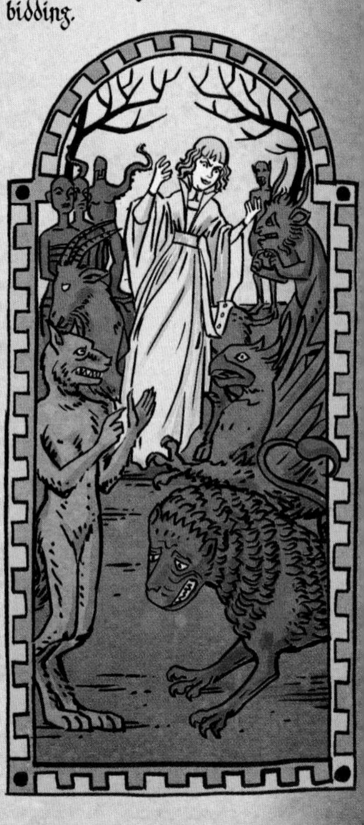

And in her twenty-fifth year, the princess' sister returned, and saved her.

The little princess was taken to wise healers, who worked their arts to give her back to herself.

But her sister was off fighting wars against shadows and demons and dread automatons, and could not be found.

Abandoned, isolated, alone, the little princess longed for the world her sister shared in. Until one day...

A knight called The Knife appeared.

The noble knight carried the little princess back, back to the Twins who had been anointed in her stead.

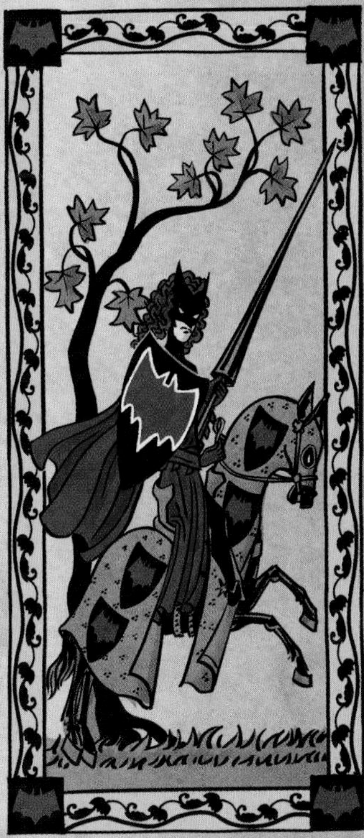

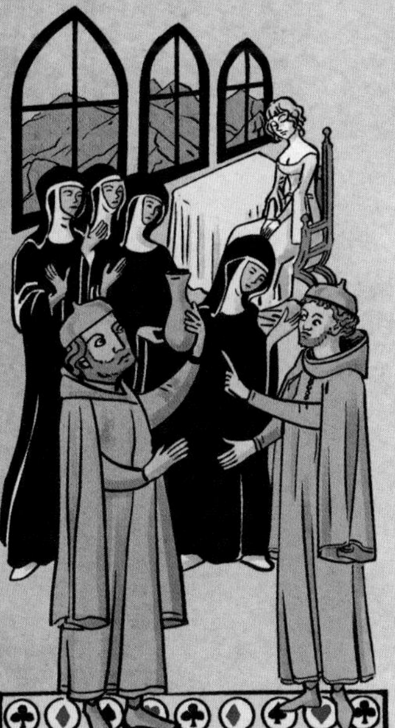

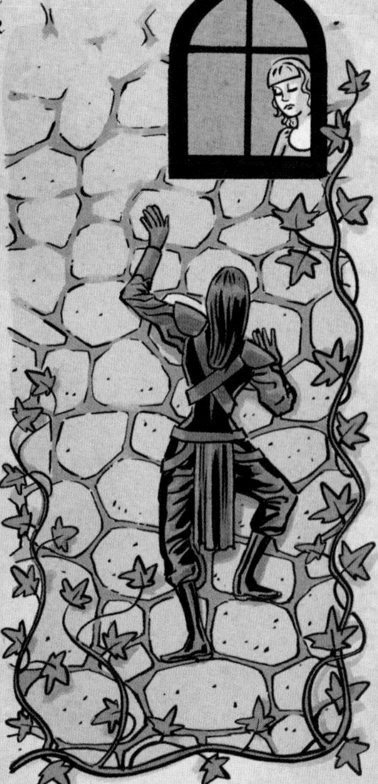

The Twins read the signs of her birth, purer and brighter than their own...and they knelt.

The Knight, the Knife, was the advisor of the princess, her great friend and grand vizier.

She, too, had been cast aside by the one she loved.

She, too, had been abandoned because of the princess' sister.

And the knight called Knife guided the princess' hand...

...and all the many hands of the monster...

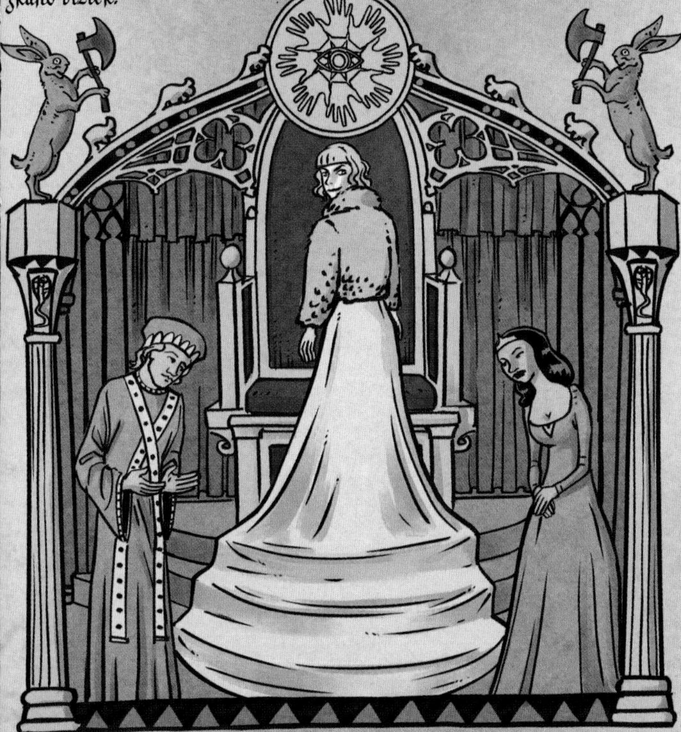

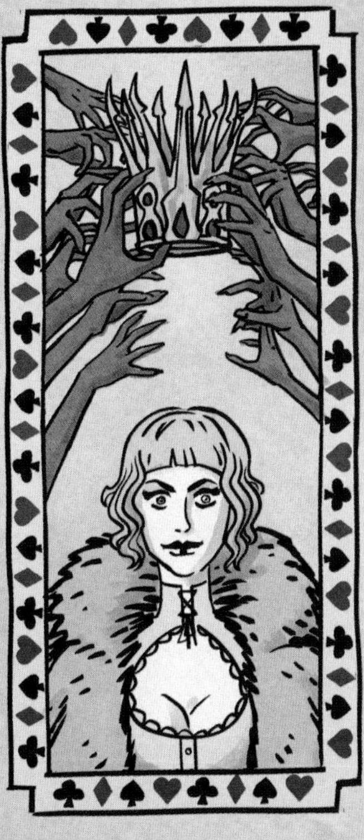

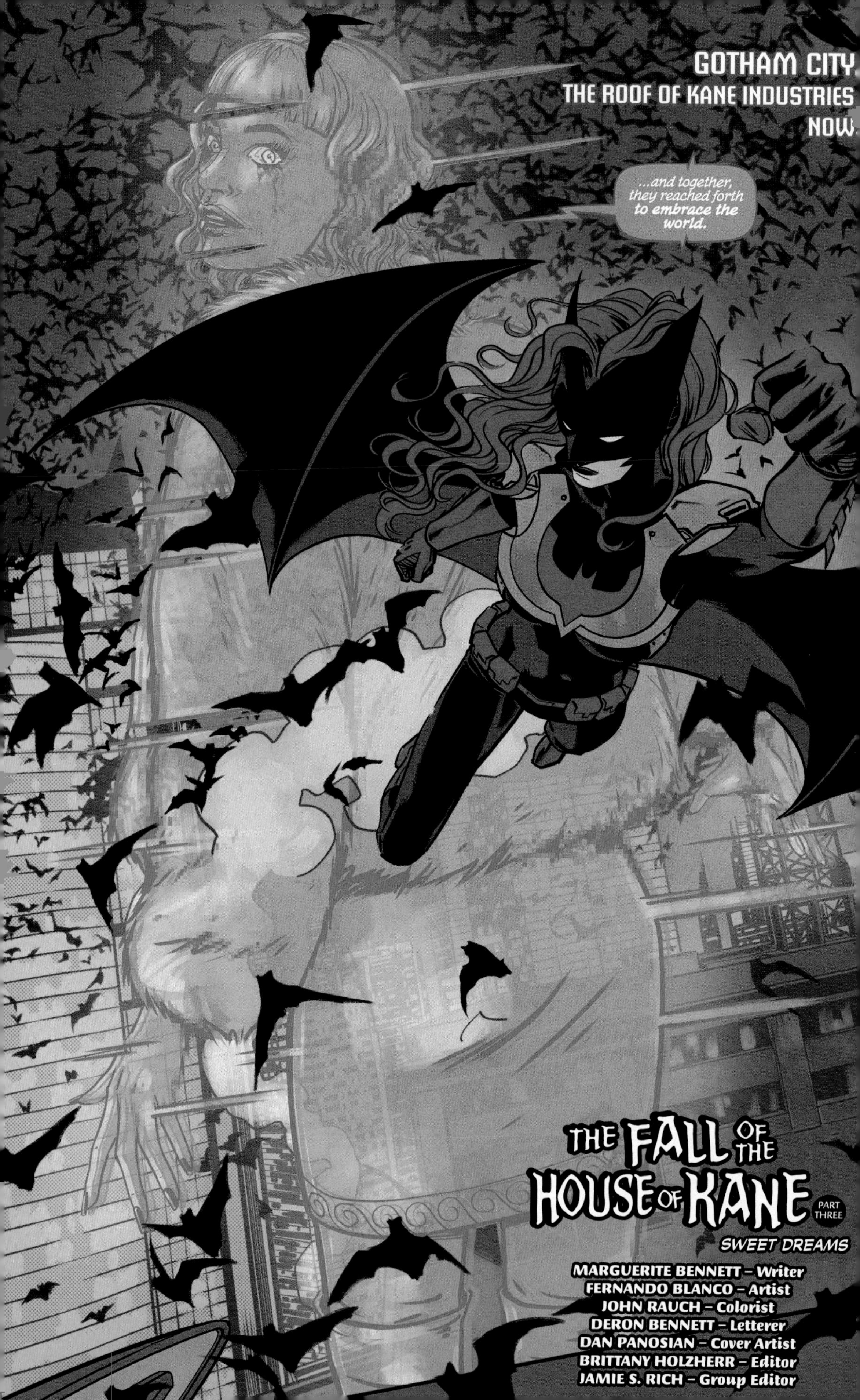
GOTHAM CITY
THE ROOF OF KANE INDUSTRIES
NOW
...and together, they reached forth to embrace the world.
THE FALL OF THE HOUSE OF KANE
PART THREE
SWEET DREAMS
MARGUERITE BENNETT – Writer
FERNANDO BLANCO – Artist
JOHN RAUCH – Colorist
DERON BENNETT – Letterer
DAN PANOSIAN – Cover Artist
BRITTANY HOLZHERR – Editor
JAMIE S. RICH – Group Editor

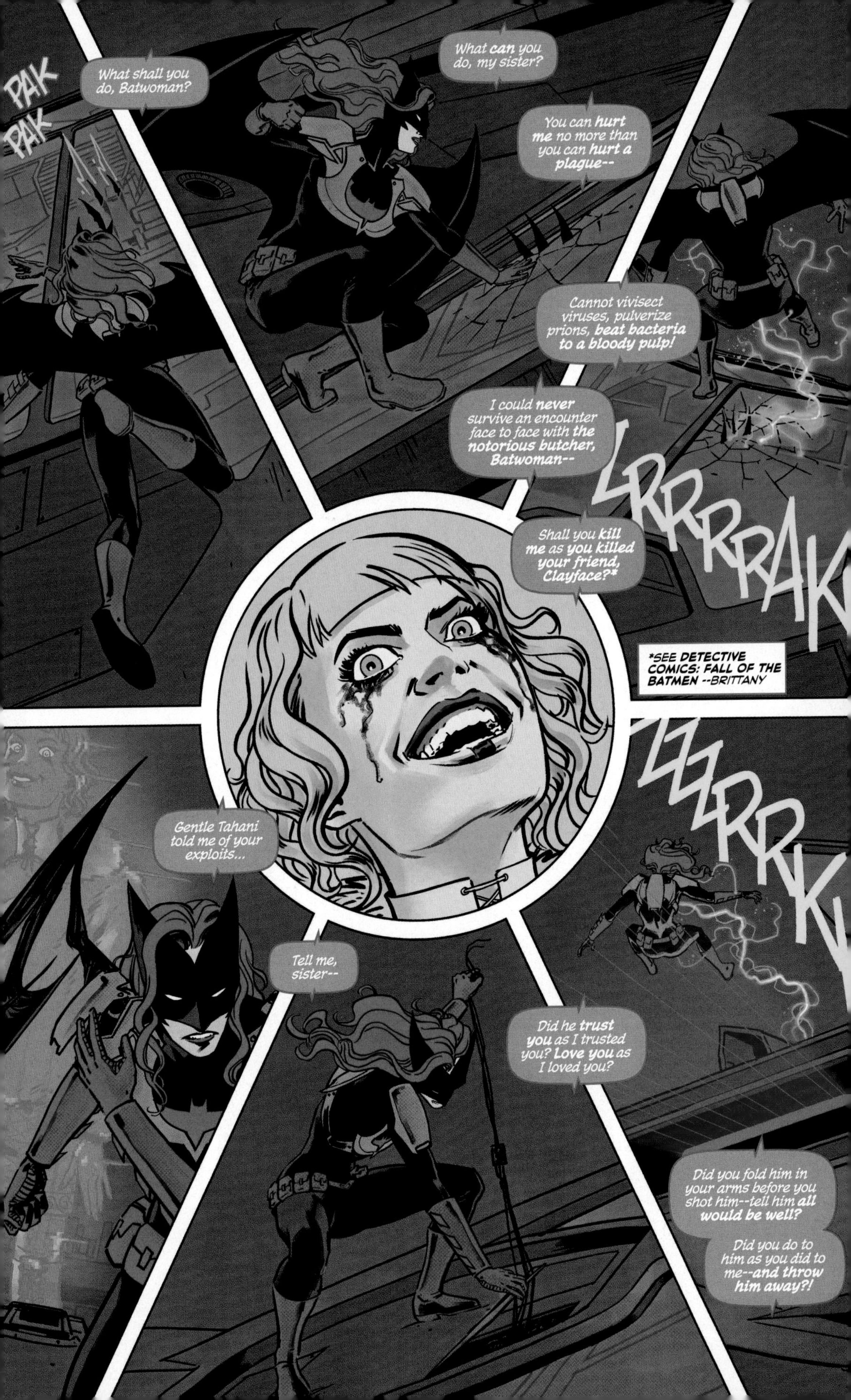
PAK PAK
What shall you do, Batwoman?
What can you do, my sister?
You can hurt me no more than you can hurt a plague--
Cannot vivisect viruses, pulverize prions, beat bacteria to a bloody pulp!
I could never survive an encounter face to face with the notorious butcher, Batwoman--
LRRRRRAK
Shall you kill me as you killed your friend, Clayface?*
*SEE DETECTIVE COMICS: FALL OF THE BATMEN --BRITTANY
ZZZRRRK
Gentle Tahani told me of your exploits...
Tell me, sister--
Did he trust you as I trusted you? Love you as I loved you?
Did you fold him in your arms before you shot him--tell him all would be well?
Did you do to him as you did to me--and throw him away?!

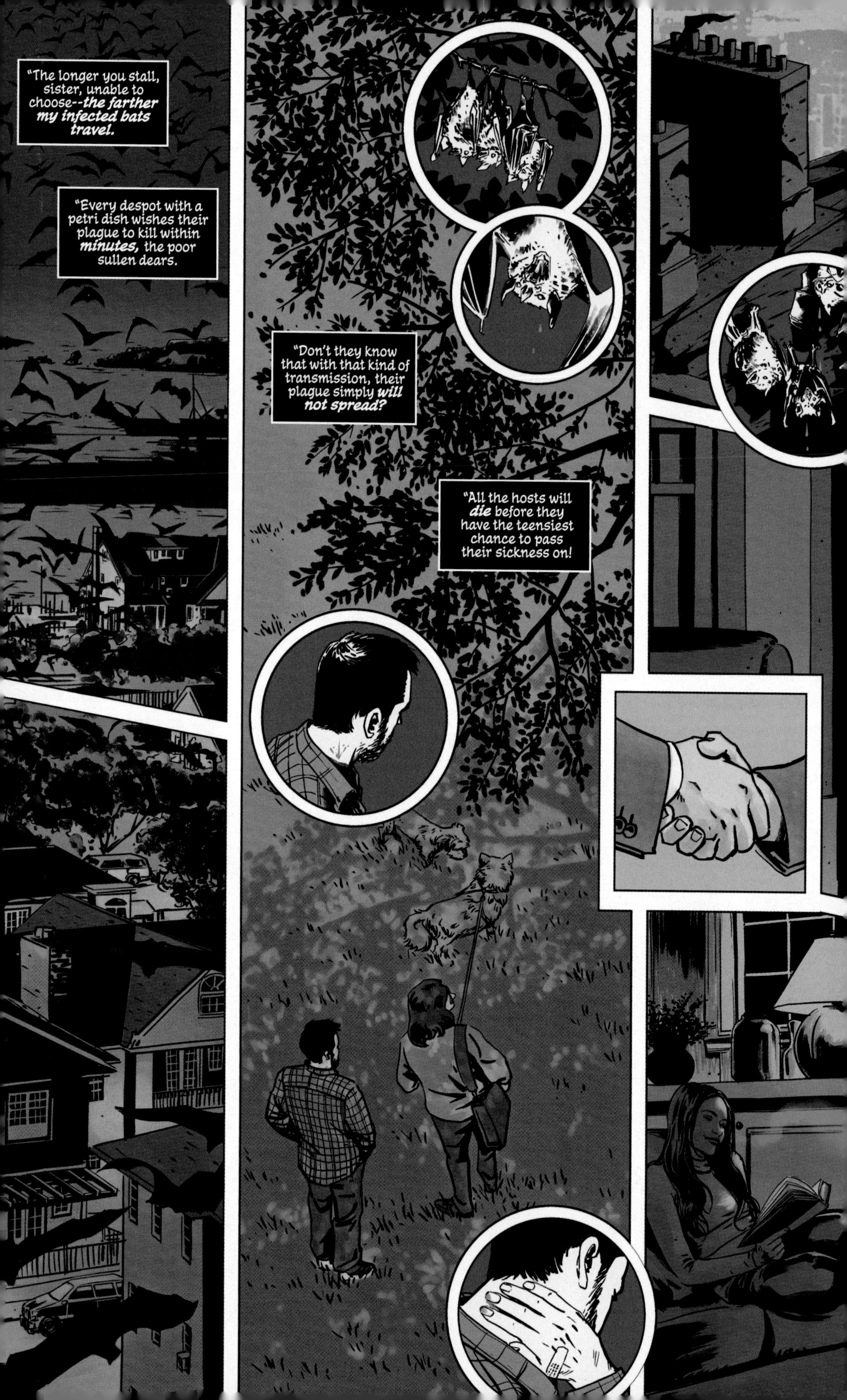
"The longer you stall, sister, unable to choose--*the farther my infected bats travel.*
"Every despot with a petri dish wishes their plague to kill within *minutes,* the poor sullen dears.
"Don't they know that with that kind of transmission, their plague simply *will not spread?*
"All the hosts will *die* before they have the teensiest chance to pass their sickness on!

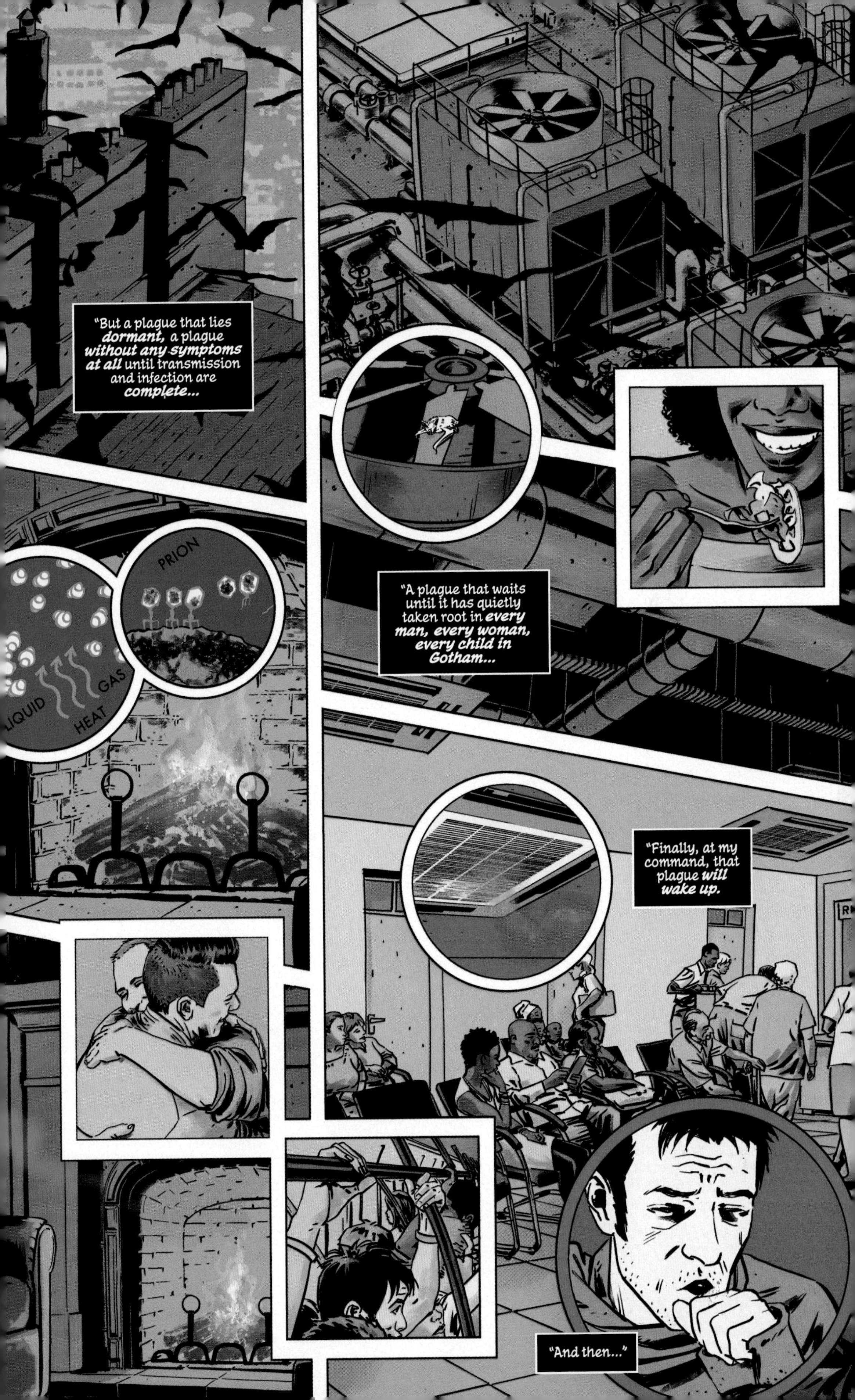
"But a plague that lies *dormant,* a plague *without any symptoms at all* until transmission and infection are *complete...*
PRION
LIQUID
HEAT
GAS
"A plague that waits until it has quietly taken root in *every man, every woman, every child in Gotham...*
"Finally, at my command, that plague *will wake up.*
"And then..."

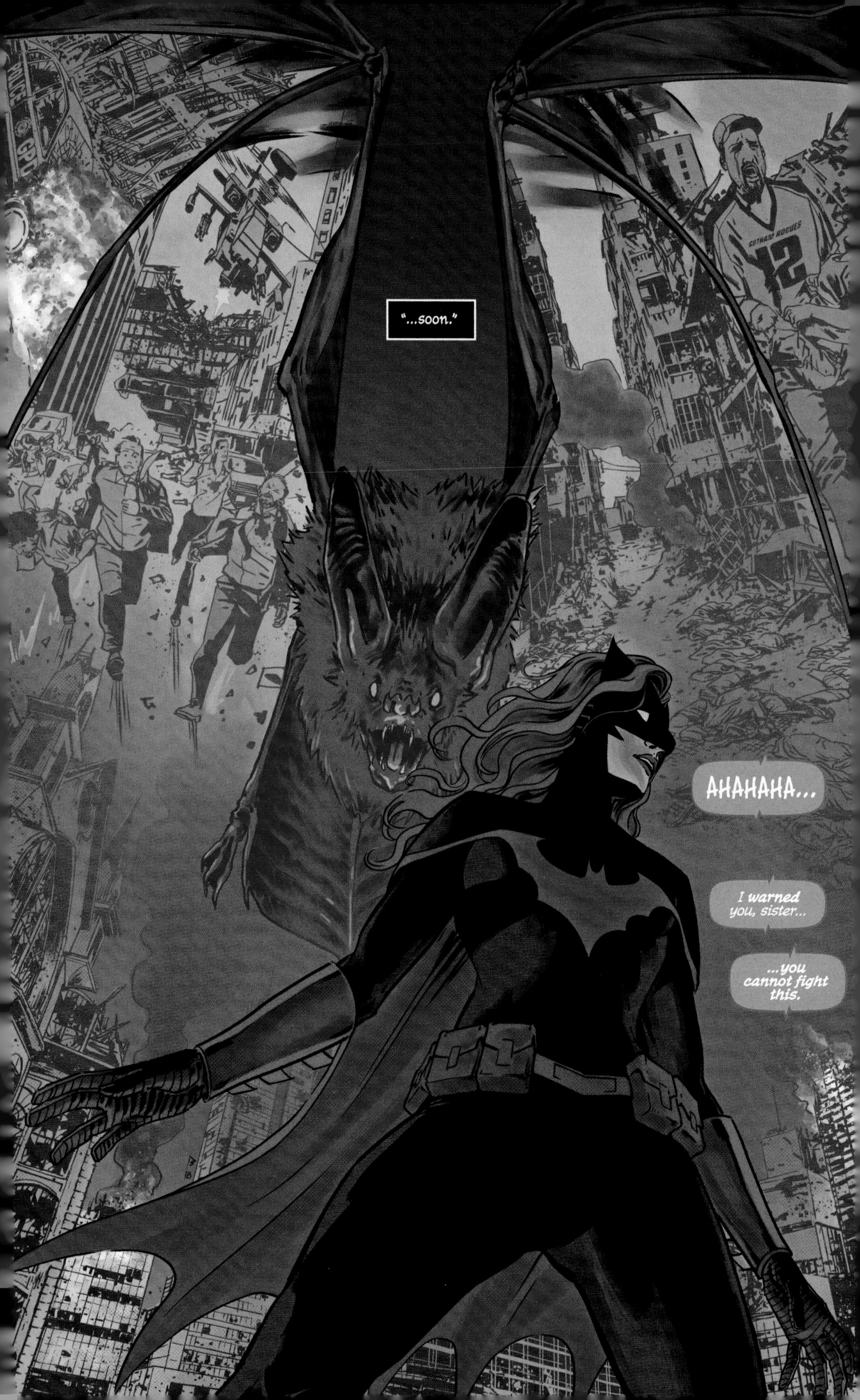
"...soon."
GOTHAM ROGUES
12
AHAHAHA...
I warned you, sister...
...you cannot fight this.

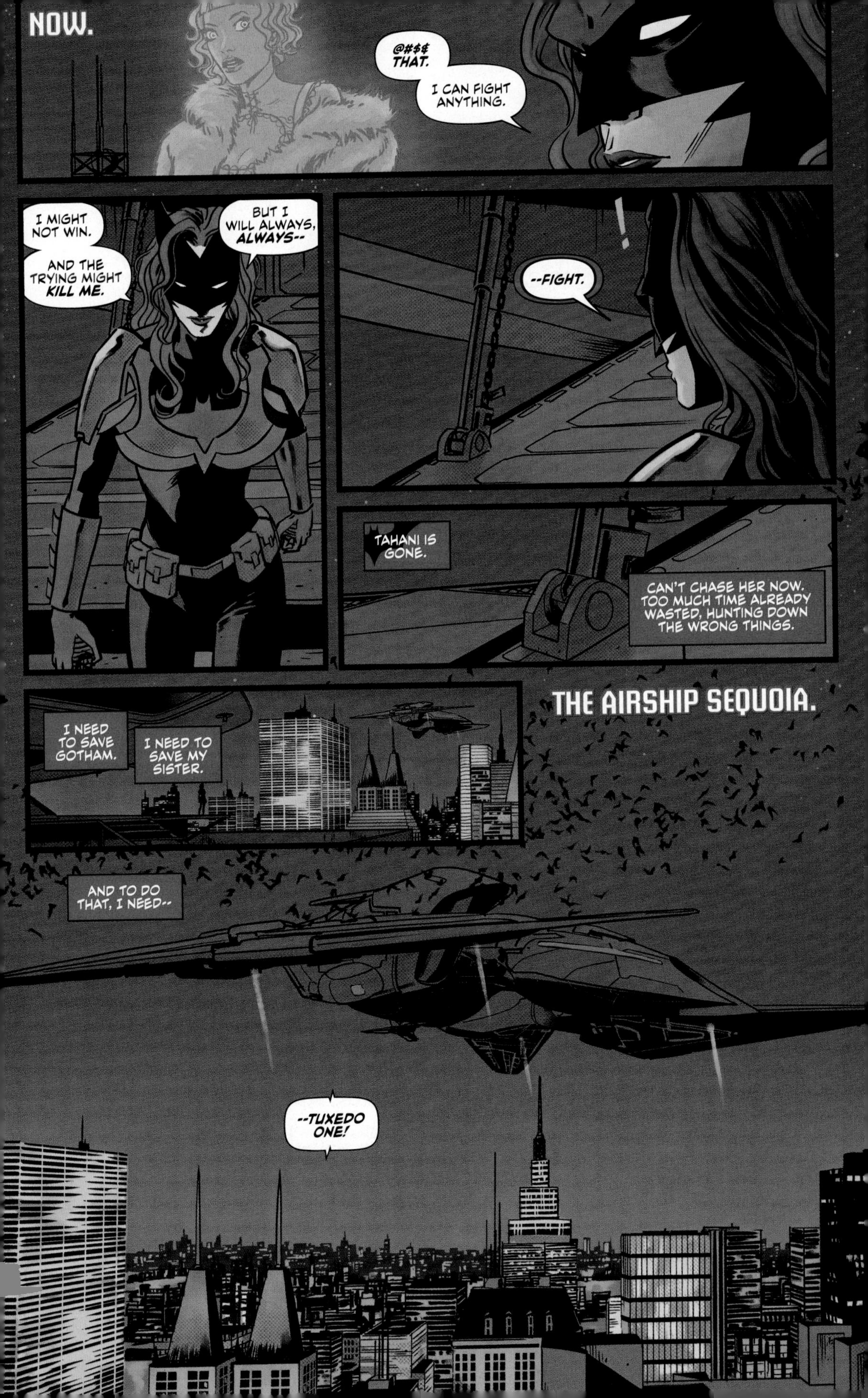
NOW.
@#$$ THAT.
I CAN FIGHT ANYTHING.
I MIGHT NOT WIN.
AND THE TRYING MIGHT KILL ME.
BUT I WILL ALWAYS, ALWAYS--
--FIGHT.
TAHANI IS GONE.
CAN'T CHASE HER NOW. TOO MUCH TIME ALREADY WASTED, HUNTING DOWN THE WRONG THINGS.
THE AIRSHIP SEQUOIA.
I NEED TO SAVE GOTHAM.
I NEED TO SAVE MY SISTER.
AND TO DO THAT, I NEED--
--TUXEDO ONE!

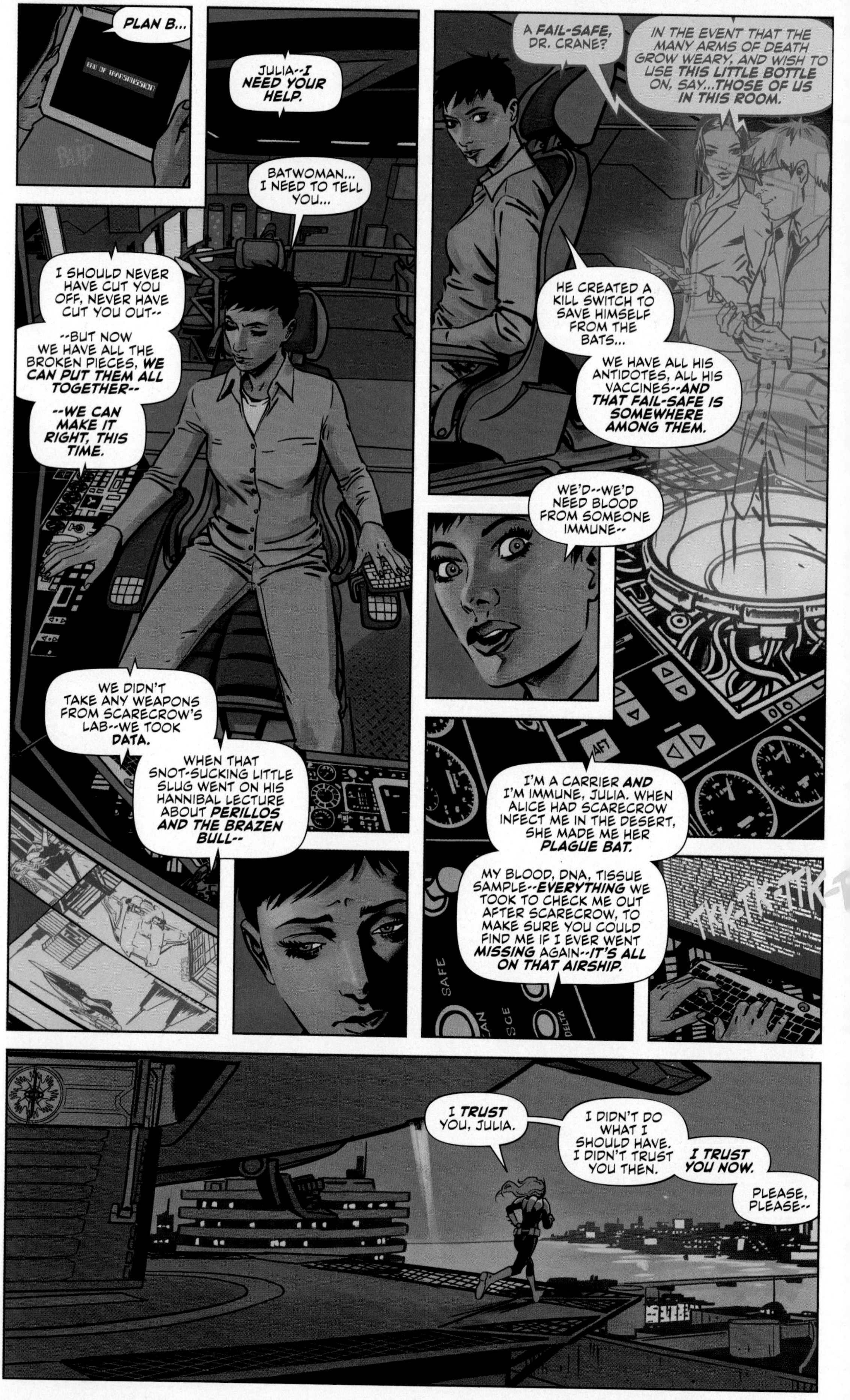

PLAN B...
END OF TRANSMISSION
BLIP
JULIA--I NEED YOUR HELP.
BATWOMAN... I NEED TO TELL YOU...
I SHOULD NEVER HAVE CUT YOU OFF, NEVER HAVE CUT YOU OUT--
--BUT NOW WE HAVE ALL THE BROKEN PIECES, WE CAN PUT THEM ALL TOGETHER--
--WE CAN MAKE IT RIGHT, THIS TIME.
A FAIL-SAFE, DR. CRANE?
IN THE EVENT THAT THE MANY ARMS OF DEATH GROW WEARY, AND WISH TO USE THIS LITTLE BOTTLE ON, SAY...THOSE OF US IN THIS ROOM.
HE CREATED A KILL SWITCH TO SAVE HIMSELF FROM THE BATS...
WE HAVE ALL HIS ANTIDOTES, ALL HIS VACCINES--AND THAT FAIL-SAFE IS SOMEWHERE AMONG THEM.
WE'D--WE'D NEED BLOOD FROM SOMEONE IMMUNE--
WE DIDN'T TAKE ANY WEAPONS FROM SCARECROW'S LAB--WE TOOK DATA.
WHEN THAT SNOT-SUCKING LITTLE SLUG WENT ON HIS HANNIBAL LECTURE ABOUT PERILLOS AND THE BRAZEN BULL--
AFT
I'M A CARRIER AND I'M IMMUNE, JULIA. WHEN ALICE HAD SCARECROW INFECT ME IN THE DESERT, SHE MADE ME HER PLAGUE BAT.
MY BLOOD, DNA, TISSUE SAMPLE--EVERYTHING WE TOOK TO CHECK ME OUT AFTER SCARECROW, TO MAKE SURE YOU COULD FIND ME IF I EVER WENT MISSING AGAIN--IT'S ALL ON THAT AIRSHIP.
SAFE
DELTA
TKTKTK
I TRUST YOU, JULIA.
I DIDN'T DO WHAT I SHOULD HAVE. I DIDN'T TRUST YOU THEN.
I TRUST YOU NOW.
PLEASE, PLEASE--

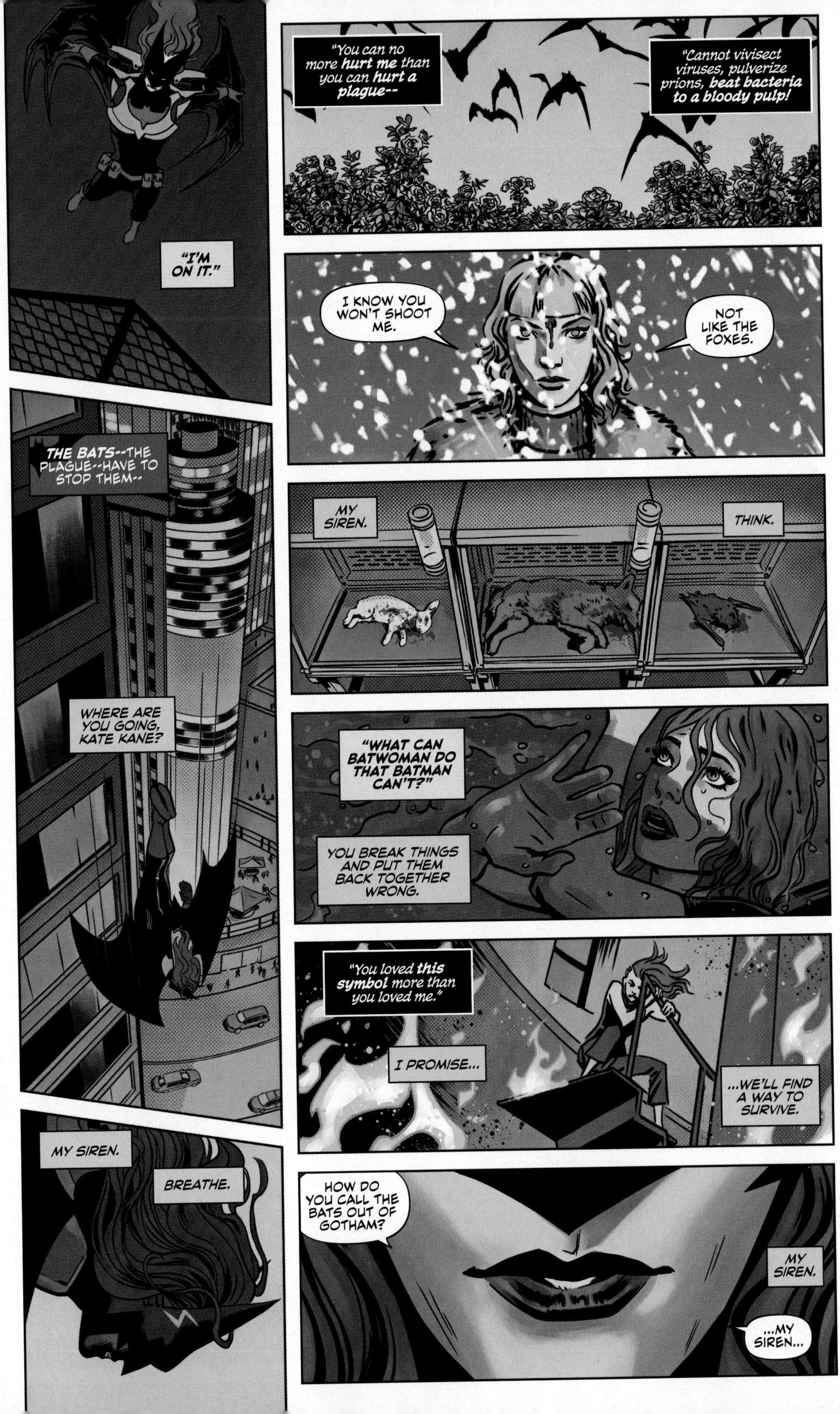
"You can no more hurt me than you can hurt a plague--
"Cannot vivisect viruses, pulverize prions, beat bacteria to a bloody pulp!
"I'M ON IT."
I KNOW YOU WON'T SHOOT ME.
NOT LIKE THE FOXES.
THE BATS--THE PLAGUE--HAVE TO STOP THEM--
MY SIREN.
THINK.
"WHAT CAN BATWOMAN DO THAT BATMAN CAN'T?"
YOU BREAK THINGS AND PUT THEM BACK TOGETHER WRONG.
WHERE ARE YOU GOING, KATE KANE?
"You loved this symbol more than you loved me."
I PROMISE...
...WE'LL FIND A WAY TO SURVIVE.
MY SIREN.
BREATHE.
HOW DO YOU CALL THE BATS OUT OF GOTHAM?
MY SIREN.
...MY SIREN...

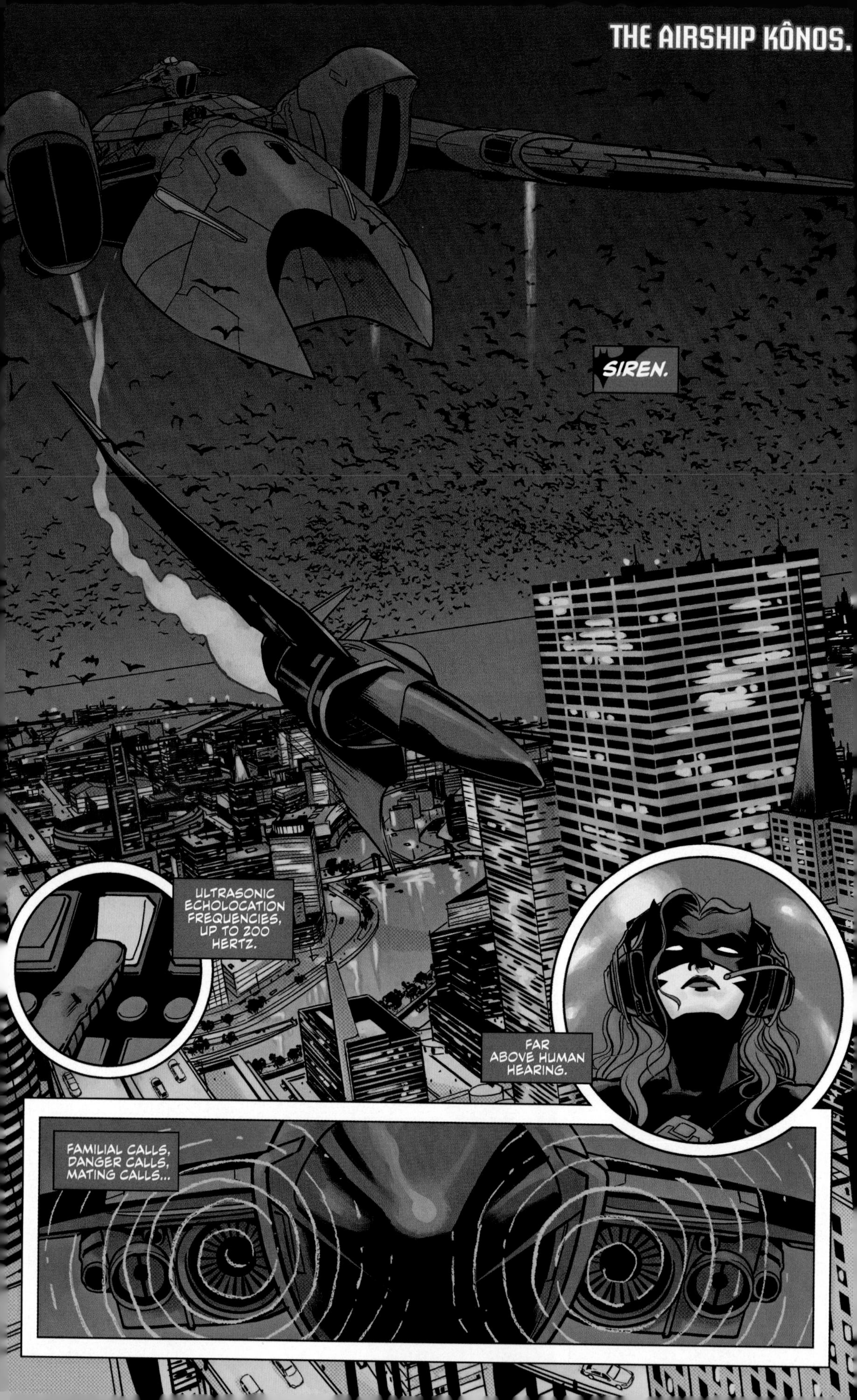
THE AIRSHIP KÔNOS.
SIREN.
ULTRASONIC ECHOLOCATION FREQUENCIES, UP TO 200 HERTZ.
FAR ABOVE HUMAN HEARING.
FAMILIAL CALLS, DANGER CALLS, MATING CALLS...

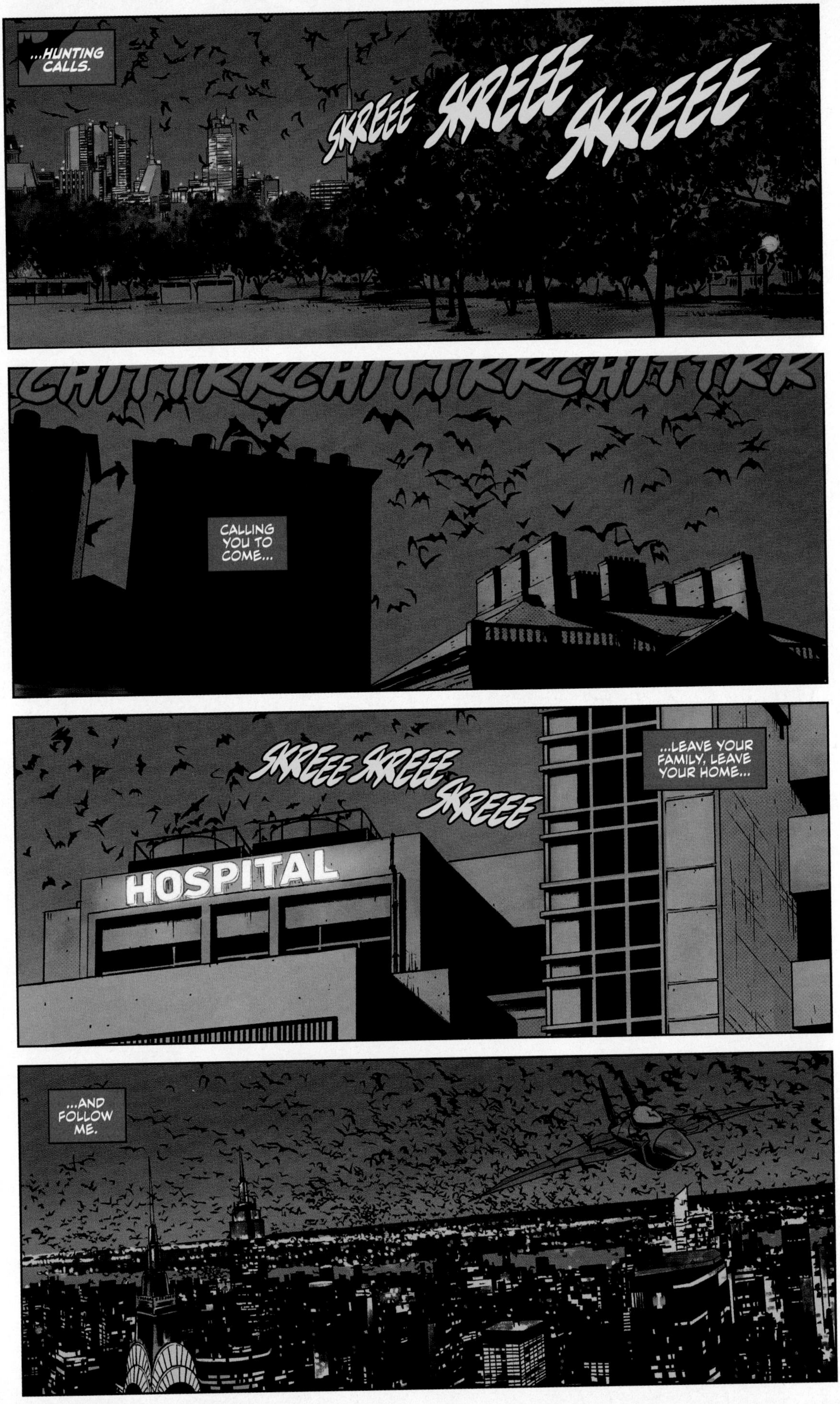
...HUNTING CALLS.
SKREEE SKREEE SKREEE
CHITTRKCHITTRKCHITTRK
CALLING YOU TO COME...
SKREEE SKREEE SKREEE
...LEAVE YOUR FAMILY, LEAVE YOUR HOME...
HOSPITAL
...AND FOLLOW ME.

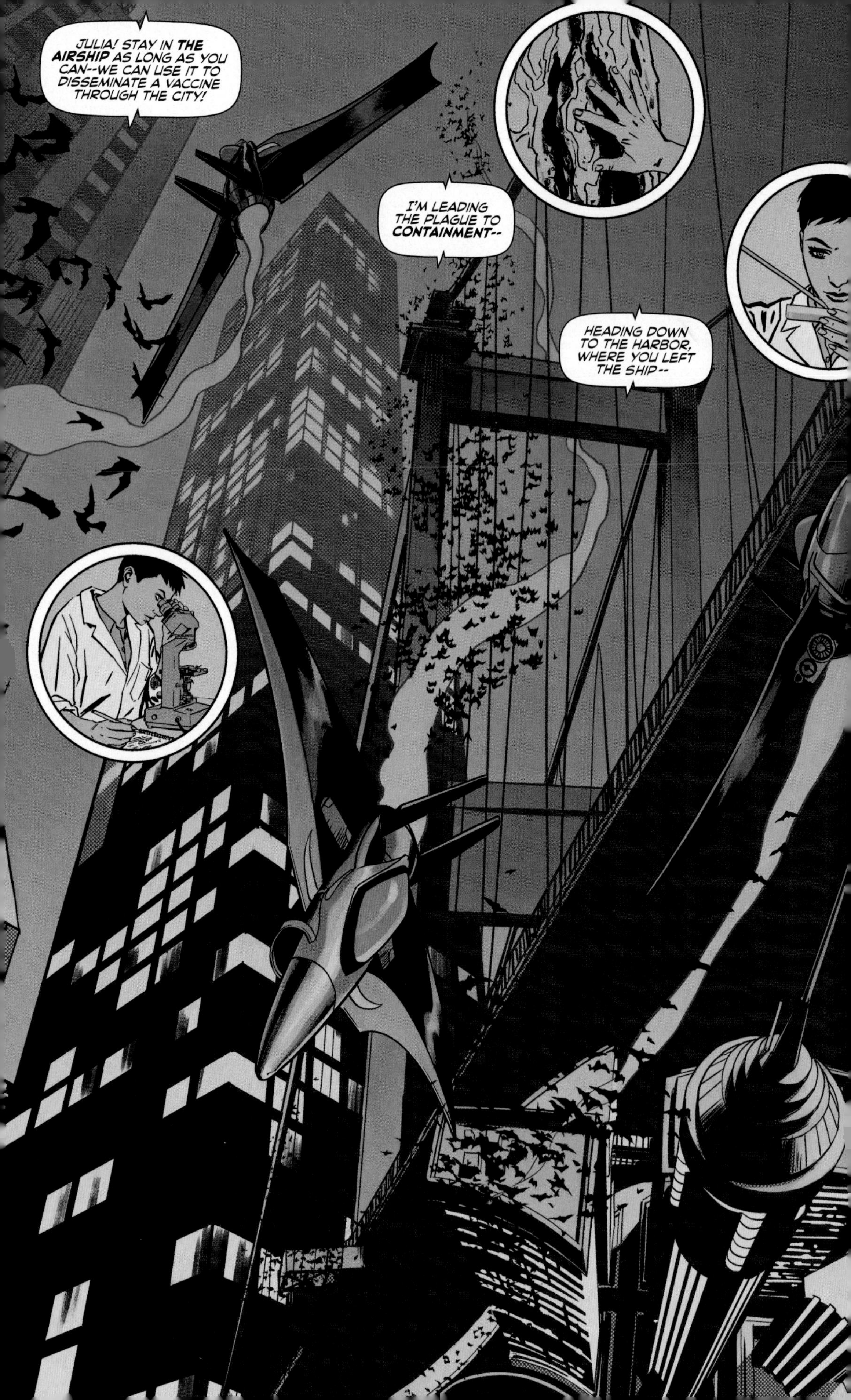
JULIA! STAY IN THE AIRSHIP AS LONG AS YOU CAN--WE CAN USE IT TO DISSEMINATE A VACCINE THROUGH THE CITY!
I'M LEADING THE PLAGUE TO CONTAINMENT--
HEADING DOWN TO THE HARBOR, WHERE YOU LEFT THE SHIP--

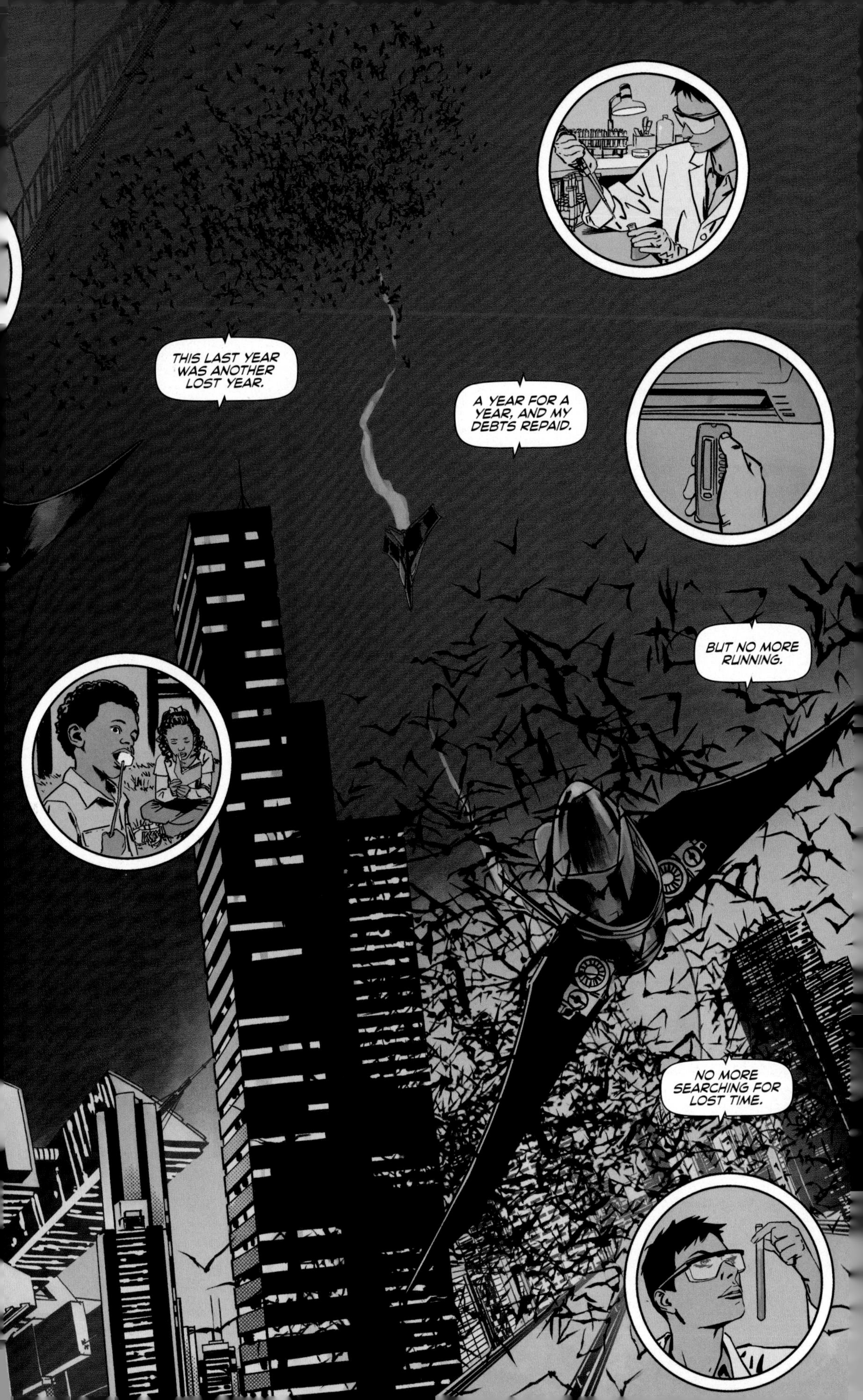
THIS LAST YEAR WAS ANOTHER LOST YEAR.
A YEAR FOR A YEAR, AND MY DEBTS REPAID.
BUT NO MORE RUNNING.
NO MORE SEARCHING FOR LOST TIME.

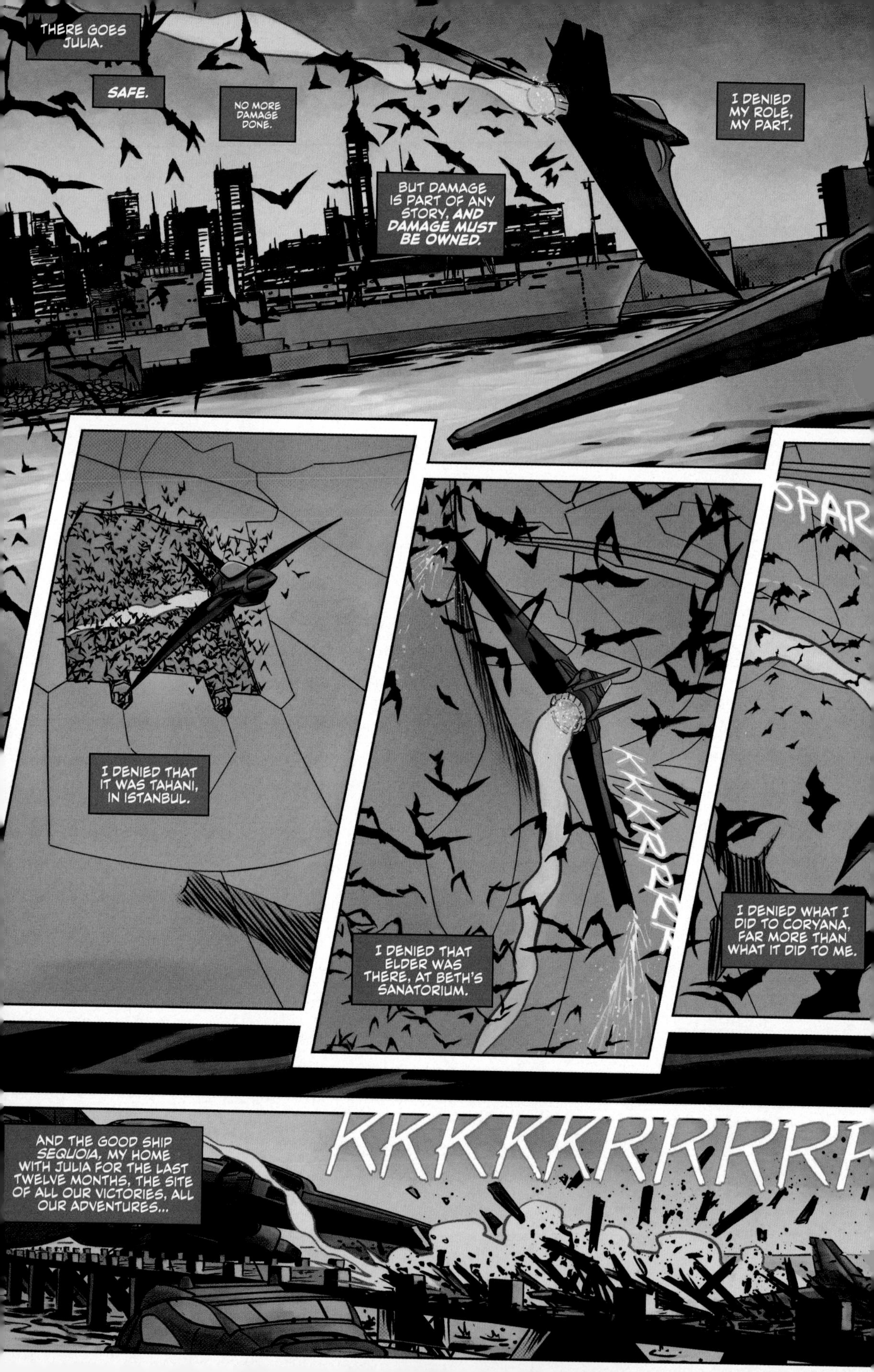
THERE GOES JULIA.
SAFE.
NO MORE DAMAGE DONE.
I DENIED MY ROLE, MY PART.
BUT DAMAGE IS PART OF ANY STORY, AND DAMAGE MUST BE OWNED.
I DENIED THAT IT WAS TAHANI, IN ISTANBUL.
I DENIED THAT ELDER WAS THERE, AT BETH'S SANATORIUM.
KKKRRRRR
SPAR
I DENIED WHAT I DID TO CORYANA, FAR MORE THAN WHAT IT DID TO ME.
AND THE GOOD SHIP SEQUOIA, MY HOME WITH JULIA FOR THE LAST TWELVE MONTHS, THE SITE OF ALL OUR VICTORIES, ALL OUR ADVENTURES...
KKKKKRRRRRR

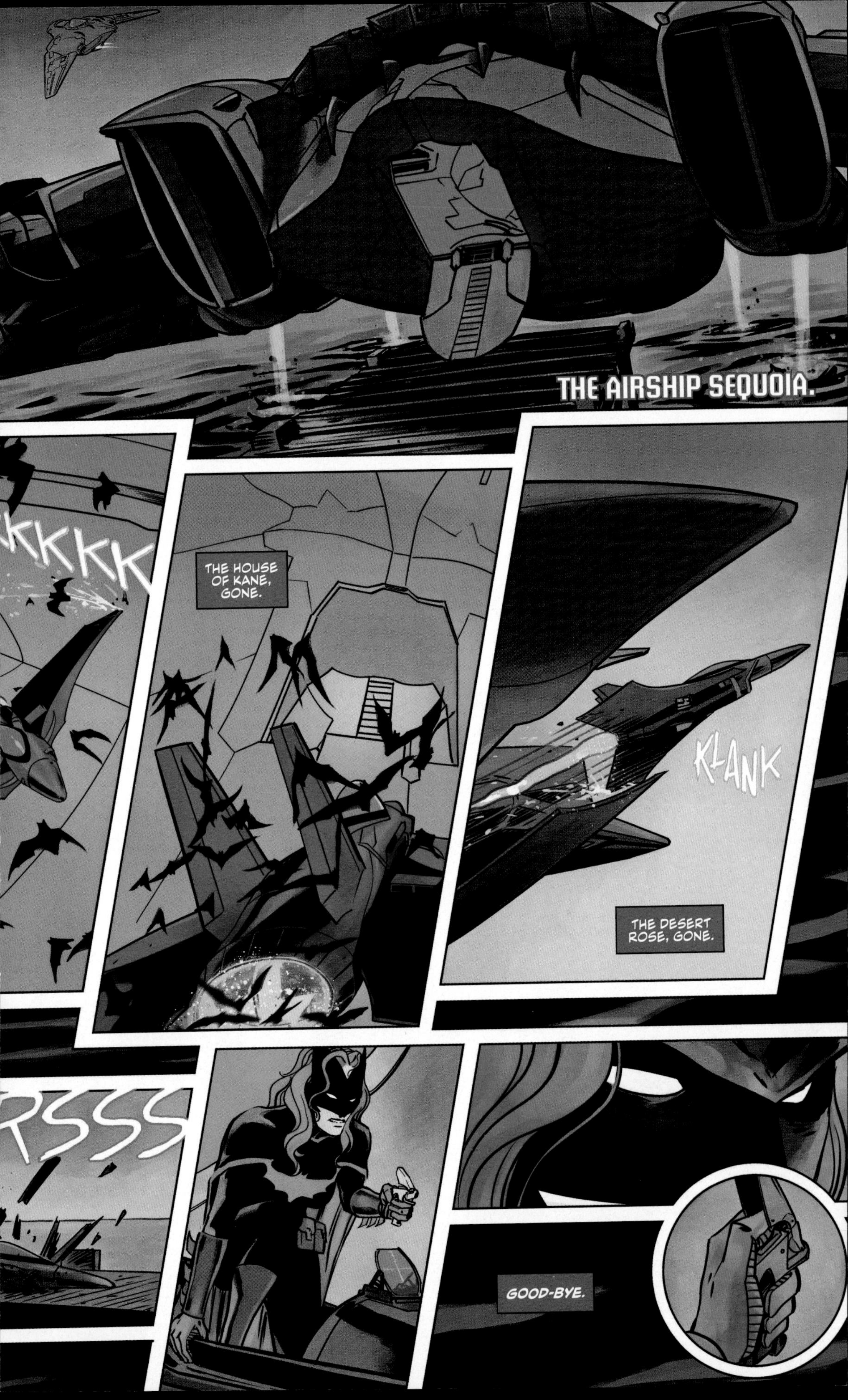
THE AIRSHIP SEQUOIA.
KKKKK
THE HOUSE OF KANE, GONE.
KLANK
THE DESERT ROSE, GONE.
RSSS
GOOD-BYE.

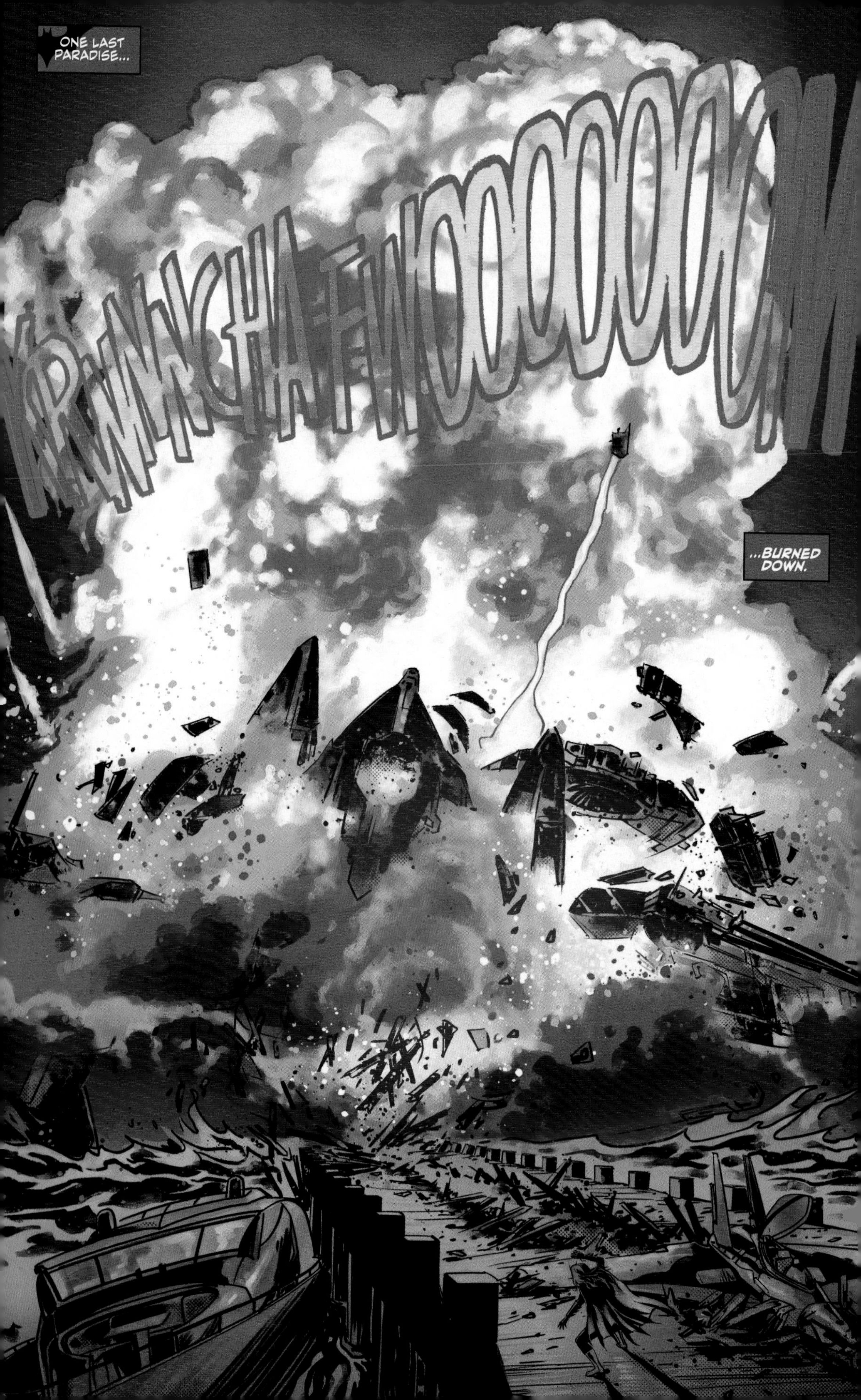
ONE LAST PARADISE...
KRANNCHA-FWOOOOOOOOM
...BURNED DOWN.

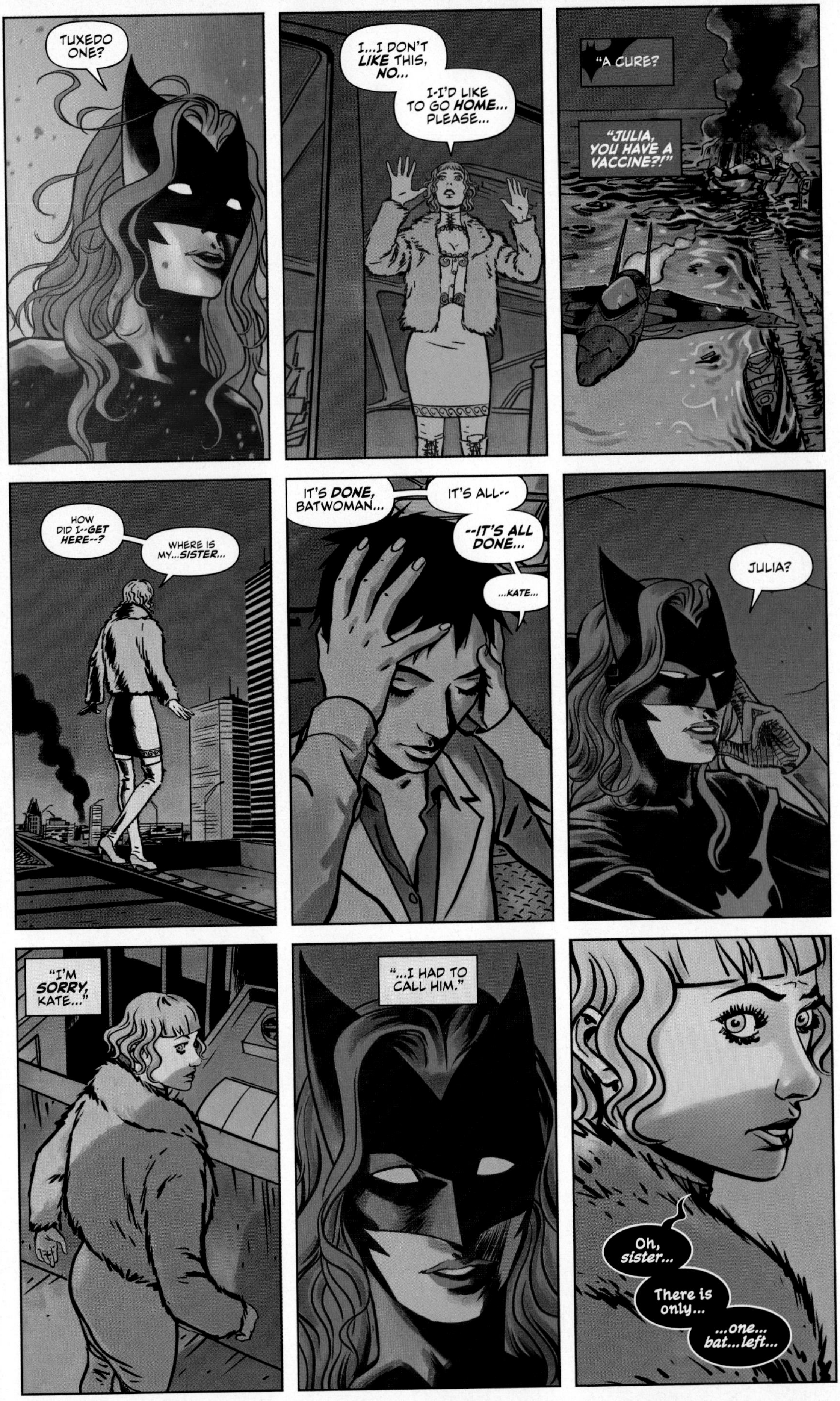
TUXEDO ONE?
I...I DON'T LIKE THIS, NO...
I-I'D LIKE TO GO HOME... PLEASE...
"A CURE?
"JULIA, YOU HAVE A VACCINE?!"
HOW DID I--GET HERE--?
WHERE IS MY...SISTER...
IT'S DONE, BATWOMAN...
IT'S ALL--
--IT'S ALL DONE...
...KATE...
JULIA?
"I'M SORRY, KATE..."
"...I HAD TO CALL HIM."
Oh, sister...
There is only...
...one... bat...left...

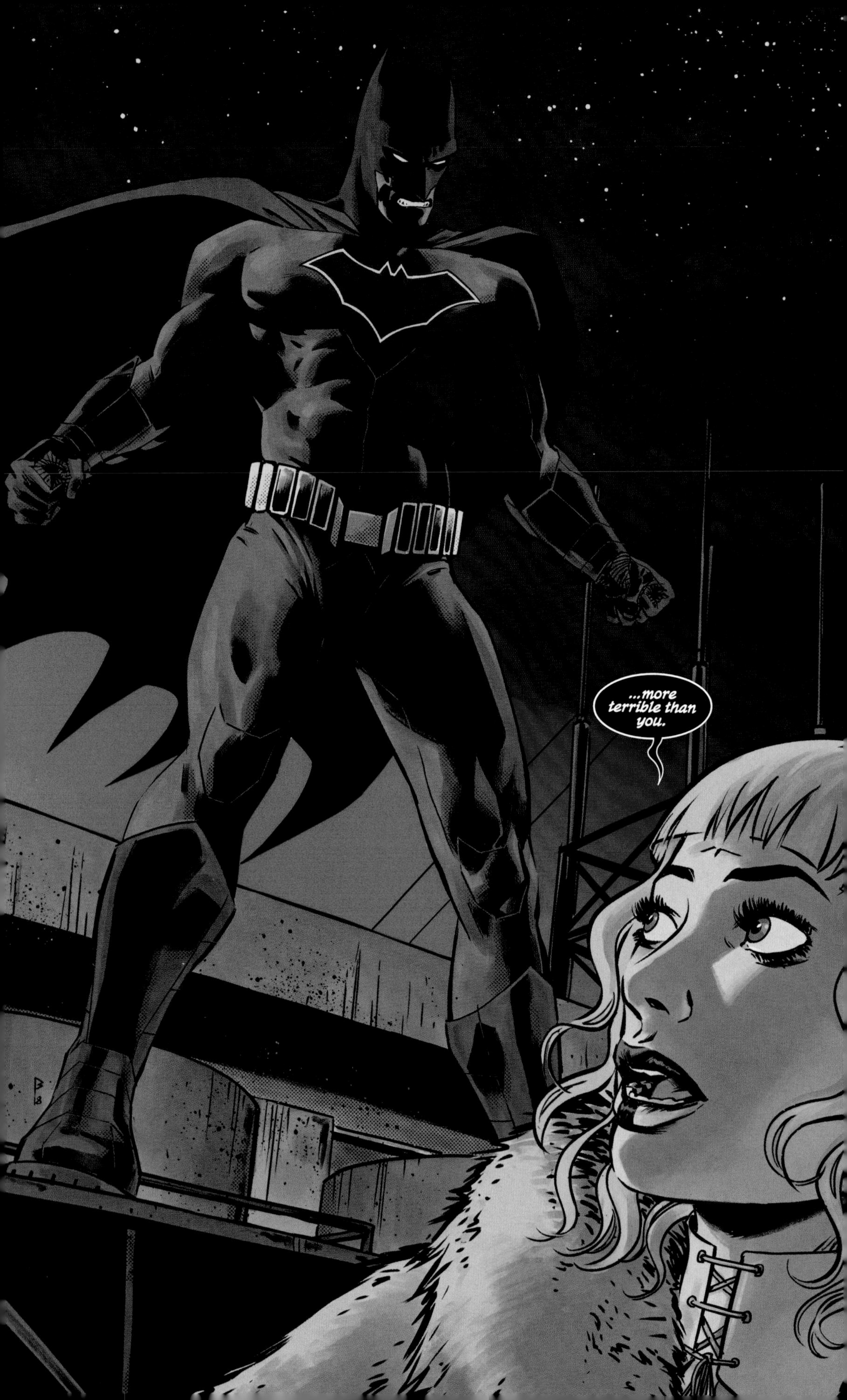
...more terrible than you.

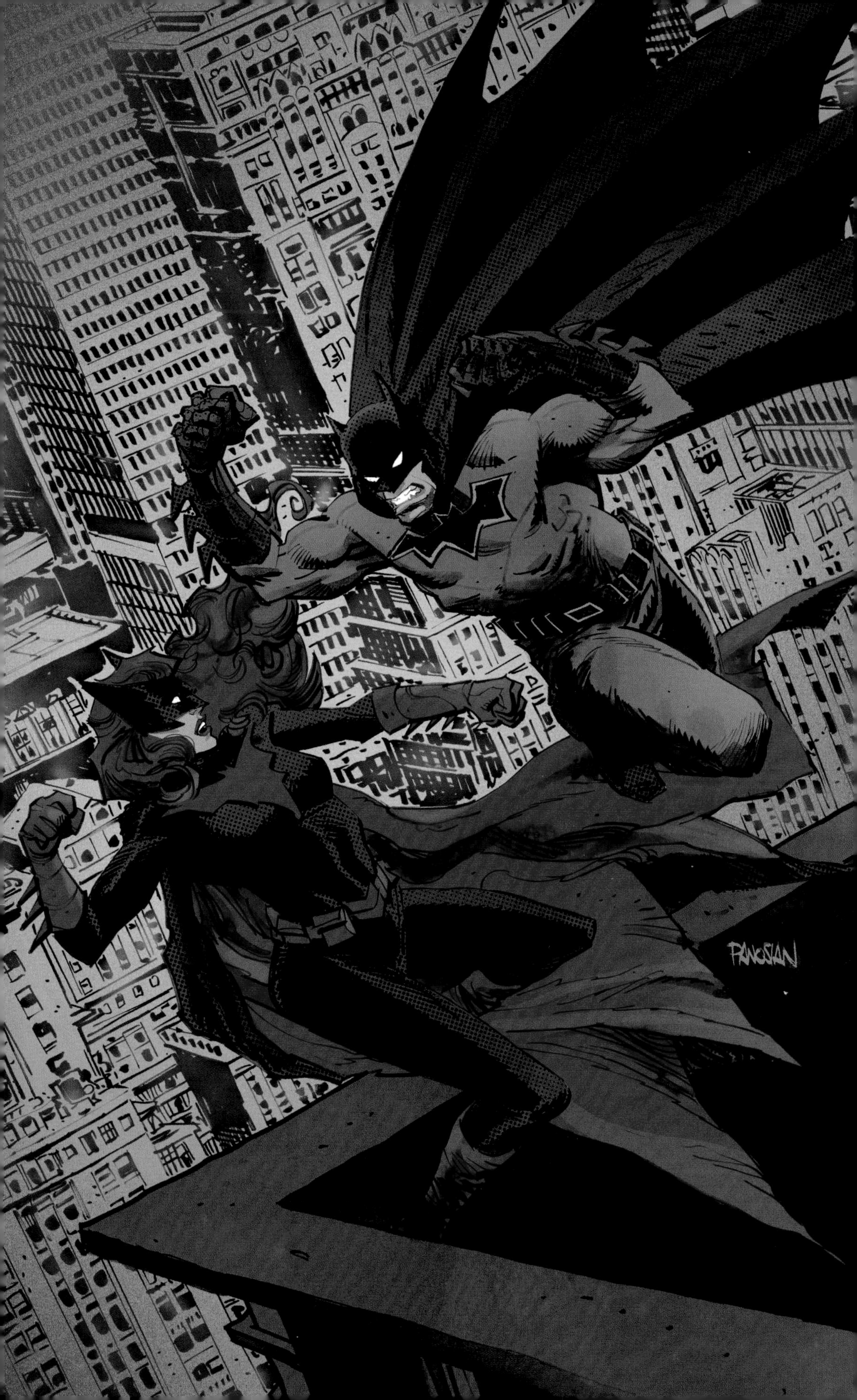
PANOSIAN

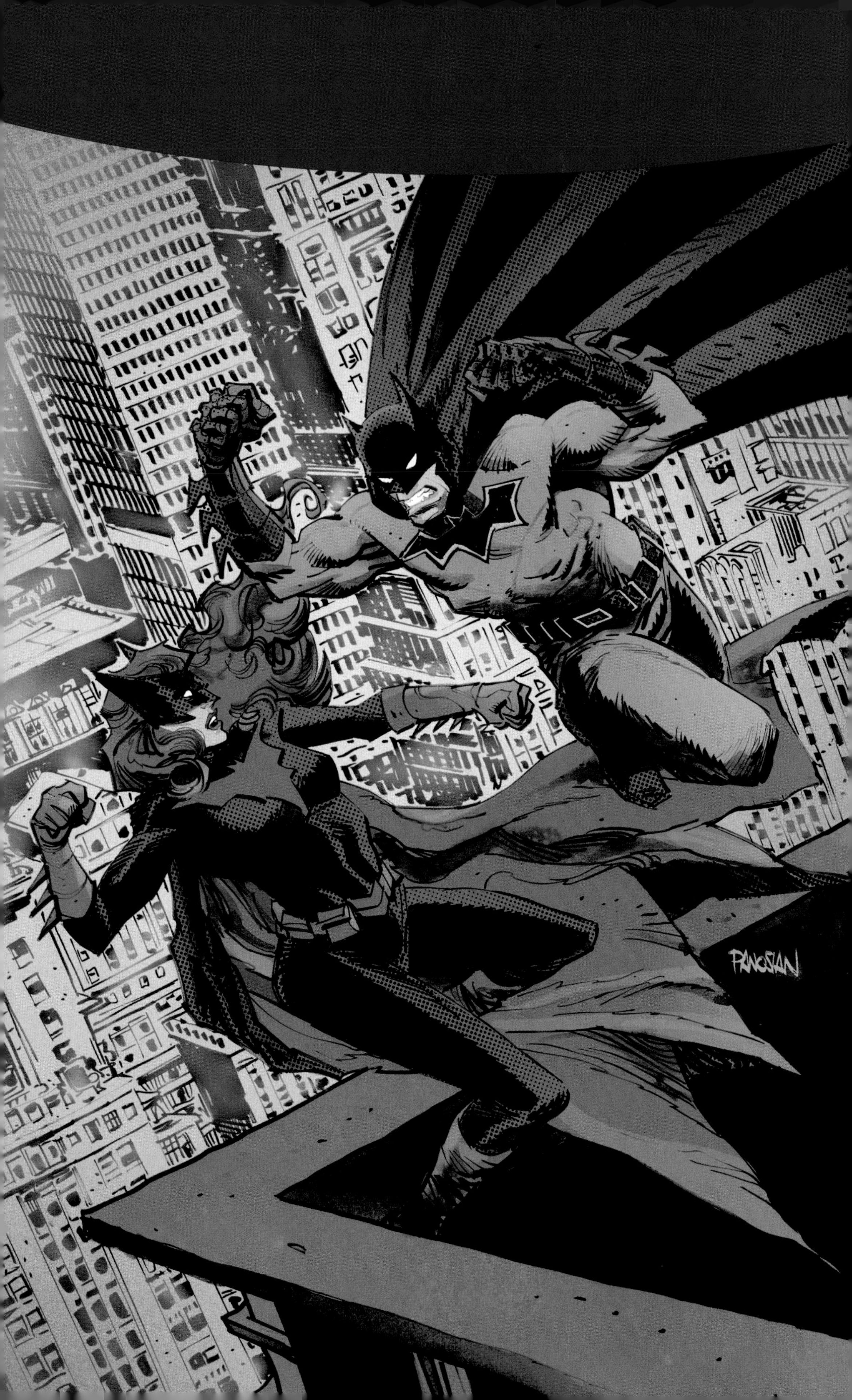
PANOSIAN

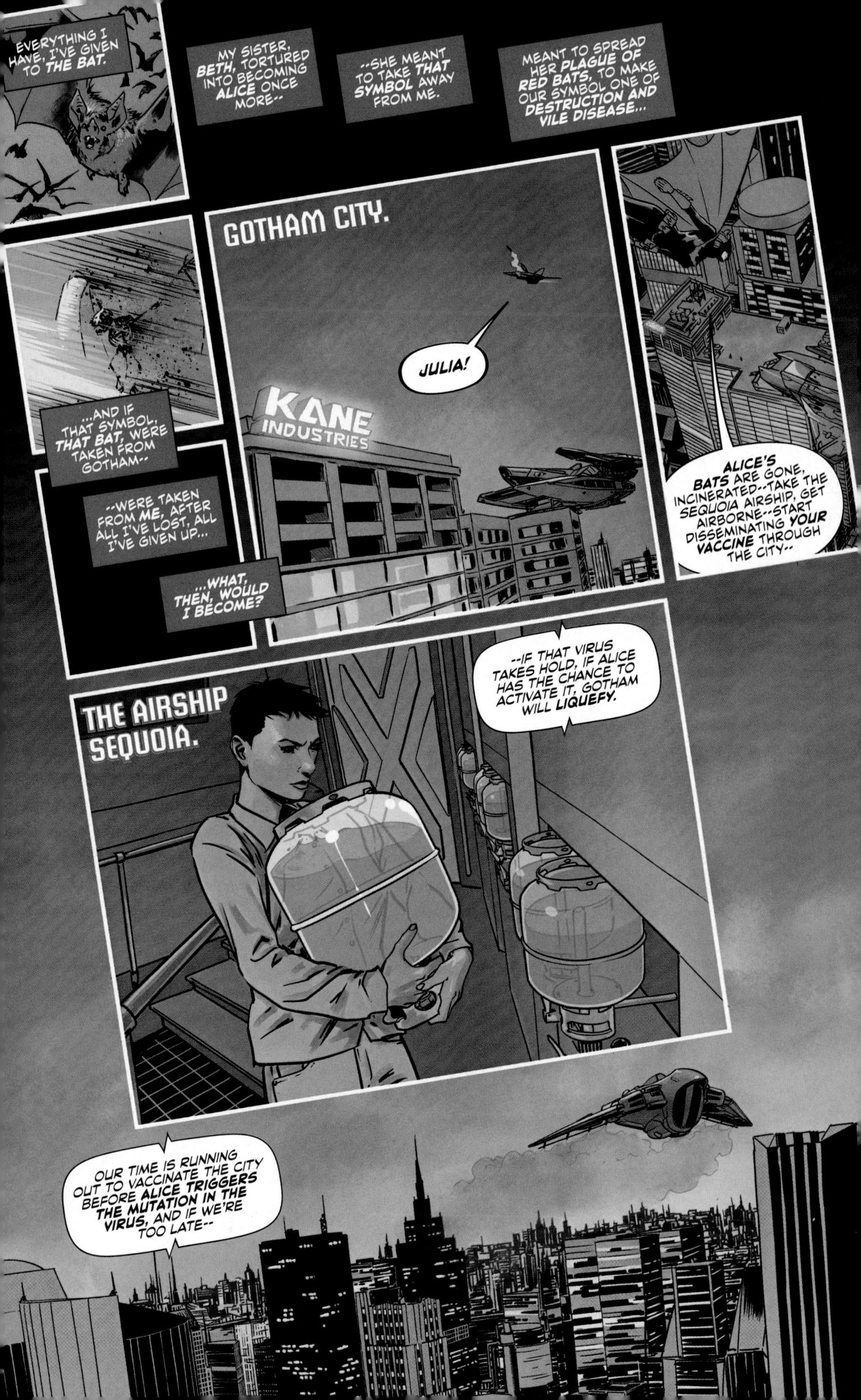
EVERYTHING I HAVE, I'VE GIVEN TO THE BAT.
MY SISTER, BETH, TORTURED INTO BECOMING ALICE ONCE MORE--
--SHE MEANT TO TAKE THAT SYMBOL AWAY FROM ME.
MEANT TO SPREAD HER PLAGUE OF RED BATS, TO MAKE OUR SYMBOL ONE OF DESTRUCTION AND VILE DISEASE...
...AND IF THAT SYMBOL, THAT BAT, WERE TAKEN FROM GOTHAM--
--WERE TAKEN FROM ME, AFTER ALL I'VE LOST, ALL I'VE GIVEN UP...
...WHAT, THEN, WOULD I BECOME?
GOTHAM CITY.
KANE INDUSTRIES
JULIA!
ALICE'S BATS ARE GONE, INCINERATED--TAKE THE SEQUOIA AIRSHIP, GET AIRBORNE--START DISSEMINATING YOUR VACCINE THROUGH THE CITY--
THE AIRSHIP SEQUOIA.
--IF THAT VIRUS TAKES HOLD, IF ALICE HAS THE CHANCE TO ACTIVATE IT, GOTHAM WILL LIQUEFY.
OUR TIME IS RUNNING OUT TO VACCINATE THE CITY BEFORE ALICE TRIGGERS THE MUTATION IN THE VIRUS, AND IF WE'RE TOO LATE--

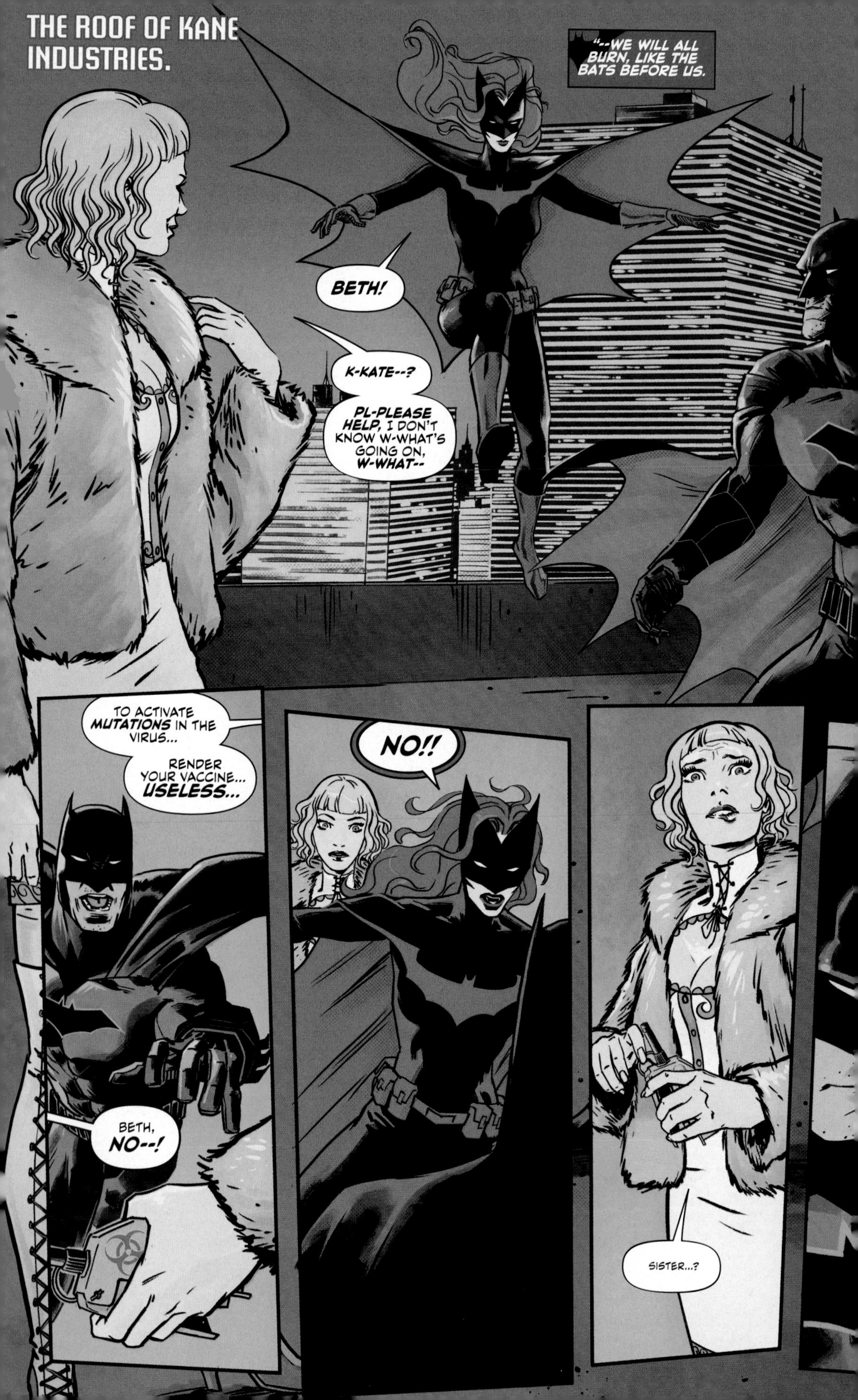
THE ROOF OF KANE INDUSTRIES.
"--WE WILL ALL BURN, LIKE THE BATS BEFORE US.
BETH!
K-KATE--?
PL-PLEASE HELP, I DON'T KNOW W-WHAT'S GOING ON, W-WHAT--
TO ACTIVATE MUTATIONS IN THE VIRUS...
RENDER YOUR VACCINE... USELESS...
BETH, NO--!
NO!!
SISTER...?

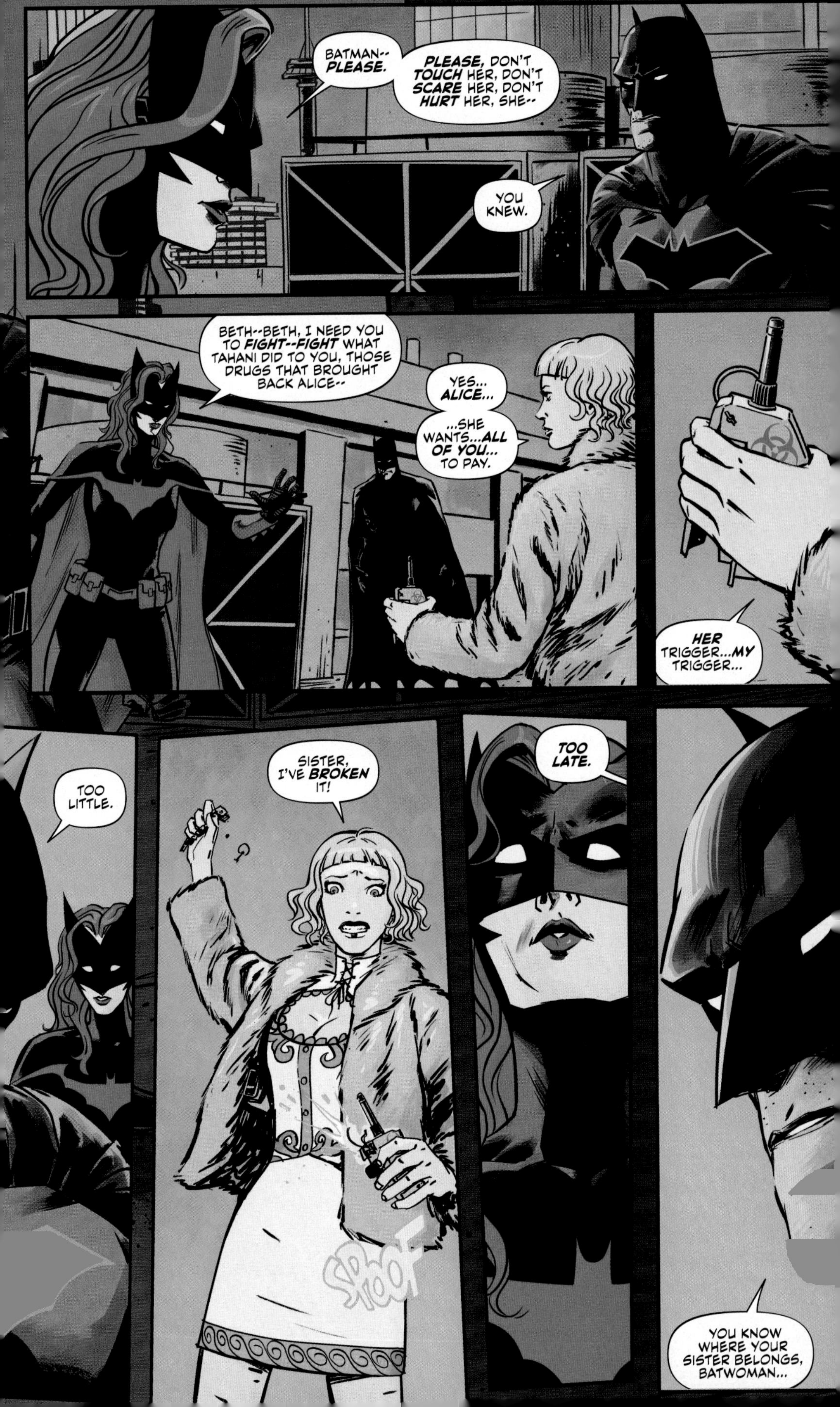
BATMAN-- PLEASE.
PLEASE, DON'T TOUCH HER, DON'T SCARE HER, DON'T HURT HER, SHE--
YOU KNEW.
BETH--BETH, I NEED YOU TO FIGHT--FIGHT WHAT TAHANI DID TO YOU, THOSE DRUGS THAT BROUGHT BACK ALICE--
YES... ALICE...
...SHE WANTS...ALL OF YOU... TO PAY.
HER TRIGGER...MY TRIGGER...
TOO LITTLE.
SISTER, I'VE BROKEN IT!
SPROOF
TOO LATE.
YOU KNOW WHERE YOUR SISTER BELONGS, BATWOMAN...

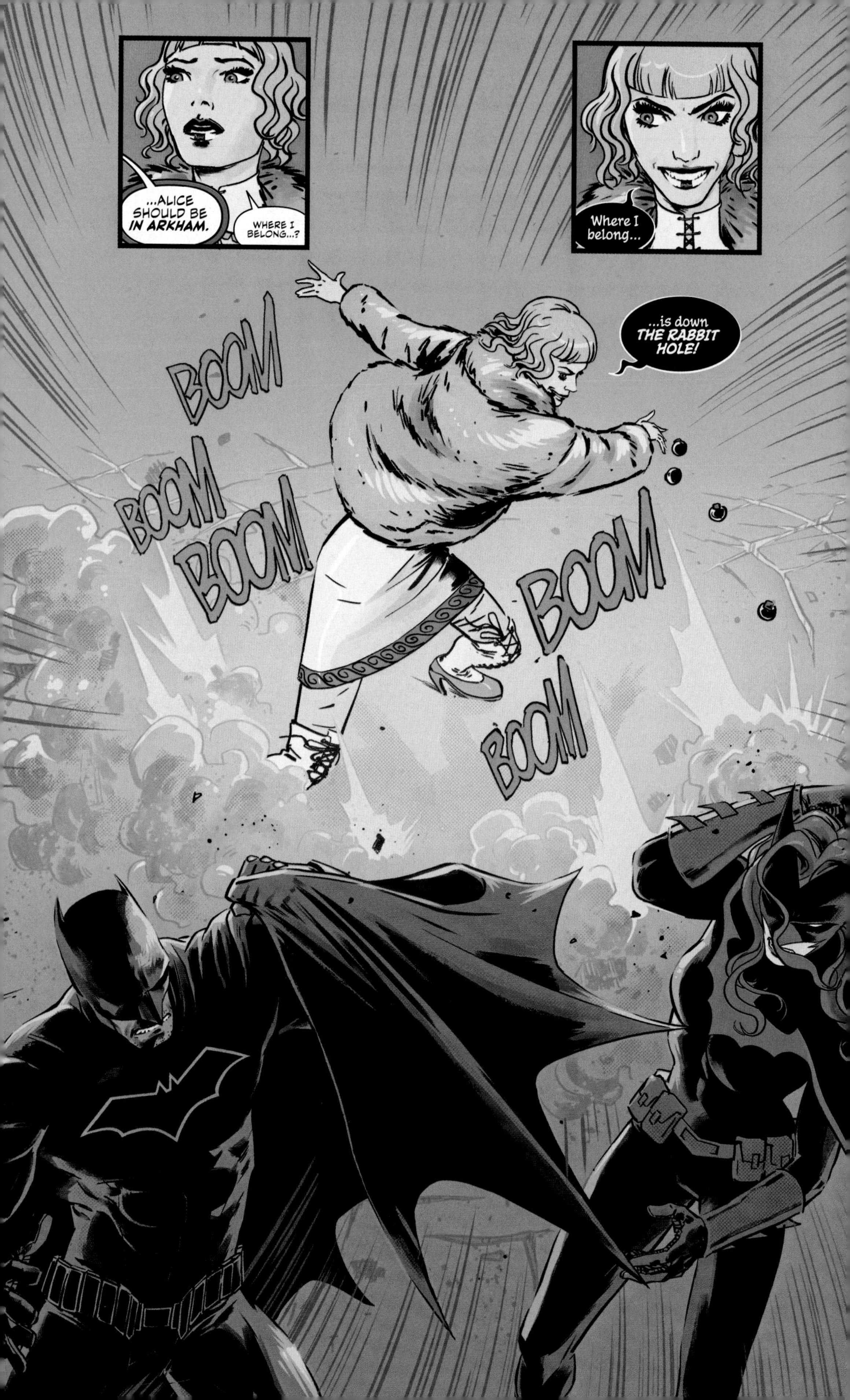
...ALICE SHOULD BE IN ARKHAM.
WHERE I BELONG...?
Where I belong...
...is down THE RABBIT HOLE!
BOOM
BOOM
BOOM
BOOM
BOOM

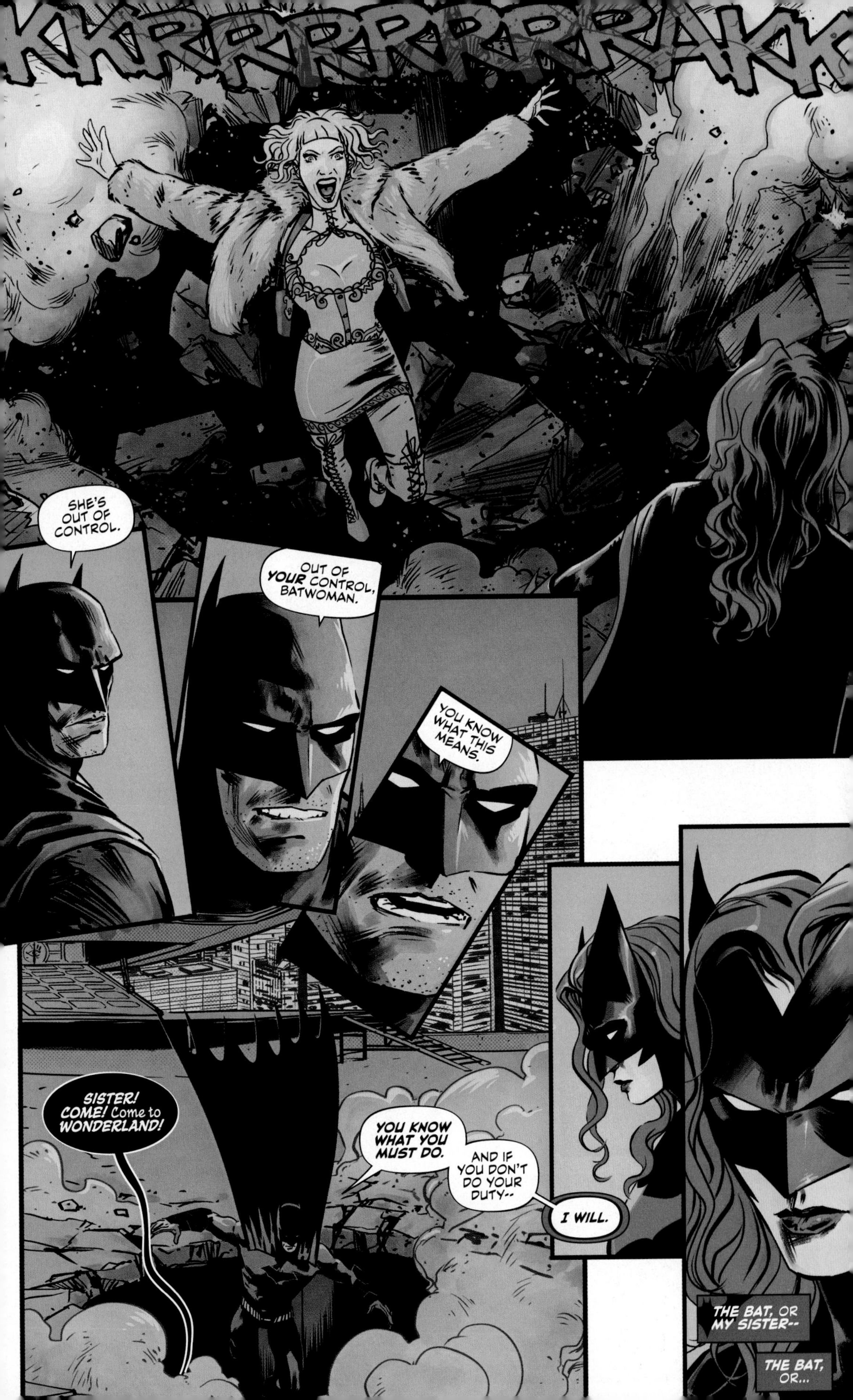
KKRRRRRRRRAKK
SHE'S OUT OF CONTROL.
OUT OF YOUR CONTROL, BATWOMAN.
YOU KNOW WHAT THIS MEANS.
SISTER! COME! Come to WONDERLAND!
YOU KNOW WHAT YOU MUST DO.
AND IF YOU DON'T DO YOUR DUTY--
I WILL.
THE BAT, OR MY SISTER--
THE BAT, OR...

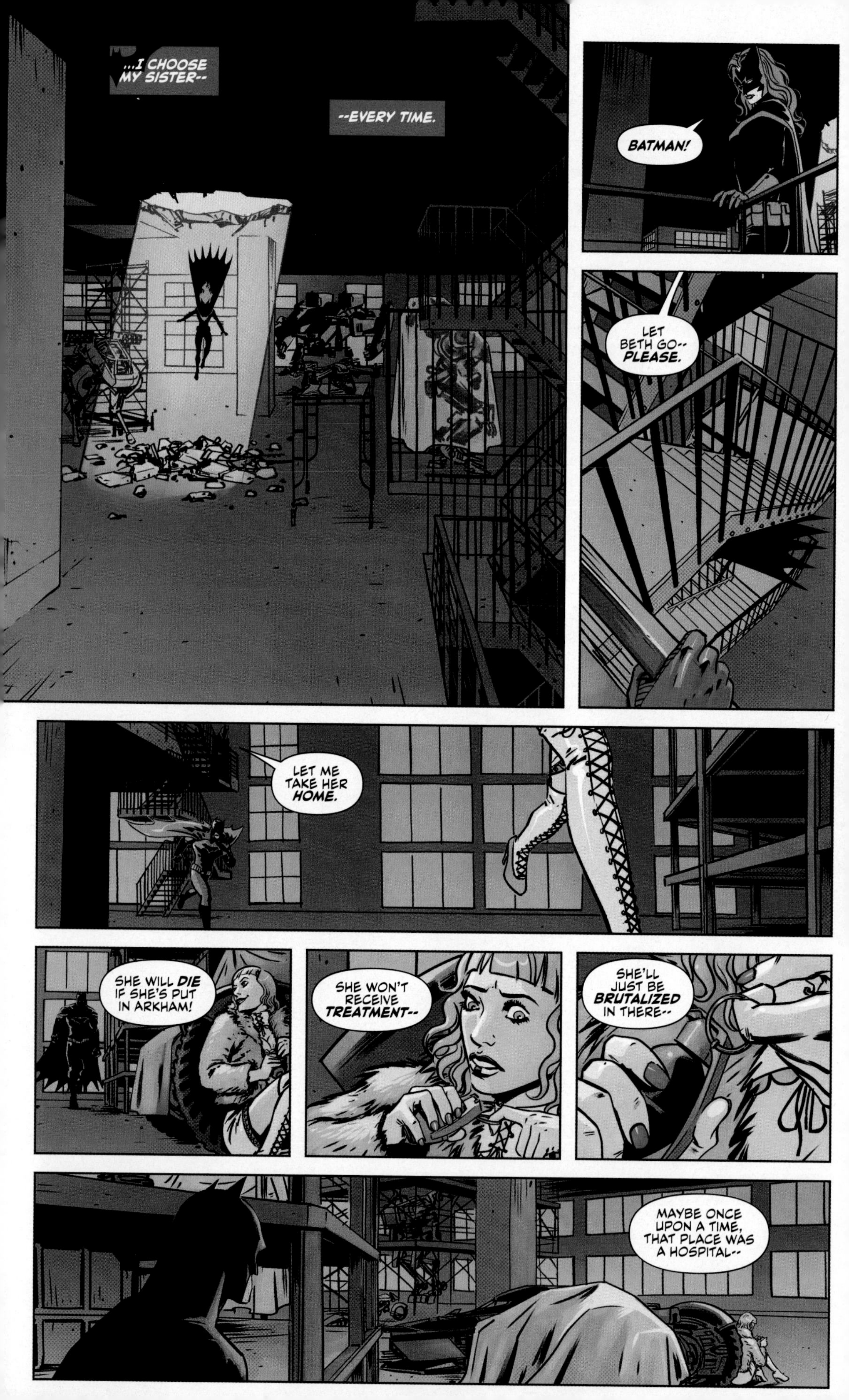
...I CHOOSE MY SISTER--
--EVERY TIME.
BATMAN!
LET BETH GO-- PLEASE.
LET ME TAKE HER HOME.
SHE WILL DIE IF SHE'S PUT IN ARKHAM!
SHE WON'T RECEIVE TREATMENT--
SHE'LL JUST BE BRUTALIZED IN THERE--
MAYBE ONCE UPON A TIME, THAT PLACE WAS A HOSPITAL--

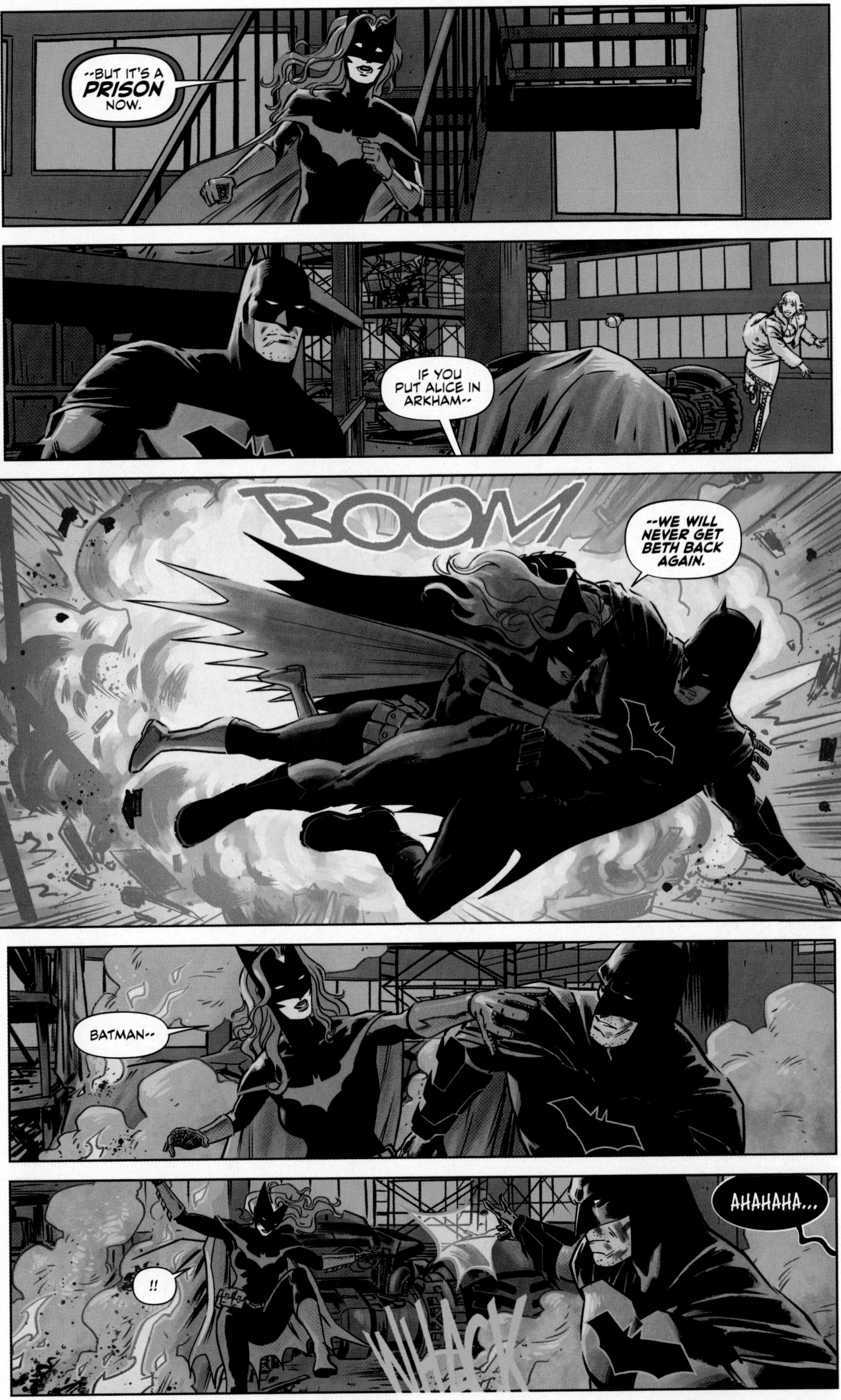
--BUT IT'S A PRISON NOW.
IF YOU PUT ALICE IN ARKHAM--
BOOM
--WE WILL NEVER GET BETH BACK AGAIN.
BATMAN--
AHAHAHA...
!!
WHACK

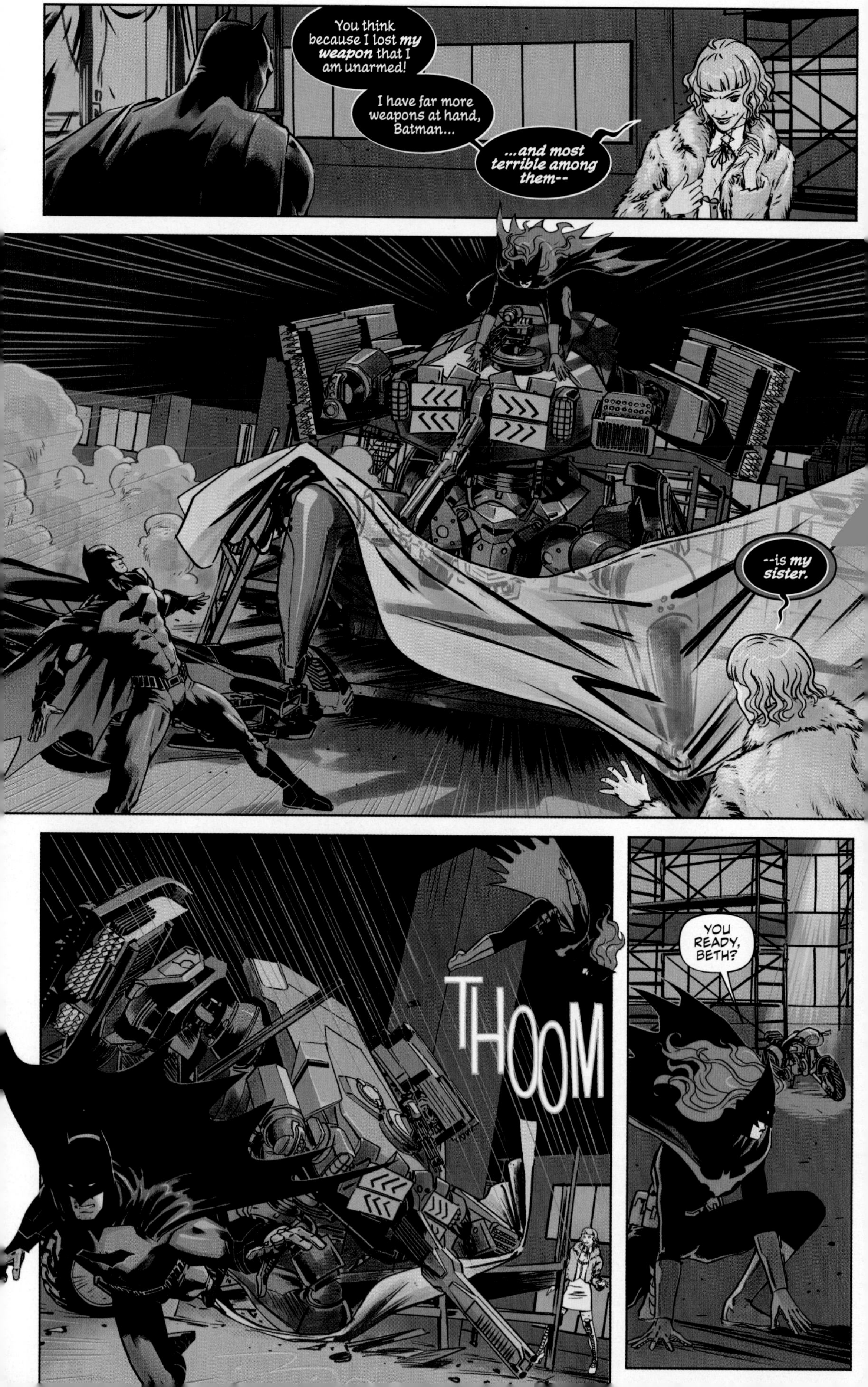
You think because I lost *my weapon* that I am unarmed!
I have far more weapons at hand, Batman...
...and most terrible among them--
--is my sister.
THOOM
YOU READY, BETH?

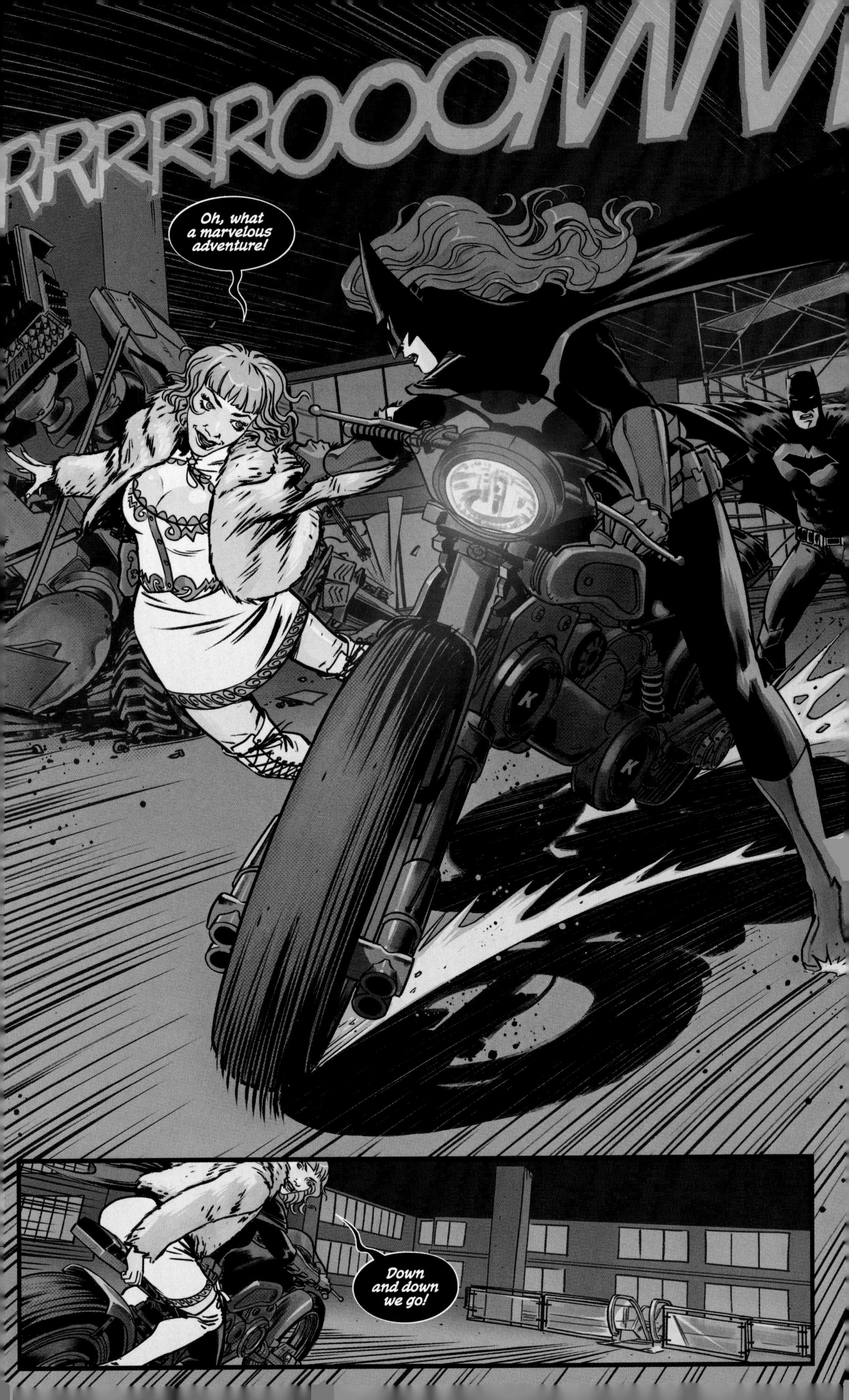
RRRRROOOOMMM
Oh, what a marvelous adventure!
Down and down we go!

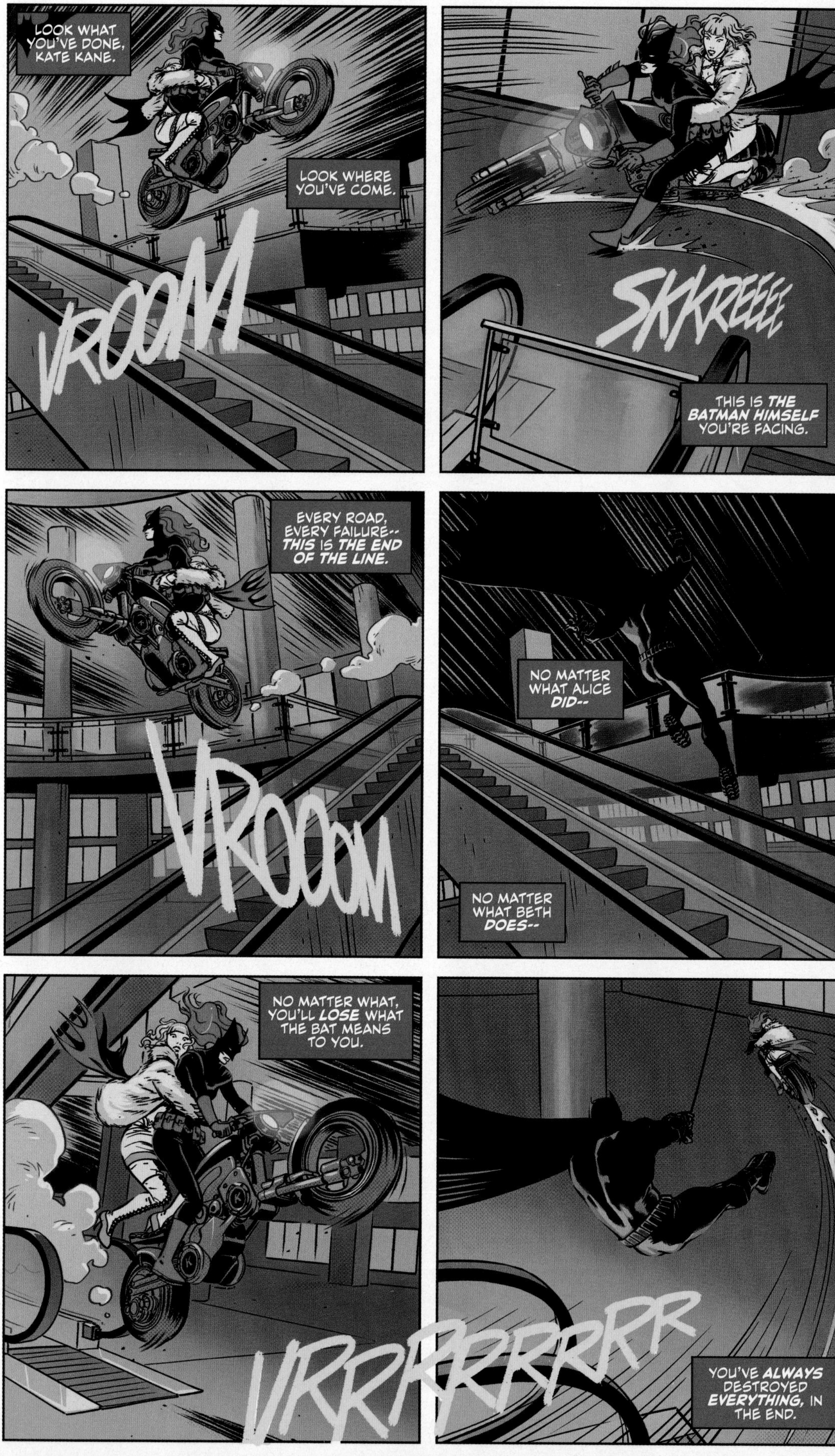
LOOK WHAT YOU'VE DONE, KATE KANE.
LOOK WHERE YOU'VE COME.
VROOM
SKKREEEE
THIS IS THE BATMAN HIMSELF YOU'RE FACING.
EVERY ROAD, EVERY FAILURE-- THIS IS THE END OF THE LINE.
VROOOM
NO MATTER WHAT ALICE DID--
NO MATTER WHAT BETH DOES--
NO MATTER WHAT, YOU'LL LOSE WHAT THE BAT MEANS TO YOU.
VRRRRRRRR
YOU'VE ALWAYS DESTROYED EVERYTHING, IN THE END.

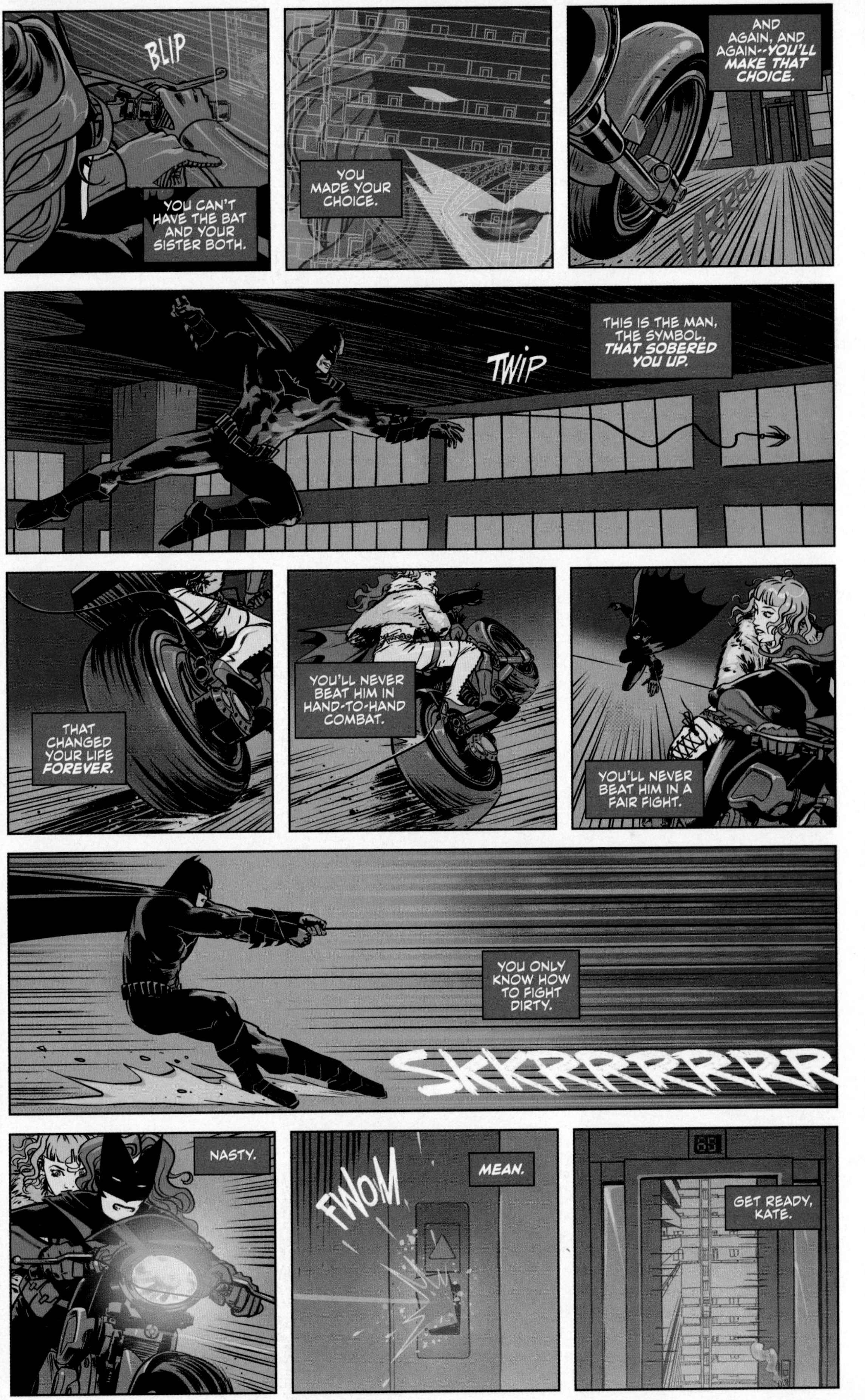
BLIP
YOU CAN'T HAVE THE BAT AND YOUR SISTER BOTH.
YOU MADE YOUR CHOICE.
AND AGAIN, AND AGAIN--*YOU'LL MAKE THAT CHOICE.*
TWIP
THIS IS THE MAN, THE SYMBOL, *THAT SOBERED YOU UP.*
THAT CHANGED YOUR LIFE *FOREVER.*
YOU'LL NEVER BEAT HIM IN HAND-TO-HAND COMBAT.
YOU'LL NEVER BEAT HIM IN A FAIR FIGHT.
YOU ONLY KNOW HOW TO FIGHT DIRTY.
SKKRRRRRRR
NASTY.
FWOM
MEAN.
GET READY, KATE.

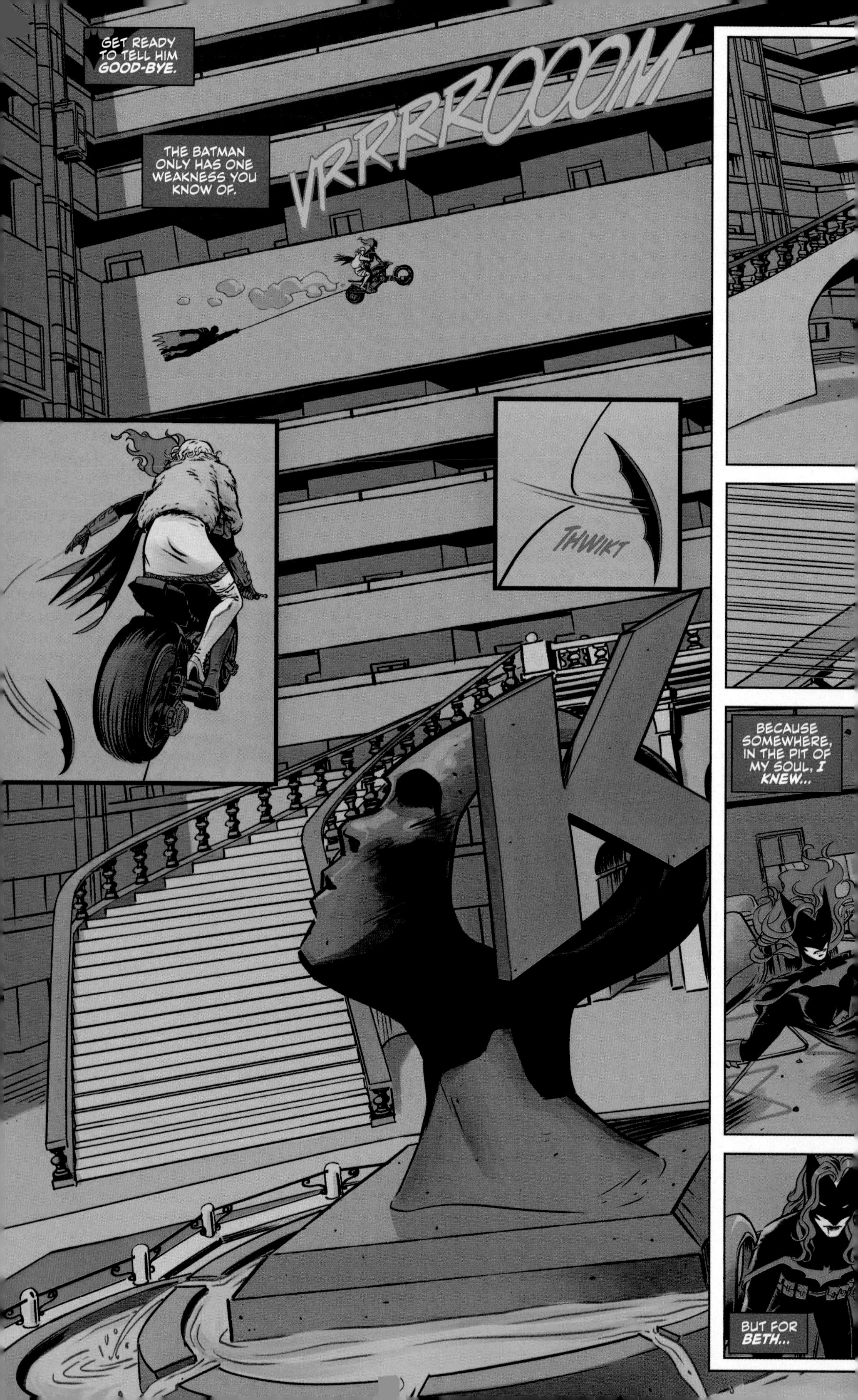

GET READY TO TELL HIM *GOOD-BYE.*
VRRRROOOOM
THE BATMAN ONLY HAS ONE WEAKNESS YOU KNOW OF.
THWIKT
BECAUSE SOMEWHERE, IN THE PIT OF MY SOUL, *I KNEW...*
BUT FOR *BETH...*

ONE WEAKNESS NO ONE ELSE HAS EVER GUESSED.

I RECORDED IT MYSELF.

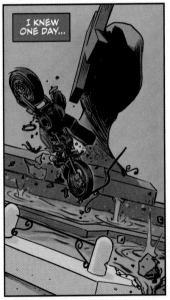

I KNEW ONE DAY...

...I'D DESTROY *THIS*, TOO.

I'LL NEVER FORGIVE MYSELF FOR WHAT I'M ABOUT TO DO.

DO IT.

JUST DO IT.

LET IT ALL END.

DOWNLOADING

98%

WE'LL ALL GO DOWN TOGETHER.

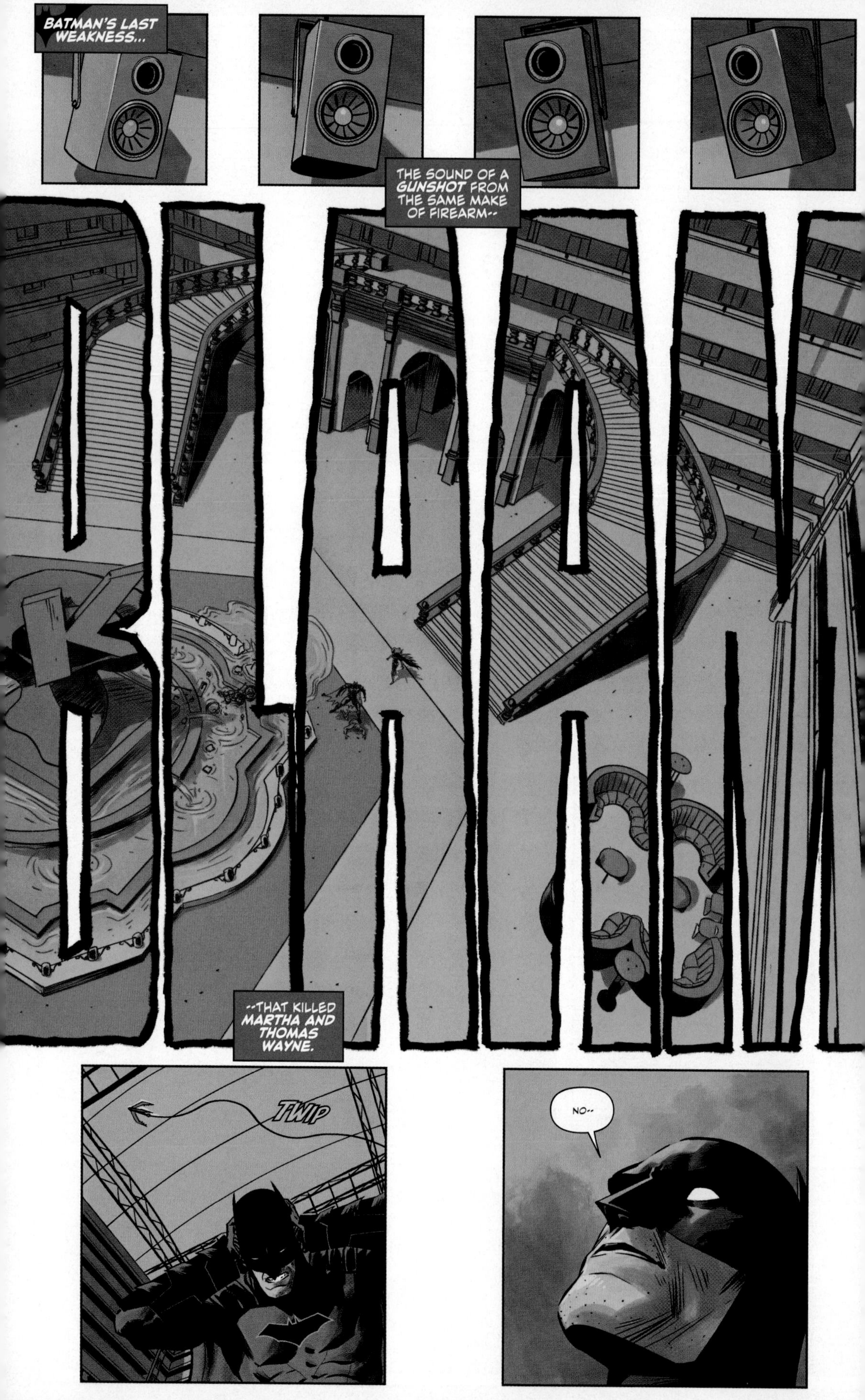
BATMAN'S LAST WEAKNESS...
THE SOUND OF A GUNSHOT FROM THE SAME MAKE OF FIREARM--
BLAM
--THAT KILLED MARTHA AND THOMAS WAYNE.
TWIP
NO--

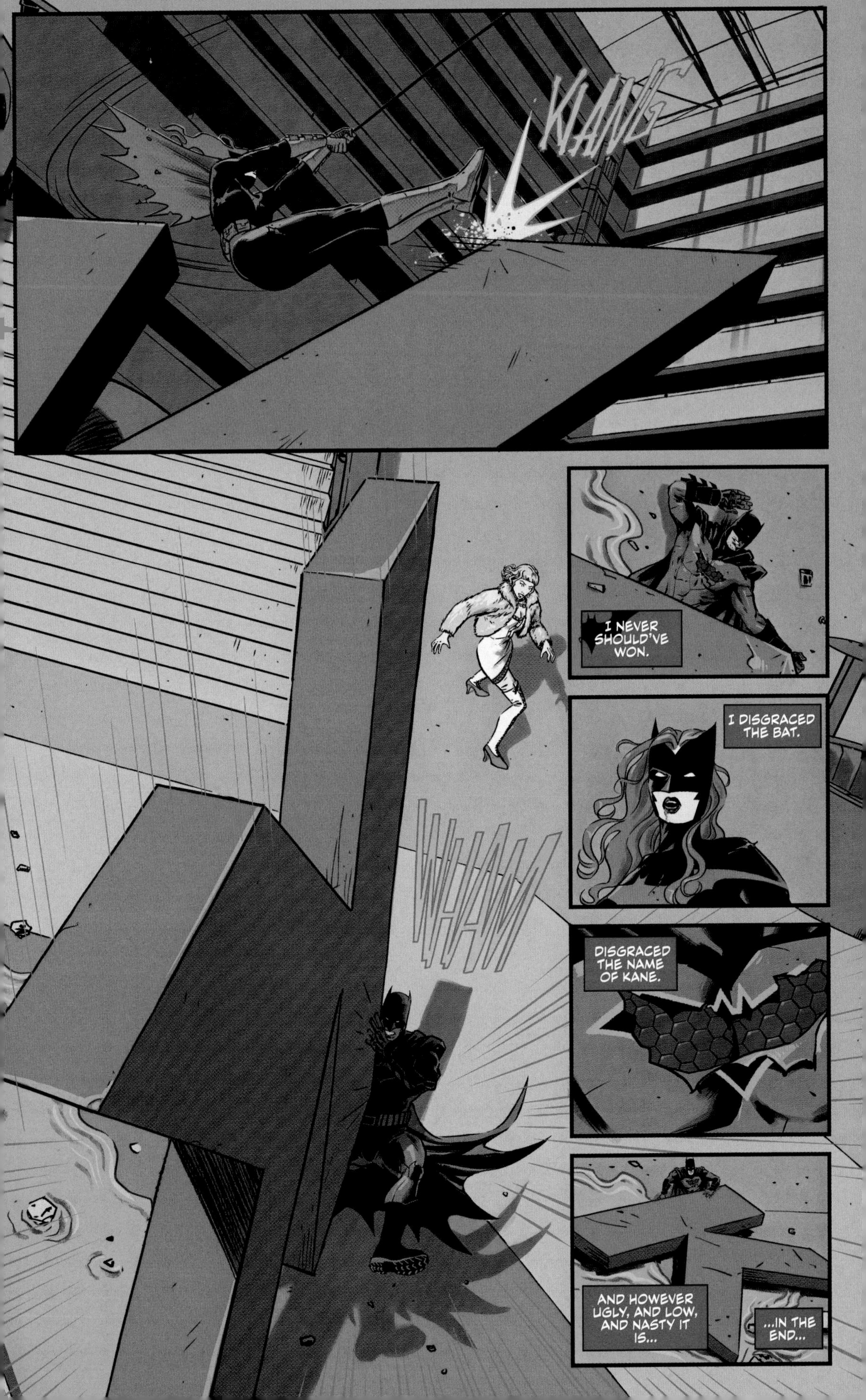
KLANG
WHAM
I NEVER SHOULD'VE WON.
I DISGRACED THE BAT.
DISGRACED THE NAME OF KANE.
AND HOWEVER UGLY, AND LOW, AND NASTY IT IS...
...IN THE END...

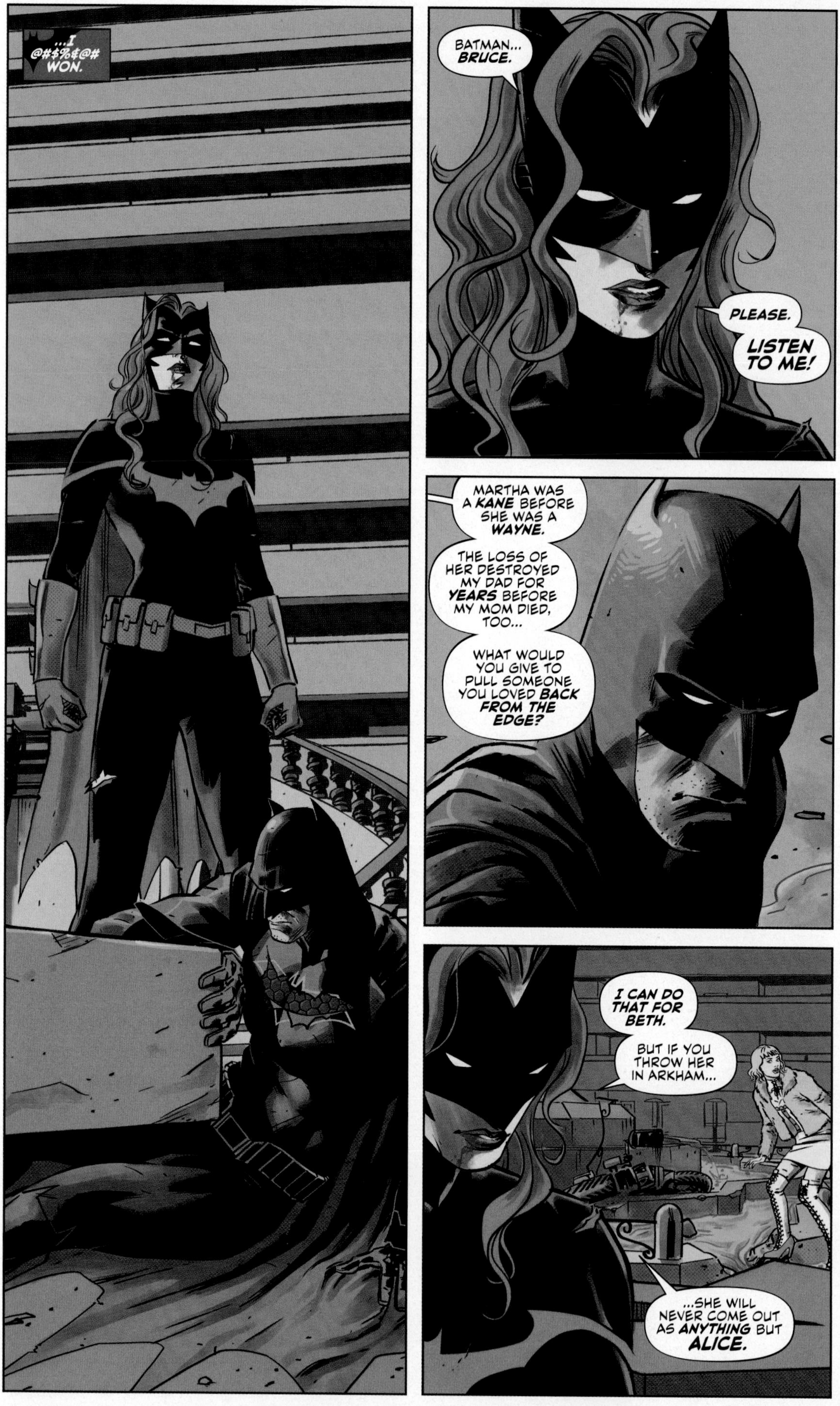
...I @#$%&@# WON.
BATMAN... BRUCE.
PLEASE. LISTEN TO ME!
MARTHA WAS A KANE BEFORE SHE WAS A WAYNE.
THE LOSS OF HER DESTROYED MY DAD FOR YEARS BEFORE MY MOM DIED, TOO...
WHAT WOULD YOU GIVE TO PULL SOMEONE YOU LOVED BACK FROM THE EDGE?
I CAN DO THAT FOR BETH.
BUT IF YOU THROW HER IN ARKHAM...
...SHE WILL NEVER COME OUT AS ANYTHING BUT ALICE.

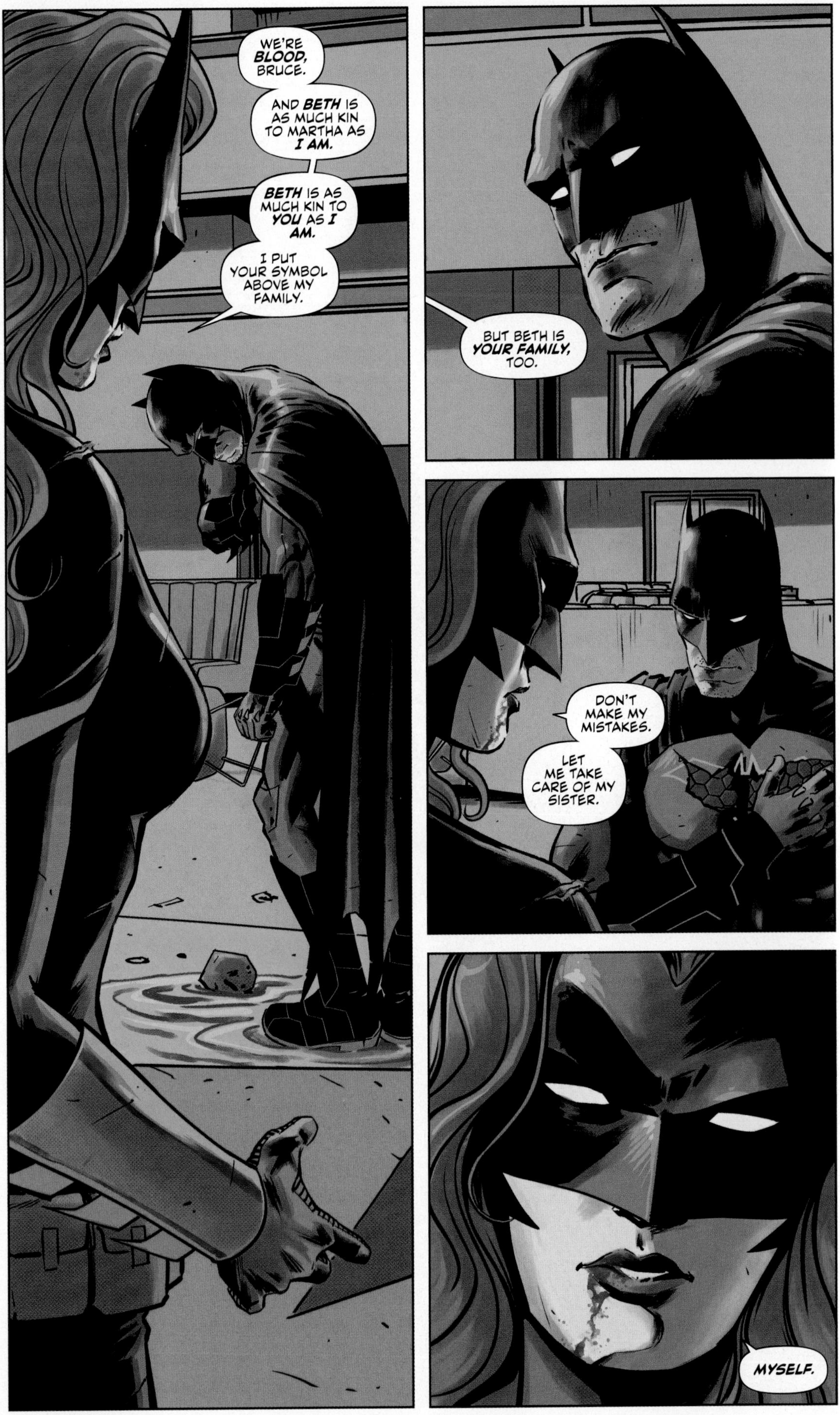
WE'RE *BLOOD,* BRUCE.
AND *BETH* IS AS MUCH KIN TO MARTHA AS *I AM.*
BETH IS AS MUCH KIN TO *YOU* AS *I AM.*
I PUT YOUR SYMBOL ABOVE MY FAMILY.
BUT BETH IS *YOUR FAMILY,* TOO.
DON'T MAKE MY MISTAKES.
LET ME TAKE CARE OF MY SISTER.
MYSELF.

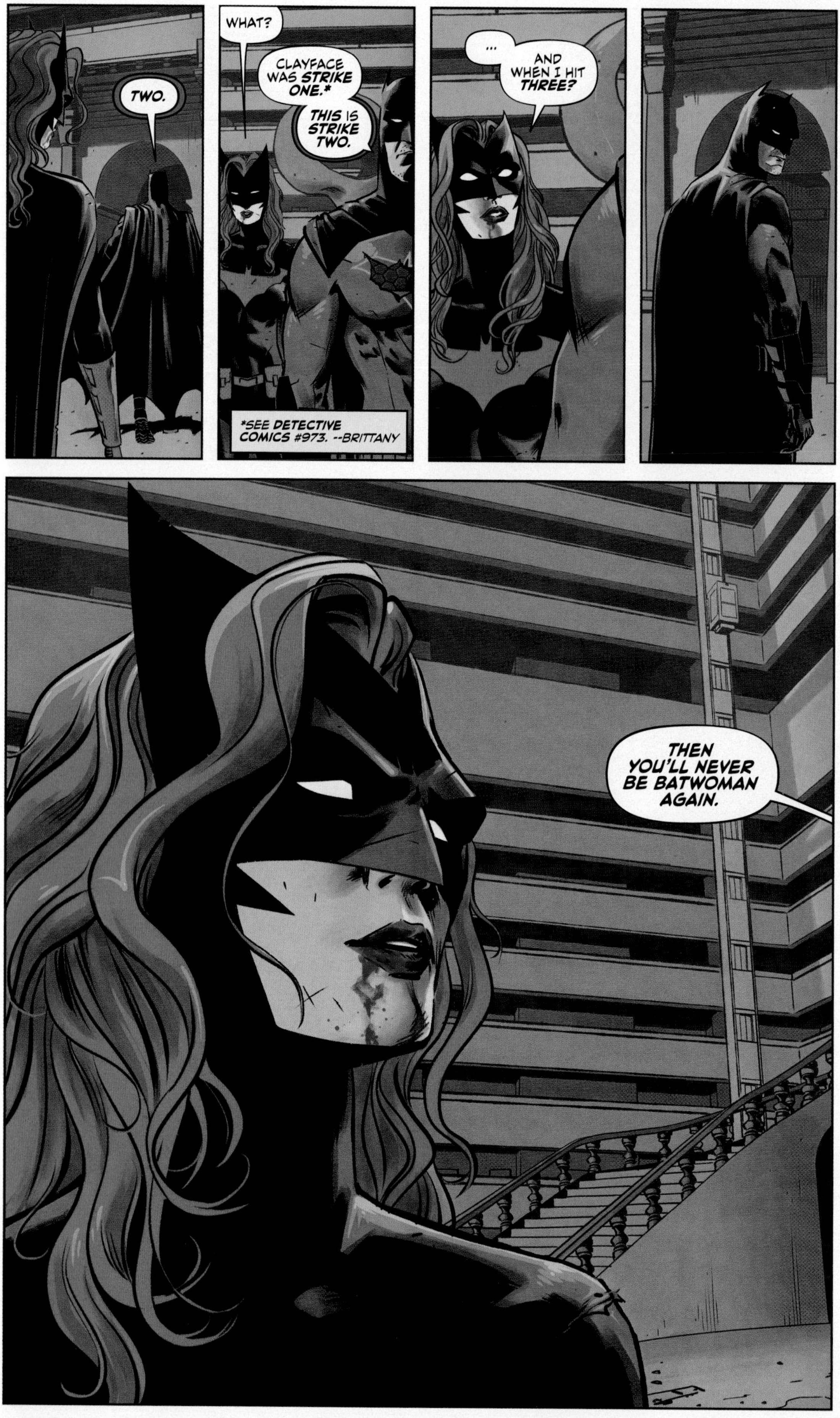
TWO.
WHAT?
CLAYFACE WAS STRIKE ONE.*
THIS IS STRIKE TWO.
*SEE DETECTIVE COMICS #973. --BRITTANY
...
AND WHEN I HIT THREE?
THEN YOU'LL NEVER BE BATWOMAN AGAIN.

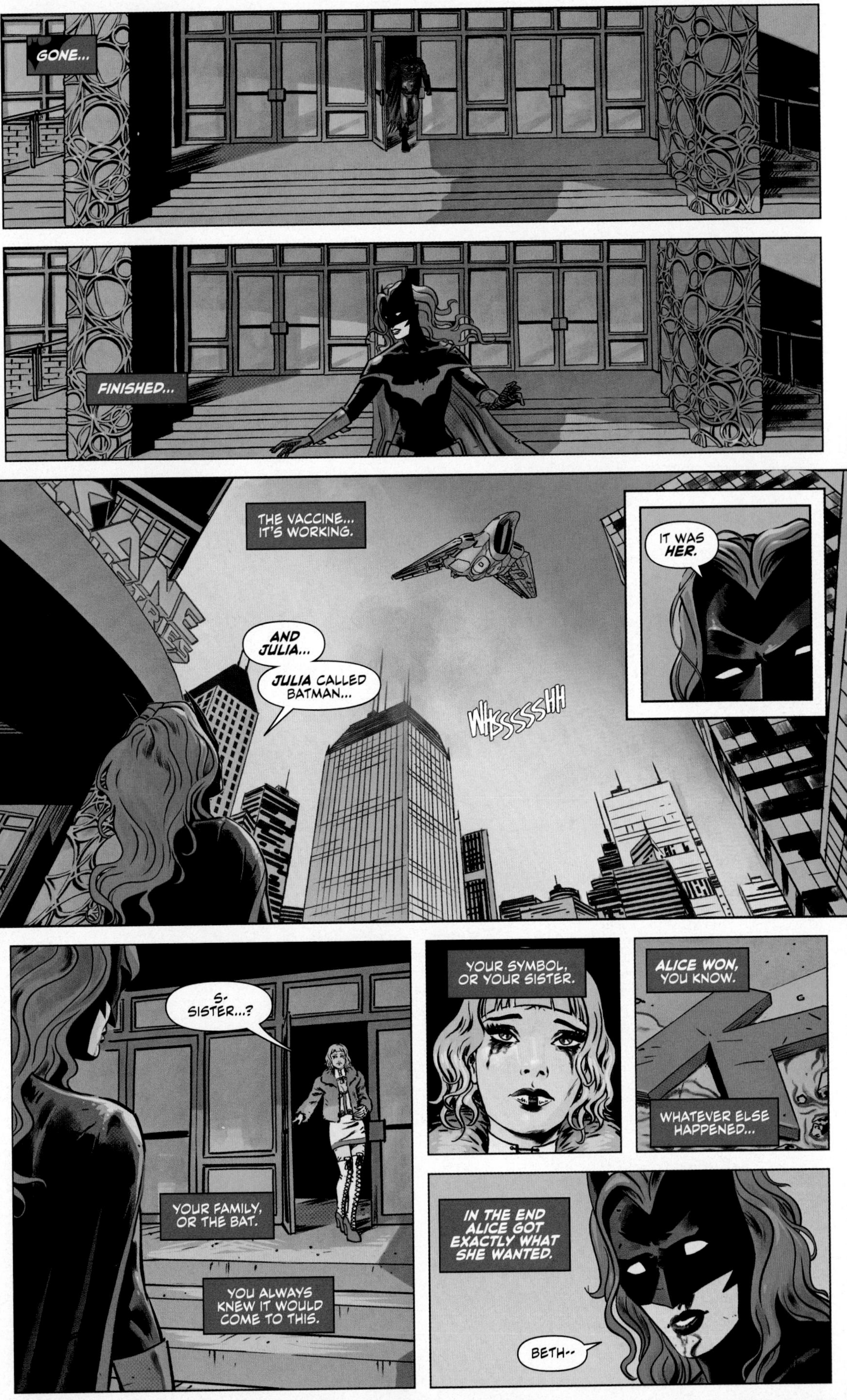
GONE...
FINISHED...
THE VACCINE... IT'S WORKING.
IT WAS HER.
AND JULIA...
JULIA CALLED BATMAN...
WHSSSSSHH
S- SISTER...?
YOUR FAMILY, OR THE BAT.
YOU ALWAYS KNEW IT WOULD COME TO THIS.
YOUR SYMBOL, OR YOUR SISTER.
ALICE WON, YOU KNOW.
WHATEVER ELSE HAPPENED...
IN THE END ALICE GOT EXACTLY WHAT SHE WANTED.
BETH--

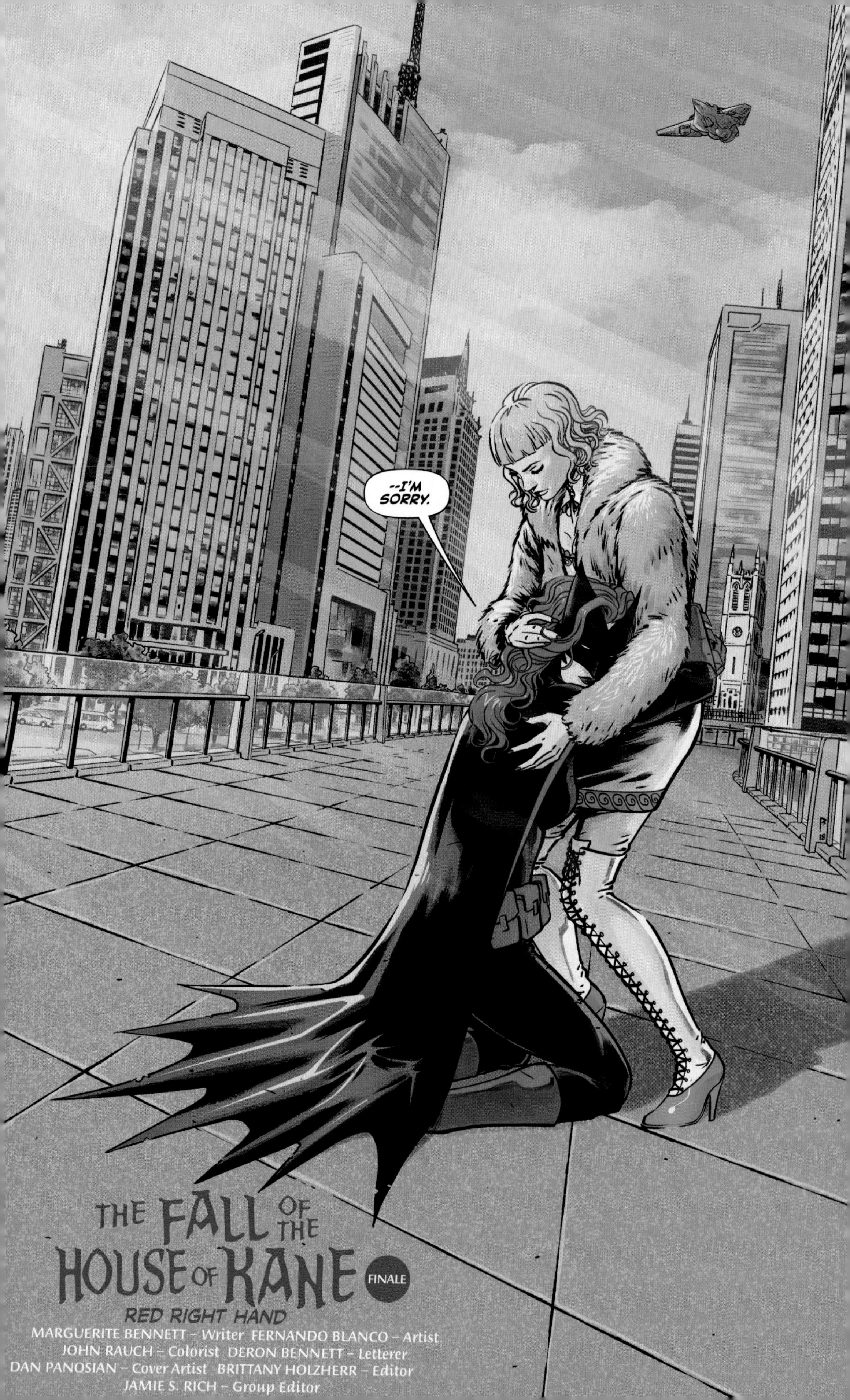
--I'M SORRY.
THE FALL OF THE HOUSE OF KANE
FINALE
RED RIGHT HAND
MARGUERITE BENNETT – Writer FERNANDO BLANCO – Artist
JOHN RAUCH – Colorist DERON BENNETT – Letterer
DAN PANOSIAN – Cover Artist BRITTANY HOLZHERR – Editor
JAMIE S. RICH – Group Editor

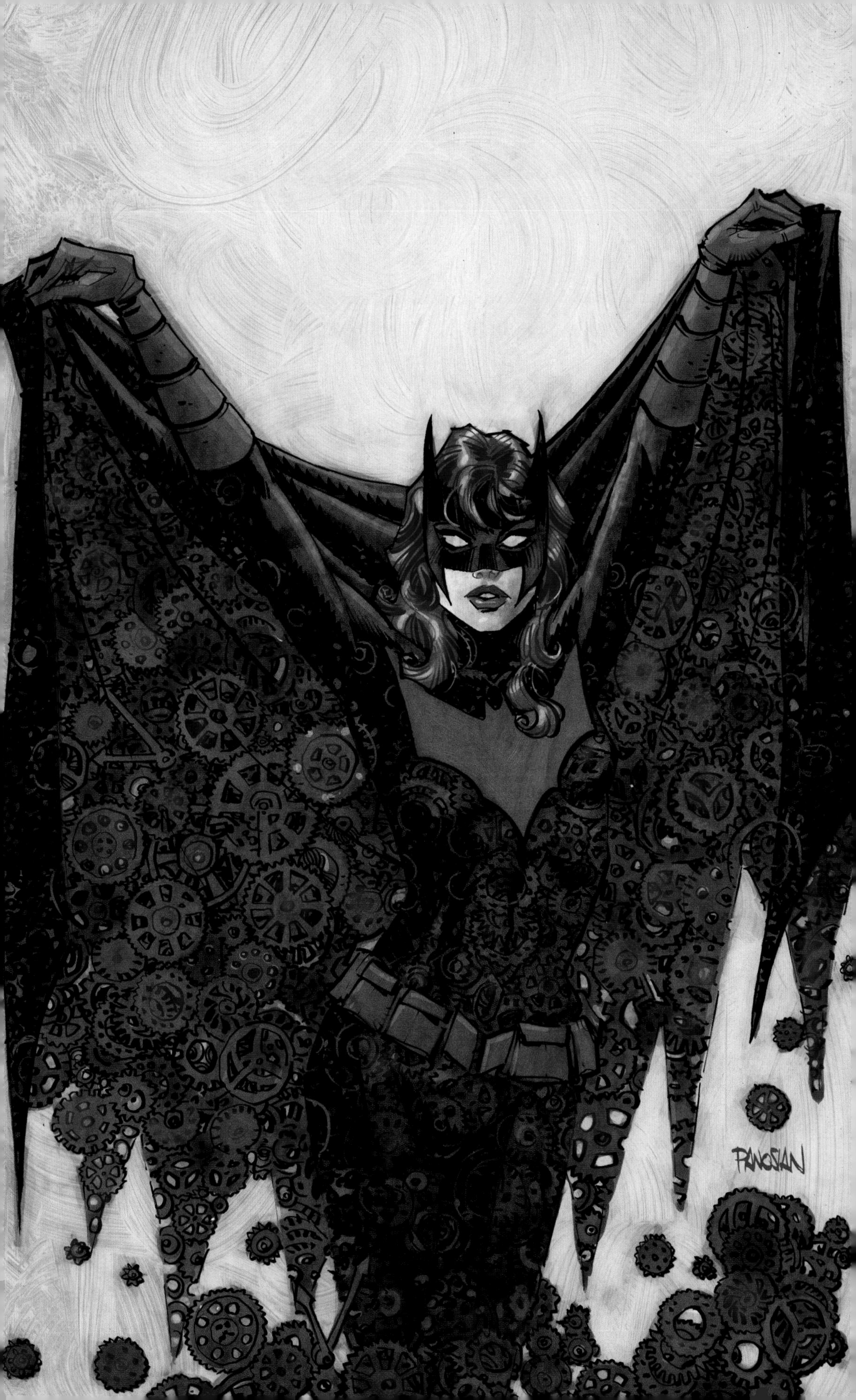
PANOSIAN

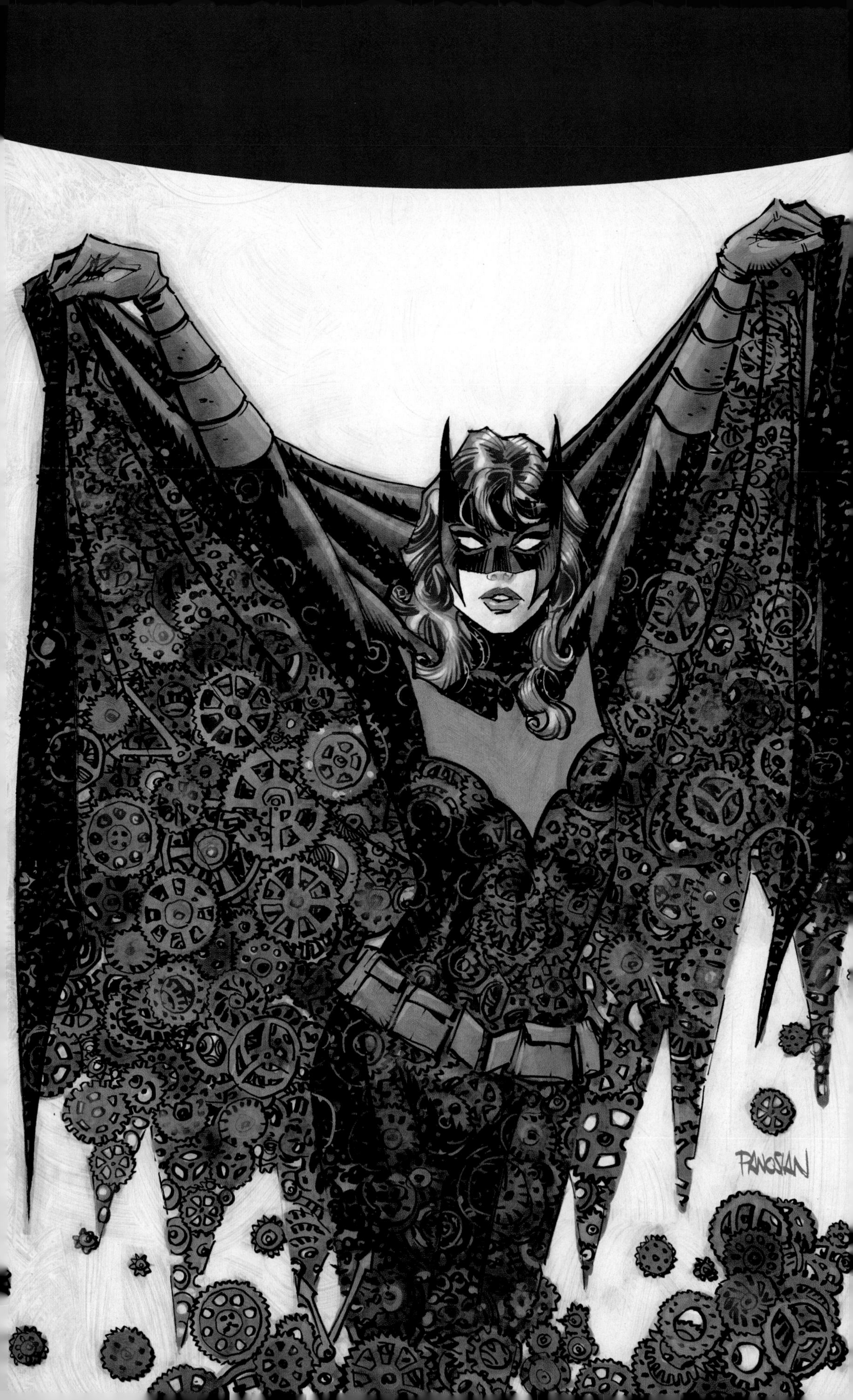
PANOSIAN

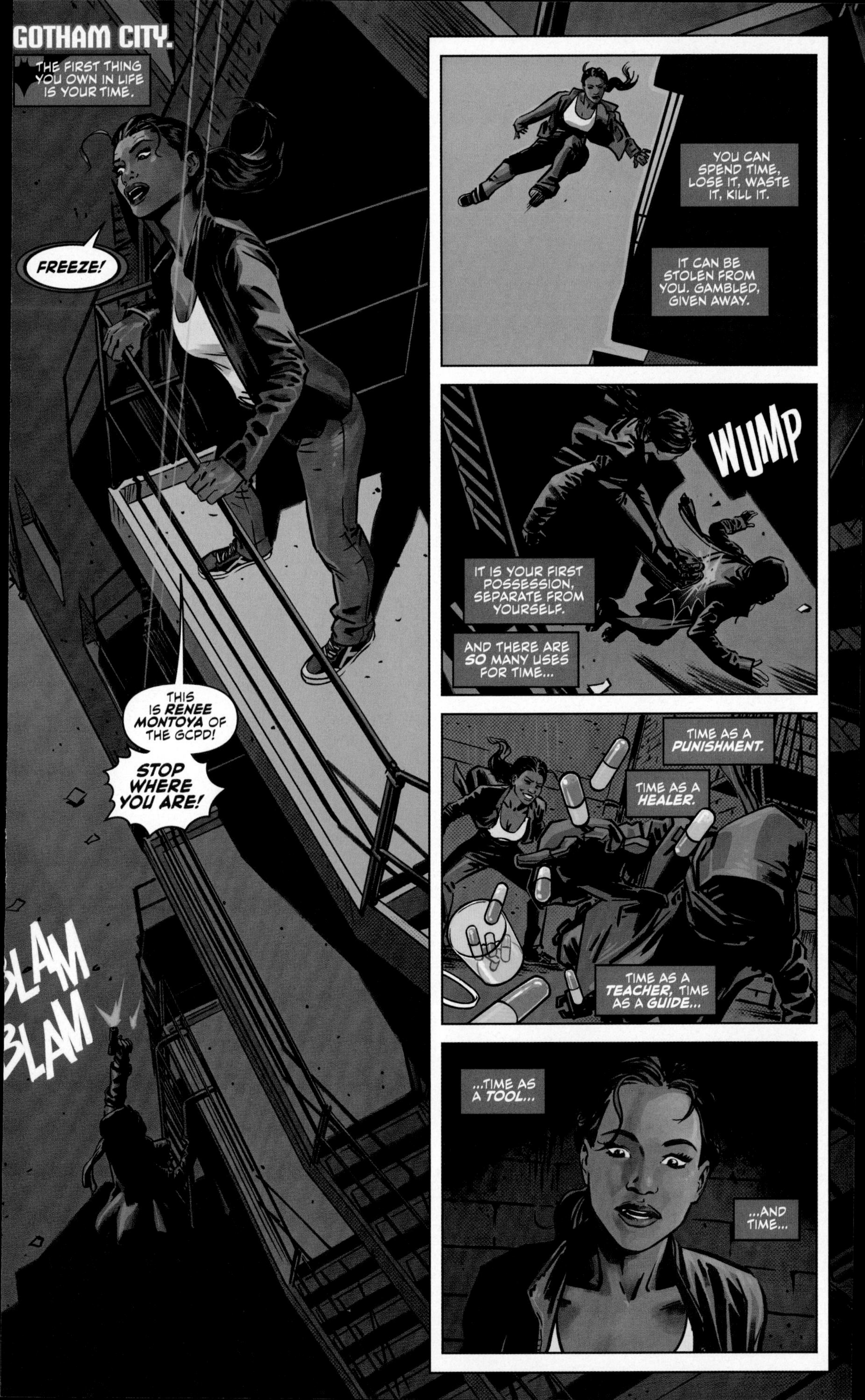
GOTHAM CITY.
THE FIRST THING YOU OWN IN LIFE IS YOUR TIME.
FREEZE!
THIS IS RENEE MONTOYA OF THE GCPD!
STOP WHERE YOU ARE!
BLAM BLAM
YOU CAN SPEND TIME, LOSE IT, WASTE IT, KILL IT.
IT CAN BE STOLEN FROM YOU. GAMBLED, GIVEN AWAY.
WUMP
IT IS YOUR FIRST POSSESSION, SEPARATE FROM YOURSELF.
AND THERE ARE SO MANY USES FOR TIME...
TIME AS A PUNISHMENT.
TIME AS A HEALER.
TIME AS A TEACHER, TIME AS A GUIDE...
...TIME AS A TOOL...
...AND TIME...

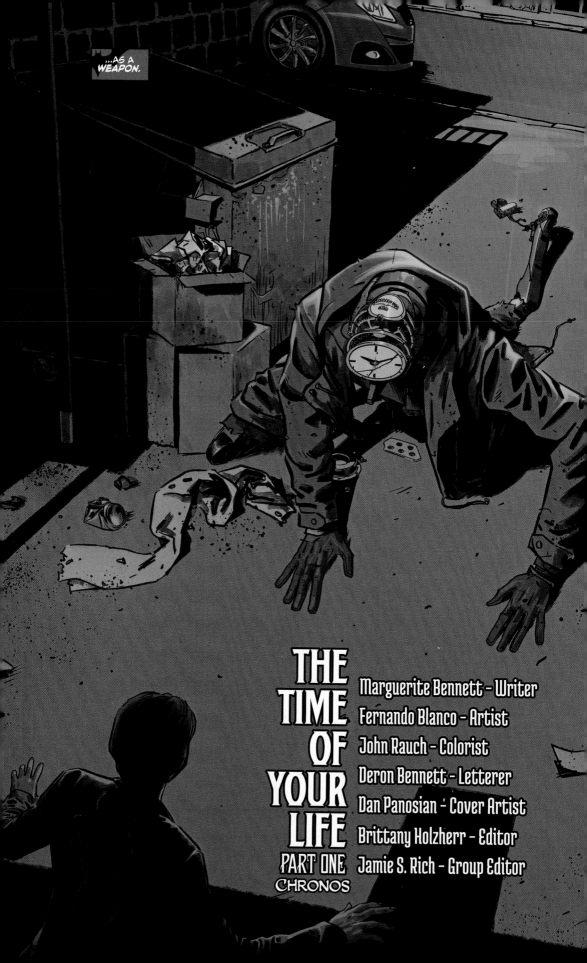

...AS A WEAPON.

THE TIME OF YOUR LIFE

PART ONE
CHRONOS

Marguerite Bennett – Writer

Fernando Blanco – Artist

John Rauch – Colorist

Deron Bennett – Letterer

Dan Panosian – Cover Artist

Brittany Holzherr – Editor

Jamie S. Rich – Group Editor

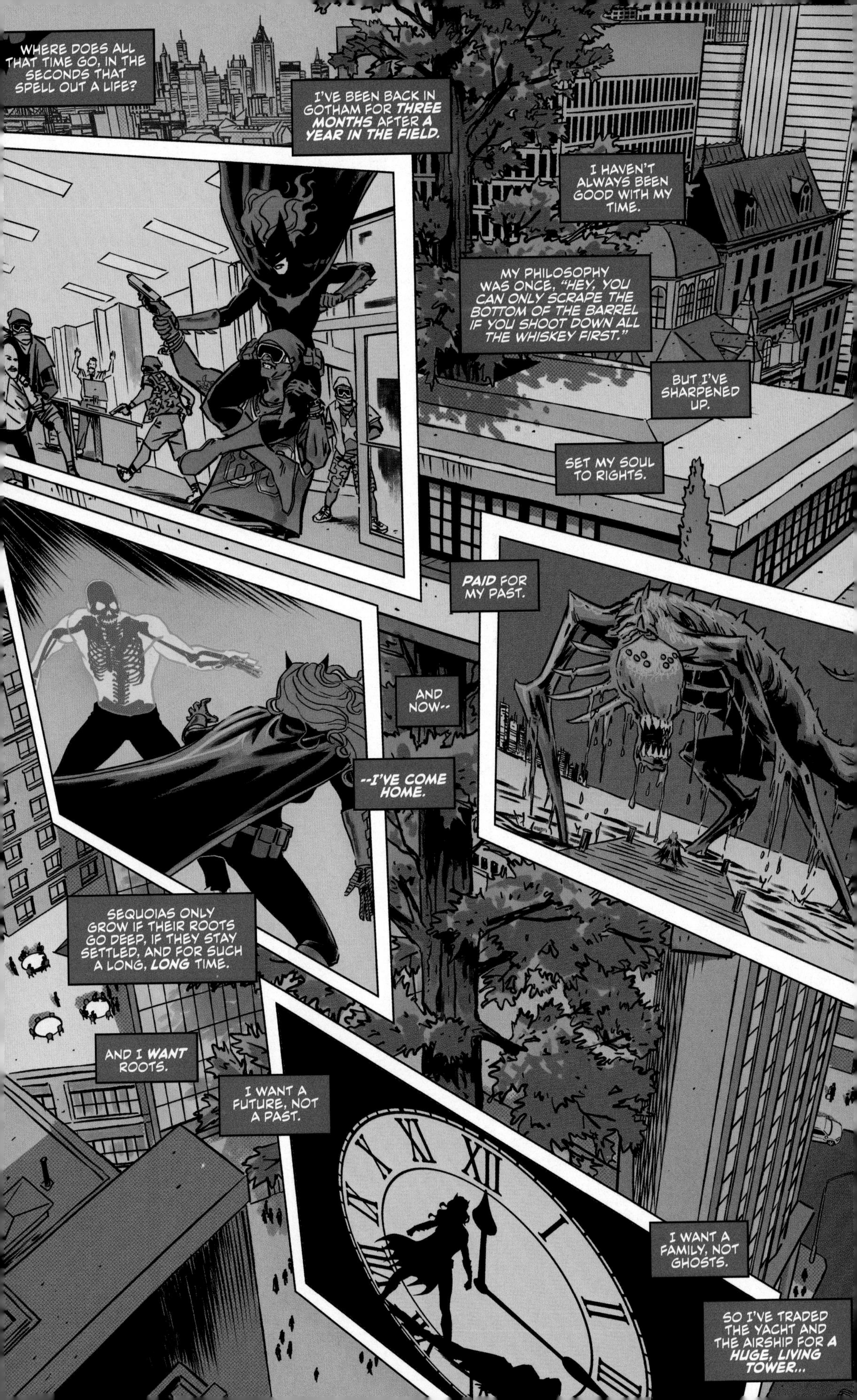

WHERE DOES ALL THAT TIME GO, IN THE SECONDS THAT SPELL OUT A LIFE?
I'VE BEEN BACK IN GOTHAM FOR **THREE MONTHS** AFTER **A YEAR IN THE FIELD.**
I HAVEN'T ALWAYS BEEN GOOD WITH MY TIME.
MY PHILOSOPHY WAS ONCE, *"HEY, YOU CAN ONLY SCRAPE THE BOTTOM OF THE BARREL IF YOU SHOOT DOWN ALL THE WHISKEY FIRST."*
BUT I'VE SHARPENED UP.
SET MY SOUL TO RIGHTS.
PAID FOR MY PAST.
AND NOW--
--I'VE COME HOME.
SEQUOIAS ONLY GROW IF THEIR ROOTS GO DEEP, IF THEY STAY SETTLED, AND FOR SUCH A LONG, **LONG** TIME.
AND I **WANT** ROOTS.
I WANT A FUTURE, NOT A PAST.
I WANT A FAMILY, NOT GHOSTS.
SO I'VE TRADED THE YACHT AND THE AIRSHIP FOR **A HUGE, LIVING TOWER...**

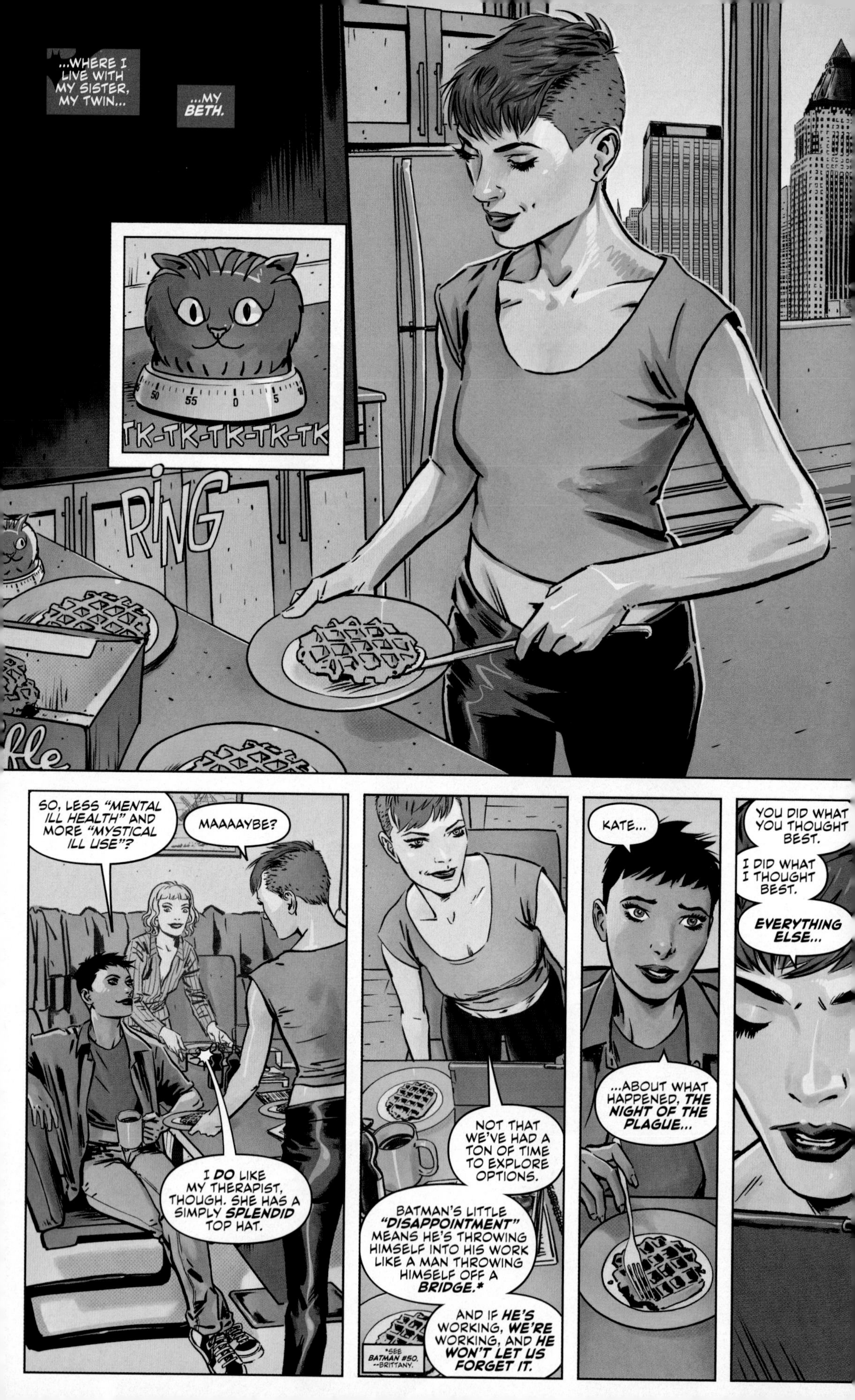

...WHERE I LIVE WITH MY SISTER, MY TWIN...
...MY BETH.
50 55 0 5
TK-TK-TK-TK-TK
RING
SO, LESS "MENTAL ILL HEALTH" AND MORE "MYSTICAL ILL USE"?
MAAAAYBE?
I DO LIKE MY THERAPIST, THOUGH. SHE HAS A SIMPLY SPLENDID TOP HAT.
NOT THAT WE'VE HAD A TON OF TIME TO EXPLORE OPTIONS.
BATMAN'S LITTLE "DISAPPOINTMENT" MEANS HE'S THROWING HIMSELF INTO HIS WORK LIKE A MAN THROWING HIMSELF OFF A BRIDGE.*
AND IF HE'S WORKING, WE'RE WORKING, AND HE WON'T LET US FORGET IT.
*SEE BATMAN #50. --BRITTANY.
KATE...
...ABOUT WHAT HAPPENED, THE NIGHT OF THE PLAGUE...
YOU DID WHAT YOU THOUGHT BEST.
I DID WHAT I THOUGHT BEST.
EVERYTHING ELSE...

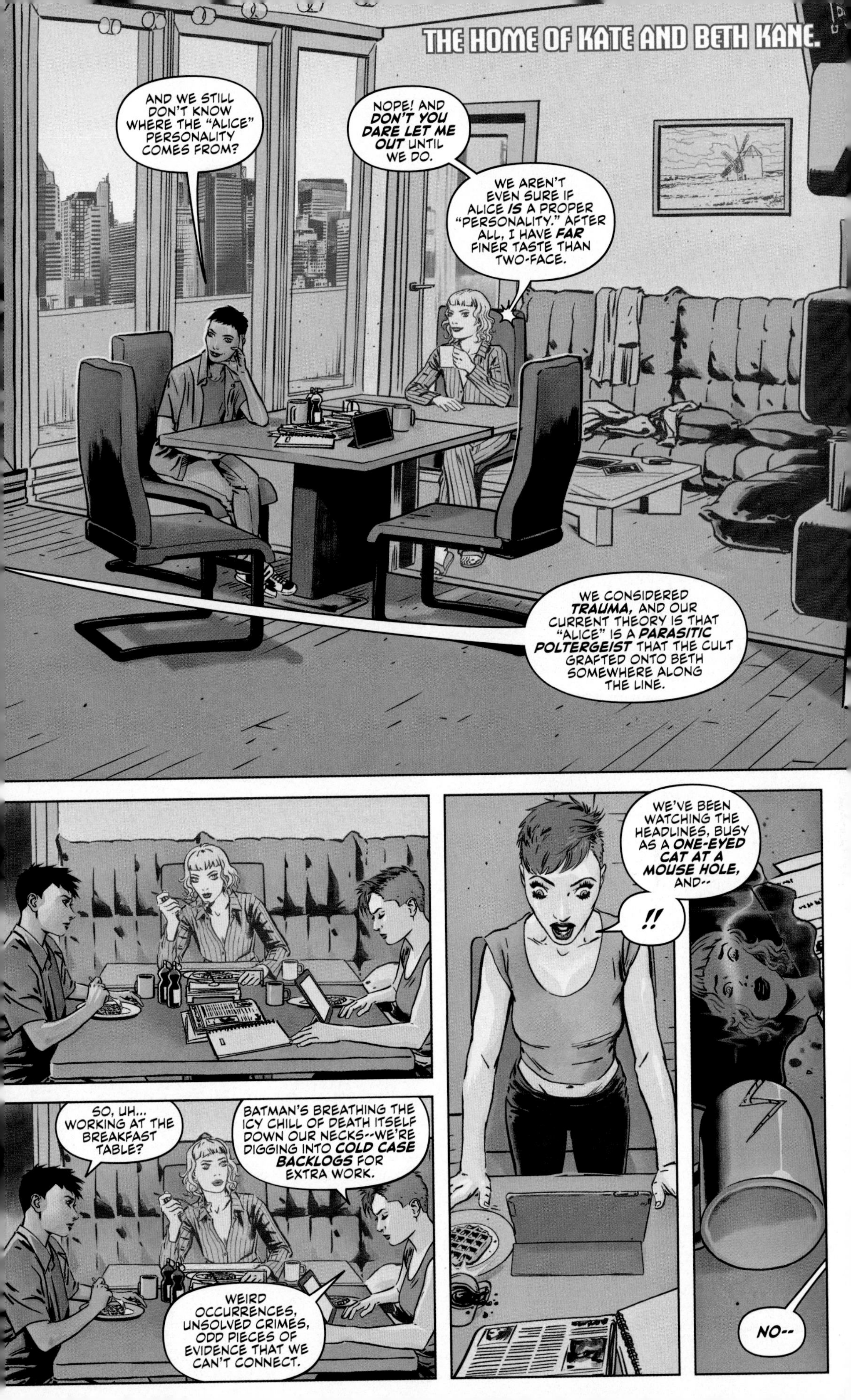
THE HOME OF KATE AND BETH KANE.
AND WE STILL DON'T KNOW WHERE THE "ALICE" PERSONALITY COMES FROM?
NOPE! AND DON'T YOU DARE LET ME OUT UNTIL WE DO.
WE AREN'T EVEN SURE IF ALICE IS A PROPER "PERSONALITY." AFTER ALL, I HAVE FAR FINER TASTE THAN TWO-FACE.
WE CONSIDERED TRAUMA, AND OUR CURRENT THEORY IS THAT "ALICE" IS A PARASITIC POLTERGEIST THAT THE CULT GRAFTED ONTO BETH SOMEWHERE ALONG THE LINE.
SO, UH... WORKING AT THE BREAKFAST TABLE?
BATMAN'S BREATHING THE ICY CHILL OF DEATH ITSELF DOWN OUR NECKS--WE'RE DIGGING INTO COLD CASE BACKLOGS FOR EXTRA WORK.
WEIRD OCCURRENCES, UNSOLVED CRIMES, ODD PIECES OF EVIDENCE THAT WE CAN'T CONNECT.
WE'VE BEEN WATCHING THE HEADLINES, BUSY AS A ONE-EYED CAT AT A MOUSE HOLE, AND--
!!
NO--

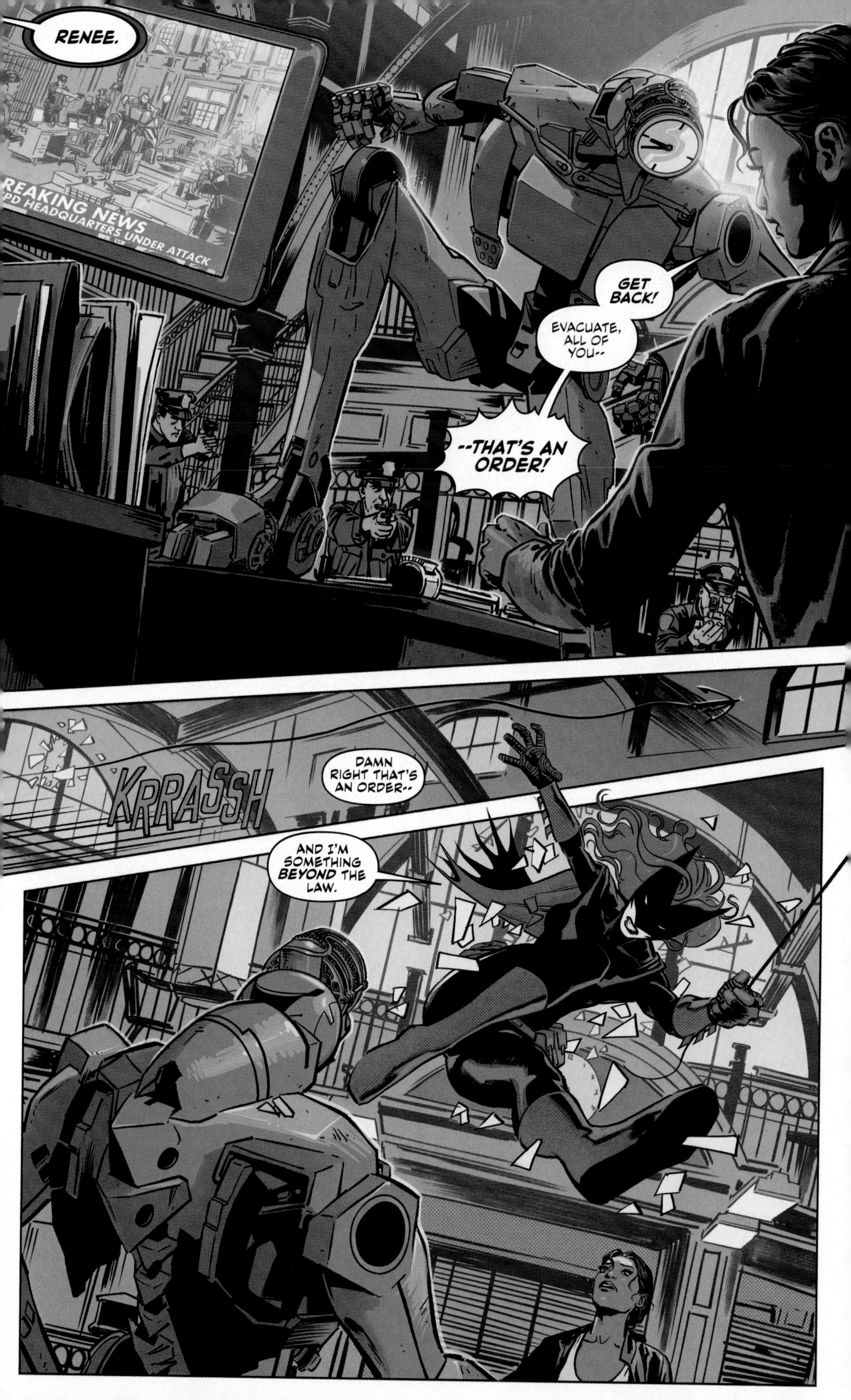
RENEE.
BREAKING NEWS
GCPD HEADQUARTERS UNDER ATTACK
GET BACK!
EVACUATE, ALL OF YOU--
--THAT'S AN ORDER!
KRRASSSH
DAMN RIGHT THAT'S AN ORDER--
AND I'M SOMETHING *BEYOND* THE LAW.

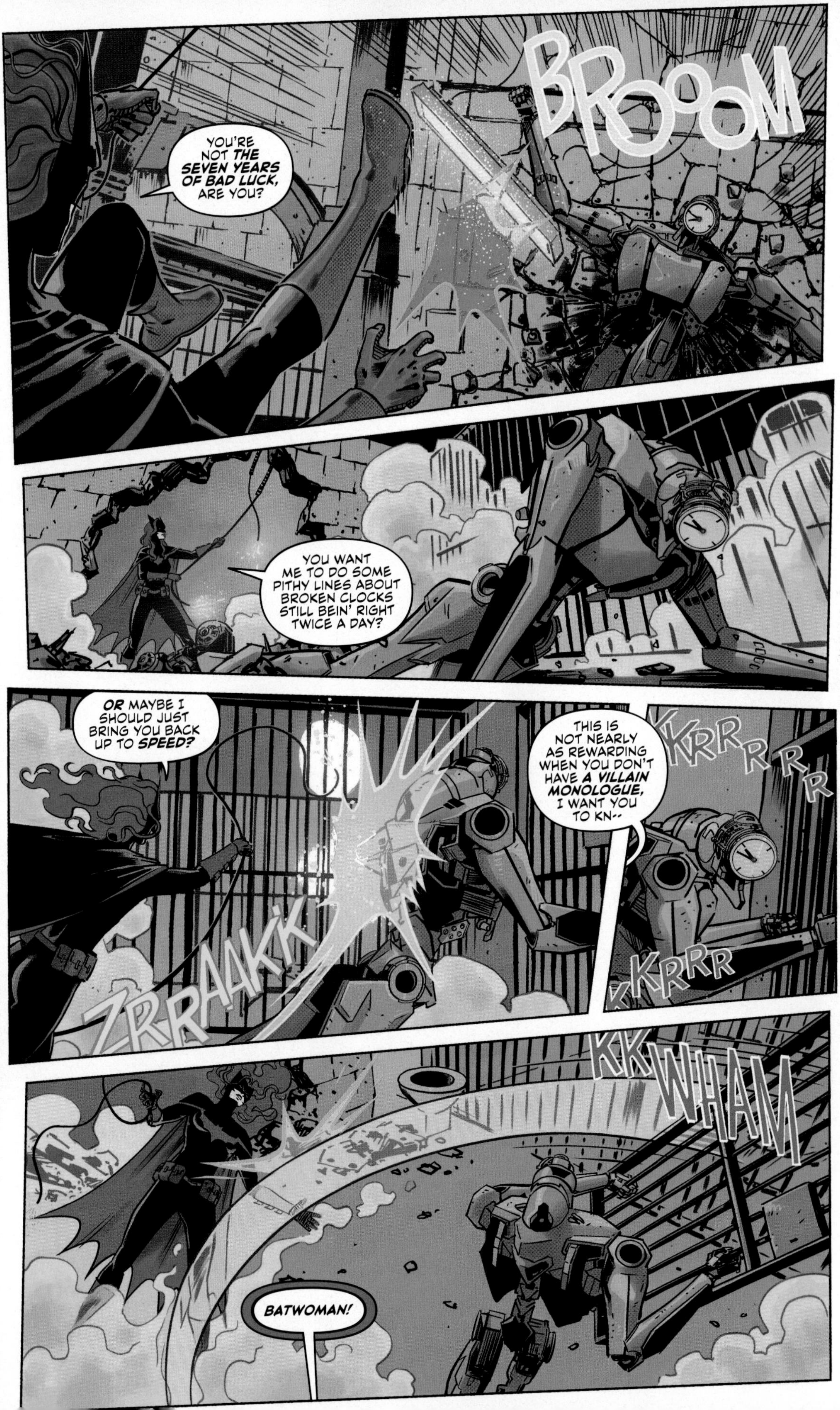
BROOOOM
YOU'RE NOT THE SEVEN YEARS OF BAD LUCK, ARE YOU?
YOU WANT ME TO DO SOME PITHY LINES ABOUT BROKEN CLOCKS STILL BEIN' RIGHT TWICE A DAY?
OR MAYBE I SHOULD JUST BRING YOU BACK UP TO SPEED?
ZRRAAKK
THIS IS NOT NEARLY AS REWARDING WHEN YOU DON'T HAVE A VILLAIN MONOLOGUE, I WANT YOU TO KN--
KKRRRRRRR
KKRRRR
KKWHAM
BATWOMAN!

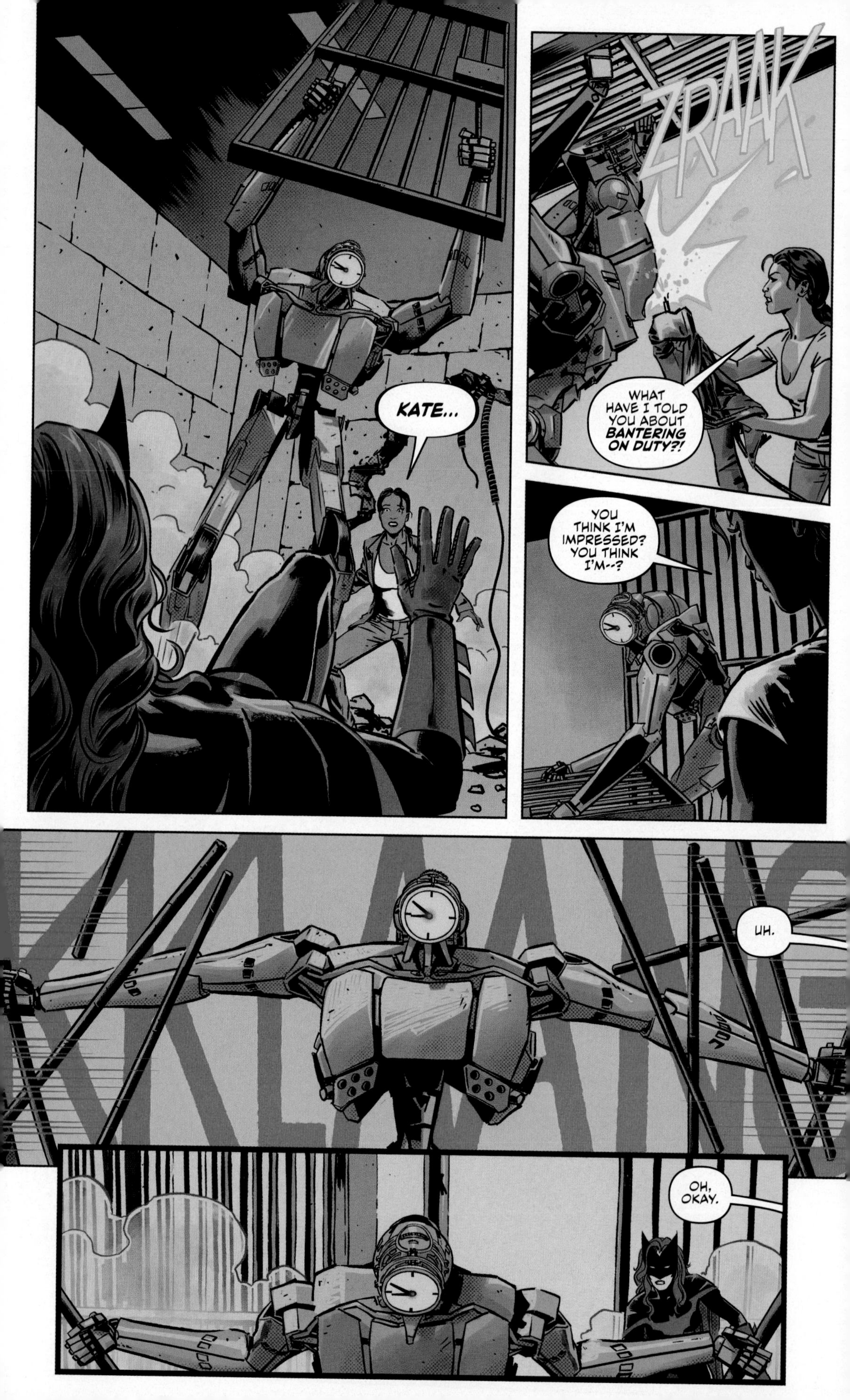
KATE...
ZRAAK
WHAT HAVE I TOLD YOU ABOUT BANTERING ON DUTY?!
YOU THINK I'M IMPRESSED? YOU THINK I'M--?
UH.
OH, OKAY.

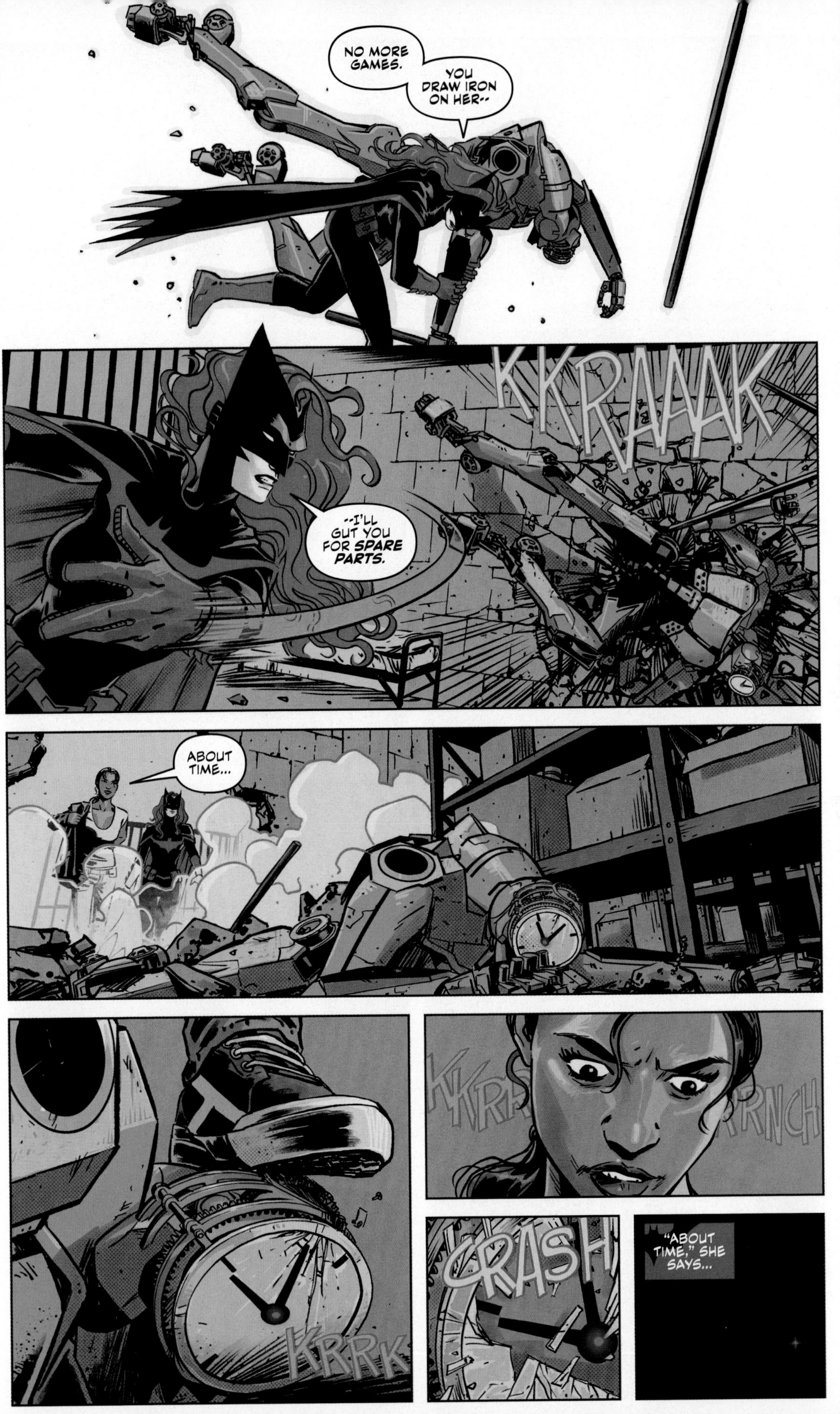
NO MORE GAMES.
YOU DRAW IRON ON HER--
KKRAAAK
--I'LL GUT YOU FOR SPARE PARTS.
ABOUT TIME...
KRRK
KKRASH
KRRNCH
CRASH
"ABOUT TIME," SHE SAYS...

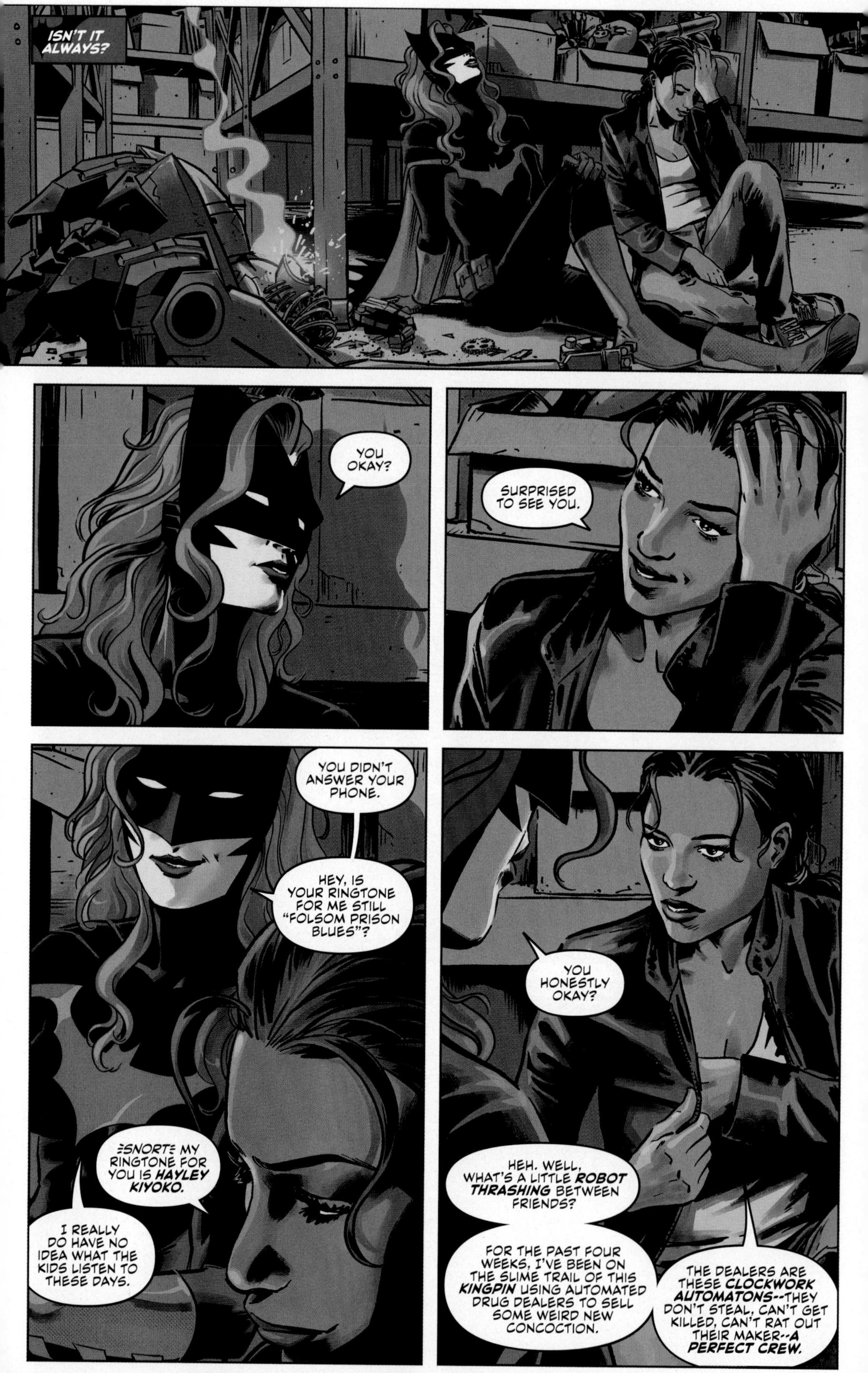
ISN'T IT ALWAYS?
YOU OKAY?
SURPRISED TO SEE YOU.
YOU DIDN'T ANSWER YOUR PHONE.
HEY, IS YOUR RINGTONE FOR ME STILL "FOLSOM PRISON BLUES"?
YOU HONESTLY OKAY?
=SNORT= MY RINGTONE FOR YOU IS HAYLEY KIYOKO.
I REALLY DO HAVE NO IDEA WHAT THE KIDS LISTEN TO THESE DAYS.
HEH. WELL, WHAT'S A LITTLE ROBOT THRASHING BETWEEN FRIENDS?
FOR THE PAST FOUR WEEKS, I'VE BEEN ON THE SLIME TRAIL OF THIS KINGPIN USING AUTOMATED DRUG DEALERS TO SELL SOME WEIRD NEW CONCOCTION.
THE DEALERS ARE THESE CLOCKWORK AUTOMATONS--THEY DON'T STEAL, CAN'T GET KILLED, CAN'T RAT OUT THEIR MAKER--A PERFECT CREW.

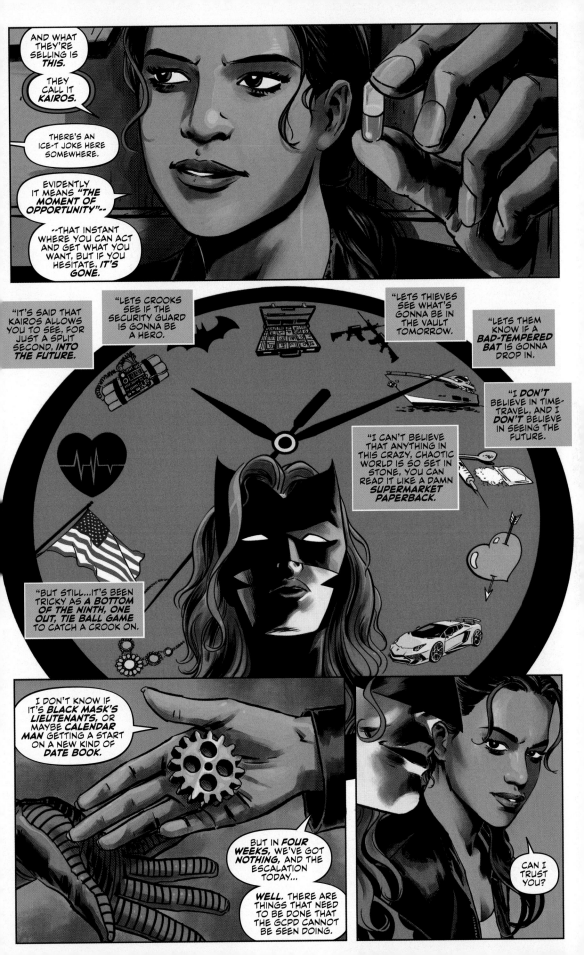

AND WHAT THEY'RE SELLING IS *THIS*.

THEY CALL IT *KAIROS*.

THERE'S AN ICE-T JOKE HERE SOMEWHERE.

EVIDENTLY IT MEANS *"THE MOMENT OF OPPORTUNITY"*--

--THAT INSTANT WHERE YOU CAN ACT AND GET WHAT YOU WANT, BUT IF YOU HESITATE, *IT'S GONE.*

"IT'S SAID THAT KAIROS ALLOWS YOU TO SEE, FOR JUST A SPLIT SECOND, *INTO THE FUTURE.*

"LETS CROOKS SEE IF THE SECURITY GUARD IS GONNA BE A HERO.

"LETS THIEVES SEE WHAT'S GONNA BE IN THE VAULT TOMORROW.

"LETS THEM KNOW IF A *BAD-TEMPERED BAT* IS GONNA DROP IN.

"I *DON'T* BELIEVE IN TIME-TRAVEL, AND I *DON'T* BELIEVE IN SEEING THE FUTURE.

"I CAN'T BELIEVE THAT ANYTHING IN THIS CRAZY, CHAOTIC WORLD IS SO SET IN STONE, YOU CAN READ IT LIKE A DAMN *SUPERMARKET PAPERBACK.*

"BUT STILL...IT'S BEEN TRICKY AS A *BOTTOM OF THE NINTH, ONE OUT, TIE BALL GAME* TO CATCH A CROOK ON.

I DON'T KNOW IF IT'S *BLACK MASK'S LIEUTENANTS*, OR MAYBE *CALENDAR MAN* GETTING A START ON A NEW KIND OF *DATE BOOK.*

BUT IN *FOUR WEEKS*, WE'VE GOT *NOTHING*, AND THE ESCALATION TODAY...

WELL. THERE ARE THINGS THAT NEED TO BE DONE THAT THE GCPD CANNOT BE SEEN DOING.

CAN I TRUST YOU?

LATER.

AND COMING UP NEXT...HAYLEY KIYOKO!

♪ ♫♫♫♫♫♫ ♪

EVEN IF BATMAN WEREN'T RIDING US WITH SPURS, I'D BE DOWN HERE, *DIGGING GRAVES*...

DOWN IN THE DEEP...

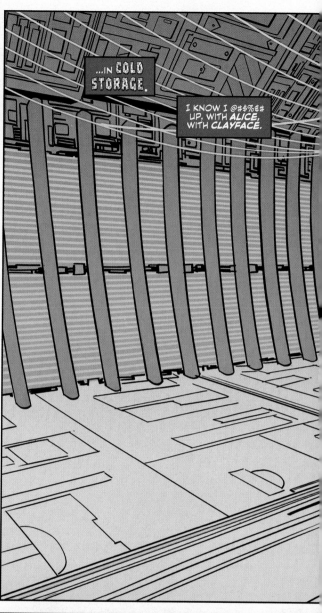

...IN **COLD STORAGE.**

I KNOW I @#\$%#\$ UP, WITH *ALICE*, WITH *CLAYFACE.*

ALL THE CASES WE COULDN'T SOLVE. *ALL* THE PUZZLING PUZZLE PIECES THAT NEVER FIT TOGETHER.

WE DON'T EVEN KNOW IF HALF THE THINGS WE'VE LOGGED ARE EVEN EVIDENCE OF A CRIME.

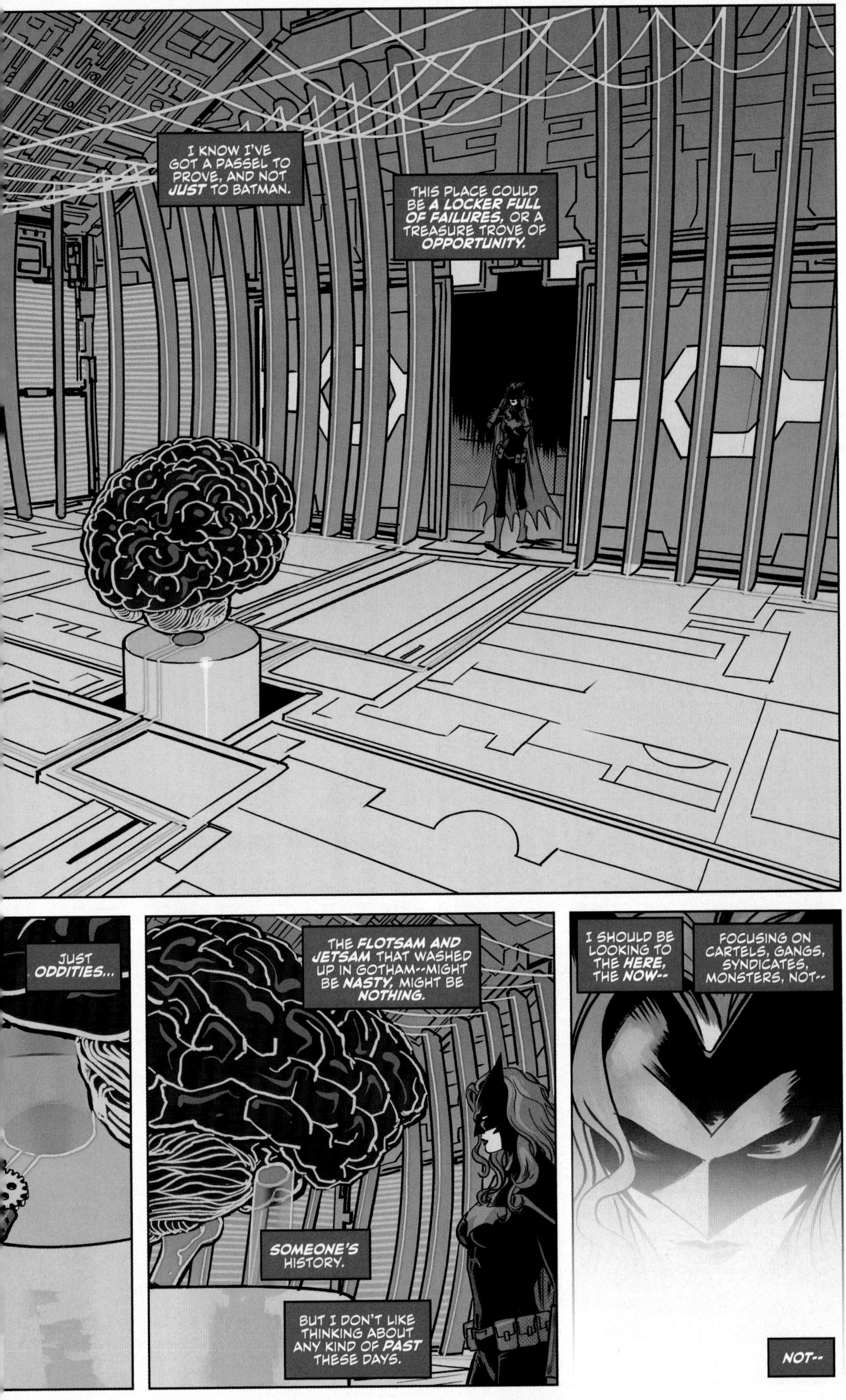
I KNOW I'VE GOT A PASSEL TO PROVE, AND NOT *JUST* TO BATMAN.
THIS PLACE COULD BE ***A LOCKER FULL OF FAILURES,*** OR A TREASURE TROVE OF ***OPPORTUNITY.***
JUST ***ODDITIES...***
THE ***FLOTSAM AND JETSAM*** THAT WASHED UP IN GOTHAM--MIGHT BE ***NASTY,*** MIGHT BE ***NOTHING.***
SOMEONE'S HISTORY.
BUT I DON'T LIKE THINKING ABOUT ANY KIND OF ***PAST*** THESE DAYS.
I SHOULD BE LOOKING TO THE ***HERE,*** THE ***NOW--***
FOCUSING ON CARTELS, GANGS, SYNDICATES, MONSTERS, NOT--
NOT--

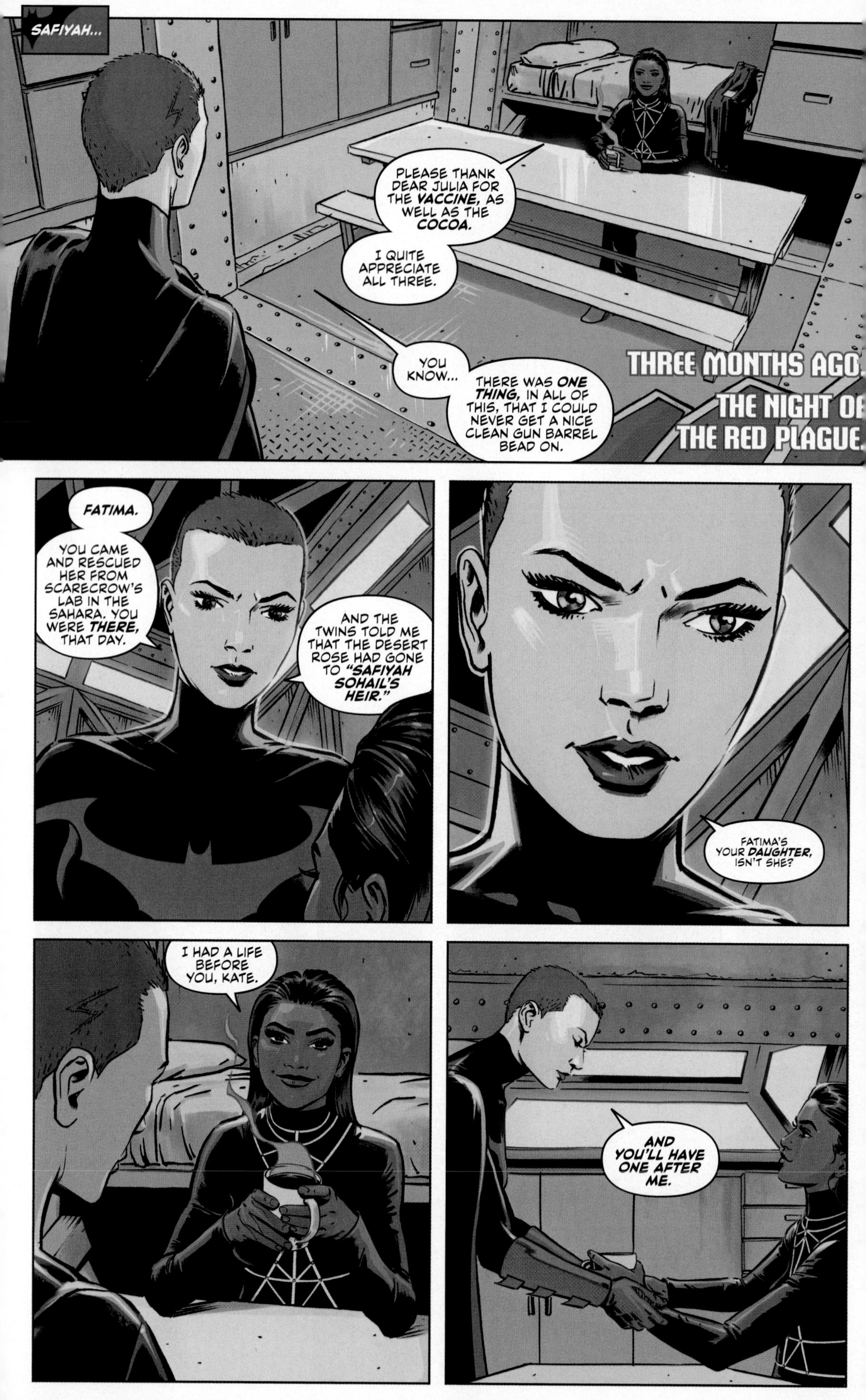
SAFIYAH...
PLEASE THANK DEAR JULIA FOR THE VACCINE, AS WELL AS THE COCOA.
I QUITE APPRECIATE ALL THREE.
YOU KNOW...
THERE WAS ONE THING, IN ALL OF THIS, THAT I COULD NEVER GET A NICE CLEAN GUN BARREL BEAD ON.
THREE MONTHS AGO:
THE NIGHT OF THE RED PLAGUE.
FATIMA.
YOU CAME AND RESCUED HER FROM SCARECROW'S LAB IN THE SAHARA. YOU WERE THERE, THAT DAY.
AND THE TWINS TOLD ME THAT THE DESERT ROSE HAD GONE TO "SAFIYAH SOHAIL'S HEIR."
FATIMA'S YOUR DAUGHTER, ISN'T SHE?
I HAD A LIFE BEFORE YOU, KATE.
AND YOU'LL HAVE ONE AFTER ME.

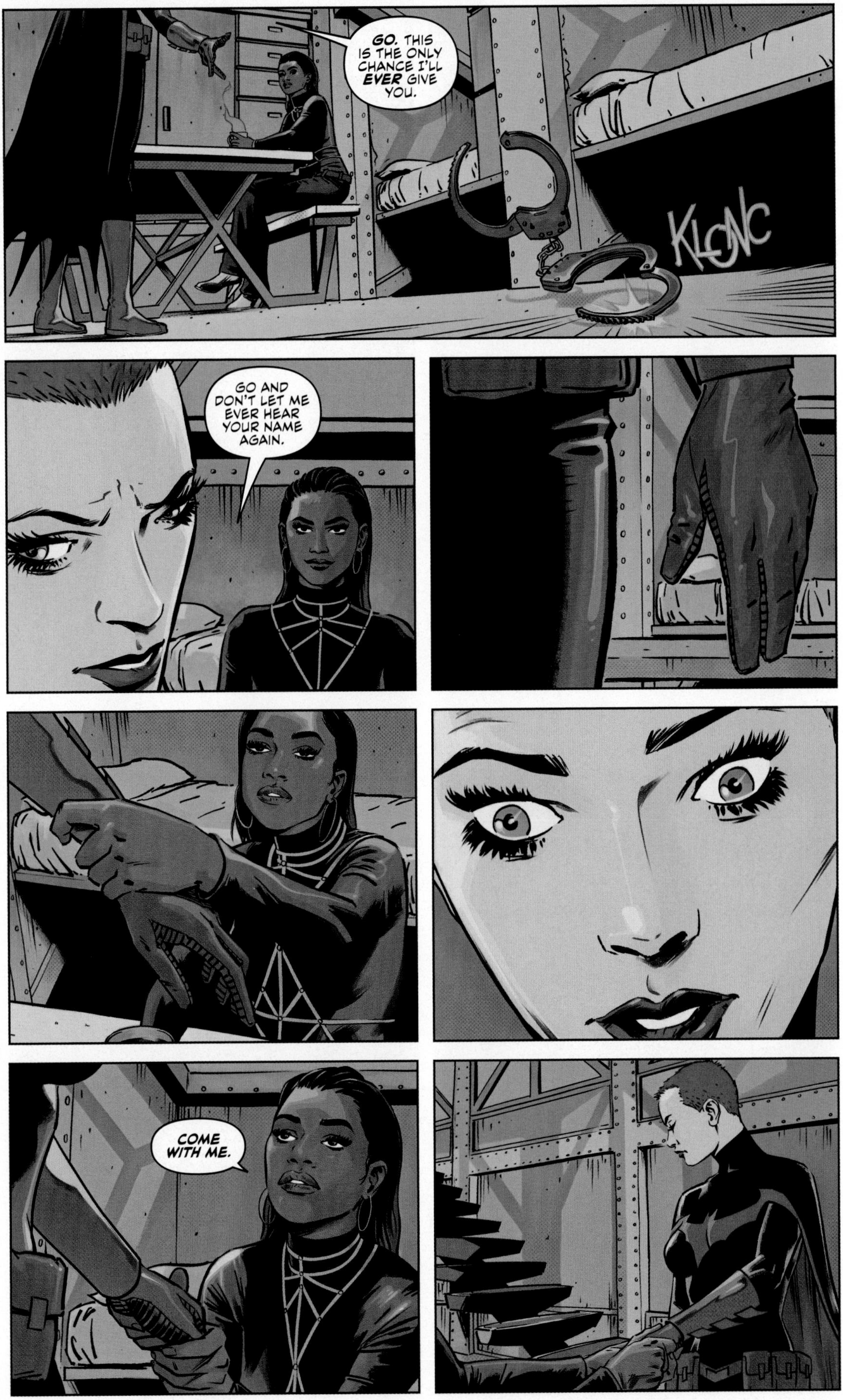
GO. THIS IS THE ONLY CHANCE I'LL EVER GIVE YOU.
KLONC
GO AND DON'T LET ME EVER HEAR YOUR NAME AGAIN.
COME WITH ME.

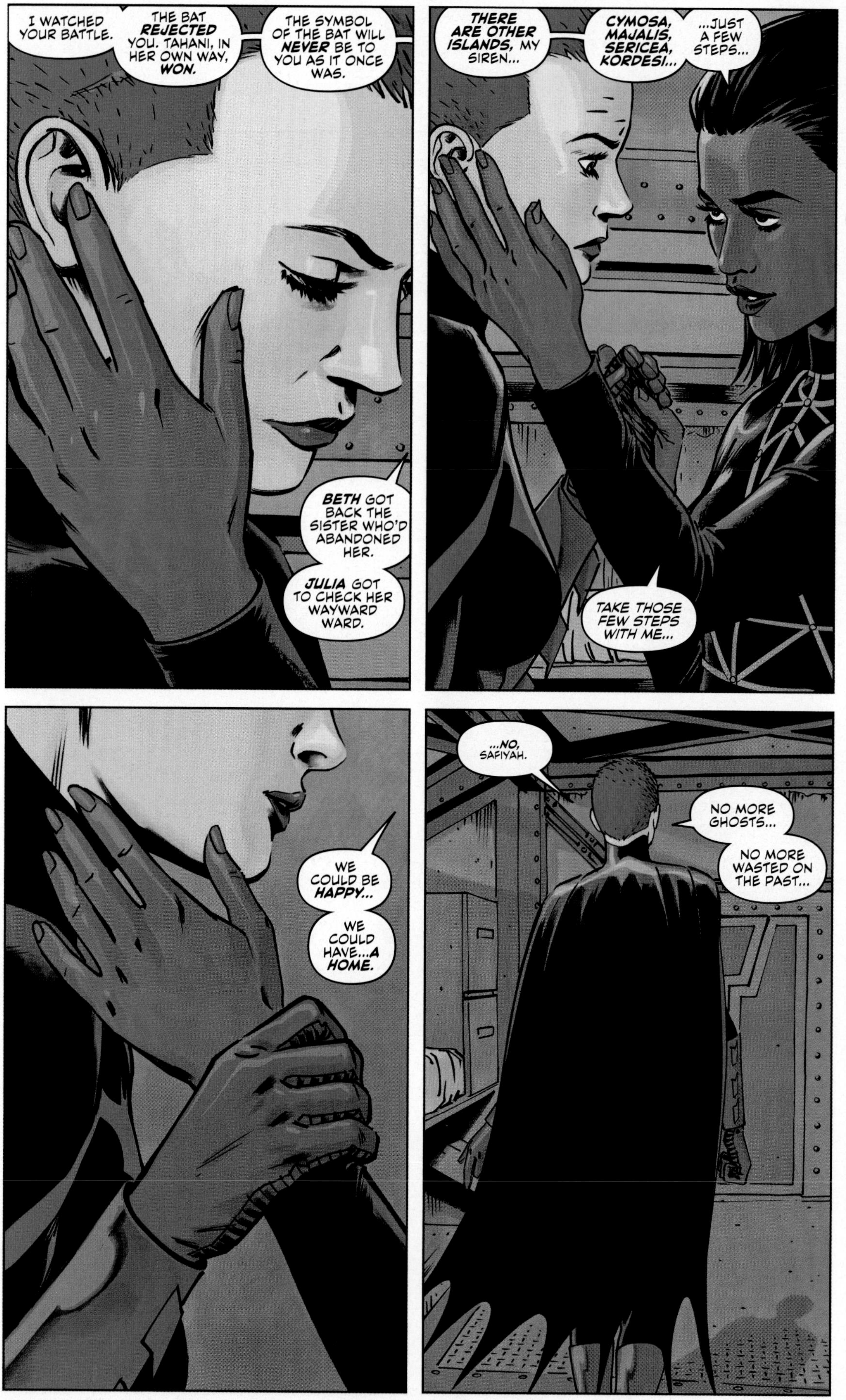

I WATCHED YOUR BATTLE.
THE BAT **REJECTED** YOU. TAHANI, IN HER OWN WAY, **WON.**
THE SYMBOL OF THE BAT WILL **NEVER** BE TO YOU AS IT ONCE WAS.
BETH GOT BACK THE SISTER WHO'D ABANDONED HER.
JULIA GOT TO CHECK HER WAYWARD WARD.
THERE ARE OTHER ISLANDS, MY SIREN...
CYMOSA, MAJALIS, SERICEA, KORDESI...
...JUST A FEW STEPS...
TAKE THOSE FEW STEPS WITH ME...
WE COULD BE **HAPPY...**
WE COULD HAVE...**A HOME.**
...**NO,** SAFIYAH.
NO MORE GHOSTS...
NO MORE WASTED ON THE PAST...

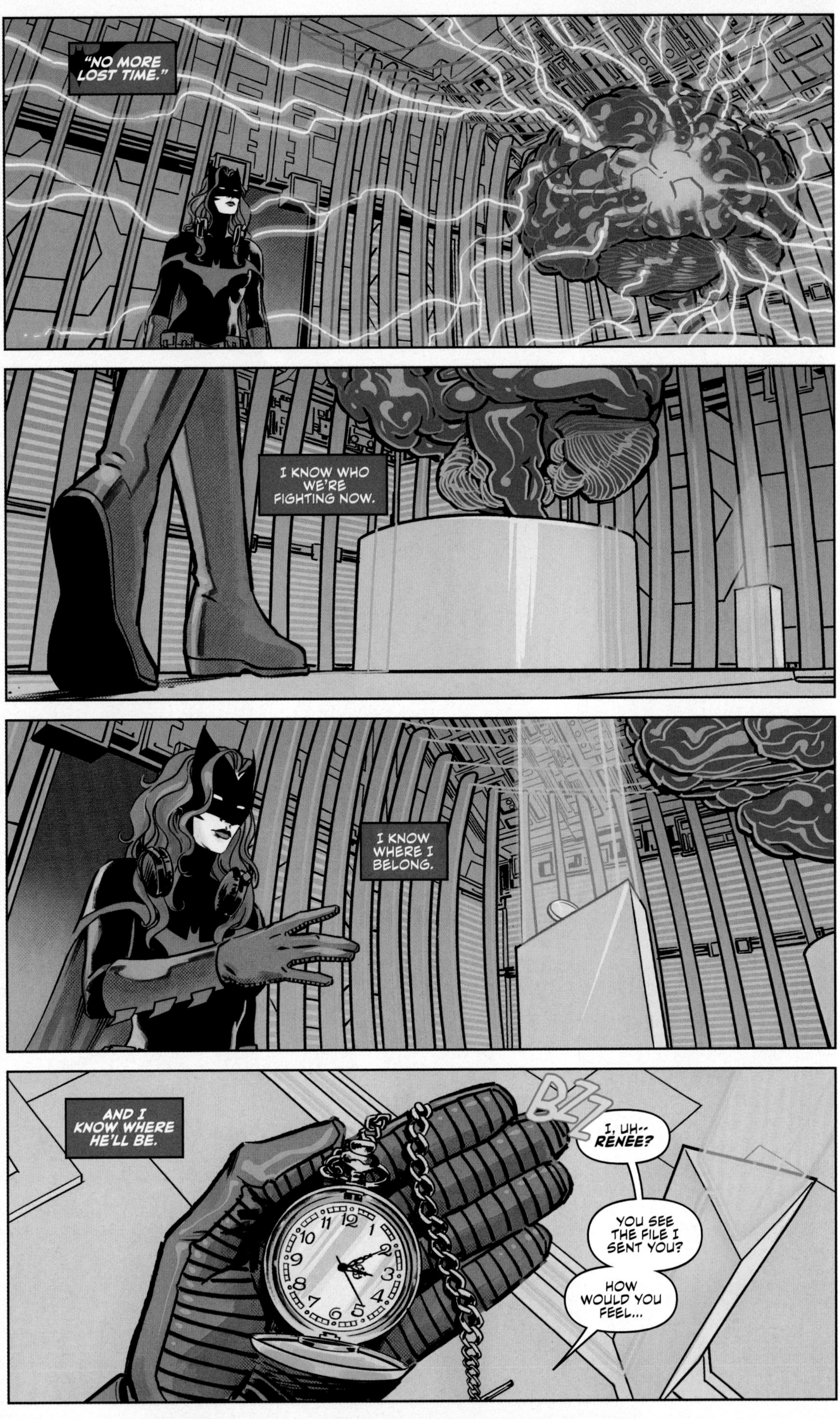
"NO MORE LOST TIME."
I KNOW WHO WE'RE FIGHTING NOW.
I KNOW WHERE I BELONG.
AND I KNOW WHERE HE'LL BE.
BZZ
I, UH-- RENEE?
YOU SEE THE FILE I SENT YOU?
HOW WOULD YOU FEEL...

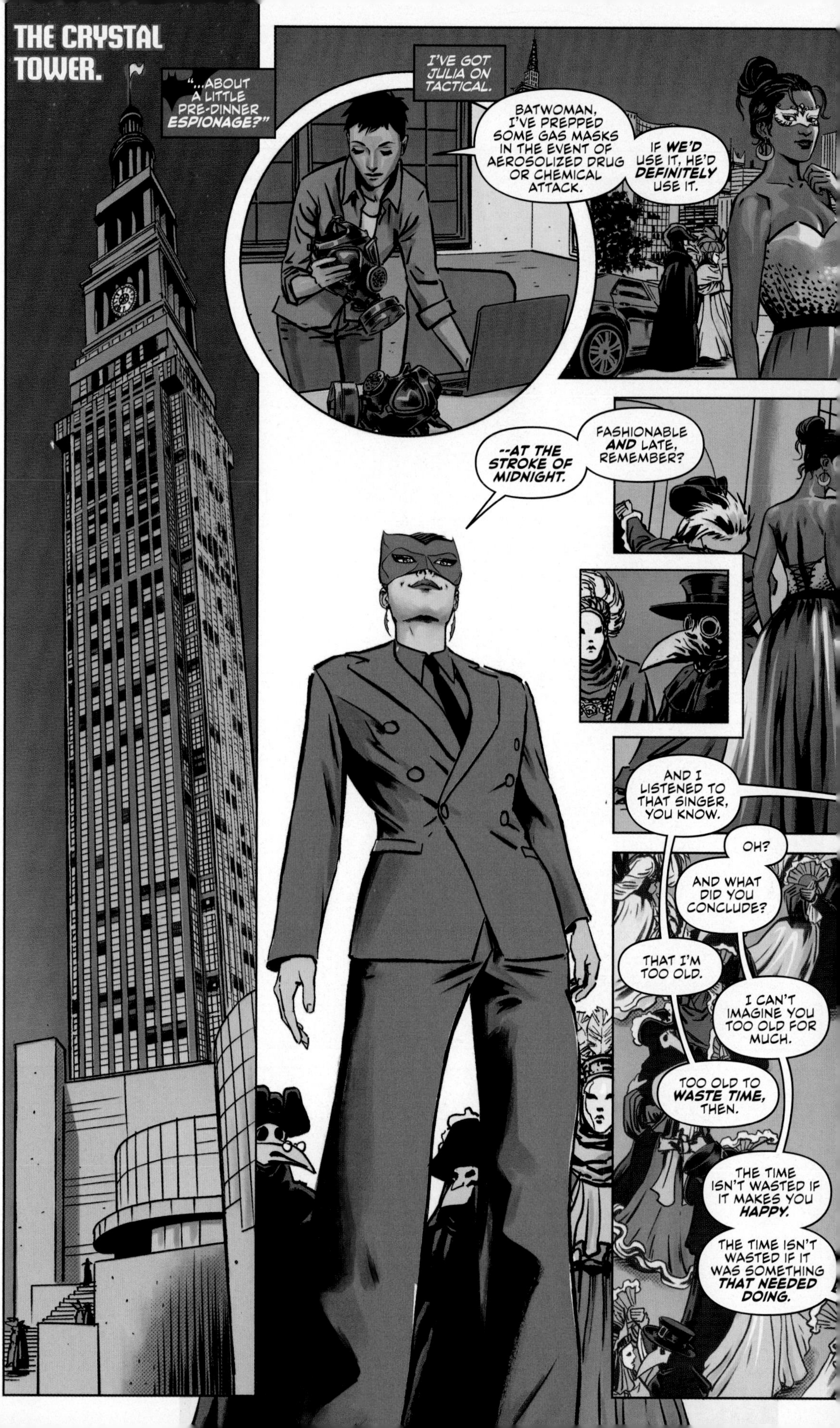
THE CRYSTAL TOWER.
"...ABOUT A LITTLE PRE-DINNER ESPIONAGE?"
I'VE GOT JULIA ON TACTICAL.
BATWOMAN, I'VE PREPPED SOME GAS MASKS IN THE EVENT OF AEROSOLIZED DRUG OR CHEMICAL ATTACK.
IF WE'D USE IT, HE'D DEFINITELY USE IT.
FASHIONABLE AND LATE, REMEMBER?
--AT THE STROKE OF MIDNIGHT.
AND I LISTENED TO THAT SINGER, YOU KNOW.
OH?
AND WHAT DID YOU CONCLUDE?
THAT I'M TOO OLD.
I CAN'T IMAGINE YOU TOO OLD FOR MUCH.
TOO OLD TO WASTE TIME, THEN.
THE TIME ISN'T WASTED IF IT MAKES YOU HAPPY.
THE TIME ISN'T WASTED IF IT WAS SOMETHING THAT NEEDED DOING.

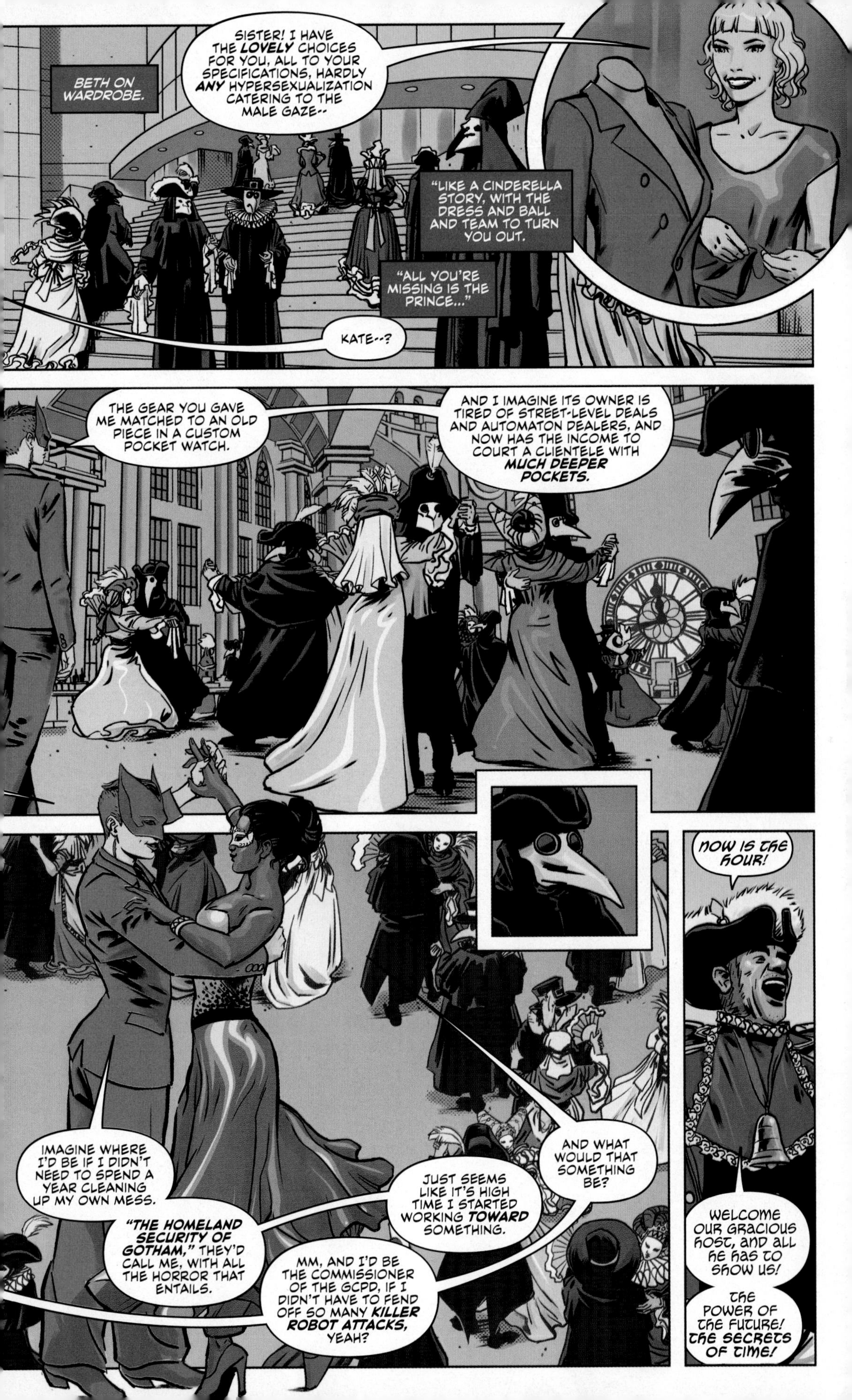
BETH ON WARDROBE.
SISTER! I HAVE THE LOVELY CHOICES FOR YOU, ALL TO YOUR SPECIFICATIONS. HARDLY ANY HYPERSEXUALIZATION CATERING TO THE MALE GAZE--
"LIKE A CINDERELLA STORY, WITH THE DRESS AND BALL AND TEAM TO TURN YOU OUT.
"ALL YOU'RE MISSING IS THE PRINCE..."
KATE--?
THE GEAR YOU GAVE ME MATCHED TO AN OLD PIECE IN A CUSTOM POCKET WATCH.
AND I IMAGINE ITS OWNER IS TIRED OF STREET-LEVEL DEALS AND AUTOMATON DEALERS, AND NOW HAS THE INCOME TO COURT A CLIENTELE WITH MUCH DEEPER POCKETS.
IMAGINE WHERE I'D BE IF I DIDN'T NEED TO SPEND A YEAR CLEANING UP MY OWN MESS.
"THE HOMELAND SECURITY OF GOTHAM," THEY'D CALL ME, WITH ALL THE HORROR THAT ENTAILS.
MM, AND I'D BE THE COMMISSIONER OF THE GCPD, IF I DIDN'T HAVE TO FEND OFF SO MANY KILLER ROBOT ATTACKS, YEAH?
JUST SEEMS LIKE IT'S HIGH TIME I STARTED WORKING TOWARD SOMETHING.
AND WHAT WOULD THAT SOMETHING BE?
NOW IS THE HOUR!
WELCOME OUR GRACIOUS HOST, AND ALL HE HAS TO SHOW US!
THE POWER OF THE FUTURE! THE SECRETS OF TIME!

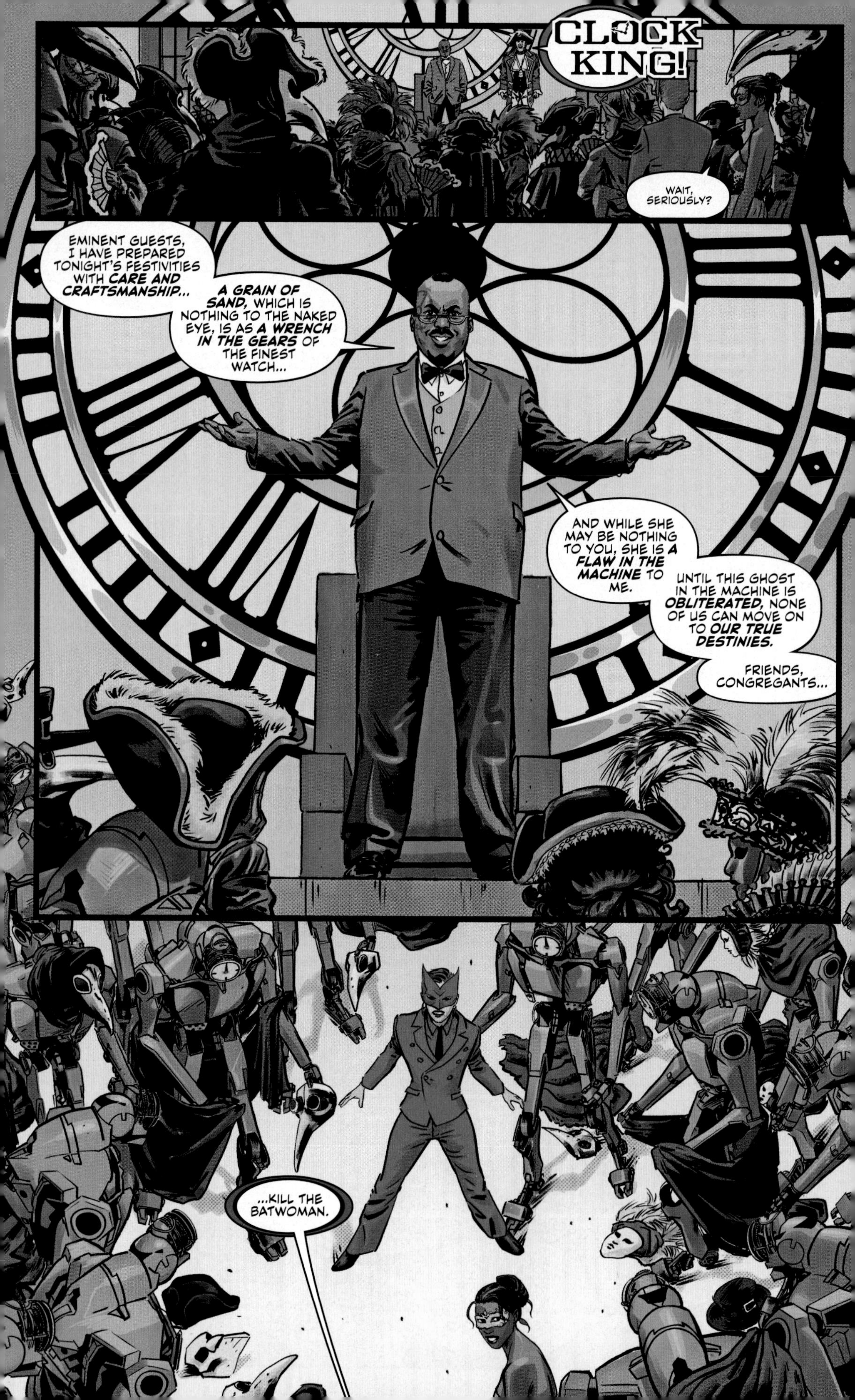
CLOCK KING!
WAIT, SERIOUSLY?
EMINENT GUESTS, I HAVE PREPARED TONIGHT'S FESTIVITIES WITH CARE AND CRAFTSMANSHIP...
A GRAIN OF SAND, WHICH IS NOTHING TO THE NAKED EYE, IS AS A WRENCH IN THE GEARS OF THE FINEST WATCH...
AND WHILE SHE MAY BE NOTHING TO YOU, SHE IS A FLAW IN THE MACHINE TO ME.
UNTIL THIS GHOST IN THE MACHINE IS OBLITERATED, NONE OF US CAN MOVE ON TO OUR TRUE DESTINIES.
FRIENDS, CONGREGANTS...
...KILL THE BATWOMAN.

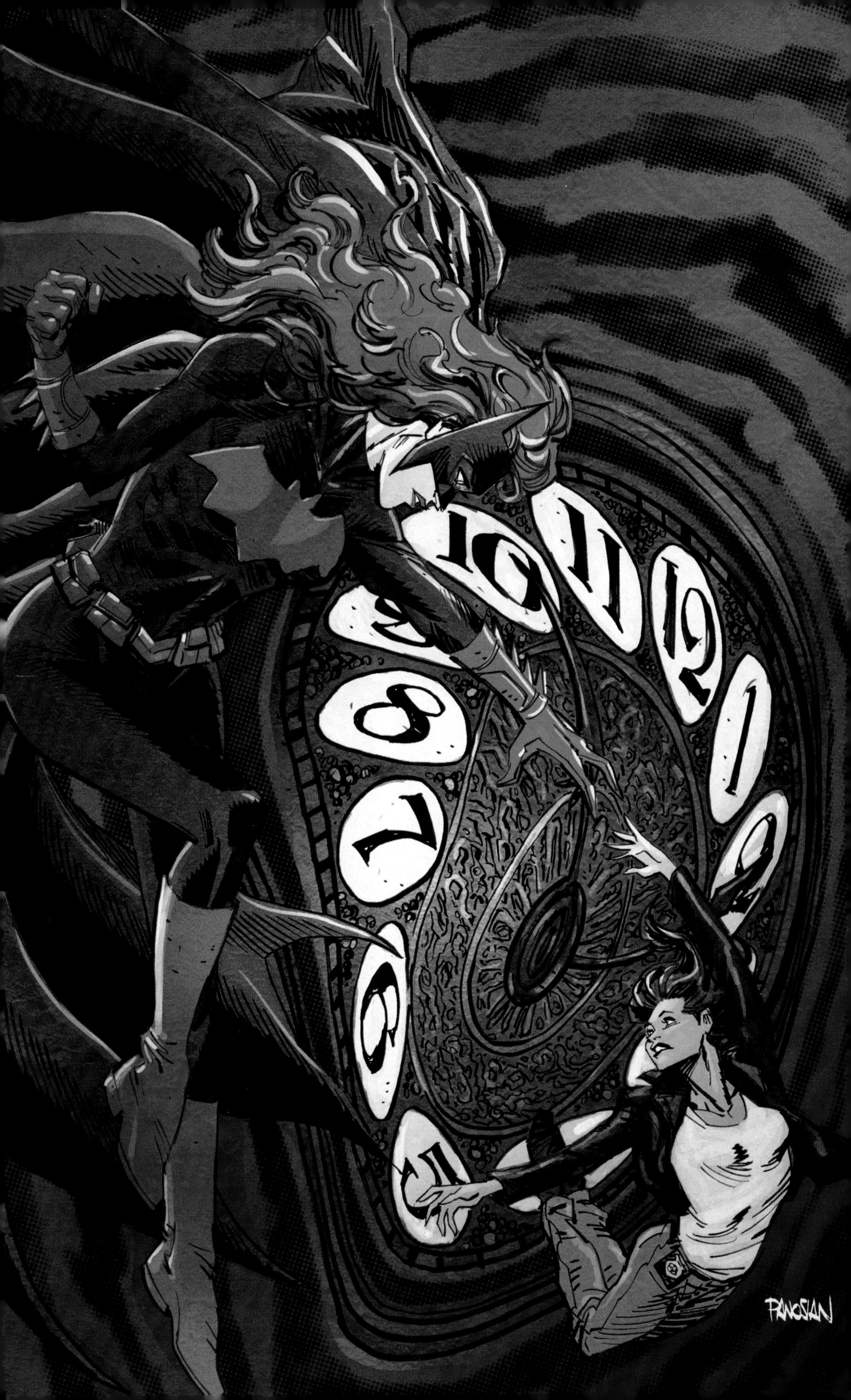
PANOSIAN

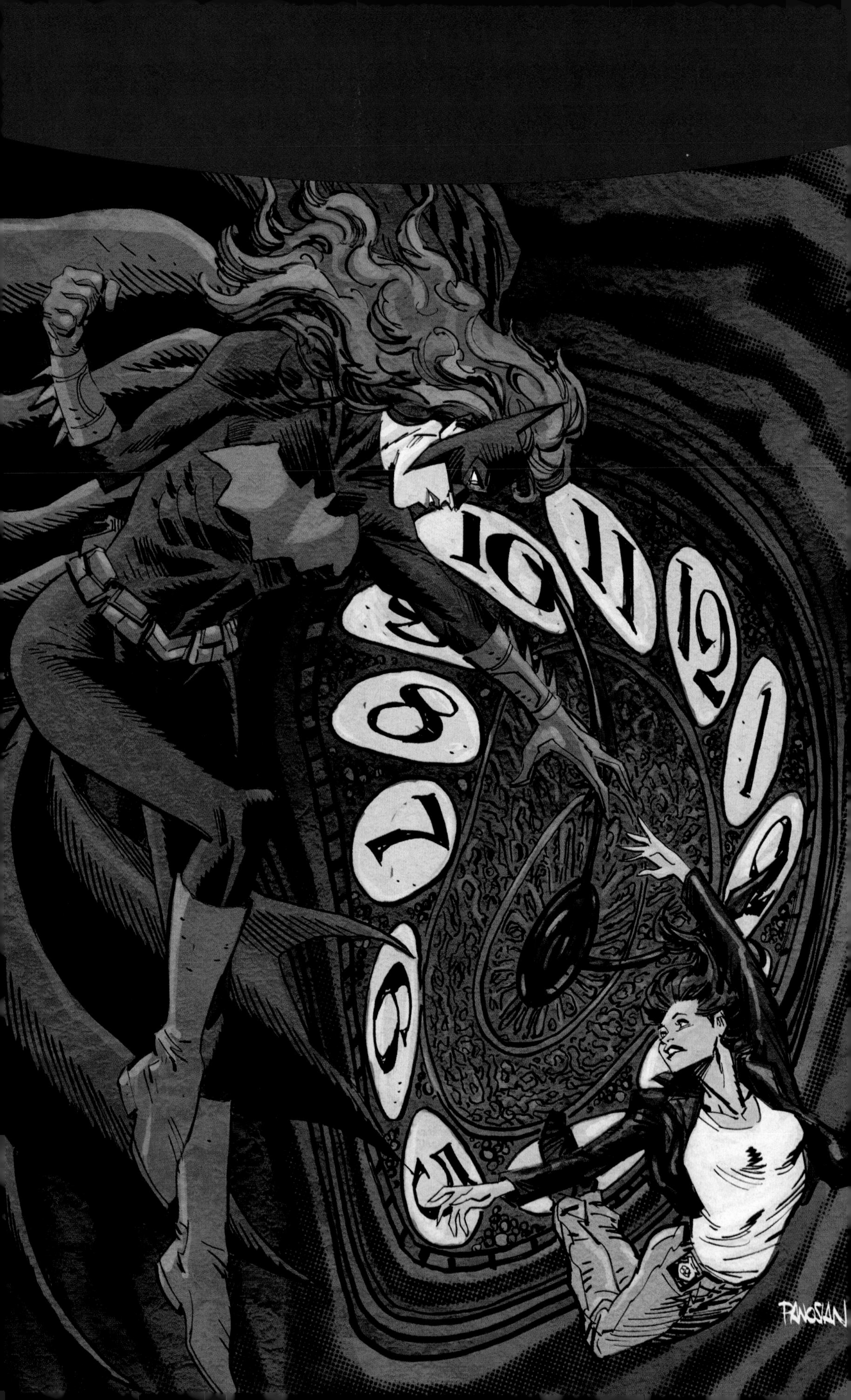
PANOSIAN

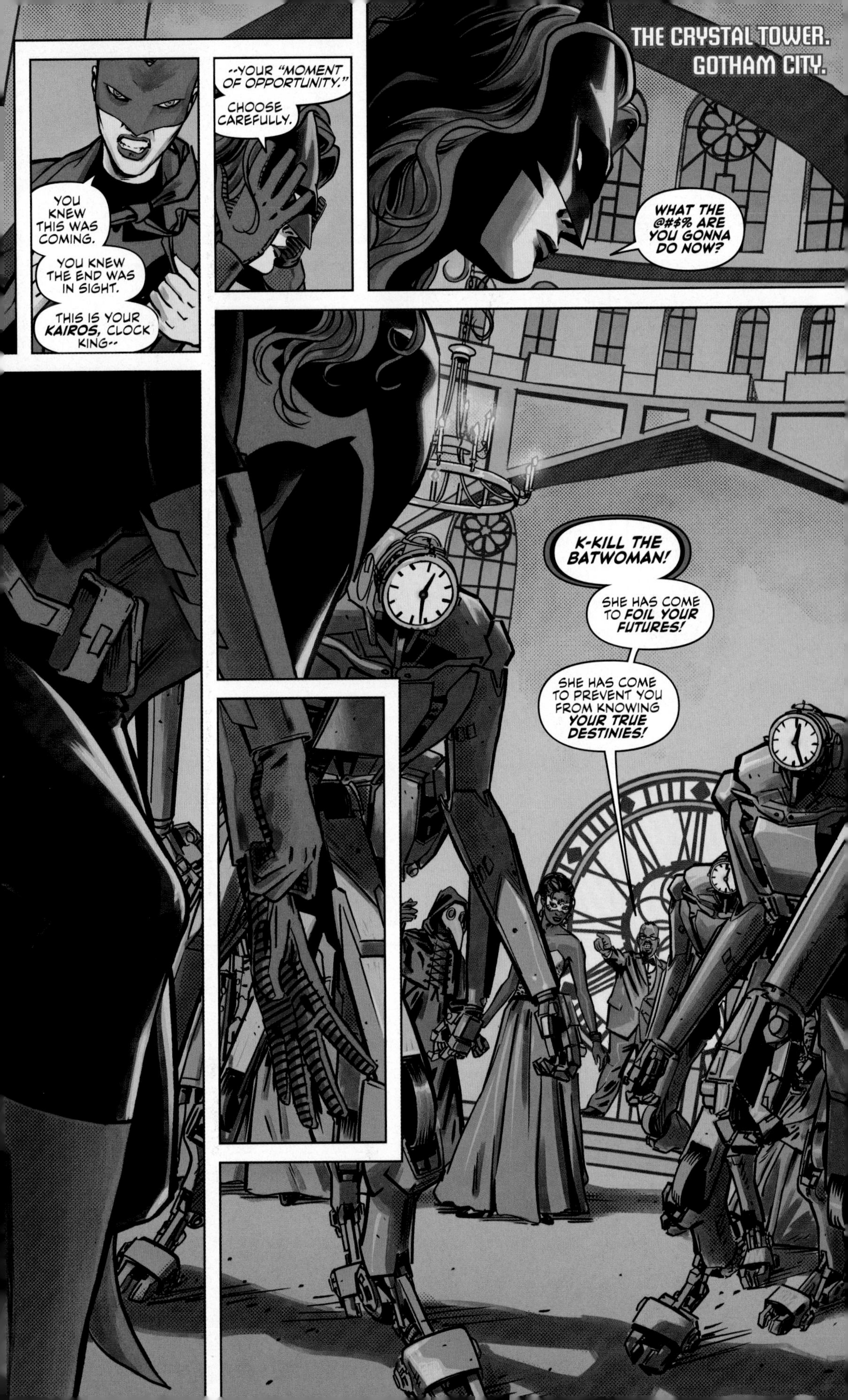

THE CRYSTAL TOWER. GOTHAM CITY.
YOU KNEW THIS WAS COMING.
YOU KNEW THE END WAS IN SIGHT.
THIS IS YOUR KAIROS, CLOCK KING--
--YOUR "MOMENT OF OPPORTUNITY."
CHOOSE CAREFULLY.
WHAT THE @#$% ARE YOU GONNA DO NOW?
K-KILL THE BATWOMAN!
SHE HAS COME TO FOIL YOUR FUTURES!
SHE HAS COME TO PREVENT YOU FROM KNOWING YOUR TRUE DESTINIES!

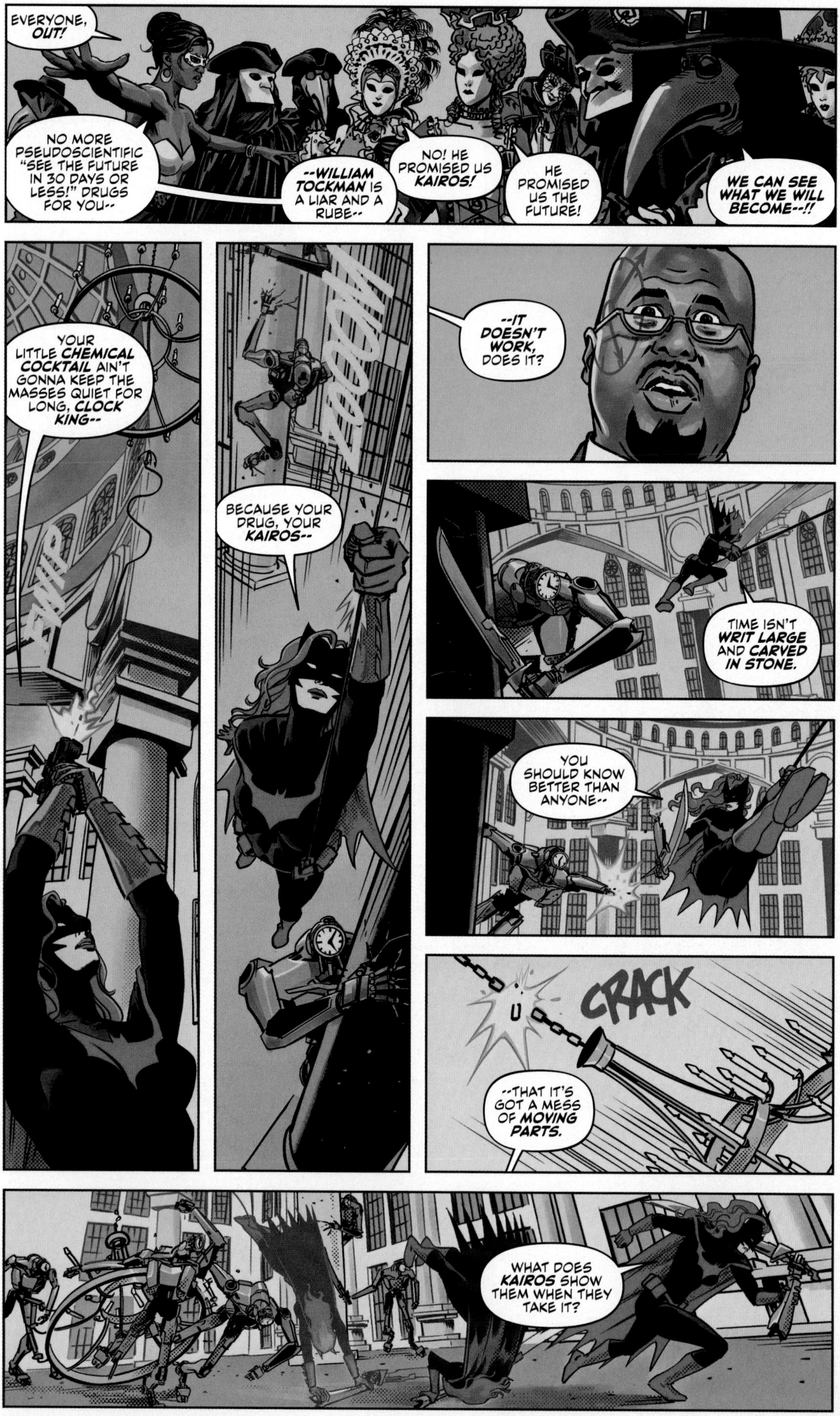
EVERYONE, OUT!
NO MORE PSEUDOSCIENTIFIC "SEE THE FUTURE IN 30 DAYS OR LESS!" DRUGS FOR YOU--
--WILLIAM TOCKMAN IS A LIAR AND A RUBE--
NO! HE PROMISED US KAIROS!
HE PROMISED US THE FUTURE!
WE CAN SEE WHAT WE WILL BECOME--!!
YOUR LITTLE CHEMICAL COCKTAIL AIN'T GONNA KEEP THE MASSES QUIET FOR LONG, CLOCK KING--
FWIP
ZOOOM
BECAUSE YOUR DRUG, YOUR KAIROS--
--IT DOESN'T WORK, DOES IT?
TIME ISN'T WRIT LARGE AND CARVED IN STONE.
YOU SHOULD KNOW BETTER THAN ANYONE--
CRACK
--THAT IT'S GOT A MESS OF MOVING PARTS.
WHAT DOES KAIROS SHOW THEM WHEN THEY TAKE IT?

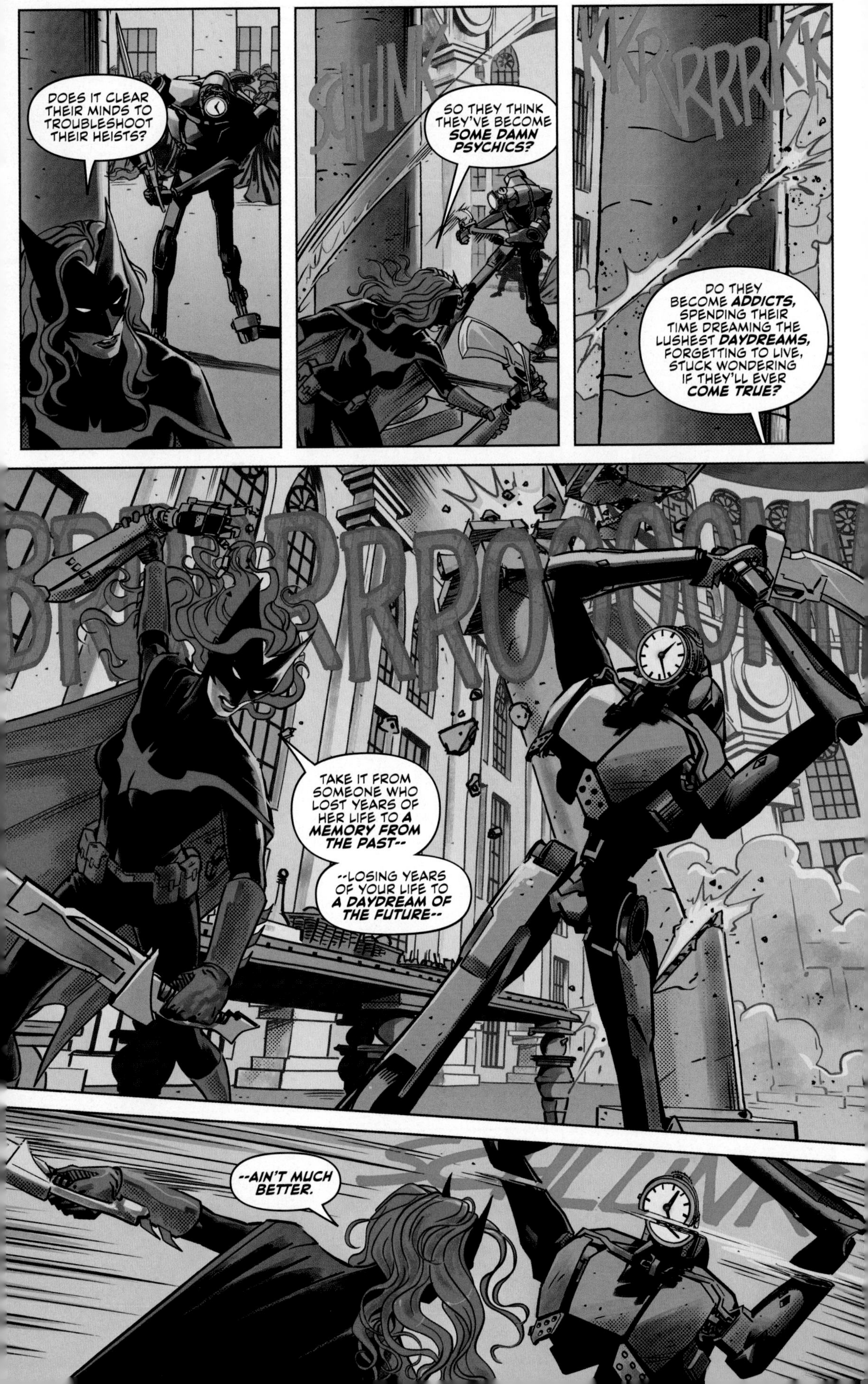
DOES IT CLEAR THEIR MINDS TO TROUBLESHOOT THEIR HEISTS?
SCHUNK
SO THEY THINK THEY'VE BECOME SOME DAMN PSYCHICS?
KKRRRRKK
DO THEY BECOME ADDICTS, SPENDING THEIR TIME DREAMING THE LUSHEST DAYDREAMS, FORGETTING TO LIVE, STUCK WONDERING IF THEY'LL EVER COME TRUE?
TAKE IT FROM SOMEONE WHO LOST YEARS OF HER LIFE TO A MEMORY FROM THE PAST--
--LOSING YEARS OF YOUR LIFE TO A DAYDREAM OF THE FUTURE--
--AIN'T MUCH BETTER.

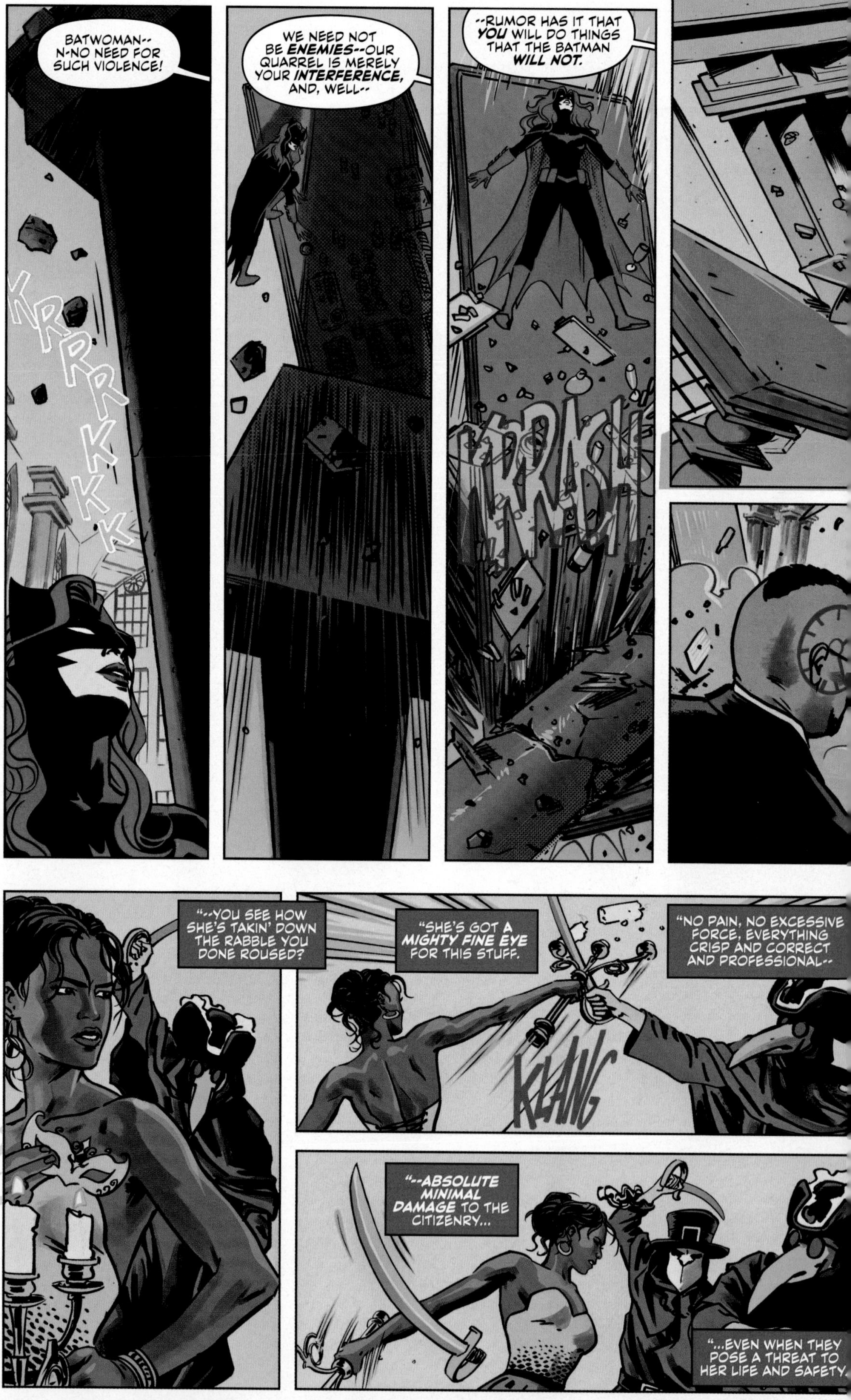
BATWOMAN-- N-NO NEED FOR SUCH VIOLENCE!
KRRRRKKKK
WE NEED NOT BE ENEMIES--OUR QUARREL IS MERELY YOUR INTERFERENCE, AND, WELL--
--RUMOR HAS IT THAT YOU WILL DO THINGS THAT THE BATMAN WILL NOT.
KRASH
"--YOU SEE HOW SHE'S TAKIN' DOWN THE RABBLE YOU DONE ROUSED?
"SHE'S GOT A MIGHTY FINE EYE FOR THIS STUFF.
"NO PAIN, NO EXCESSIVE FORCE, EVERYTHING CRISP AND CORRECT AND PROFESSIONAL--
KLANG
"--ABSOLUTE MINIMAL DAMAGE TO THE CITIZENRY...
"...EVEN WHEN THEY POSE A THREAT TO HER LIFE AND SAFETY.

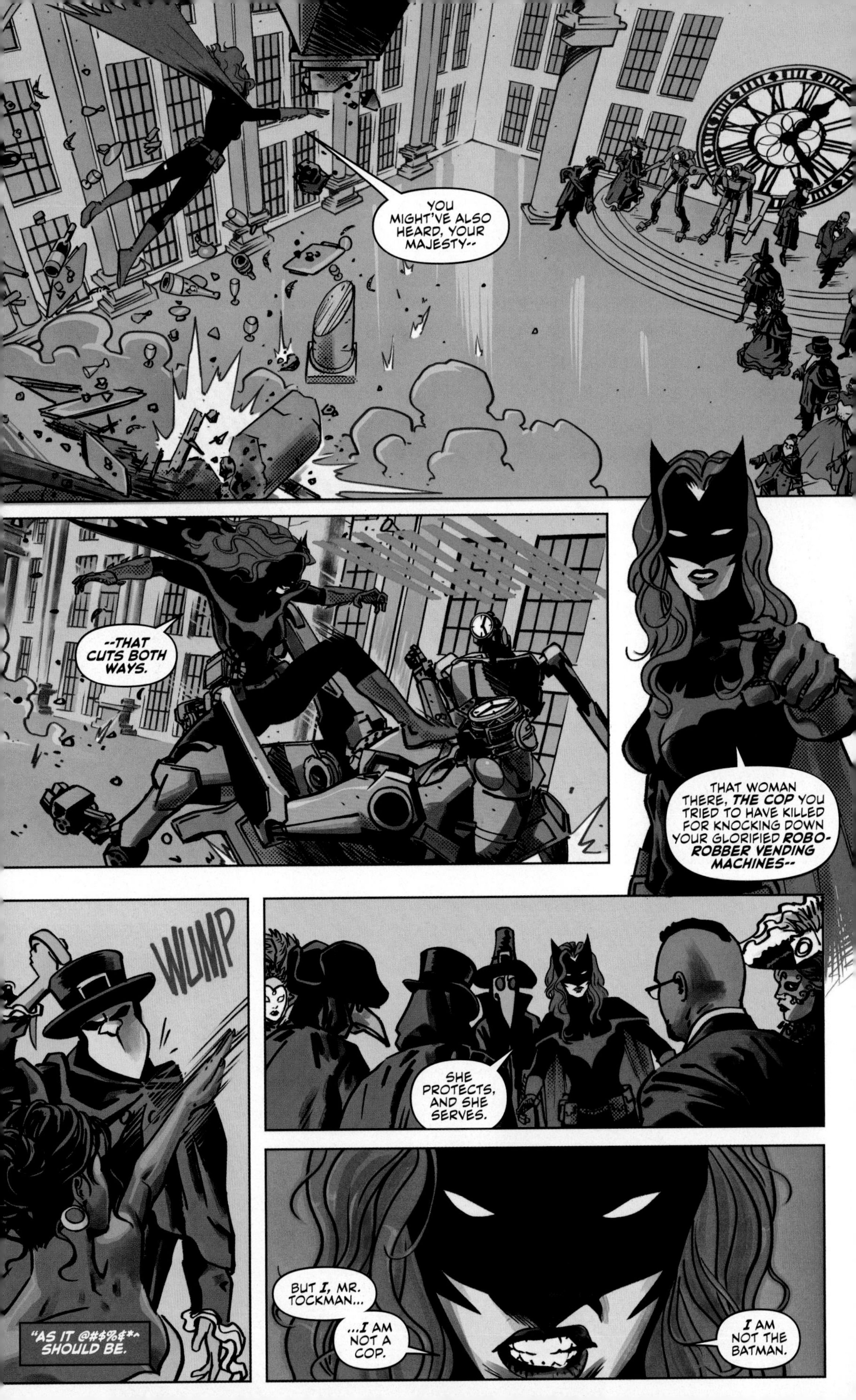
YOU MIGHT'VE ALSO HEARD, YOUR MAJESTY--
--THAT CUTS BOTH WAYS.
THAT WOMAN THERE, THE COP YOU TRIED TO HAVE KILLED FOR KNOCKING DOWN YOUR GLORIFIED ROBO-ROBBER VENDING MACHINES--
WUMP
"AS IT @#$%¢*^ SHOULD BE.
SHE PROTECTS, AND SHE SERVES.
BUT I, MR. TOCKMAN...
...I AM NOT A COP.
I AM NOT THE BATMAN.

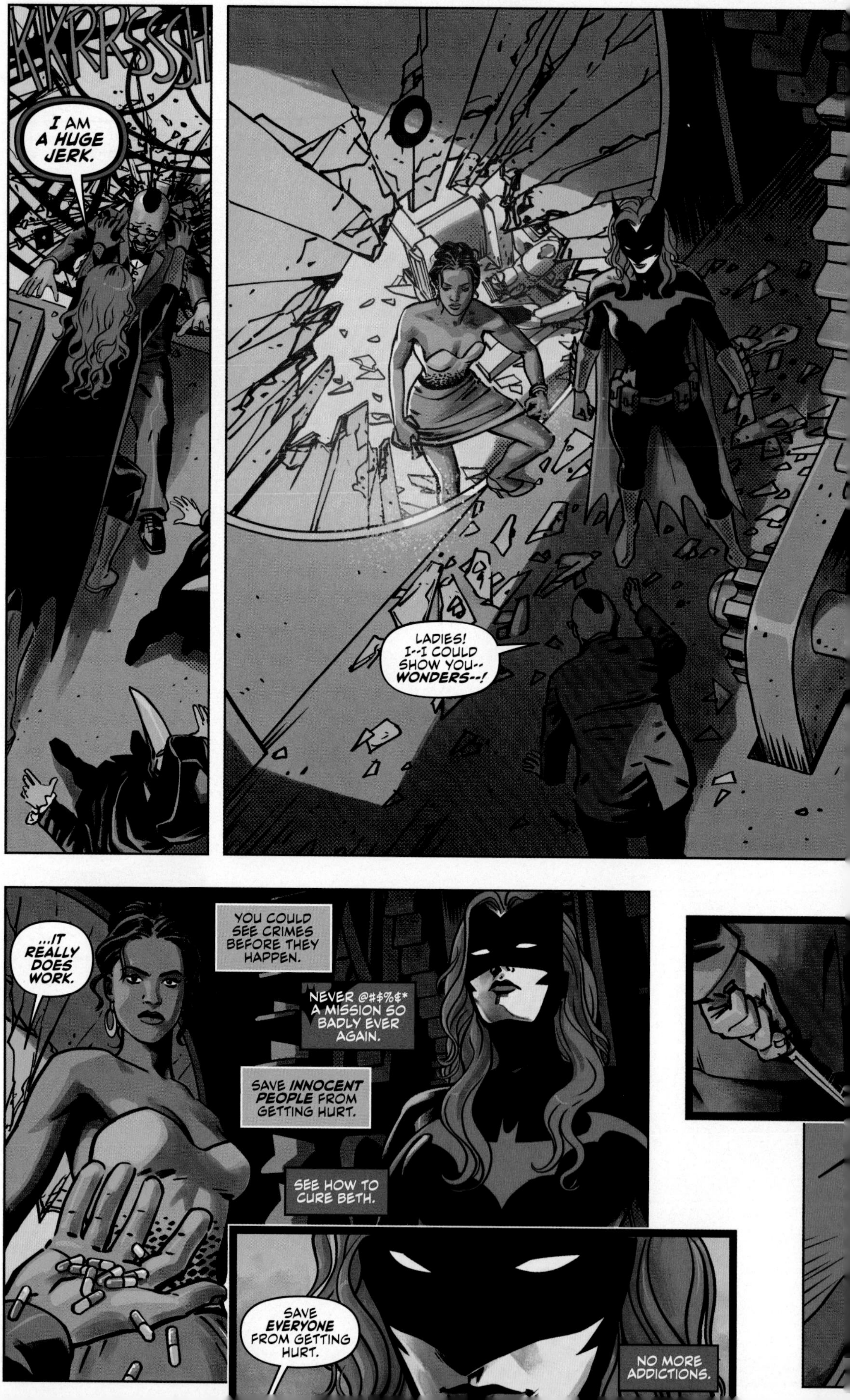
KKRRSSSH
I AM A **HUGE** JERK.
LADIES! I--I COULD SHOW YOU-- **WONDERS--!**
...IT REALLY DOES WORK.
YOU COULD SEE CRIMES BEFORE THEY HAPPEN.
NEVER @#$%¢* A MISSION SO BADLY EVER AGAIN.
SAVE **INNOCENT PEOPLE** FROM GETTING HURT.
SEE HOW TO CURE BETH.
SAVE **EVERYONE** FROM GETTING HURT.
NO MORE ADDICTIONS.

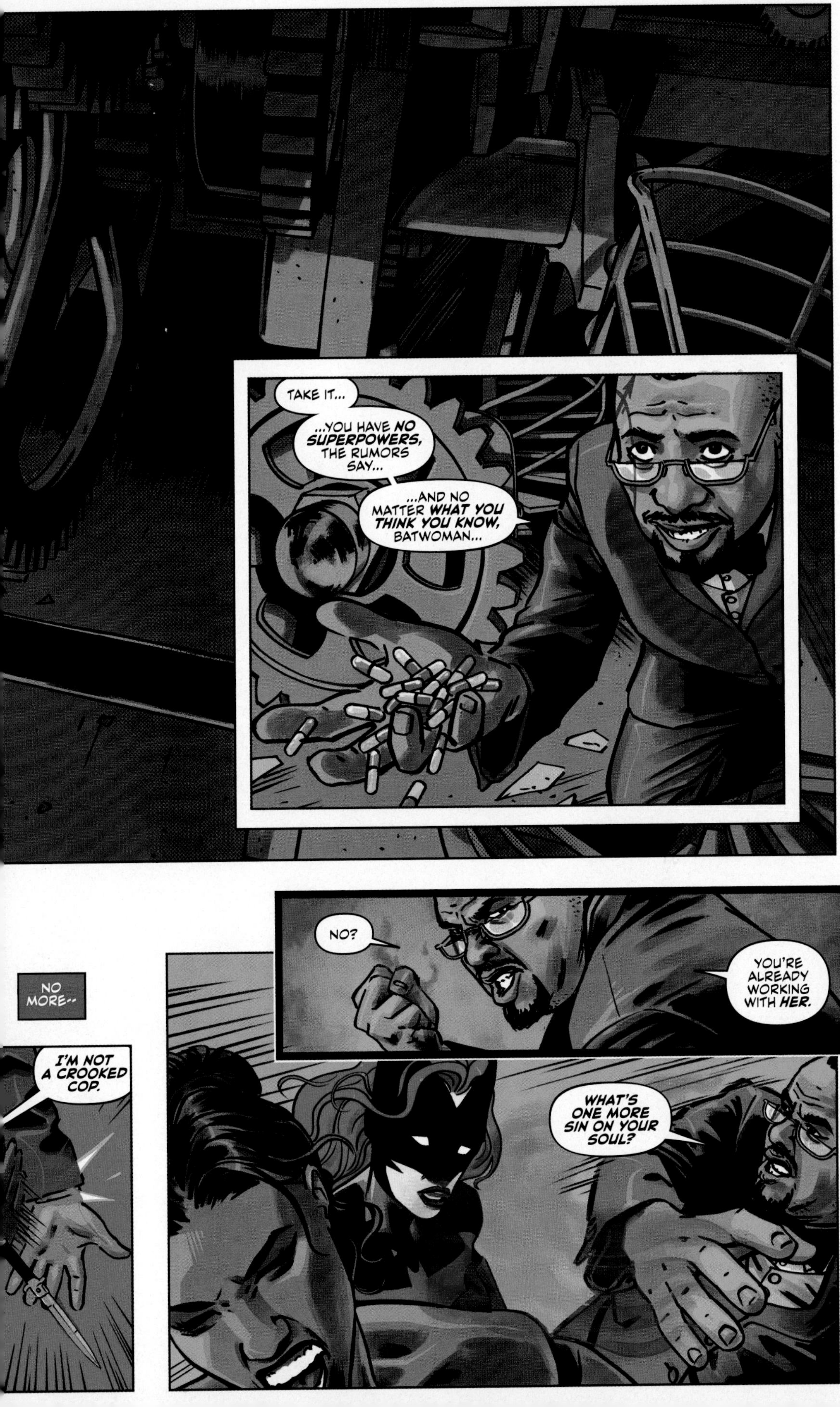
TAKE IT...
...YOU HAVE NO SUPERPOWERS, THE RUMORS SAY...
...AND NO MATTER WHAT YOU THINK YOU KNOW, BATWOMAN...
NO?
YOU'RE ALREADY WORKING WITH HER.
NO MORE--
I'M NOT A CROOKED COP.
WHAT'S ONE MORE SIN ON YOUR SOUL?

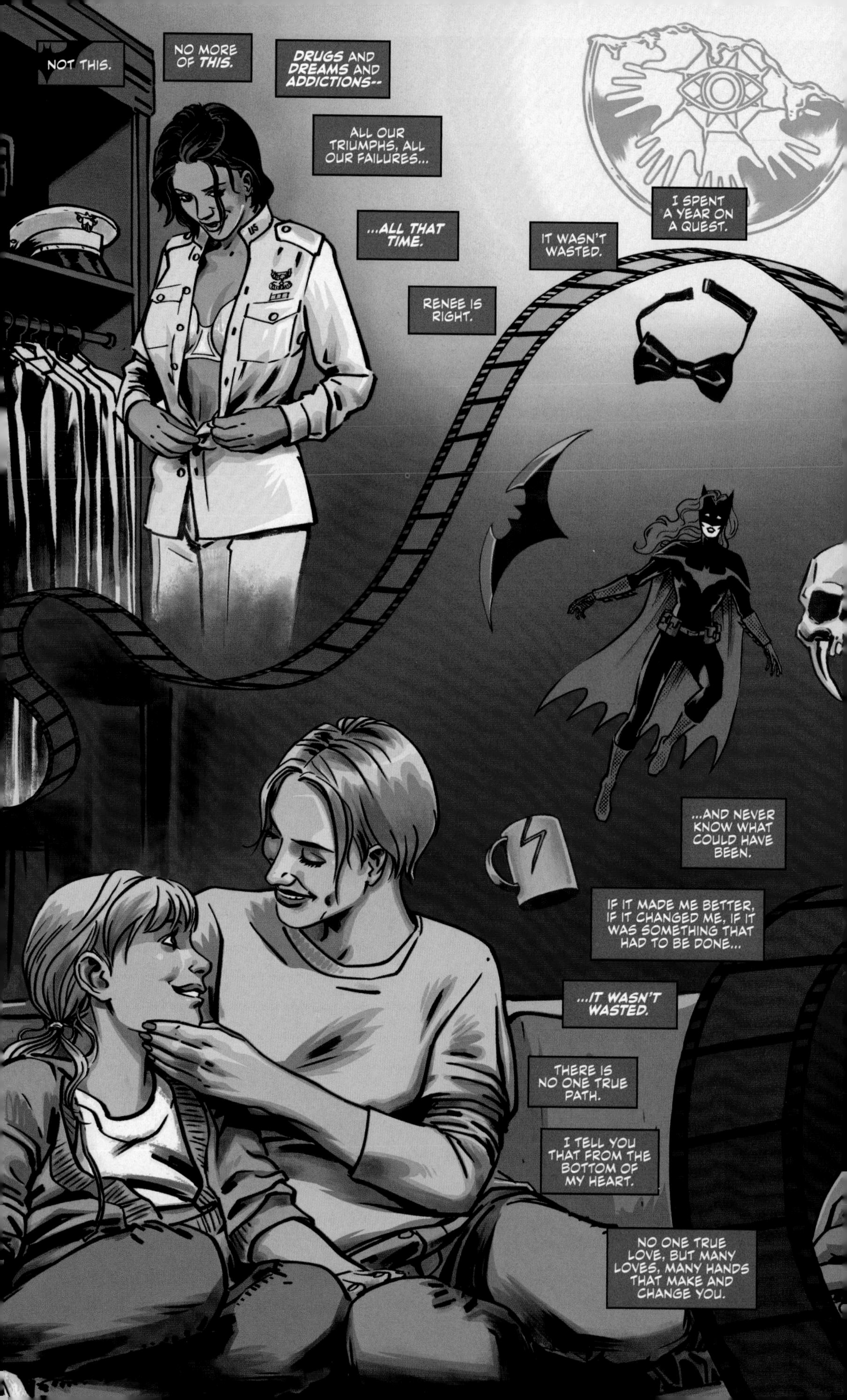
NOT THIS.
NO MORE OF *THIS.*
DRUGS AND *DREAMS* AND *ADDICTIONS--*
ALL OUR TRIUMPHS, ALL OUR FAILURES...
...ALL THAT TIME.
RENEE IS RIGHT.
IT WASN'T WASTED.
I SPENT A YEAR ON A QUEST.
...AND NEVER KNOW WHAT COULD HAVE BEEN.
IF IT MADE ME BETTER, IF IT CHANGED ME, IF IT WAS SOMETHING THAT HAD TO BE DONE...
...IT WASN'T WASTED.
THERE IS NO ONE TRUE PATH.
I TELL YOU THAT FROM THE BOTTOM OF MY HEART.
NO ONE TRUE LOVE, BUT MANY LOVES, MANY HANDS THAT MAKE AND CHANGE YOU.

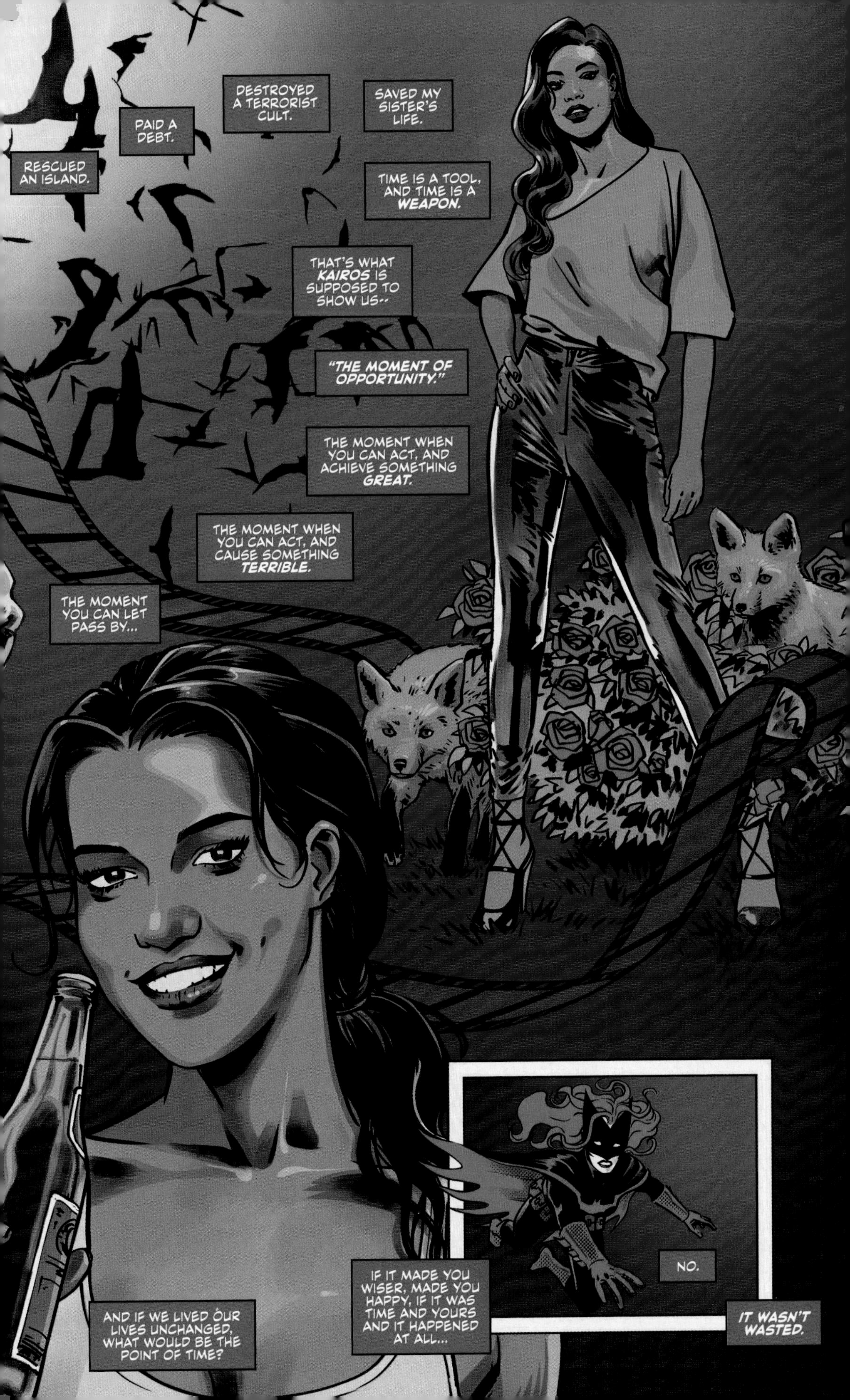
RESCUED AN ISLAND.
PAID A DEBT.
DESTROYED A TERRORIST CULT.
SAVED MY SISTER'S LIFE.
TIME IS A TOOL, AND TIME IS A WEAPON.
THAT'S WHAT KAIROS IS SUPPOSED TO SHOW US--
"THE MOMENT OF OPPORTUNITY."
THE MOMENT WHEN YOU CAN ACT, AND ACHIEVE SOMETHING GREAT.
THE MOMENT WHEN YOU CAN ACT, AND CAUSE SOMETHING TERRIBLE.
THE MOMENT YOU CAN LET PASS BY...
AND IF WE LIVED OUR LIVES UNCHANGED, WHAT WOULD BE THE POINT OF TIME?
IF IT MADE YOU WISER, MADE YOU HAPPY, IF IT WAS TIME AND YOURS AND IT HAPPENED AT ALL...
NO.
IT WASN'T WASTED.

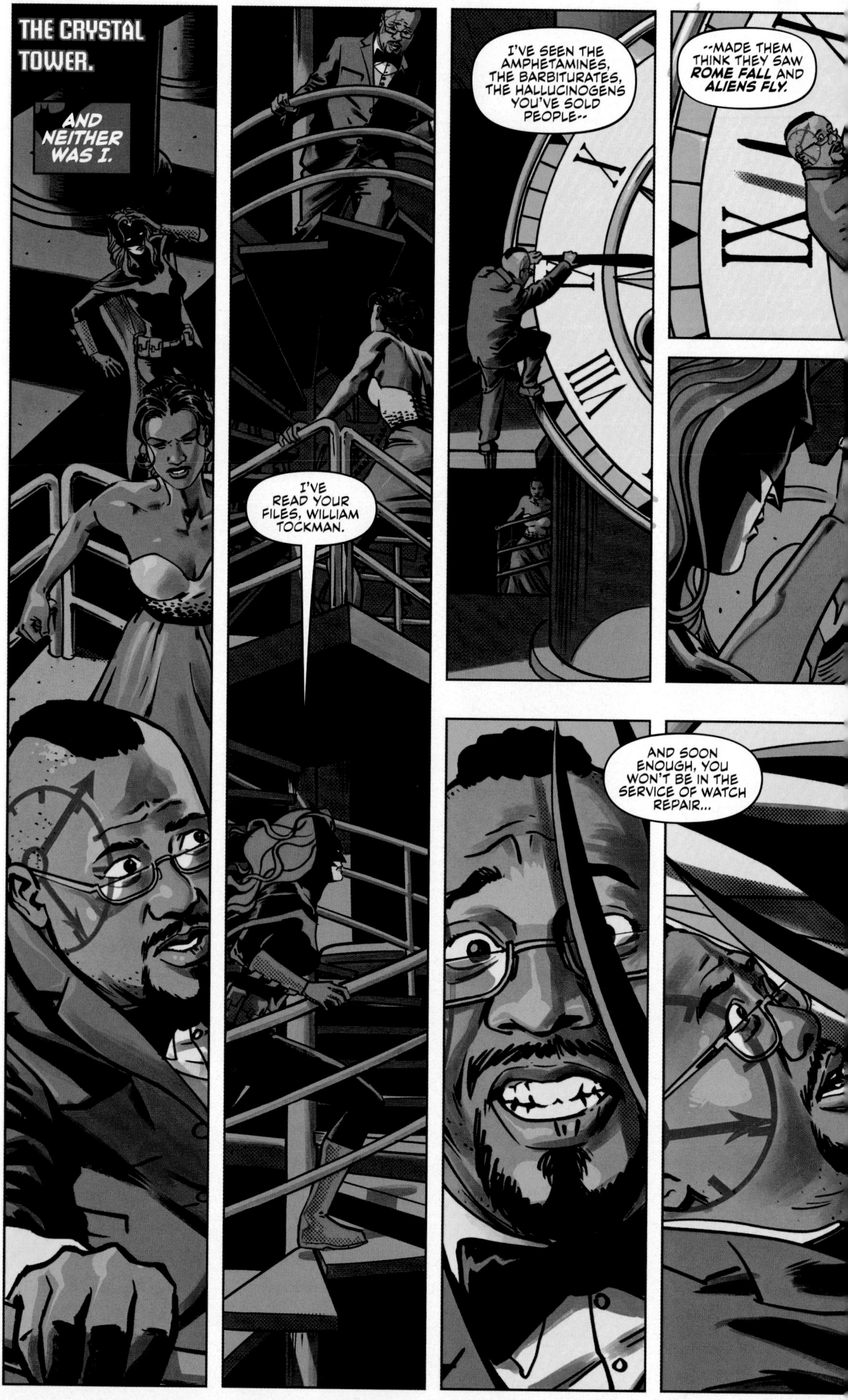
THE CRYSTAL TOWER.
AND NEITHER WAS I.
I'VE READ YOUR FILES, WILLIAM TOCKMAN.
I'VE SEEN THE AMPHETAMINES, THE BARBITURATES, THE HALLUCINOGENS YOU'VE SOLD PEOPLE--
--MADE THEM THINK THEY SAW ROME FALL AND ALIENS FLY.
AND SOON ENOUGH, YOU WON'T BE IN THE SERVICE OF WATCH REPAIR...

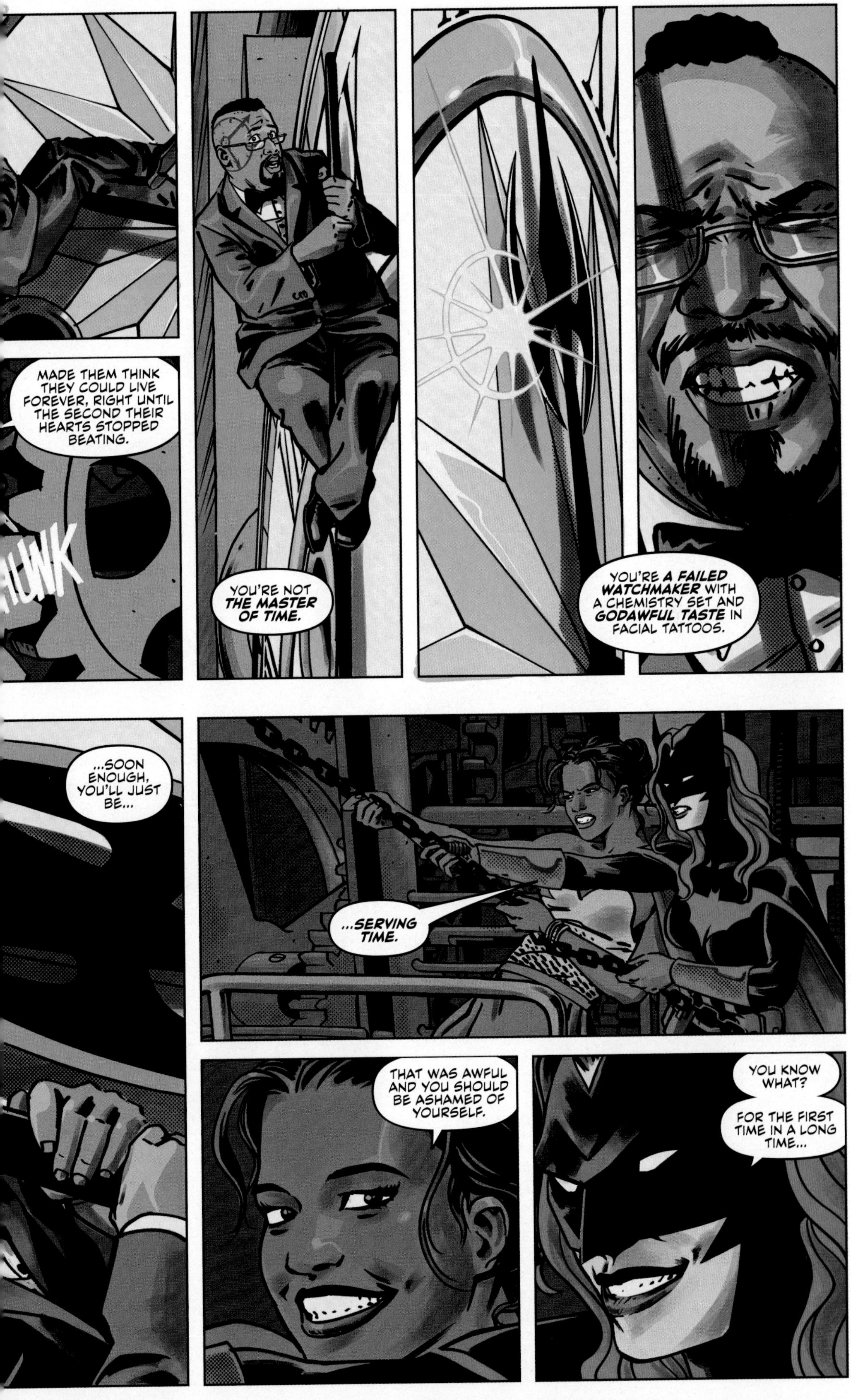
MADE THEM THINK THEY COULD LIVE FOREVER, RIGHT UNTIL THE SECOND THEIR HEARTS STOPPED BEATING.
HUNK
YOU'RE NOT THE MASTER OF TIME.
YOU'RE A FAILED WATCHMAKER WITH A CHEMISTRY SET AND GODAWFUL TASTE IN FACIAL TATTOOS.
...SOON ENOUGH, YOU'LL JUST BE...
...SERVING TIME.
THAT WAS AWFUL AND YOU SHOULD BE ASHAMED OF YOURSELF.
YOU KNOW WHAT?
FOR THE FIRST TIME IN A LONG TIME...

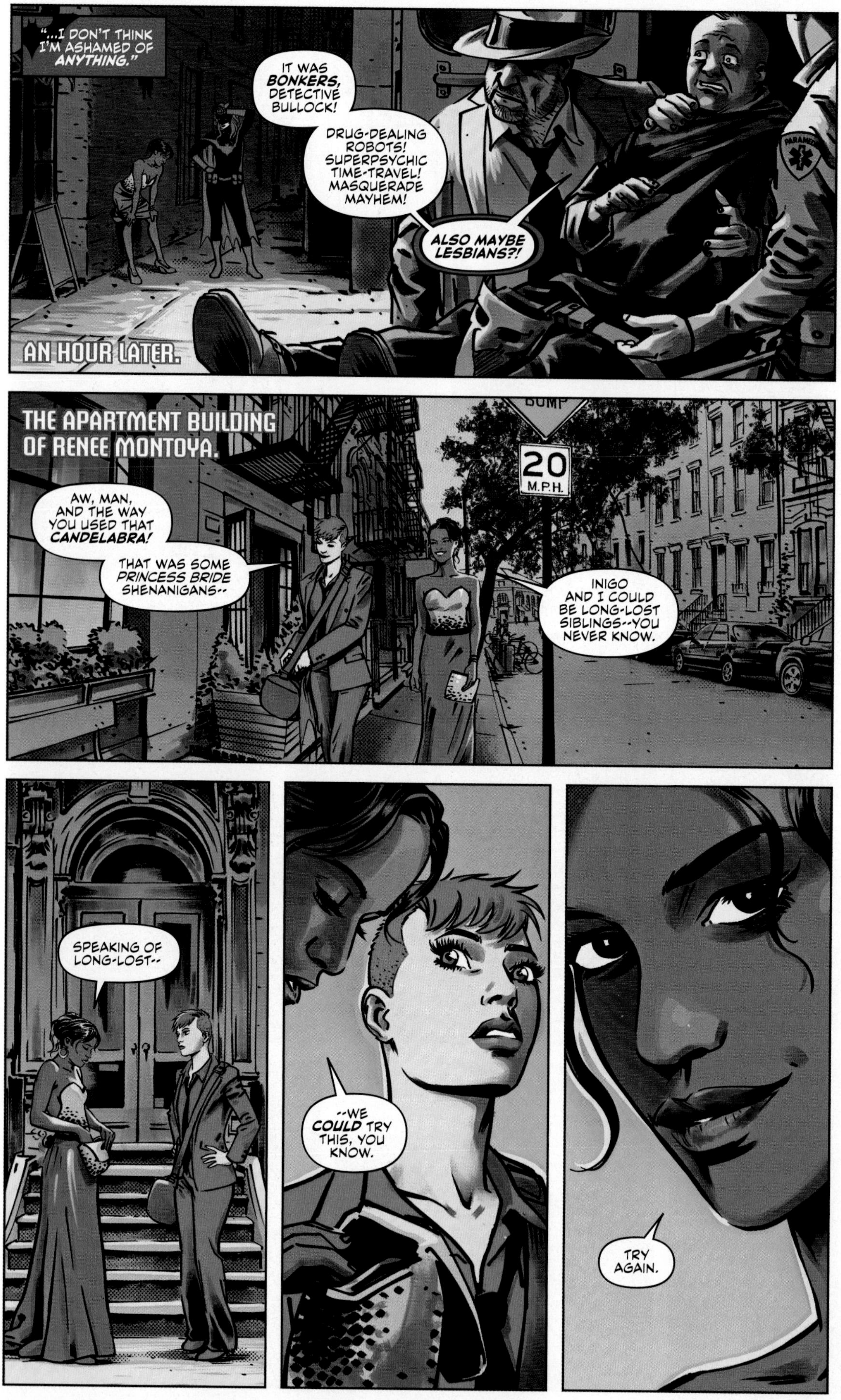
"...I DON'T THINK I'M ASHAMED OF *ANYTHING.*"
IT WAS *BONKERS,* DETECTIVE BULLOCK!
DRUG-DEALING ROBOTS! SUPERPSYCHIC TIME-TRAVEL! MASQUERADE MAYHEM!
ALSO MAYBE LESBIANS?!
AN HOUR LATER.
THE APARTMENT BUILDING OF RENEE MONTOYA.
BUMP
20
M.P.H.
AW, MAN, AND THE WAY YOU USED THAT *CANDELABRA!*
THAT WAS SOME *PRINCESS BRIDE* SHENANIGANS--
INIGO AND I COULD BE LONG-LOST SIBLINGS--YOU NEVER KNOW.
SPEAKING OF LONG-LOST--
--WE *COULD* TRY THIS, YOU KNOW.
TRY AGAIN.

NO... WHAT AM I SAYING?

NOT *AGAIN*.

NO MORE *"AGAIN,"* TIME-IS-A-FLAT-CIRCLE *NONSENSE*.

KATE KANE...

WHAT WOULD YOU SAY TO *A FIRST DATE?*

SPICY KBBQ DOWN ON 14TH...

...OR YOU COME OVER, AND I MAKE *HONEY-BUTTER FRIED CHICKEN.*

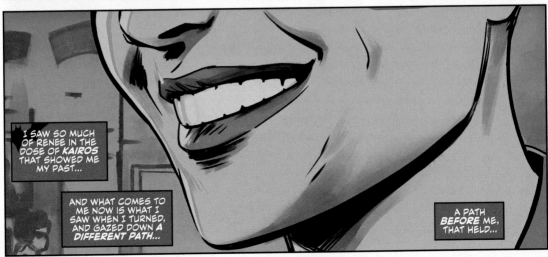

I SAW SO MUCH OF RENE IN THE DOSE OF *KAIROS* THAT SHOWED ME MY PAST...

AND WHAT COMES TO ME NOW IS WHAT I SAW WHEN I TURNED, AND GAZED DOWN *A DIFFERENT PATH...*

A PATH *BEFORE* ME, THAT HELD...

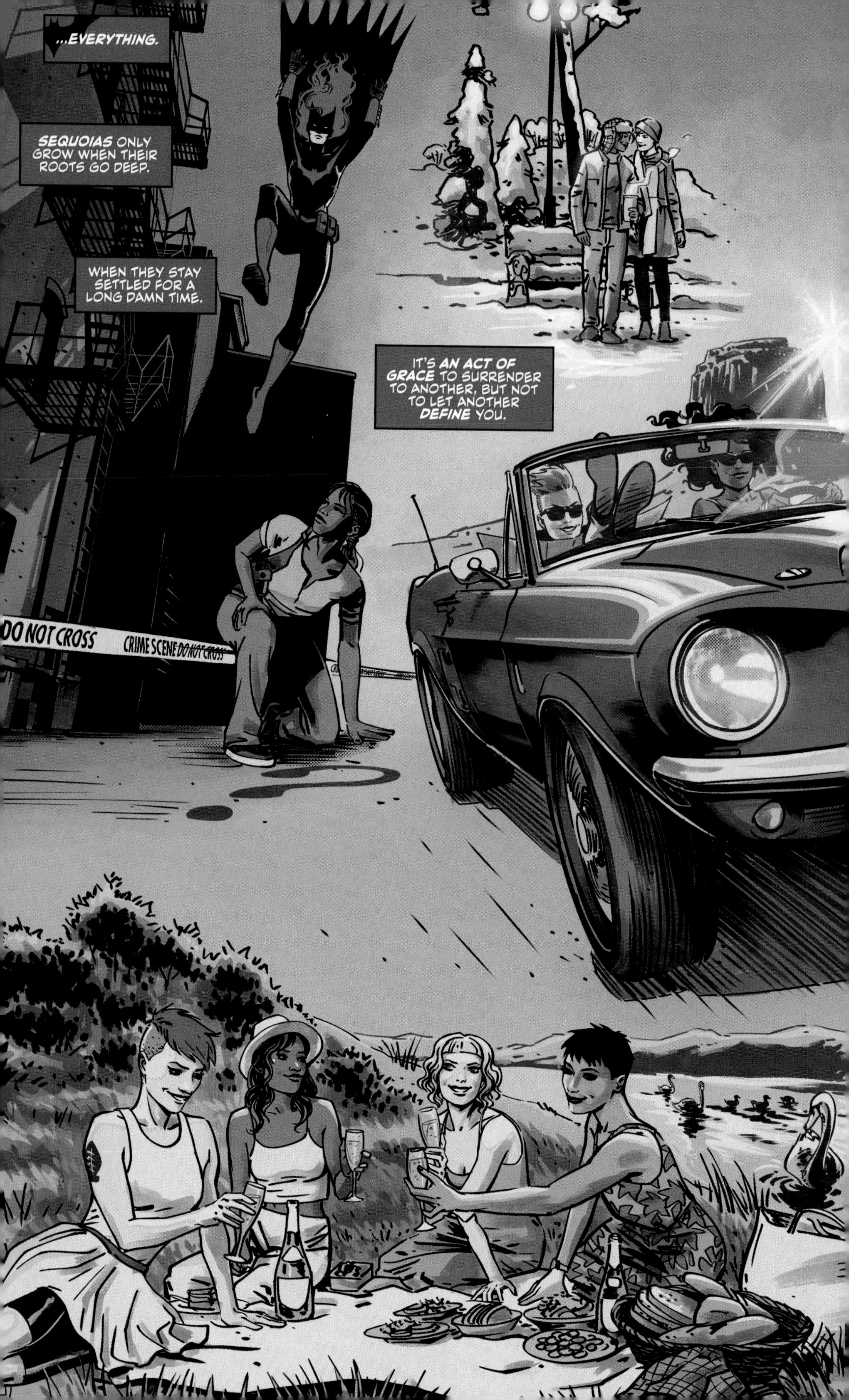
...EVERYTHING.
SEQUOIAS ONLY GROW WHEN THEIR ROOTS GO DEEP.
WHEN THEY STAY SETTLED FOR A LONG DAMN TIME.
IT'S AN ACT OF GRACE TO SURRENDER TO ANOTHER, BUT NOT TO LET ANOTHER DEFINE YOU.
DO NOT CROSS
CRIME SCENE DO NOT CROSS

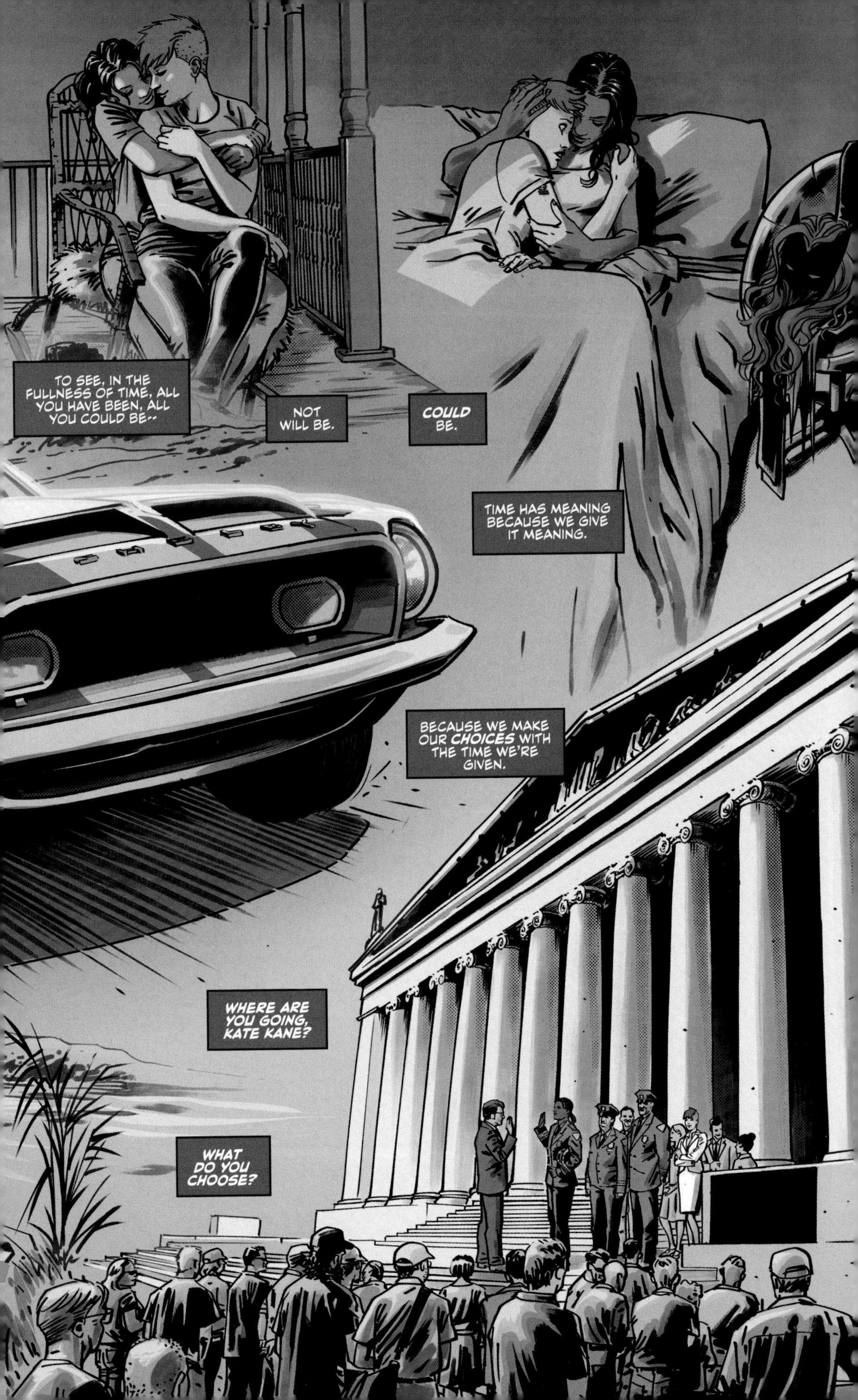
TO SEE, IN THE FULLNESS OF TIME, ALL YOU HAVE BEEN, ALL YOU COULD BE--
NOT WILL BE.
COULD BE.
TIME HAS MEANING BECAUSE WE GIVE IT MEANING.
BECAUSE WE MAKE OUR *CHOICES* WITH THE TIME WE'RE GIVEN.
WHERE ARE YOU GOING, KATE KANE?
WHAT DO YOU CHOOSE?

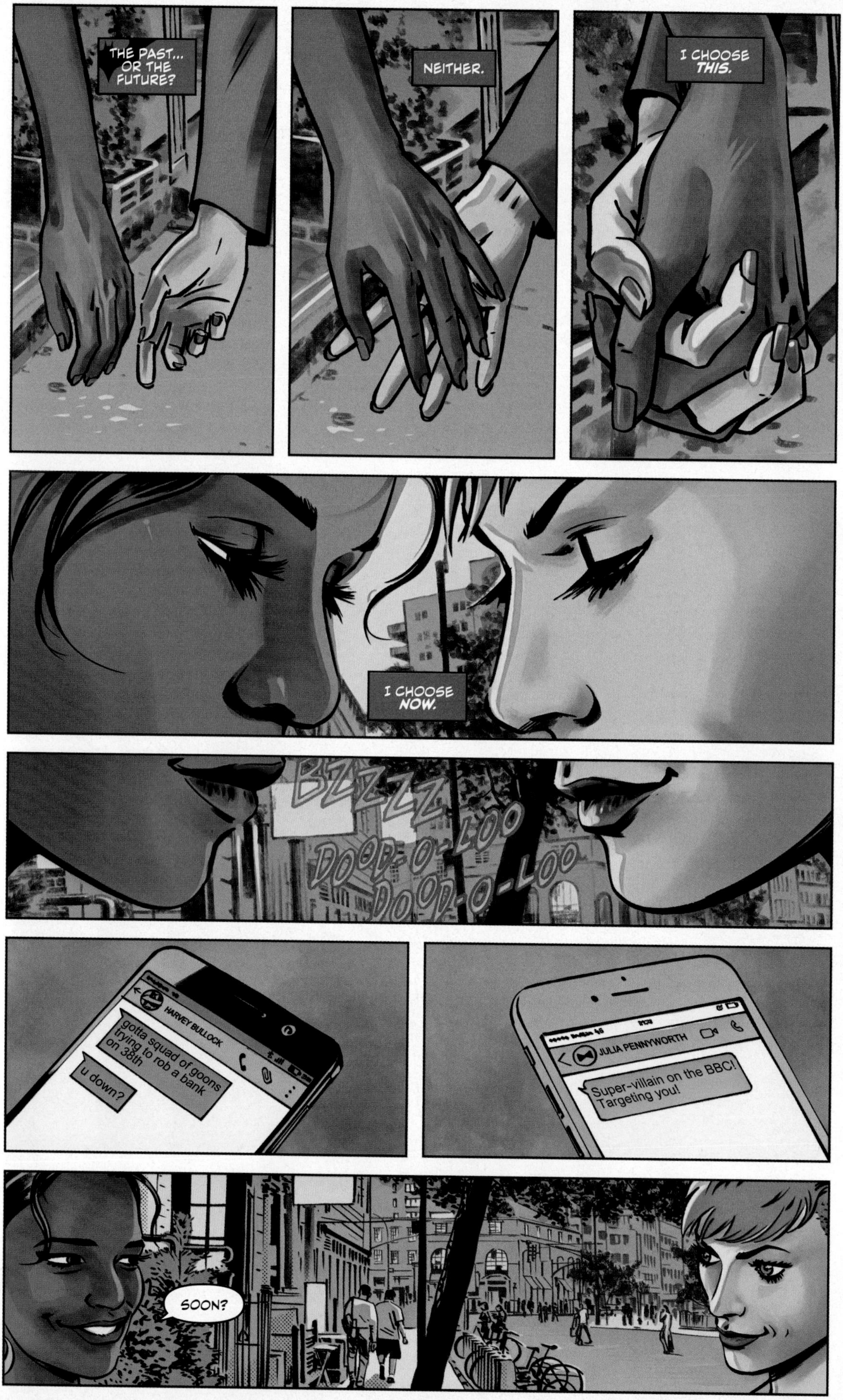
THE PAST... OR THE FUTURE?
NEITHER.
I CHOOSE THIS.
I CHOOSE NOW.
BZZZZ
DOOD-O-LOO DOOD-O-LOO
HARVEY BULLOCK
gotta squad of goons trying to rob a bank on 38th
u down?
JULIA PENNYWORTH
Super-villain on the BBC! Targeting you!
SOON?

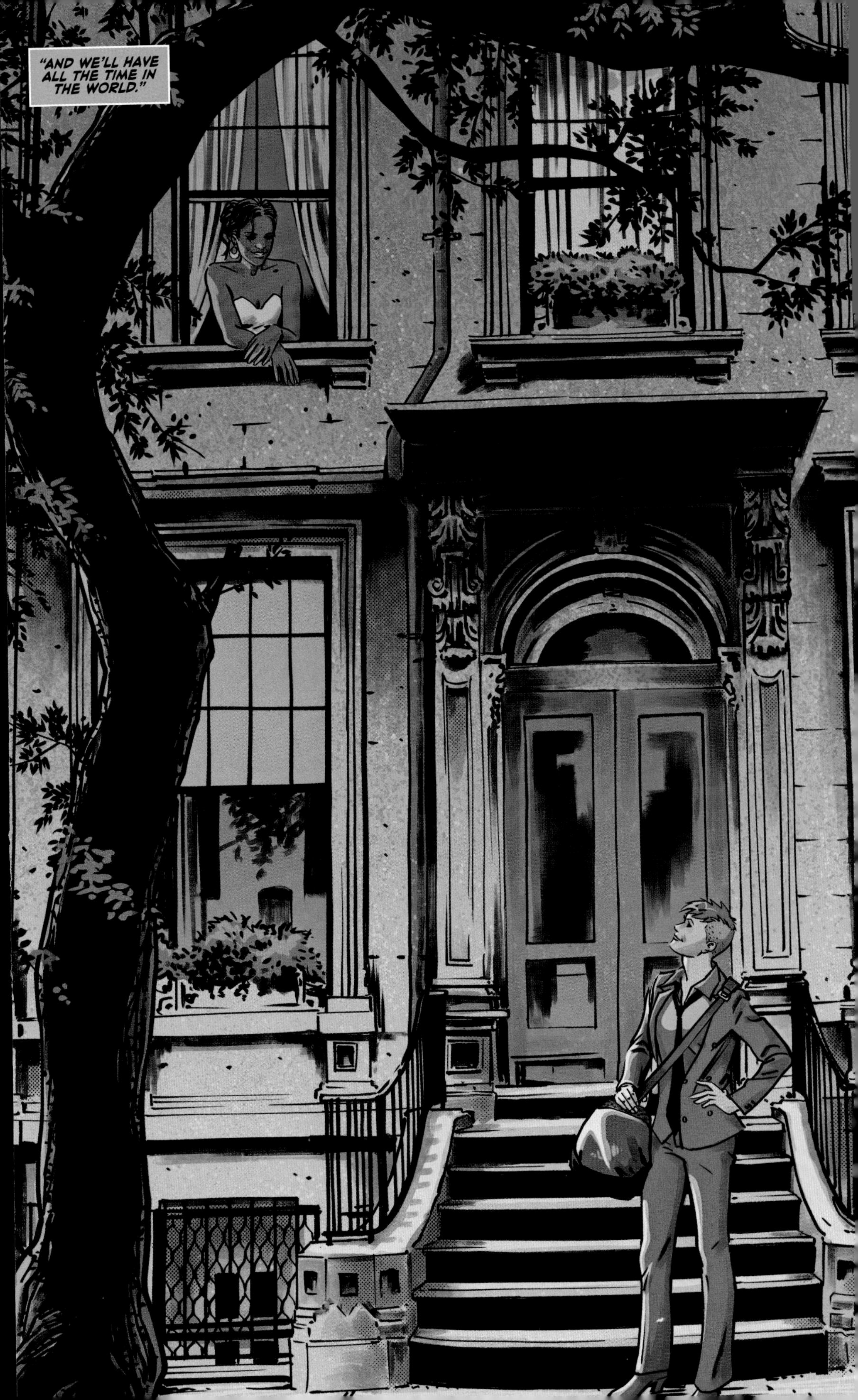
"AND WE'LL HAVE ALL THE TIME IN THE WORLD."

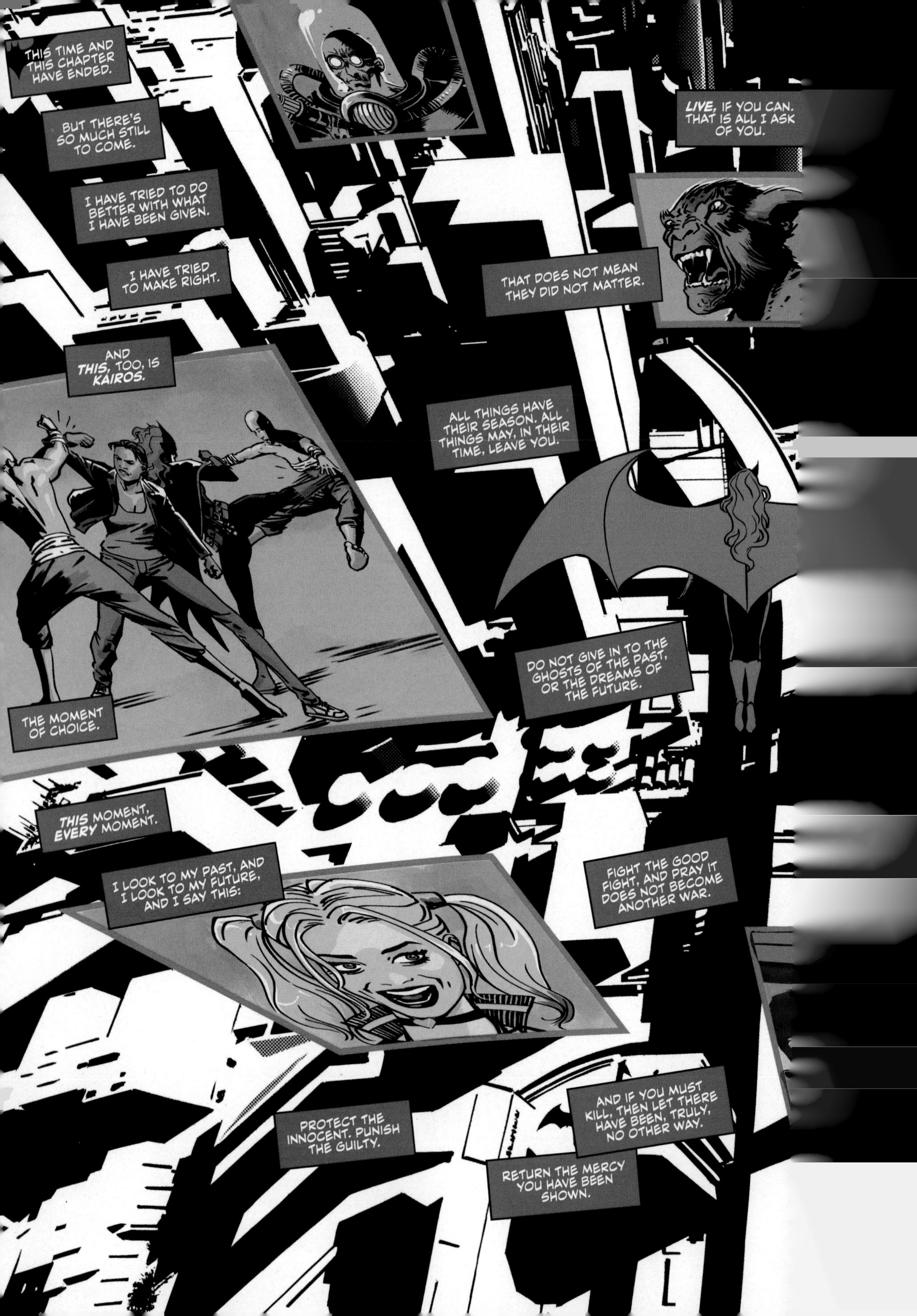
THIS TIME AND THIS CHAPTER HAVE ENDED.
BUT THERE'S SO MUCH STILL TO COME.
I HAVE TRIED TO DO BETTER WITH WHAT I HAVE BEEN GIVEN.
I HAVE TRIED TO MAKE RIGHT.
LIVE, IF YOU CAN. THAT IS ALL I ASK OF YOU.
THAT DOES NOT MEAN THEY DID NOT MATTER.
AND THIS, TOO, IS KAIROS.
ALL THINGS HAVE THEIR SEASON. ALL THINGS MAY, IN THEIR TIME, LEAVE YOU.
THE MOMENT OF CHOICE.
DO NOT GIVE IN TO THE GHOSTS OF THE PAST, OR THE DREAMS OF THE FUTURE.
THIS MOMENT, EVERY MOMENT.
I LOOK TO MY PAST, AND I LOOK TO MY FUTURE, AND I SAY THIS:
FIGHT THE GOOD FIGHT, AND PRAY IT DOES NOT BECOME ANOTHER WAR.
PROTECT THE INNOCENT. PUNISH THE GUILTY.
AND IF YOU MUST KILL, THEN LET THERE HAVE BEEN, TRULY, NO OTHER WAY.
RETURN THE MERCY YOU HAVE BEEN SHOWN.

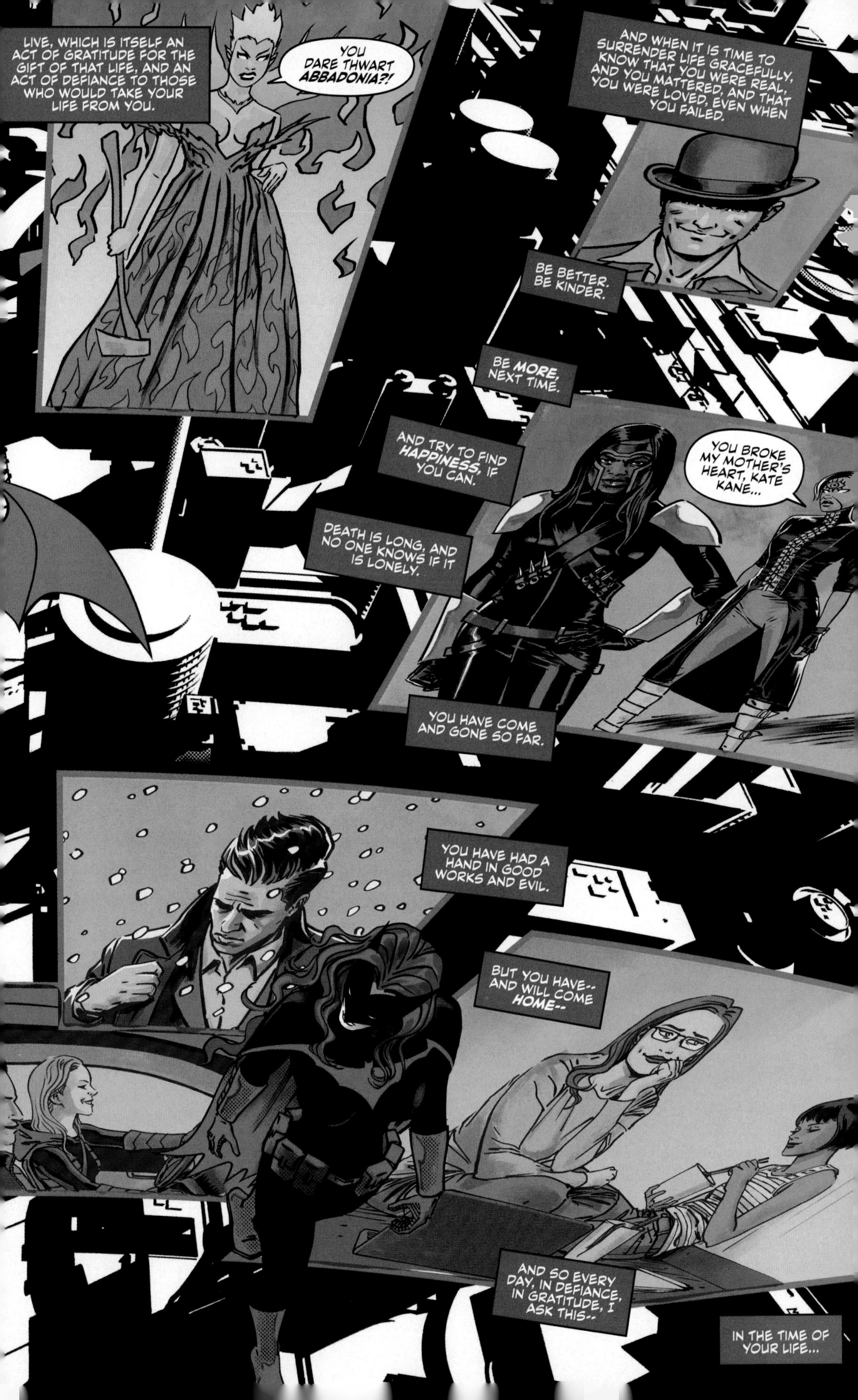

LIVE, WHICH IS ITSELF AN ACT OF GRATITUDE FOR THE GIFT OF THAT LIFE, AND AN ACT OF DEFIANCE TO THOSE WHO WOULD TAKE YOUR LIFE FROM YOU.
YOU DARE THWART ABBADONIA?!
AND WHEN IT IS TIME TO SURRENDER LIFE GRACEFULLY, KNOW THAT YOU WERE REAL, AND YOU MATTERED, AND THAT YOU WERE LOVED, EVEN WHEN YOU FAILED.
BE BETTER. BE KINDER.
BE MORE, NEXT TIME.
AND TRY TO FIND HAPPINESS, IF YOU CAN.
YOU BROKE MY MOTHER'S HEART, KATE KANE...
DEATH IS LONG, AND NO ONE KNOWS IF IT IS LONELY.
YOU HAVE COME AND GONE SO FAR.
YOU HAVE HAD A HAND IN GOOD WORKS AND EVIL.
BUT YOU HAVE-- AND WILL COME HOME--
AND SO EVERY DAY, IN DEFIANCE, IN GRATITUDE, I ASK THIS--
IN THE TIME OF YOUR LIFE...

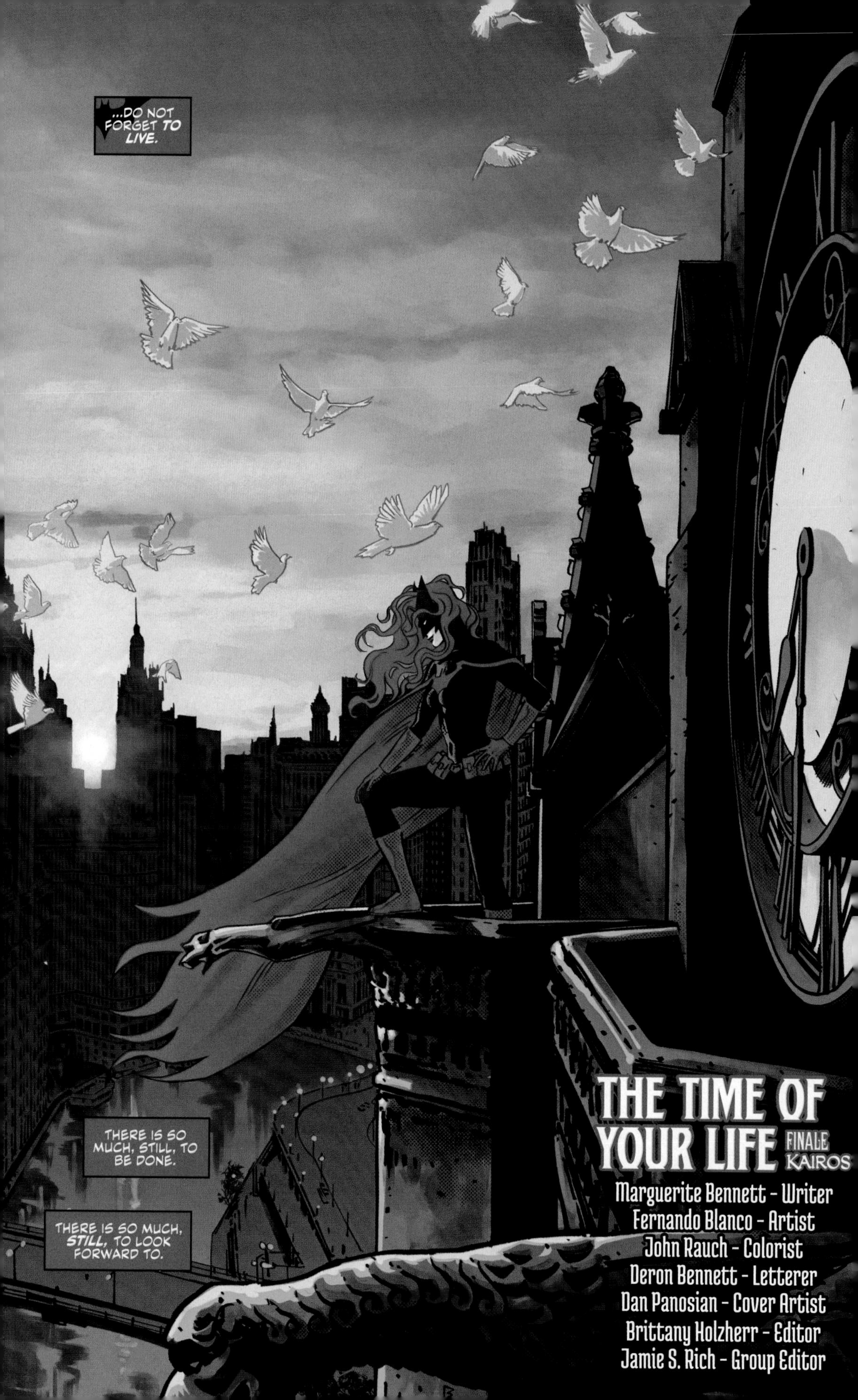
...DO NOT FORGET TO LIVE.
THERE IS SO MUCH, STILL, TO BE DONE.
THERE IS SO MUCH, STILL, TO LOOK FORWARD TO.
THE TIME OF YOUR LIFE FINALE KAIROS
Marguerite Bennett - Writer
Fernando Blanco - Artist
John Rauch - Colorist
Deron Bennett - Letterer
Dan Panosian - Cover Artist
Brittany Holzherr - Editor
Jamie S. Rich - Group Editor

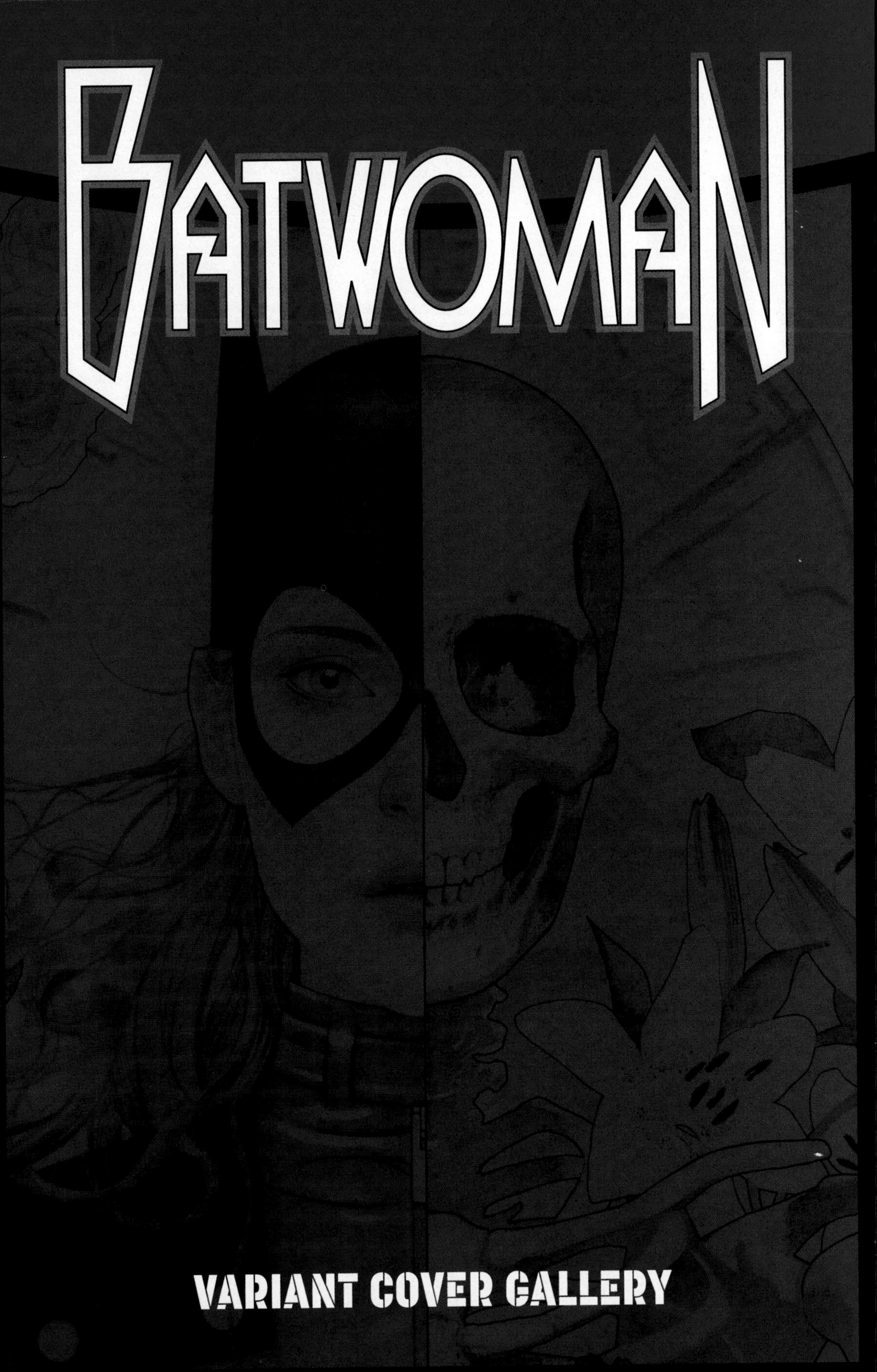
BATWOMAN
VARIANT COVER GALLERY

BATWOMAN #12 variant cover by MICHAEL CHO

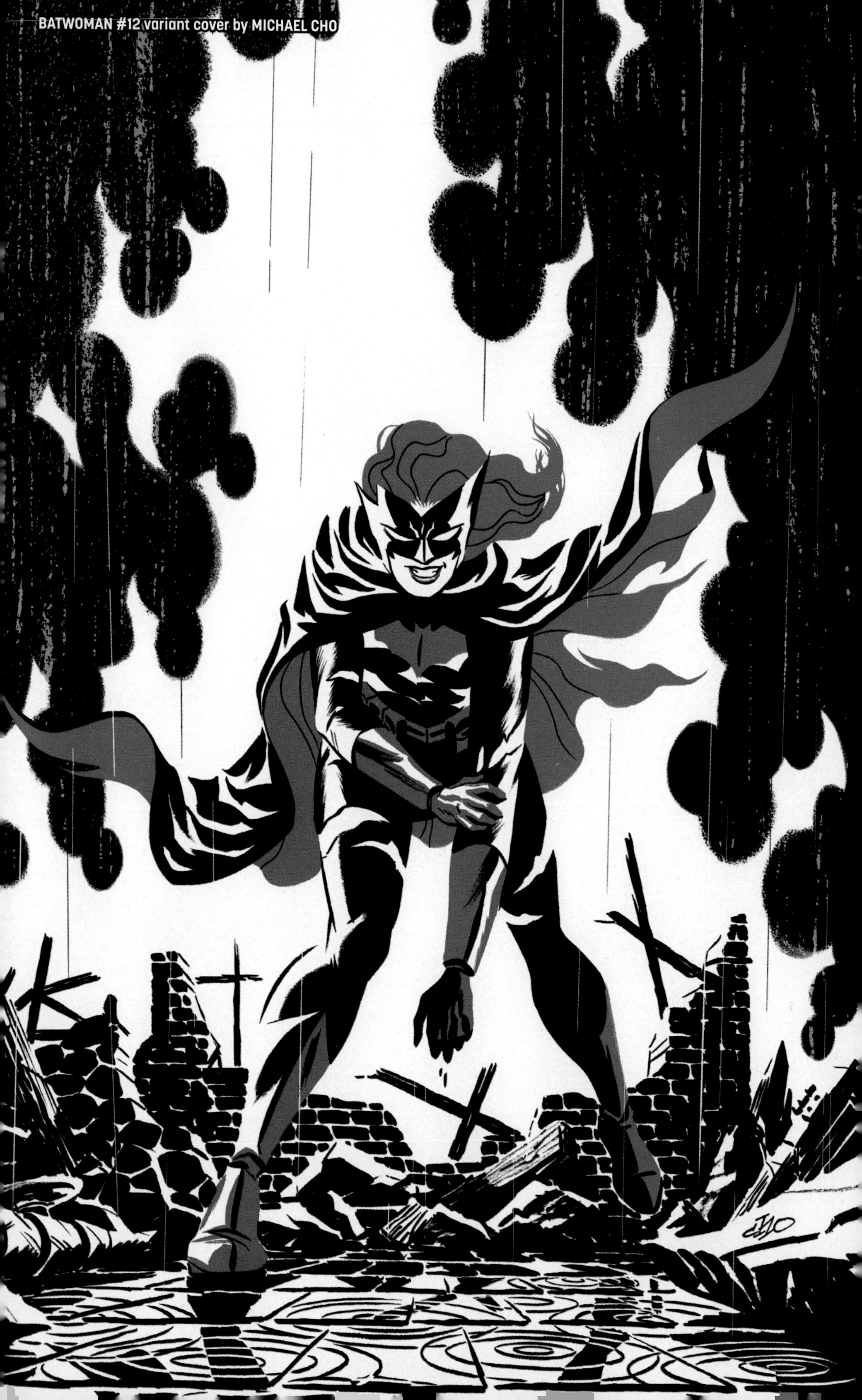

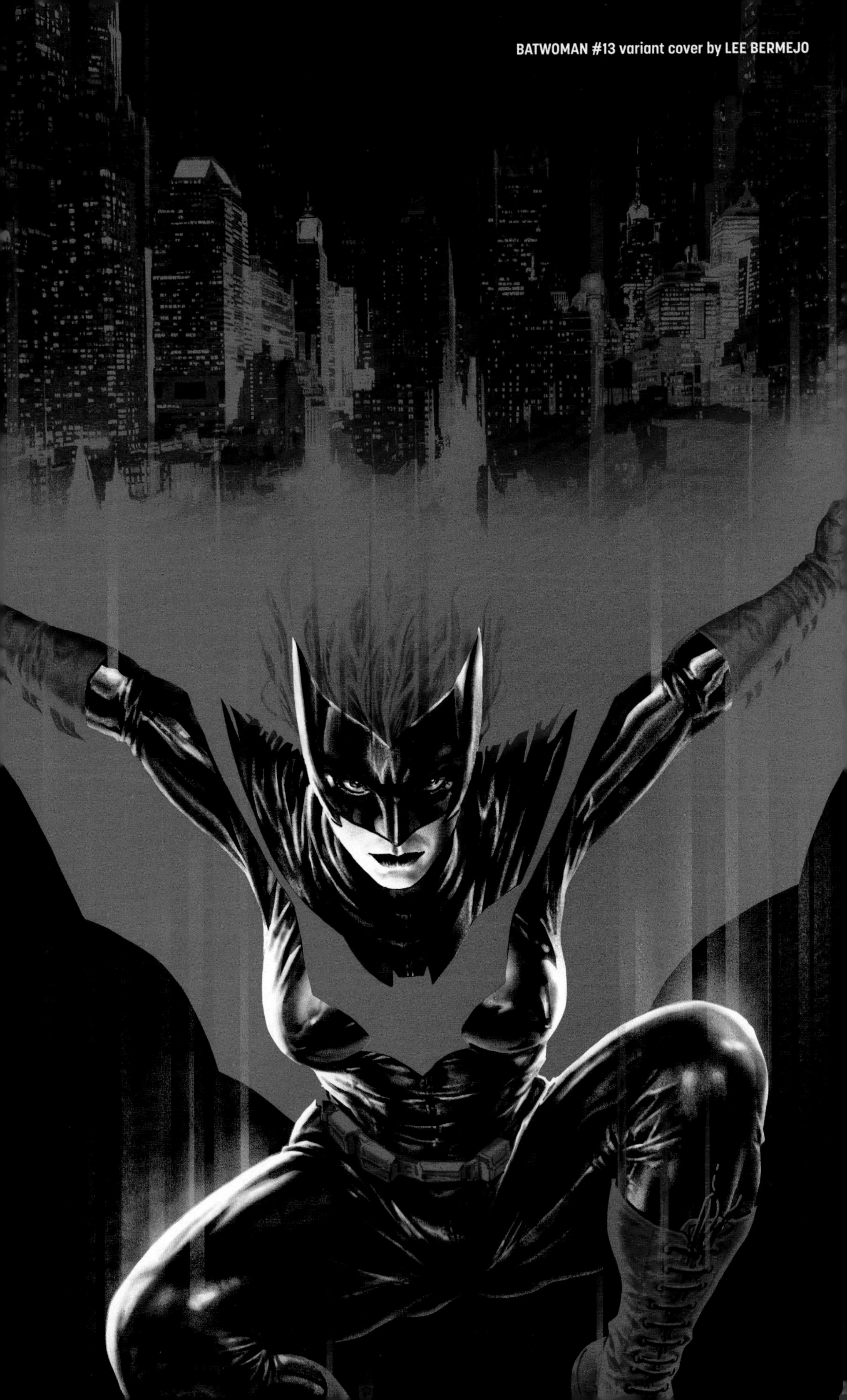

BATWOMAN #13 variant cover by LEE BERMEJO

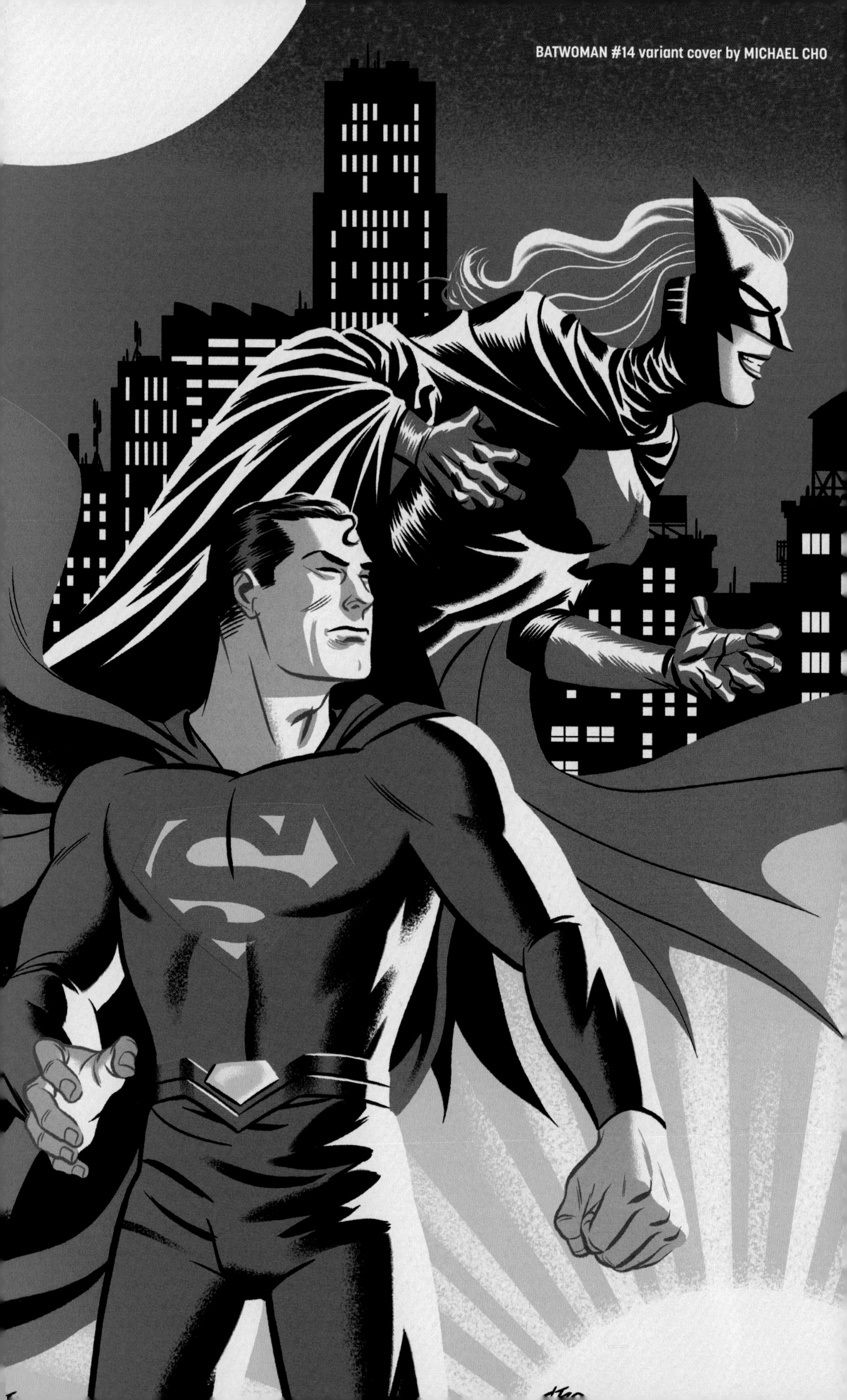

BATWOMAN #14 variant cover by MICHAEL CHO

BATWOMAN #15 variant cover by RAFAEL GRAMPÁ

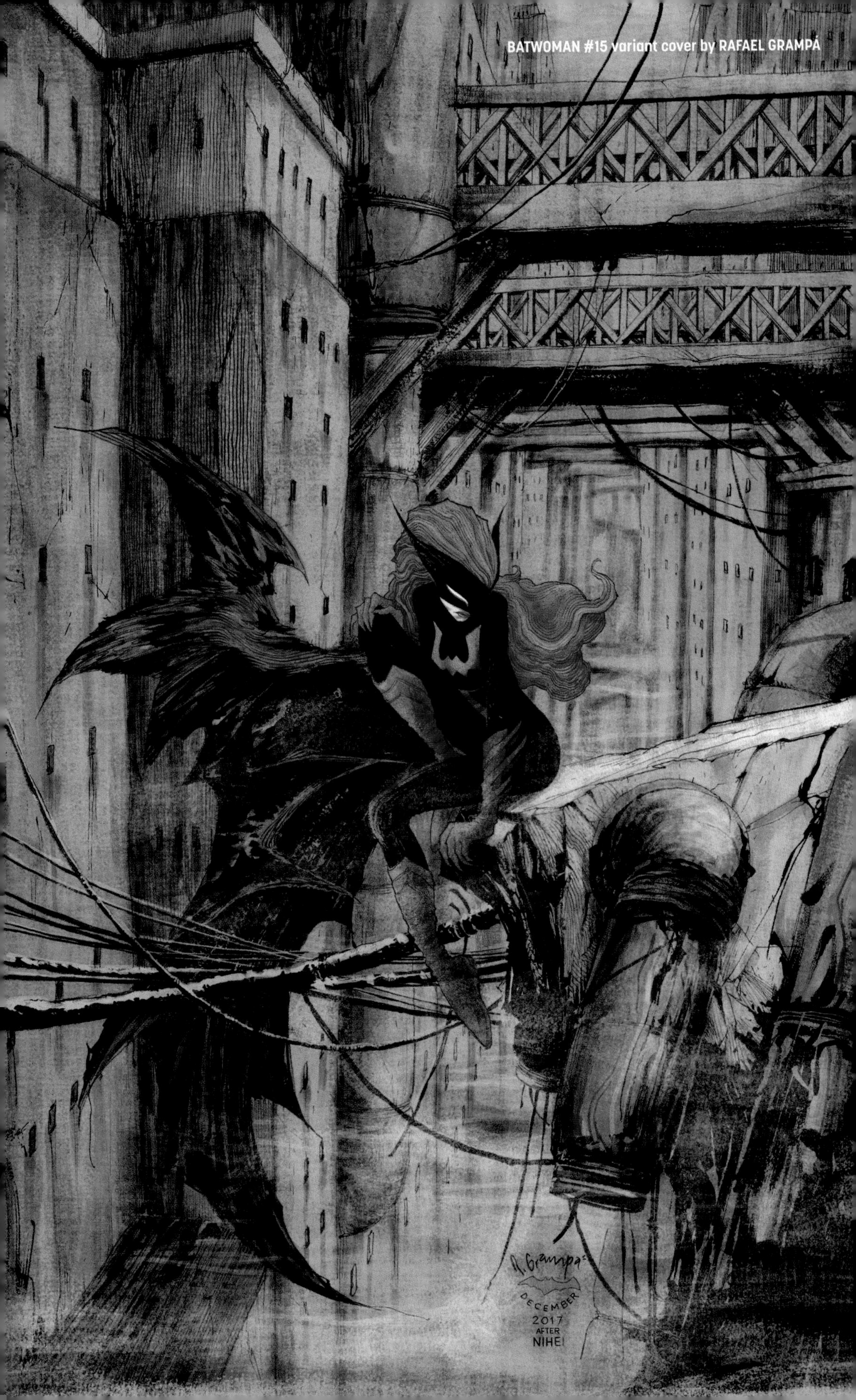
R. Grampá
DECEMBER
2017
AFTER
NIHEI

BATWOMAN #16 variant cover by MICHAEL CHO

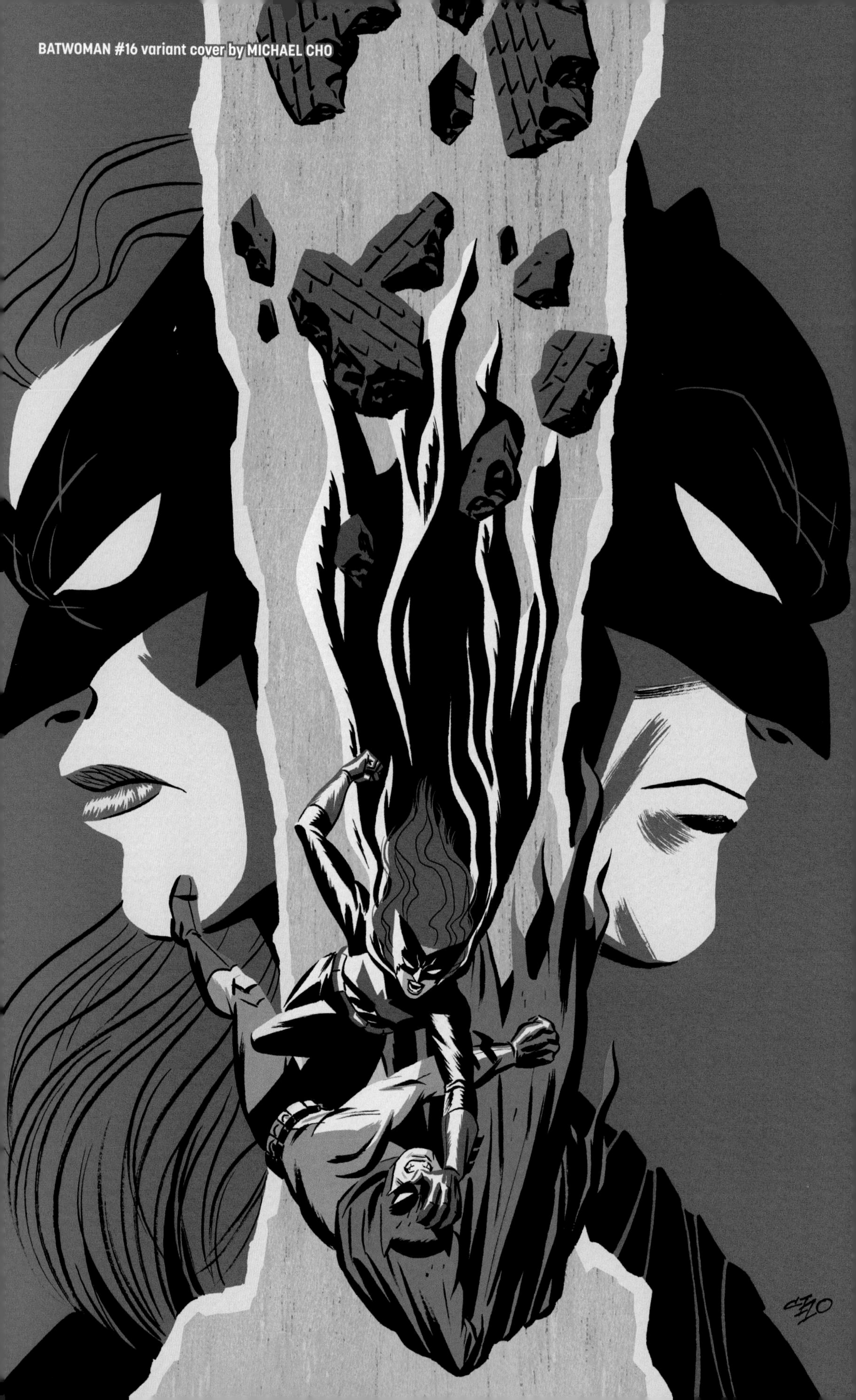

BATWOMAN #17 variant cover by MICHAEL CHO

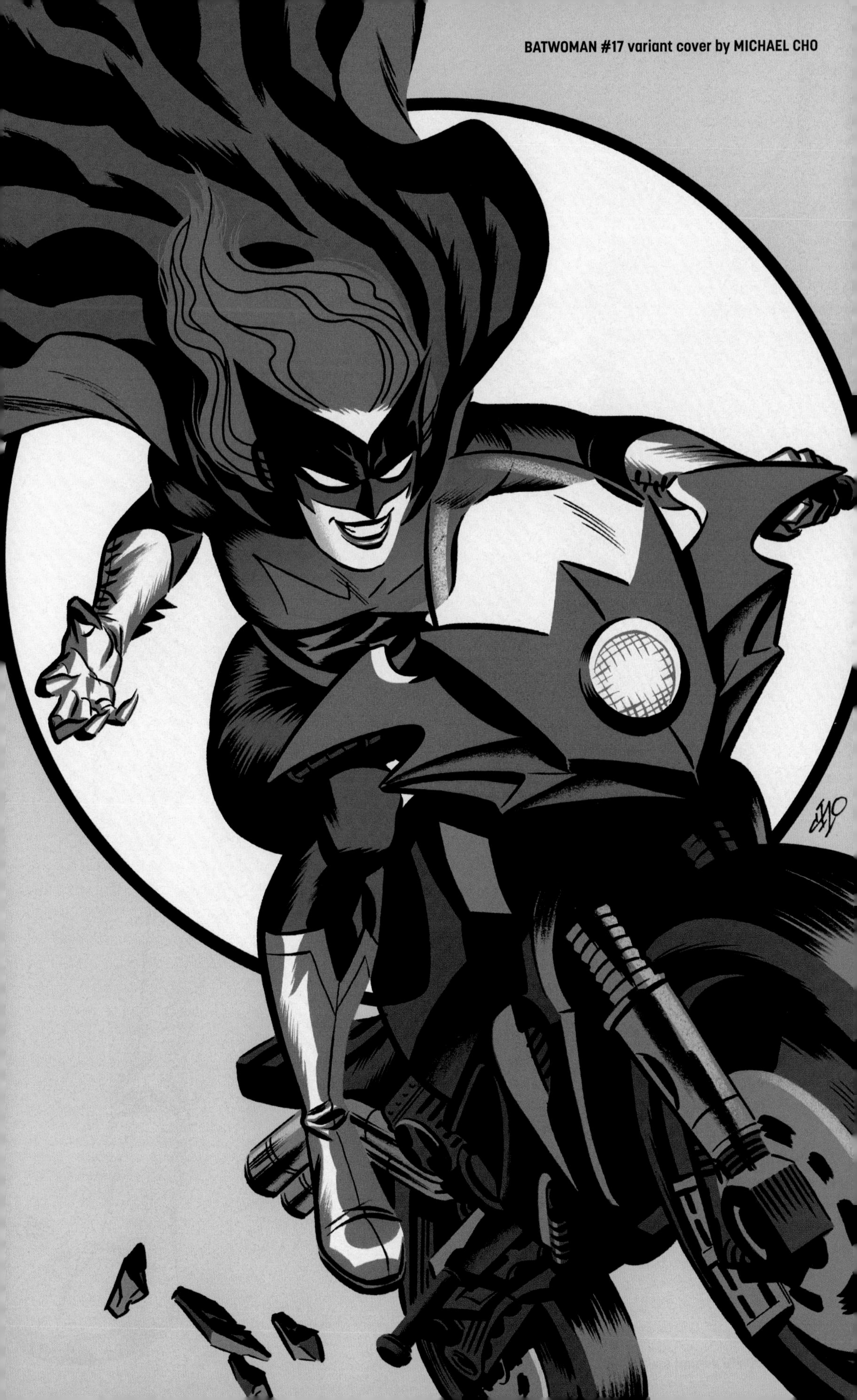

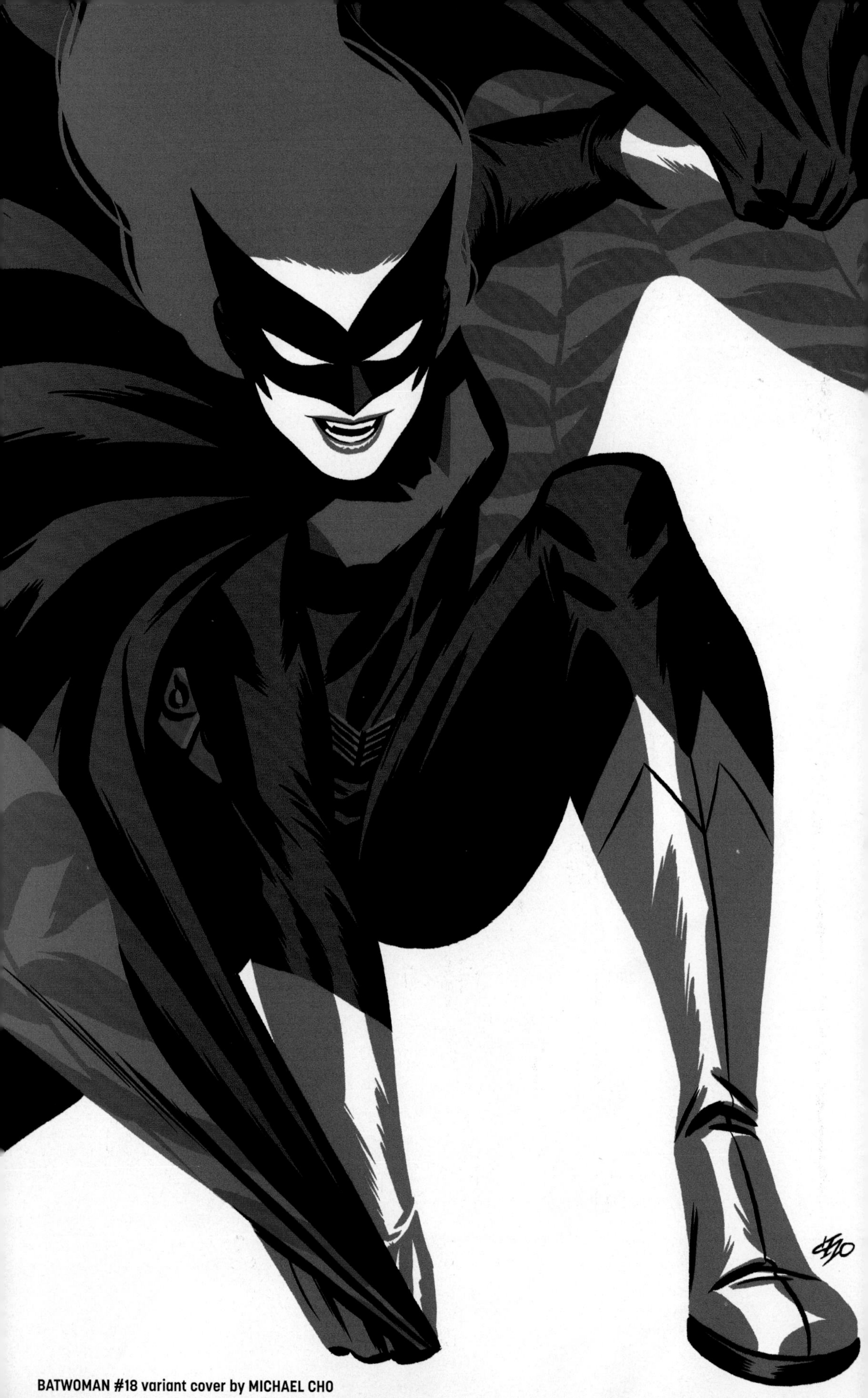

BATWOMAN #18 variant cover by MICHAEL CHO

"Batman is getting a brand-new voice."
– USA TODAY

"A great showcase for the new team as well as offering a taste of the new flavor they'll be bringing to Gotham City." **– IGN**

DC UNIVERSE REBIRTH
BATMAN

VOL. 1: I AM GOTHAM
TOM KING
with DAVID FINCH

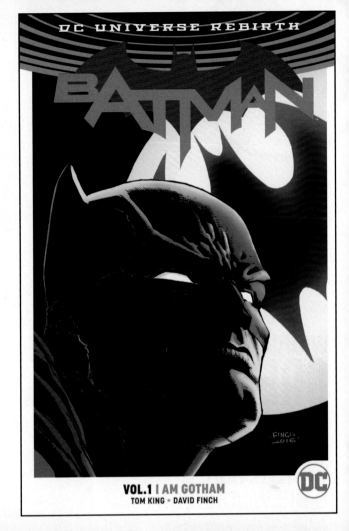

DC UNIVERSE REBIRTH

BATMAN

VOL.1 I AM GOTHAM
TOM KING ★ DAVID FINCH

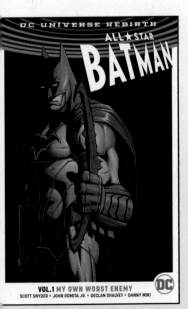

ALL-STAR BATMAN VOL. 1:
MY OWN WORST ENEMY

NIGHTWING VOL. 1:
BETTER THAN BATMAN

DETECTIVE COMICS VOL. 1:
RISE OF THE BATMEN

WONDER WOMAN BY
GREG
RUCKA
with J.G. JONES
& DREW JOHNSON

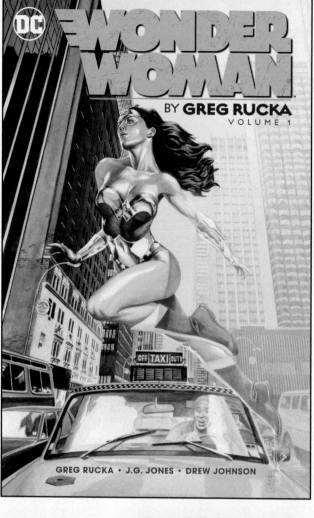

GREG RUCKA • J.G. JONES • DREW JOHNSON

BATWOMAN: ELEGY
with J.H. WILLIAMS III

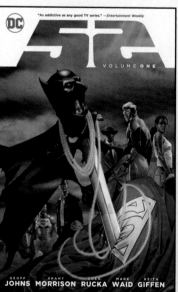

52 VOL. 1
with VARIOUS ARTISTS

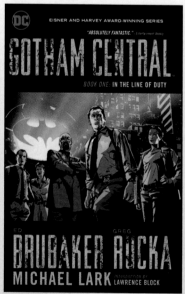

GOTHAM CENTRAL BOOK ONE
with ED BRUBAKER
& MICHAEL LARK